The Rise of the Consumer in Modern China

By Wang Ning

Paths International Ltd

社会科学文献出版社
SOCIAL SCIENCES ACADEMIC PRESS (CHINA)

Contents

Chapter One

Theoretical Viewpoint, Research Framework and Methodology

There have been tremendous changes in Chinese society over the past half century, especially in the last three decades. During the most recent thirty years not only have there been revolutionary changes in consumer behavior, furthermore the role of consumption in driving the evolution of society has become un-ignorable. It has become valuable to study and analyze the changes in Chinese consumption before and after the reforms from a sociological perspective, considering the role of consumption in these social changes. This book intends to examine the Chinese urban consumption system and the evolution of the ideological concept of consumption by analyzing governmental documents, using a qualitative research methodology.

Examination of the Theoretical Viewpoint

As a research object, consumption must be studied from a certain theoretical point of view. It is obvious that different subjects need to be studied from different viewpoints. For instance, philosophy, economics, management, politics, psychology, social geography, social history, media research and feminism all provide different research perspectives for consumption studies. Even within each subject, there are different genres of theories and a variety of viewpoints. Similarly, in consumption research, sociology provides a different perspective from that of other disciplines. To establish a comparatively high level starting point for our research, we must examine all historical genres of sociological theory and viewpoints that have been used to examine consumption. Then we will be able to find the best point of view.

We must point out that economics is the most rigorous and complete foundation for consumption research. For example, marginal utility theory and consumption function theory both provide mathematical models of consumption. To derive these models, simplified and idealized assumptions have to be made. It is necessary to simplify the various variables that may affect consumption and discard the "irrelevant" ones. This achieves accuracy and precision in modeling the consumption function. Such precise mathematical modeling of consumption behavior is without doubt a great achievement, but it pays a price. Take for instance consumption function theory. Since John Maynard Keynes established that consumption is a function of current income,[1] multiple theories have been put forward to refine and improve the consumption function, such as Dusenberry's comparative income theory, Irvin Fisher's life cycle hypothesis and Milton Friedman's permanent income hypothesis.[2] Yet the explanatory power of these theories is limited. It is confined to the economic level of consumption: consumption becomes how to best allocate and utilize an individual's or family's permanent income to achieve optimal utility, depending on the person's or family's stage of life. Other dimensions of consumption are excluded from these theories of consumer economics. However, such "other dimensions" are not only inherent components of consumption behavior but also are important factors in explaining it. The theory of consumer economics seems to explain the quantitative aspects of how individuals or families consume (e.g., how much consumption, the level of consumption, and the structure of consumption). But it lacks qualitative explanations (e.g., how does one consume and what is the experience of the consumption). Understanding consumption from a qualitative perspective is equally important. To certain extent, research in sociology and anthropology are responses to the oversimplifying tendencies of consumption economics. As pointed out by Nicosia and Mayer, consumer behavior is not only influenced by economic and psychological factors, but also affected by social elements (e.g., the system arrangement, cultural values, etc.)[3] According to Douglas and Isherwood, consuming a certain object is not only the process of maximizing utility from an economic perspective, but also a behavior of social communication, pattern recognition, establishing and maintaining mutually beneficial relationships and ceremonies. Consumption is not only an economic activity but also cultural and social one. The study of consumer behavior should not concentrate on the merely economic aspects, but examine its social and cultural significance.[4]

As the theory of consumer economics mainly focuses its explanations of an individual's or family's consumption on their income and economic condition, with assistance of mathematical modeling to make it more thorough and complete, and out of respect for the division of academic labor, it is unnecessary for sociology and anthropology to repeat what economics has done. (Which is analyzing income or economic resources to explain people's consumption behavior.) In fact there are hardly any sociologists or anthropologists doing this.[5] They more often analyze consumer society and its cultural dimensions from the perspective of their own field of sociology or anthropology. Of course, an explanation of consumption cannot be made without examining income and economic factors. Economic theories are fully developed in this area, and sociology and anthropology can naturally borrow from them. But consumer behavior and related phenomena, especially their "qualitative" aspects, cannot be understood by considering only income and economic factors. They are integral parts of the processes of society, systems and culture. So they can and must be analyzed with assistance of sociology and anthropology. Sociology and anthropology offer their own perspectives on the study of consumption. Among current theories and schools, the most influential ones are the "Theory of Social Stratification", the "Theory of Control of Capital", the "Theory of Romanticism" and the "Theory of Cultural Globalization".

A. Theory of Social Stratification

"Social Stratification" refers to the generalization I made about theories of social distinction, social imitation and the contest for status, which is relevant to the field of consumption sociology. Not only are people's consumption levels and consumption patterns determined by their class position and condition, their consumption itself is a process of shaping, constructing and enhancing their social status. From the viewpoint of social stratification, consumption is not only a result of class division, it is at the same time a process of constructing class – it consolidates and legitimizes at the symbolic level the status of the structural level.

Consumption constructs hierarchy because consumption activities are competitions for social status. Such competitions are mainly reflected in the symbolic aspects of consumption. Obtaining and using consumer goods are symbols of social status, so consumption activities have become competitions for symbolic resources (e.g., status and prestige) as related to one's structural class location. Therefore consumption has become an activity of social interaction, social communication, social classification and social competition. In details, this school has three theories: "Status Competition Theory", "Social Imitation Theory", and the "Theory of Social Distinction".

1. Status Competition Theory

The status competition paradigm can be traced back to Veblen. Veblen analyzed how the upper class displays its economic and social status through conspicuous consumption, and the social consequences of this status competition. He believed that people's social status depended on whether they could avoid "vulgar" productive work, or distance themselves as much possible from productive work. The consumption of time and goods can provide such distance. Wasting time and goods by showing off is the most obvious manifestation of people keeping their distance from productive work. So the more distant a person's leisure activities are from productive work (e.g., fashion, arts, sports, gaming, etc.), the more it proves the person's superior economic and social status. At the same time, people can show their distance from productive work through conspicuous consumption and luxury. For example, cumbersome skirts or white suits require much investment to obtain and further effort to keep up with the fashion. These are all ways to provide distance. Consumption of luxuries by housewives and servant's is "proxy consumption" by the master. It circumstantially attests the master's economic status. Evidently, conspicuous consumers do not buy products because of their intrinsic value. They consume them in order to prove their own superiority and financial status and to provoke other's envy and jealousy. It goes without saying that one's monetary position is always relative to that of others. To obtain relative superiority, people compete by conspicuous consumption[6]. Veblen's concept of conspicuous consumption has had strong influence on the studies of consumption. Economists call the phenomenon of satisfying pride and showing off status by high-price consumption the "Veblen Effect".[7]   The consumption in conspicuous consumption theory contains activities to demonstrate rank and compete for status. The theory has become an important research model in the sociology of consumption.

The status competition paradigm is summarized by Juliet Schor in her work outlining a new theory of American consumerism. In her book "The Overspent American", Schor describes how American "new consumerism" began. In the past, Americans used their neighbor's consumption as the reference standard for themselves. Today's American consumers are different. They use those far above their own status as their reference group. Advertising and the media have elevated many of these reference groups. What is advertised on TV is often the lifestyle pursued by the middle and upper classes, or even the super-rich. But audiences take it as the ordinary American's lifestyle. That is to say, by watching TV, audiences have internalized a higher standard of "the normal lifestyle". Around this standard, consumers begin to compete each other. The stronger the competition becomes, the more money Americans spend. And they become poorer. The reason is that the objects of their comparisons have also been raising their living standard. But people can never catch up with the reference group's wealth and the rate of change of their lifestyle. Consequently, consumers become anxious, frustrated, and unsatisfied. To maintain their desired lifestyle and living standard, Americans are forced to tap into their leisure time in order to make more money. As a result, many Americans work too much and do not get enough rest. American's competitive consumption has fallen into an irrational cycle.

2. Theory of Social Imitation

Simmel discussed the social operating mechanism of fashion in his book "Fashion

Philosophy". He believes that fashion is the lower class's behavior in continuously pursuing the upper class, while at the same time it is kind of dynamic social game of "cat and mouse" used by the upper class to increase its distance from the lower classes through continuous invention and update.[9] In Veblen's conspicuous consumption theory, people pursue conspicuous consumption to demonstrate their superiority to others, i.e., to "differentiate" themselves from others. In real life, however, there often exists the phenomenon of "much alike". "Much alike" is achieved through imitation. From Simmel's perspective, the power of consumption is not only in "differentiating" but also in "much alike". What Veblen described as conspicuous consumption is intended to distance one from others ("differentiating"), while Simmel's imitation intends to eliminate this distance. In other words, the way to eliminate the distance between one's self and the upper class is to copy and imitate the upper class's consumption patterns. According to Simmel, "differentiating" and "much alike" constitute the two kinds of power in consumption. "Differentiation" is the upper class's power in consumption. It intends by its behavior to increase the distance from the "ordinary" classes. "Much alike" is therefore the power of consumption held by the middle and lower classes. It intends to shrink the distance to the upper class. The method of shrinking is to imitate the upper clas's consumption behavior. The combination of the two becomes fashion. Fashion is the continuously interacting process of imitation and anti-imitation (innovation). However, there always exists a time lag between imitation and innovation. That is to say, after the middle and lower classes imitate the upper clas's consumption behavior, the upper class will discard the fashion that was copied. The upper class continues to maintain the distance from the middle and lower classes via innovation in consumption. Such cat and mouse movement gives fashion its features of being dynamic, transient, perishable and continuously ramifying. These features of fashion catered to the psychology of the middle class in the nineteenth century, with their insecurity and strong desire for change. Moving social boundaries between classes, greatly reduced social dynamic obstacles, along with fashion evolving from being expensive to cheap, led fashion to spread and frequently change.[10] Simmel's "fashion theory" emphasizes fashion itself as being "top down"; Grant McCracken has generalized it to a "trickle down theory".[11]

3. Theory of Social Distinction

Pierre Bourdieu's "Social Distinction Theory" differs from the theory of status competition and the theory of social imitation. Consumers in social distinction theory are not what Veblen described as "conspicuous consumers" characterized by narcissism and the desire to influence others. They are also different from Simmel's middle class that pursues fashion from a lack of self-confidence. Like both Veblen and Simmel, the theory of social distinction points out that consumption is an activity in the fight for social status. But this struggle has changed its character from using consumption to display legitimate and superior taste to highlight social status, to using consumption to highlight given functions of cultural capital by the new middle class. According to Bourdieu, consumption is a type of cultural activity. It reflects taste and style. So-called taste is a set of preference choices constrained by culture. In other words, it is the cultural paradigm of choice and preference. Bourdieu believes that taste can be seen as a kind of resource. With such resources, an individual, group or class can establish or raise its social position. Taste therefore has classification effect. Simply because different groups and classes have different habits and temperaments, different groups and classes have different tastes. Through consumption we demonstrate our own taste, and to certain extent, it reflects our social status, which contains the portfolio of our economic capital and cultural capital. This means that social stratification and cultural classification, to certain extent, have their own internal consistency.

Since taste has a function in differentiating social classes, how is taste used to indicate people's social status as being high or low?   This involves the legitimacy of taste. People having high economic capital see expensive cultural consumption (for example, vacations at luxury hotels) as high grade. People having high degree of cultural capital but lacking economic capital, try to legitimize inexpensive but elegant cultural activities. (For instance, backpackers travel to the third-world countries to experience the authentic local culture.) Therefore, people possessing different forms of capital struggle with "legitimacy rating" of taste. Cultural consumption is not only influenced by social status, but in itself shapes the class position.[12]

Unlike Bourdieu, Jean Baudrillard sees consumption as a category of purely symbolic activities. Consumption is the "systematic activity of controlling symbols" and "to become the objects of consumption, objects become symbols".[13]   So the real purpose of consumption does not reside in using objects or satisfying needs (which is only the premise of consumption). What matters is its symbolic meaning. The symbolism of consumption shows our social status. The class relationship can be transformed into a symbolic relationship. Consumption therefore follows the logic of "social distinction".[14]

"Social Stratification" goes successfully far beyond economics. It sees the influence of social structure, social relationships and social process on consumer behavior. It reveals the social, symbolic and structural aspects of the consumption process. It has expanded and deepened the vision of consumption research. However, the paradigm of the theory is unable to explain the scope and extent of constructive consumption. It is unable to reveal the premise of the constructive role of consumption. Obviously, in a different overall social structure, the constructive role of consumption is different. For example, in capitalist society and in socialist society, the constructive role and constructive methods are obviously different. In the West, using lipstick is a way of construct female identity. But during the Culture Revolution in China, putting on lipstick was an action of self-disgrace. When using social stratification theory to explain Chinese consumption, it is essential to understand the applicability of the theory, which determines its external validity.

B. Theory of Capital Control

Among the western theories of contemporary consumer behavior and consumerism, the theory of "Capital Control" developed by western Marxists (especially the Frankfurt school) has had comparatively strong influence. According to this theory, to increase its own value and meet its need for expanding production, by means of culture industry using advertisement and consumer media,[15] capital creates an ideology[16] of "happiness", "cheerfulness", "consuming" and "cultural dominance".[17] It artificially stimulates and produces a variety of "false" needs.[18] Consumers are satisfied by short period of happiness each time after they consume. At the same time, it reinforces the capitalist ruling order and alienation of labor. In the view of the Frankfurt School, consumption is a mechanism by which capital controls labor. While capital gives workers unreal "happiness" and "freedom", it deprives them of the condition of real happiness and freedom.

The theory of capital control reveals the non-autonomous aspect of consumption and its vulnerability to manipulation in a society with inequality and other disparities. It goes beyond the vision of behaviorism. The theory sees consumption as culture (consumerism), and links culture to constitutional conditions to analyze capital's role in shaping culture. The theory is deepened in revealing to certain extent the fact that inequalities in the social structure affect consumption. Nevertheless, one of its hidden premises is that the consumer is passive and easily cheated. The theory assumes that consumers follow manufacturer's intentions and routine in buying, which is subject to discussion as well.[19] Regardless of the effectiveness of the theory in explaining consumerism in western society,[20] the theory is undoubtedly insufficient to explain contemporary Chinese consumer behavior and consumerism. Huizhen Dai believes that Chinese consumer experience is often built upon the group memory of the poor living condition before the economic reform. Therefore it is given a positive meaning.[21] Honge Zheng also lists some special characteristics of Chinese consumerism: first, it leans heavily on reciprocity of consumption, and it over-emphasizes "face" in consumption; Second, consumption to enhance one's job or professional position has become very common; third, organizational overspending and abuse of public funds becomes rampant.[22] Obviously, traditional culture, corruption and the derivatives of various "hidden rules" are particular national conditions, all of which are elements in forming Chinese consumerism.

C. Theory of Romanticism

The theory of romanticism is Campbell's generalization of the sociology of consumption. He considers the mystery of contemporary consumerism is that people assume the grass is greener on the other side, change their minds upon seeing different things, and continuously pursue new and innovative products. And they can never satisfy their own desire. Campbell believes that mainstream economics can neither explain the unsatisfiability of modern desire, nor the reason for people's persistence in pursuing new products. A simple question is: if existing products can satisfy people's needs and the benefits of new products are uncertain, why do people still chase the new and discard the old? There are three explanations of this phenomenon: Instinct Doctrine, Control Theory, and the Veblen Perspective. Campbell does not believe any of the three answer the question effectively: (1) Instinct doctrine sees people's desire as animal instinct. It cannot explain however, if they have the same animal instincts, why people are different from each other, and why do people's consumption desires change over time. It cannot explain either why people, either out of love or self-control, give up some biological or instinctual needs. (2) The theory of control sees consumer's desires being the result of business's control through advertising. The theory assumes that consumers are passive, and they can only be activated by media information. But it cannot explain why, with the same advertising information, some consumers can react differently than others. Campbell believes that advertising is only one of many factors influencing consumer desire, not the sole factor; consumers react to advertisements selectively and with purpose, and not the collection of advertising as a whole. (3) The Veblen perspective sees desire being a byproduct of people's pursuit of social position and competition for status. It explains why people are not satisfied with their current status. Veblen ignored the variety of possibilities in pursuit of social position. That is also to say, wealth may not necessarily be the sole determining factor in obtaining high social status. In fact, in modern society social stratification is not along a single dimension, but is multi-dimensional.

Traditional (pre-modern) consumerism lies in the fact that traditional people's consumption desires are satisfiable, comparatively stable and repeatable, while modern consumer's desires are dynamic and endless. The reason for this is that modern consumerism reflects a kind of hedonism of independent imagination. In traditional hedonism, the image of a product comes mainly from memory. The pleasure of consumption is to review such memory. The difference in modern hedonism is that its main characteristic is that of imagination. It is an imaginary hedonism. The pleasure of consumption is the imagination of experiencing novelty. It is not the memory of experiencing prior consumption. The hedonism embodied in modern consumerism is built upon the fantasy of desire. Novel products provide raw materials for such imaginary hedonism. Consumers who are not satisfied with reality transfer their fantasy to new objects of desire. This creates a continuous desire for new and hitherto unknown products. According to Campbell, this imaginary hedonism explains the endless desire of modern consumption and its continuous pursuit of novelty. Imaginary hedonism also reformulates the "Romantic Ethic" of modern consumption. As Weber's used protestantism to interpret the spirit of modern capitalism, Campbell believes that the romantic ethic explains the spirit of modern consumerism. If the Protestant ethic is one of the cultural conditions for capital accumulation, the romantic ethic is one kind of cultural power in market expansion.[23]

Campbell emphasized the freedom that culture has in influencing consumer behavior. He pointed out the role of the romantic ethic in forming modern consumerism. His perspective overcomes the shortcomings of social stratification theory and capital control theory in that they ignore the comparative independence of culture. But he did not give adequate explanation of the structural causes of consumer culture and how consumer culture and that structure interact.

D. Theory of Cultural Globalization

All of above are theories of consumption sociology for developed western countries. They must be tested to see if they are suitable for developing countries. Mainstream economic theories cannot easily explain the disconnection of consumer culture or consumerism from the economic development level of developing countries. Some scholars looking at this from the perspective of cultural globalization, attribute the rise of third-world countrie's consumerism to the role models provided by the U.S. and other western developed nations. This type of theoretical perspective is summarized as "theory of cultural globalization".

Belk at the University of Utah in the U.S. points out that traditional economic theories have difficulties in effectively interpreting the rise of consumerism in third-world countries, because the consumer culture has exceeded the economic development level in those countries. Obviously, the rise of consumerism in the third-world does not follow traditional economic logic. It has followed another logic. On the one hand, the western lifestyle has been disseminated with assistance of the media in third-world countries. On the other hand, urbanization in third-world countries has destroyed traditional attitudes toward displays of social status by one's neighbors. In other words, arousing the neighbor's jealousy has become acceptable. This change of community structure has enabled the penetration of developed countrie's consumer culture into the third-world. Belk believes that this penetration has led to negative social consequences. For example, consumers in these countries may sacrifice the basic needs of nutrition to their pursuit of luxury goods and conspicuous consumption. Furthermore, as consumption has become a more individual activity, the sense of community has weakened.[24]

Feffery James has discussed the relationships between consumption and development, and consumption and globalization. He analyzed a proposition by Ragnar Nurkse, the "International Demonstration Effect". The effect refers to the attractiveness of rich countrie's standard of consumption in poor countries. It leads to imitation by the people in poor countries. James believes that one inadequacy in Nurkse's proposition is that he ignores the changes of values by the citizens in developing countries during modernization and the influence of such modernization on the citizen's preferences for products from developed countries. How to explain this process? In Jame's view, Veblen's conspicuous consumption theory can help. Conspicuous consumption or status competition is a kind of high-income taste, but with help from globalization, such taste has been transferred to the third-world countries. How did such taste transfer take place? James believes there are several mechanisms playing a role. Education is one kind of transfer mechanism of value, because it instills western and American values and their standard of conduct into the young people of third-world countries. Foreign enterprise is another kind of mechanism, because corporate management enforces upon local employees a "respectable" dress code and a uniform standard of conduct. Advertisement is also an important mechanism, because it encourages people to replace social objectives with personal goals, and to relate products to social position. It often disseminates the lifestyle of the developed countries to third-world countries without any filtering, arousing the impulse of the local residents to imitate wealthy foreigners and local elites. Last, since the colonial period, the interactions of citizens of third-world countries with the Europeans or North Americans have had a seductive effect on those countries, leading them to imitate American or European lifestyles. James believes that this seeking of social status by citizens of the developing countries has had a negative effect on social welfare, because lower-income group's pursuit of conspicuous consumption and social status has caused them to sacrifice their basic needs. And the poor do always fall behind the rich in the competition for status.[25]

Sklair has proposed the "Global System Model". In this model, multinational companie's expansion and their capitalist control of the media, has led the diffusion of consumerism worldwide (including to the third-world countries). He believes that the global system is composed of economic, political, cultural and ideological systems. At economic level, the primary institution is the multinational enterprise. At political level, the primary institution is transnational capitalism. This includes transnational company management, state bureaucracy around the world, politicians who favor capitalists and members of the professions, and the consumer elite (business and media). At the cultural and ideological level, the primary institutions are multinational mass media companies and advertising agencies. These agencies are united to create the culture and ideology of consumerism; that is, a set of attitudes, values and practices built upon advertising by a mass media that permeates the whole of society in encouraging continuous consumption.

Under Sklair's global system model, the diffusion of values and beliefs in developing countries is primarily promoted by global capitalists and transnational corporations. For example, Hollywood has played a key role in the process of consumerism's expansion worldwide. Sklair believes that in the global system, information flow between the first-world and the third-world countries is unbalanced. By dominating the international media, transnational media companies have transformed the global audience into consumers of multinational corporation's products. The reason they have accomplished this is that these North American and European multinational corporations control of the global flow of information and have raised barriers to entry in the communications and entertainment industries: because of the high costs of communication technologies and also the rapid changes in these technologies, third-world countries have neither the interest nor ability to establish a strong public media sector. Thus global information flows have become unbalanced. The flow of information from developed to developing countries, controlled by multinational companies, has led to the successful spread of the culture and ideology of consumerism to developing countries. It has caused the consumers of developing countries to admire and become dependent on the products of multinational companies. It consumes resources that could be used for their own development, creating negative consequences for third-world countries.[26] Using this research framework, Sklair studied consumerism in Shanghai.[27]

It is unique in treating consumption in developing countries from a global perspective. Indeed, for many developing countries, multinational corporations and their sales and marketing campaigns are a kind of external power fostering the rise of consumerism, which should not be ignored. However, the theory has its limitations. It ignores the "inherent factors" in developing countries. More importantly, if we do not differentiate the former Soviet Union, Eastern Europe and China, nations that are transitioning from a planned economic system to a market economic system, we obscure many important differences among them. Because of these differences, using the theory to explain consumerism for countries undergoing this transformation is like "looking at flowers across the fog" or "scratching through boots to relieve an itch".

Comparison of Theoretical Perspectives

If the study of consumption is limited to countries with democratic politics and market economies, the above theoretical perspectives appear to have considerable explanatory power. However, if the research objects of consumerism are transformational countries like the former Soviet Union, Eastern Europe, China, etc., the defects in the above perspectives will be apparent. One key condition affecting consumerism in transformational countries is state itself, but the state is absent in the above theories. To put everything together, the research perspective of the sociology of consumption can be generalized into the following model. (Single arrows do not necessarily mean the lack of mutual interaction between the two, but they are used to refer to the relationship between explanatory objects and objects being explained. This convention is used similarly in the following.) (Figure 1-1):

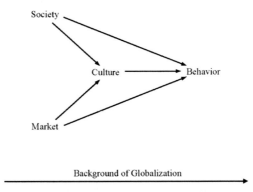

Figure 1-1   Theoretical Perspective of Western Sociology on Consumption

The theory of social stratification emphasizes the role of "social" elements, i.e., it emphasizes the role of social interactions and social relationships that influence consumer culture and consumer behavior. The theory of capital control emphasizes the influence of market elements, highlighting the comparative independence of consumer culture and its influence on consumer behavior. The theory of cultural globalization emphasizes the factor of "globalization", which gives a new interpretation of capital control from a global perspective. It has extended the scope of capital control from domestic to international. Obviously, there is no presence of the state itself in models based on the above theories. The reason is that the above theories are limited to research on capitalist countries or market economy countries, less on transformational countries such as former Soviet Union, East Europe and China. In capitalist countries with democratic political systems, the role of the state is constrained; it is not all-powerful. In the former Soviet Union, Eastern Europe and China, the state itself plays a role unmatched in other countries. These countries are obviously different from "ordinary" third-world countries. They have their own unique development paths and features. Although it is convenient to combine these countries with others in the third-world, it can lead to serious problems with the validity of research results. The transformational countries form their own genre and have become important research objects contributing to the growth of human knowledge. To overcome the shortsightedness of current theories of sociology of consumption, it is necessary to include these transformational countries into the scope of research and to seek out and explore their unique features in order to complete, enrich and correct the existing theoretical frameworks. Since the totalitarian state is a common feature of former the Soviet Union, Eastern Europe and China, and in totalitarian countries the state has omnipresent influence on social life and social structure, to explain the consumer behavior in these countries, the above theoretical model must be corrected and modified to include the role of the state (Figure 1-2):

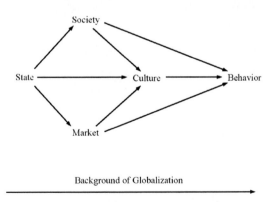

Figure 1-2   Revision of Theoretical Perspective

With this theoretical background, research on changes in consumption in China has outstanding significance. Existing western theories cannot explain completely the changes in consumption in China, which has created an excellent opportunity to acquire new knowledge. Based upon restricting the scope of the original theoretical perspective, such research anticipates new types of changes in consumption. It enhances our understanding of the changes in diversity of consumption. It also suggests a new theoretical model. Simultaneously, this research helps formulate a local sociology of consumption theories.

As the name implies, transformational countries involve a restructuring of the social system. During this transformation, the state plays a leading role. Therefore such restructuring is based upon the country's leadership. From this perspective, it is impossible to ignore country's leadership in researching changes in consumption systems and consumer culture. In this type of country, the state played a positive role in establishing a planned economic system and eliminating the market mechanism. The state played another key role in leading the transformation to a market economy. Because of the state's intervention in the market and society, the roles of market and society are re-ordered, which from an individual's perspective, influences their consumption concept and behavior.

A major difference between transformational countries and others is the condition of culture formation. In developed western countries, although the state plays a role in culture formation, its influence is comparatively limited. Society has comparatively high autonomy and independence, thus it is a more important factor in culture formation. In contrast, in the former Soviet Union, East Europe and China, society was controlled by the state, lacking autonomy and independence. A market economy hardly existed. The emergence of globalization is blocked (there was limited interaction between these countries and the rest of the world), therefore, the major influences and forces on culture come primarily from the state. This means that before transformational countries begin to transform themselves, they lack what Campbell describes as the cultural soil of high-degree independence. On the contrary, in these countries, culture has become an important channel for the state's influence on society. The state can change and control society by shaping and controlling culture.

Considering the special feature of the state's influence in transformational countries, this book focuses on how the state influences resident's consumer behavior. In detail, it discusses how the state influences society's social structures via institutional arrangements, and therefore the state's impact on consumption and consumer behavior. The state's influence on consumption is also the subject of the dialectical argument between this book and the main existing western sociologies of consumption. The influence on consumption by factors such as "society", "market" and "culture"—mature theories in western sociology of consumption—are briefly discussed but are not the emphasis of this book.

This book is not the first to emphasize the influence of the state on consumption arrangements and concepts. Scholars such as Dai Huisi and others have analyzed specific examples in daily life from the perspective of the relationship between the state and society. They explored the origin of the Chinese urban consumption revolution and the rise of consumer independence.[28] Zheng Hong –E also analyzed the influence of the nation's consumption polices on urban resident's consumption experience and attitudes.[29] This book is a new attempt to analyze the reciprocal relationship between the state and its citizens on the social structure and the influence of this relationship on consumer's attitudes and behavior. Another unique characteristic of this book is that it does not analyze consumption alone, instead it considers the linkage between consumption and labor. This means analyzing how the state treats consumption and labor through institutional arrangements, shaping the corresponding social structure, and therefore influencing people's concept of consumption and consumption behavior. Thus changes in the consumption system and consumption culture reflect the changes of relationship between the state and its citizens.

Research Framework

Unlike in western countries, in the former Soviet Union, Eastern Europe, China and other transformational countries, consumption is more influenced by the state and the social structure that is shaped by the state. The research framework of this book is centered on the relationship between the state and social structure, and its influence on consumption. The role of the state is mainly reflected in institutional arrangements and how these institutional arrangements create a corresponding social structure that influences the concept of consumption and consumer behavior.

In the totalitarian countries with planned economic systems, individual consumption is not merely a private matter. What people consume, how much they consume and how they consume, to great extent are affected by the institutional arrangements of the state. The first reason is that at global level, most countries implementing socialist planned economic systems are starting from a condition of economic backwardness. The second reason is that these countries have an ideological incentive to catch up with the capitalist countries, marshaling all social resources to do so. Therefore, in these countries, reducing consumption of resources and increasing the production of resources have become inevitable choices in order to realize the countrie's ambitious goals starting from conditions in which material resources are lacking. In making these two choices, China is not exceptional but is the most prominent. So on one hand, the state has made institutional arrangements to curb consumption, on the other hand, it also implemented "super economic incentives" (mental stimulation) as a way to encourage people to work actively to increase economic production. This shows that from the state's perspective, curbing consumption must be connected with labor stimulation. Since the two have inherent tension, the state must arrange certain means in order to overcome the conflict between the two. Obviously, studying the policies (or institutional arrangements) imposed upon consumption by the state cannot be done without considering the state's policies (or institutional arrangements) for labor stimulation.

What means does the state use to resolve the conflict between curbing consumption and stimulating labor? From a historical point of view, there are at least two methods. One is a military-like institutional arrangement. Institutes in the city and People's Communes in the countryside are all organized on similar military lines, so as to enhance the state's "right of command" upon people's labor. The second is a quasi-religious institutional arrangement. Ideological and political efforts in institutionalizing the urban and rural areas perform the function of shaping and unifying the people's beliefs, ideas and attitudes. They therefore create a unique social structure with a religious colour. In such a social structure, the ideas of dedication and frugality are "married" and the state's "persuasive rights" (or "power of calling") is affirmed. These two rights of the state cannot be isolated. Command power secures persuasive rights. And persuasive rights promote the successful exercise of command power (for instance: "do whatever the party calls upon you to do").

The institutional arrangements made to curb consumption form one part of the military-like institutional arrangements. Taking the city as an example, the institution system, household registration system, records system, food and oil supply system with their ration certificates, all force individuals to be tied to institutions. Individuals are sheltered by institutions, but they also rely upon institutions. Such an arrangement enables the state to exercise its power to the maximum extent. With such power, the state can set up systems to curb citizen's consumption in urban and suburban areas.

How to guarantee that citizens do not become slack and lazy (a kind of soft resistance) after curbing their consumption? This is a real problem that the national leadership has to face. Obviously, to remove the tension between curbing consumption and labor stimulation, it must rely upon other means, one of which is a deep transformation of people's beliefs, concepts, attitudes and motivations. This involves fundamental changes in people, to wit, the creation of a new sacred body or social structure. To achieve this, state relies upon its own sacred ideological image to create the citizen's new social structure (and psychological structure).

The fundamental character of this sacred ideology is that it makes individuals replace their personal goals with the state's objectives. They not only see the state's objectives as their own individual targets, and further adopt such targets as their own beliefs.[30] Partially this works because the state has set up obstacles in the system to prevent individuals from pursuing their own interest. But this is far from enough to make individuals to adopt the state's goals as their own beliefs. To achieve this result, the state must make nation's goals sacred. The state must make people feel that if they are separated from the nation's goals, they would not have a meaningful life. One side effect of making the nation's goals sacred is to make individual's objectives small. Instilling sacred ideology in the citizens of the nation, leads to a double effect. On one hand, it makes individuals connect the pursuit of naked self-interest with "shame". On the other hand, it makes people feel lofty by their dedication to and sacrifice for their country. From this perspective, Hedonic consumption is considered morally ugly (e.g., "pleasure seeking"), and selfless dedication to work is considered to demonstrate moral beauty (e.g., "labor glory", and "the noblest of workers"). The ugliness of consumption and the beauty of work are naturally intertwined. Obviously, the sacred ideology has assisted the state in implementing its strategic objective of catching up with capitalism in an environment where material resources are lacking.

Only by understanding such a sacred ideology, can we really understand people's consumption attitudes. To study the consumption attitudes and consumer behaviors of citizens of totalitarian countries, we have to consider the impact of the sacred ideology on citizen's social system and its further relationship to consumption attitudes. Since pursuing personal gain and enjoyment is perceived by sacred ideology as "shameful", frugality is recognized and accepted by sacred ideology as the only legitimate consumption behavior. At the same time, because of the sacred ideology, people are neither slacking off, nor merely muddling through even when they are constrained by the state's policy of curbing consumption. Thus the contradiction between curbing consumption and stimulating labor is minimized to great extent with the help of the social structure of sanctity.

However, the effectiveness of establishing a sacred ideology to resolve the contradiction between curbing consumption and stimulating labor relies upon the inherent consistency of the sacred ideology. It means that this kind of ideology cannot contain inherent contradictions and conflicts. Otherwise, it would lose its sacredness. Once it loses its sacredness, it loses its power. So what does the inherent consistency of sacred ideology include? First, the object of faith cannot have flaws. Second, promise and result must be consistent. On the first point, during the Cultural Revolution, negative phenomena such as the "Violent Incidents", the "Lin-Biao affair", and "Back-Door Activities", etc., made people lose faith in the objectives which they worship and believe (i.e., a "split"). The sacred ideology starts to show cracks and inconsistency. On the second point, beliefs advertised by the state are often interpreted as commitments to be fulfilled. If the commitment is fulfilled but the promise not kept, a crisis of faith occurs. In the mid to late period of the Cultural Revolution, when residents in urban areas experienced increasing poverty, this led to the occurrence of such a crisis. Naturally to certain extent, the Cultural Revolution was the major event that caused the sacred ideology to collapse and be destroyed. The "inconsistency" of the sacred ideology led to the social system being caught in a spiritual crisis. Consequently, the conflict between curbing consumption and stimulating labor becomes more apparent. This causes a crisis of labor motivation among urban residents that leads to further shortages of goods. In response, it forces the strengthening of curbs on consumption. As a result, the lack of consumer goods and the crisis of labor motivation led to a vicious cycle. Consequently, the state fell into a crisis of legitimacy resources.

It was in this environment that national leaders who were "let down" or ousted during the Cultural Revolution and reemerged afterwards, began the process of reform and "opening up". On the surface, the origin of the reform and opening up would seem to depend upon individual's unique experiences, subsequent beliefs and preferences. But in essence, the start of reform and opening up is intrinsically linked to the dissolution of the sacred ideology and the depletion of the state's legitimacy resources. Since the sacred ideology has the role of creating "legitimacy resources" for the state, once it fades, it causes a crisis. This crisis makes the conflict between curbing consumption and stimulating labor apparent. Soft resistance of urban residents begins to spread. Slacking off starts to occur. The motivation of labor decreases. Therefore, whether one is in the upper class or the lower class, there was the experience of unprecedented crisis. The state experiences a legitimacy resources crisis, and this leads to failure of original labor incentives (i.e. "sacred motivations"). Consequently, the state loses the means to implement its objectives. As to the lower class, it is the shaking of belief. Such shaking makes the originally acceptable poverty unbearable, and the latter in return exacerbates the crisis of belief. Once the crisis of beliefs occurs, labor motivation falls into a crisis as well. Life prospects seem dim. People's resentment increases. The "April Fifth Movement" in 1976 is just such an external reflection of a belief crisis and feeling of resentment.

It can be said that reform and opening up is one kind of systemic arrangement for re-selecting labor incentives after traditional methods for reconciling consumption curbs and labor motivation all fail. These reform methods are critical in recovering and rebuilding the state's legitimacy resources. No state can be indifferent when its legitimacy resources fall into crisis. Giving up long-running policies to curb consumption is important in restructuring the state's legitimacy resources. The legitimacy resources upon which the state relies have changed to different kinds. They have moved away from types mainly based upon "state objectives and promises" to ones based upon "improving individual materialistic interests". From the temporal perspective, the exit from a legitimacy crisis follows the path of how to improve the people's living standard: One, honor the state promises and improve people's living conditions in order to restore and restructure the state's legitimacy resources. Two, in order to improve people's standard of living, there must be stimulation of people's enthusiasm for work and an increase in labor productivity. Three, in the circumstance of the fading of the sacred ideology and failure of quasi-religious motivation, in order to increase labor productivity, alternative policies must be considered. One choice is to change old, rigid and closed-end economic system (reform and opening up), the old "big pot" and "iron rice bowl" as well as the imbalanced relationship of "right", "responsibility" and "benefits" among individuals, enterprises and local and central government. Only under this premise, the individual beliefs and preferences of the state's leaders can be fully effective. During the change of policy, material incentives and the improvement in people's living standard become the new labor incentives. Four, with respect to such initiatives, the citizen's social structure has undergone a secular transformation. It is transformed from a sacred object (or ascetic object) to a secular object (or consumption object). In labor motivation, people do not take national goals as their personal ones; instead they see their individual goals as the purpose of work. Labor incentives are also changed from quasi-religious motivations to secular motivations. Five, with respect to country's retreat from all-encompassing social control, the people's consumption has becomes more independent. Consumer culture therefore arises.

It is very obvious that research on consumer behavior during social transformation cannot be limited to describing consumption itself. The study of consumption should follow the lines of the transformation of social structure. On one hand, the changes in consumption involve the transformation of the whole economic system. In order to study the changes in consumption, we must study the changes of the various systems related to consumption, of which the most important are the changes in the consumption system and the labor incentives system. Since the state is the main sponsor of systemic changes, its behavior must be analyzed in order to understand the changes in the other systems. The state's major behavior is in fact the behavior of the agents who implement the state's power (i.e., the state leadership's beliefs and conduct). On the other hand, changes in consumption include changes in consumer attitudes. The changes in consumer attitudes relate to the changes in the citizen's social structure. Studies of consumer attitudes cannot limit themselves to only in describing consumer attitudes, but they must be examined in connection with the changes in the citizen's social structure. In these structural changes, changes in consumer attitudes and concept of labor are intrinsically linked. The changes of these two are closely related to the morphological changes of belief at the core of the social structure.

Clearly, the reason why western theories of consumption sociology are very limited in their ability to explain the changes in consumption in transformational countries is because of they ignore the role of the state and the state ideology's influence on consumption. In transformational countries, if we neglect the state's role, many phenomena are very difficult to explain. So it is with the explanation of consumption. That is why this book intends to study the changes of consumption in China from the perspective of the state and the state sponsored ideology. From this perspective, this book adopts the following research framework (Figure 1-3). (In Figure 1-3, single arrows represent relationship of including influencing direction and change flow. Double arrows represent mutual relationships.)

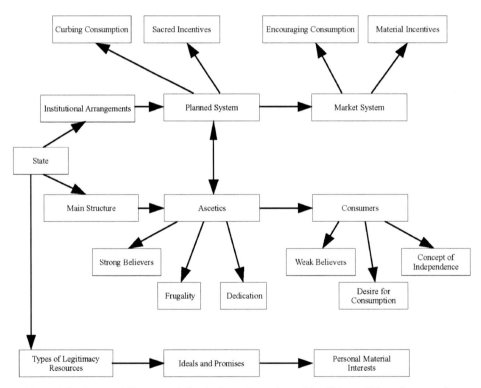

Figure 1-3　Research Framework for the Transformation of the Chinese Urban Consumption System and Changes in Consumer Attitudes

Each chapter of this book follows the above framework. The second chapter discusses the planned economy before the reform and opening up, its institutional arrangements and path taken around urban consumer life and labor incentives. The third chapter discusses the formation of social structure (ascetic subjectivity) corresponding to the policy of curbing consumption and the subsequent occurrence of crisis. The fourth chapter analyzes the start of reform and opening up, and how the state implemented its systemic transformation process around consumer life and labor incentives. The fifth chapter studies the transformational processes of the social structure along with the changes in the consumption system and labor incentives. That is the social structure's transformation from ascetic subjectivity to consumer subjectivity. The sixth chapter discusses the imbalances of consumer society and the phenomenon of the "double track". The seventh chapter summarizes the views of this book and explores some issues in more depth.

Research Methodology

This book is a longitudinal study. Since the topic covers a long time span, during which many events have taken place and some records already been lost, in order to answer the diachronic and longitudinal research questions, the author has adopted three methods: government document analysis, qualitative analysis and second-hand statistical analysis.

A. Government Document Analysis

In China, since the state is the maker and administrator of the national formal system (including the consumption system), research on the formal system is in fact research of the state's policy behavior. In a sense, it is the study of the state itself. But the state is not an abstract entity. It consists of people with power. The state itself is not an executor, rather the state's action is the exercise by certain groups of the state's power.[31] Therefore, to study the state, it is impossible not to "bring people back to the state".[32]   In China, although the policy-making process involves the interests of all parties, the country's leadership (e.g., the CPC Central Committee Political Bureau Standing Committee) and key national leaders have played pivotal and even decisive roles in developing and arranging policy. These leaders cannot be treated as normal action takers. They should be considered as "macro-actors".[33]   Therefore, taking China as an example, studying the state's actions, to great extent, is the study of the state's leadership and core leader's actions. Their policy beliefs, concepts and decision-making, have maneuvered the country's policy direction. So analysis of national leader's reports and lecture notes is methodologically significant, as they in fact represent the intellectual development of the national leaders when they develop and establish the country's policies. When I mention in this book the executor of state power, I mainly refer to the central government (which includes CPC Central Committee and National State Council and all subsidiaries).

The state's policy development and arrangements can have important, deep and widespread influence on society. For instance, centralized purchasing and marketing has had an impact on Chinese society for decades. The decision to launch the Cultural Revolution has had profound influence on the advancement of China's society. But where do the materials on the state's systemic arrangements or policies come from? They come from the party and central government's literature archive. By analyzing government documents (noted as "government document" below), we can understand the institutional arrangements of the state (i.e., the central government), and the considerations and thinking processes behind these institutional arrangements. In this sense, government documents (including party, central committee and state council policy documents) are very useful sources. They give proofs of our understanding of institutional arrangements and directions. And these proofs are easy to obtain.

Regarding labor incentives and the consumption system, I have indexed and analyzed important and relevant documents since the founding of the nation. Because there are so many government documents, analyzing the material involves selection. The filtering rule I have adopted is whether in real life, these policies played a constraining role in the choices made by the actors. That is to say, whether these policies form consistent institutional arrangements. Government documents are divided into three categories. One category is the "decision" or "notice" type of document (e.g., a decision about centralized purchasing and marketing). Another category is the "report" type of document (e.g., a party central committee conference resolution, central government working reports, the Party and central government leader's formal statements at formal meetings, etc.). Another category is the so-called "speech" documents. This includes the speeches made at formal occasions (e.g., Party and central government leader's speeches when they receive foreign guests that were not published at the time; speeches delivered at CPC Central Committee Political Bureau meetings, such as Ma Zedong's speech on centralized purchase and marketing) and informal occasions (e.g., Deng Xiaoping's "Southern Tour" speeches, etc.). The first two kinds of documents ("decision/notice" and "report") represent the central government leadership's formal policy and settled decisions. Analysis of these documents uses "qualitative analysis". As for the "speech" type of documents, the analysis uses "thematic analysis" and "scenarios analysis". First, from the standpoint of the Party and county's core decision makers, according to the interested parties at that time, the circumstances and their perceptions (perceived reality), we seek to understand how they are thinking and consequently the reasons for a policy decision. Then, within the prevailing social situation, we analyze the philosophical logic and development behind the policy decision. Although "speech" documents are not as formal as the "decision/notice" type and "report" type, they are significant in understanding the policy formulation process, its basis and development by the Party and state.

Many government documents are quoted in this book. The purpose of these quotations is to provide "textual evidence" to support the theoretical points being discussed. In doing so there is risk — it may give the reader the feeling that the materials are being "piling on". Readers who experienced the Cultural Revolution may resent the quoting of so much of the nation's leader's speeches. Nevertheless, I insist on using "textual evidence" much as possible to support the points presented. By doing so, the book is less readable, but it gives a stronger "sense of evidence".

B. Qualitative Analysis[34]

When collecting material on the changes in social structures, I mainly used interviews. There are many efforts by western scholars using qualitative analysis to study sociology. It has proved to be an effective method.[35] There are two kinds of materials for qualitative analysis: one is visual (observation and ethnographic data, photos etc.), the other is verbal (recorded interviews and transcripts).[36] Researchers using qualitative analysis can collect visual materials for study (e.g., Malinovsky, of the Chicago School), and they can collect audio materials for their research (e.g., Roman Duncan). Since the collection of visual materials requires the scholar to be at the scene, it is an impossible task to collect the materials for events that have already become historical. Therefore, the materials in this book about the changes in social structure come mainly from verbal materials, i.e., interviews.

How to study the changes of the social structure and consumer attitudes via qualitative analysis? One effective way is to use group comparison. Following Mannheim's view of sociology, by studies of generational groups, we can find the differences and similarities between previous generations and the current one.[37] The inheritance of culture is not only within a single generation but also across generations. Across generations of inheritance, culture has been conserved and continued. Cultural changes are also intergenerational. There are of course cultural changes within the same generation. But intergenerational cultural changes are more obvious.

The discussion on cultural differences in intergenerational groups by Mannheim,[38] provides the methodological foundation of our study of cultural changes and social structure. From 1949 to the present, there have been three generations. The first generation was the workforce either before the liberation or immediately after the liberation. The second generation was the workforce that was born and grew up after the liberation but before the reform and opening up. The third generation was the group that was born and grew up after the reform and opening up, or the people who joined the workforce after the reform and opening up. However, since our focus is on a "conceptual generation", the definition of generation is determined by the social structure and its ideology. At the same time, the reform and opening up transformed the social structure and its ideology. To simplify the studies of culture and the changes of social structure, we simply divide people into two generations: the "old and strong generation" and the young generation. The landmark event dividing these generations is the beginning of the reform and opening up. Those who grew up and joined the workforce before the reform and opening up, are considered the old and strong generation. Those who grew up and joined the workforce after the reform and opening up are the young generation. Such simplification of intergenerational groups is made so that it is easier to see the influence of the reform and opening up on intergenerational ideology (i.e., the social structure). To the old and strong generation, their "first layer" (experience of growing up) of life took place before the reform and opening up. To the young generation, their first layer of life experience took place after the reform and opening up. Part of the young generation had their first layer of life experience spanning the Cultural Revolution to the reform and opening up. This rough intergenerational categorization is helpful in simplifying the process of material collection. At the same time, it is also helps to overcome the problem that with short intergenerational timespans it can be hard to see differences (for instance, under the influence of re-socialization, many middle-aged people have an ideology closer to that of young people).

In consideration of this, we drew two sample groups in our qualitative interviews. One is a group of the old and strong generation, the other is a group of the young generation. There were 39 people interviewed from the old and strong generation. 78 people interviewed from the young generation. In total, there were 117 people (125 separate interviews) (See Appendix). The reason that there were so many fewer interviews with the old and strong generation as compared to the young generation, was because of the greater homogeneity across the old and strong generation. Although we followed the principle of combination of maximally varying cases in the sampling, we still discovered that this generation has a very high degree of homogeneity. By comparison, the degree of homogeneity in the young generation is much lower, and the degree of heterogeneity much higher. To maximize the usable information in material collection, in addition to the strategy of combining maximally varying cases, we tried to increase the number of people interviewed from the young generation. We did a second interview with some of them. During the interview, we used a progressive multi-stage sampling method. The amount of data sampled was based upon the principle of maximum combination of variation. We could thereby maximize the amount information from the interviews. Deciding how much information to acquire was a contingent process. When we felt sufficient information was obtained, we would end the interview.

The interview outline for the young generation group versus the old and strong generation group are partially the same, which makes them easier to compare. Differences are due to the fact that there are incomparable areas between the two groups. Logically, the consistency and similarity of the young generation and the old and strong generation groups reflect the inheritance relationship of culture and ideology. The differences between the two reflect changes in, and even the fracture of, culture and ideology.

Interviews were done in three rounds. The first round of interviews were done in 2002 and took a few months. Totally 27 people (Group C) were interviewed. The second round of interviews went on for a few months in 2004. The third round was in 2005~2006 for a few months as well. The first round of interview was of an exploratory nature. Based upon the first round, we modified the interview plan by increasing the number of interviews of the old and strong generation (Group A). At the same, we changed and made additions to the question outline used in the first round.

Due to the circular nature of a qualitative study, the interview outline must often be modified during implementation. The reason is that the questions being researched may become clearer during the process, as more material is collected and the interaction between the research goals and available information evolves. As a result, the interview outline as originally prepared may not be complete and must be modified. People who have done qualitative studies know that it is rare to see the "Linear Research Model" applied single-mindedly to qualitative research. It is inevitable during the practice of qualitative research that we need to continuously clarify and modify the research questions and at the same time constantly modify the interview outline.

Since I have focused my time mainly on analyzing government materials, I trained interviewers to conduct the interviews (see appendix). I drafted the interview outline and revised it based upon the analysis of the interviews. With a few exceptions, the interviewers have taken my course on Qualitative Research Methodology. Before the interviews were conducted, I did group training for the interviewers and discussed special topics and procedures. The interviews were done in semi-structured format. This method was used because it fits research in which different groups (generations) are compared. After the materials were gathered through the semi-structured interviews, analysis was done using the theme coding method.

The author provided recording equipment to the interviewers (some of interviewers provided their own voice or MP3 recorders). The interviewers recorded their interviews. Interview time was from 30 minutes to about 2 hours (the longest is 3 hours); most were between one and one-and-half hours. Generally, the recorded interviews were transcribed by the interviewers, though some were done by others. I then analyzed the transcripts. The analysis of the material used the qualitative sources analysis software NVivo 2.0. This made the process very convenient and effective.

The interviews took place in Guangzhou and the surrounding area. The people interviewed were residents of the Guangzhou area. However this does not mean that they were born and grew up there. In fact, due to the increase of migration, most people interviewed came from other areas. Many of them are Guangzhou residents who moved there in recent years. Nevertheless, I cannot claim that this sample for qualitative research is representative from a statistical point of view. In fact, if so-called representativeness is a kind of "statistical representativeness", qualitative research does not need such representativeness, since this is not the goal of qualitative research.

Because the interview data from the Guangzhou area does not represent the entire country, how globally applicable is this research? To answer this question, we must understand the achievable goal of qualitative research. As mentioned above, the sample size used in qualitative research is too small to meet the representativeness required of samples in quantitative research. It would be self-deceiving and misleading for the readers if we attempted to claim the small samples in qualitative research met the representativeness required of the samples (samples representing the whole) in quantitative research. Then, what kind of value does qualitative research bring us? What is its goal?

The role of samples used in qualitative research is different from that in quantitative research. In quantitative research, the samples represent the whole. The reason is simple, because the sizes of the samples are very small. Samples for qualitative research are not necessarily representative of a particular whole with a clearly defined boundary. They are intended to reveal what kind of phenomenon is going on, what categories it has, what factors there are and their interrelationships, etc. The questions qualitative research focuses on versus the questions quantitative research focuses on are of two different kinds. Take consumerism as an example. One of the questions quantitative research is interested in is how to measure consumerism in a population. Once the measurement standard is set, sampling is conducted that will be able to tell the percentage of the population that has a consumerist tendency. The conclusion of the sample can be generalized. Qualitative research does not answer such questions with statistical inference. Again take consumerism as an illustration. One of the questions it is interested in is, what is consumerism? What are its major elements? How many categories can it be divided into? What background, conditions and factors lead to consumerism? What are its consequences? These kinds of questions have nothing to do with statistical inference. They are suitable for qualitative research to resolve. As long as the samples used in qualitative research are sufficient to answer these questions, the goal of which is to enumerate the elements of certain types or conceivable categories, and to clarify the relationships among all the elements, the objectives of qualitative research are achieved.

Since qualitative research usually takes a smaller number of samples, it does not follow the logic of quantitative sampling. Because of the very small sample sizes, regardless of how the procedures of quantitative research are followed, small samples make it difficult to satisfy the representativeness required by quantitative research. In fact, qualitative research does not need such representativeness, as it is not its goal. Its goal is to explain exactly which phenomena exist, their properties and attitudes, and the relationships between these properties and attitudes. So long that it helps to enumerate a certain phenomenon's properties and altitudes (or elements) and their mutual relationship, the sample used in qualitative research it achieves its goal. The standard in measuring the samples of qualitative research is not the representativeness from statistical sense, but is to determine whether the "data saturate" and whether they helps to reach "theoretical saturation". Because of this, qualitative research mainly follows the logic of "objectives sampling" or "theoretical sampling" instead of the logic of probability sampling. If sampling for quantitative research is considered a stage in a linear model of the research process, sampling for qualitative research is a process. This process is expanded as the collection of information and analysis of material is expanded (circular research model).

Since the small sample sizes in qualitative research cannot follow the sampling logic of quantitative research, sampling for qualitative research is often focused on a particular place (e.g., a particular city). Certainly, such places must be typical. Take for example studies of Chinese consumerism. Quantitative research must follow the probability principal by statistically sampling all urban and rural areas, which makes the sample representative of the overall population. The conclusion drawn from a sample is the percentage of the population that has consumerism tendency, which can be generalized to that of the country's overall population. In contrast, qualitative research is different. It cannot be used to answer questions requiring statistical inference. It researches the question: What phenomenon is consumerism? What properties and altitudes does it have? What are the relationships between these properties and altitudes? To answer these questions, qualitative research sampling must be conducted in a particular geographic area. In another word, consumerism in this area must be comparatively prominent and typical.

Because of this, the subjects interviewed in this book are mainly in the Guangzhou district. We do not attempt to use these data to represent the whole country. But with these data, we intend to explain what ascetic culture and consumerist culture are respectively, and what each contains in terms of properties and altitudes, and their inter-relationships, how ascetic culture was transformed into consumerist culture, and so on. Undoubtedly the interview information from the Guangzhou area can answer these questions. First, with regard to ascetic culture, because of the general homogeneity of people's ideology across the country before the reform and opening up, the interview materials from Guangzhou are typical (and Guangzhou has advantages over other provinces by being geographically close to Hong Kong). Second, with regard to researching consumer culture, since commercially Guangzhou is ahead of other areas, and was in the vanguard of the reform and opening up, its consumer culture is quite typical of the country as a whole. Thus Guangzhou is a perfect place for research on consumer culture. It can be said that Guangzhou is an ideal model for studying cultural changes, in particular ascetic culture's movement to certain level of consumer culture. The conclusions of research on this model can be extrapolated and have some external implications. As to how far these conclusions can be extrapolated, or how large the external implications are, readers should use their own judgment according to the particular local circumstances. In fact, since the country has a common culture, even with cultural differences among different areas and cities, there are levels of "family resemblance" (Wittgenstein). The differences between individual areas and cities are like differences in the physical characteristics between brothers and sisters. Although such differences exist, people can still recognize the similarity of the appearance between brothers and sisters. In this sense, the interview information from the Guangzhou area is illustrative. Its universal meaning does not lie in its "representing" the whole, but it illustrates why in China there are certain phenomena and processes. Its lack of representativeness does not mean that it is not typical. Being typical should not be confused with being representative.[39] Furthermore, since I live in Guangzhou, it was very convenient operationally to choose Guangzhou as the interview location.

By studying consumerism we do not mean to assert that all or majority of the people pursue consumerism. In fact, in any developed place, including the most developed United States of America, there are shockingly poor people and poverty. The study of Chinese consumer culture and consumerism does not necessarily mean that poor groups and the culture of frugality associated with the poor do not exist in major Chinese cities (such as Guangzhou). What this book intends to reveal is how consumer culture has migrated from an ascetic culture, what properties and altitudes it has, its internal structure and what consequences it may lead to.

The other difficulty qualitative research faces is that people interviewed to great extent narrate their own personal experiences (i.e., the problem of data validity). This is exactly what qualitative research faces "characterization of crisis". This issue can be distinguished into two different parts: First, the description of experiences or facts has constructive nature. Such constructive nature is a condition of self-existence. It is not practical to attempt to recover the "original reality" in an absolute sense. Any reality is bound to be constructive. But any reality, being constructive, is only an approximation of "original reality", and it can never be recovered completely. Second, the constructive nature of narration is different from the issues of deliberate distortion and fabrication. The former is an ontological problem. The latter is methodological issue, which can be avoided with assistance of certain process. How to avoid it then? First, researchers must understand how the interview environment affects the interview conversation. Just as Habermas's pursued the "ideal conversation environment", researchers must pursue "an environment for telling the truth". Second, through re-visiting topics (or repeating an interview), examine whether there is consistency or contradiction between the topics covered twice within the interview. Third, we can "triangulate" the interview materials and other types of materials to examine the effectiveness of the interview information.

One impression people have of qualitative research is that it is subjective and arbitrary. That is to say, its reliability and effectiveness can be problematic. This is a long debated question in the academic world overseas. I agree with many scholar's point of view that we cannot completely reproduce the standards of quantitative research when we measure the reliability and effectiveness of qualitative research. The emphasis of qualitative research is more on the reliability and effectiveness of the process. The reason for this is the character of qualitative research itself (being difficult to standardize and quantify). In research methods, shortcomings and advantages are always intertwined. Therefore, credibility and effectiveness are exactly the advantages of qualitative research (it is detailed, in depth, thorough).

In qualitative research, one of most problematic issues is its "selective plausibility". For instance, in writing reports, the interview materials consistent with a particular theory that the author leans toward, are often used as the support and proof of the theory. Materials contradicting or in conflict with the theory are intentionally avoided and ignored. Through such subjective selection and filtering of materials, a proof is fabricated for an insubstantial theory. In order to overcome this question logically and as a matter of process, foreign scholars (e.g., Roman Duncan) have proposed the method of "analysis of the induction". The procedure is that after drawing a conclusion from a preliminary analysis of the material, one must examine intentionally the materials for cases that are contradictory to or in conflict with the theory. Each time one comes across such a case in the materials, reflect on why the original theory cannot explain these counter-examples and then modify the original theory so that the theory and materials are consistent. Repeat this process again and again until no more counter-examples are found. In writing this book, the author has used this method in order to improve the validity of the theory.

To enable readers to determine whether the analysis in this book is effective, I use as frequently as possible the original quotes of the people interviewed as evidence. Doing this has a risk, as it may cause the reader to feel that the author is "piling on" the materials. The reason I still chose to do so, is to enhance the reader's confidence that the details of the materials support the conclusions. This makes the materials and proof "speak for themselves". At the same time, to reduce the impression of "piling on", each time original quotes are used, there are no more than three examples or cases (from the original interviews with three people).

Finally, I want to explain the indexing of the interview information in this book. After quoted paragraphs, I note the code number of the person being interviewed. For example: A01-M-75. Here, the first code "A01" represents the sequence, the middle letter "M" represents male (F represents female), "75" represents the age of the person being interviewed (if the age is unknown, tx is used to represent retired or 60p representing more than 60 years old).

C. The Analysis of the Second-Hand Data

Three aspects are involved when studying consumption changes from vertical perspective: First, material history, which is the changes in consumption level and consumption structure; Second, the history of the spirit, belief and the evolution of customs; Third, the history of systems, which is changes in the macro-consumption model. The perspective adopted in this book is to mainly study the changes in macro-consumption and consumer ideology from the point of view of system changes and ideology (social structure) shift. As has been mentioned previously, research on system changes is primarily undertaken by analysis of government documents, following the decisions of "macro action-takers" to research the evolutionary path of the system. Research on ideological changes is done mainly by collecting information from interviews on people's beliefs, ideology and attitudes, and searching for the context of ideology changes by qualitative evaluation of this information. In addition to the perspectives of system change and ideology shift, the perspective of material history is helpful in understanding system history and ideological history. Therefore, the author also analyzed the history of consumption of some goods. This explains from another perspective the macro-consumption model and changes in consumer ideology. Here, material history is seen as an external manifestation of system and ideological history. Statistics on the history of goods, come mainly from country's statistical department's records and include statistics on material goods production, consumption and upgrades. These statistics are second-hand data.

The analysis of the second-hand data must consider whether the statistical standards meet the research objectives. Sources of statistics in this book are principally the country's statistical bureau's statistical yearbooks. Although some of the statistical standards do not exactly meet our needs, they have great reference value because there are no other comparable statistics. Secondly, in the analysis of the second-hand data we must consider objective of the collectors who gathered the original data and the quality of these data. The statistics used in this book are published by the national statistics bureau. Regardless of data quality, one thing certain is the consistency of the data across all statistical yearbooks. That is to say, the statistics from year to year are comparable. These statistics therefore help us understand the objective history and trends of materialistic consumption.

Besides the statistics from the national statistic bureau, the book also uses consumption research data from colleagues and peers in China, especially research data on consumer behavior, persuasibility and ideology. These increase the credibility of the research conclusions.

Basic Concepts and Terminology

A. System and Consumption System

Following North's definition, system refers to "a society's rules of the game, or more formally, as the constraints designed by people and used to construct people's interactions with each other. They are composed of formal rules (statue law, common law, regulations), and informal rules (customs, code of conduct, self-discipline code of conduct) as well as the execution features of the two."[40] Zhiwei Ni also pointed out that systems "are a set of interrelated rules and specifications for dominating society. They are composed of formal and informal social constraints. These constraints shape executive's choice-set".[41] This book follows the "system" defined by North's new economic system. However, this book only analyzes the formal system of consumption and does not discuss information systems. In the book, the consumption system refers to the formal arrangements by the state to control private and collective consumption through consumer policies or administrative command and regulations. These arrangements formulate the constraints on the residents in their series of consumption choices. In other words, the real life effective consumption policies of the state form the formal consumption system. In this book, another name for consumption system is "macro-consumption pattern".

B. Culture, Consumption Culture, Consumer Culture, Consumerism

Culture is the concept with the most ambiguity and it is used frequently. The American anthropologists Kroeber and Kluckhorn summarized 164 definitions of "culture" in their book from 1952. This book adopts one of most often used definitions, which is to consider culture as a system of beliefs, regulations, values and concepts that controls and adjusts people's behavior and relationships. The so-called consumption culture is the system of people's beliefs, values, concepts and attitudes around consumption behavior and consumption relationships. In this sense, consumption culture contains not only the concept of pleasure, but also the concept of frugality.

To distinguish it from the more common term "consumption culture", I use "consumer culture" to refer to the symbolic value system related to the modern market economy, which expresses personal inclination, pleasure-orientation and performance-orientation.

In this book, I define consumerism as a modern form of desire, which is different from the traditional one, which is comparatively fixed, stationary and stable. Consumerism is a kind of dynamic, changeable, and endless form of desire. In this form of desire, people believe that the living standards they "should have" may be higher than what they can afford.

C. Consumption, Consumer Goods, Consumer

"Consumption" has different meanings in different scenarios. During the period of the planned economy, consumption referred to the amount or share of products that people could obtain and consume (often planned production) to satisfy their needs. Consumer goods are usually those products that meet basic needs and are allocated from the state's planned production (and partially from farmers market supplies). Consumers use coupons to purchase these products for consumption at prices specified by the state. During the period of planned economy, there are no "consumers" as defined in the modern market economy. And the concept of "life" seems to capture the features of "consumers" better during the period of planned economy. For example, the information about consumption in the <<National Statistical Yearbook>> is categorized under "People's Lives".

With the gradual transformation of the planned economy into a market economy, the meaning of consumption has changed. Consumption is no longer citizen's purchase, use or consumption of the products provided from country's planned production, it has become a process of consumer's making free choices to purchase, use, own, collect or consume the products provided by the market, at the market price. At the same time, consumption is not only the consuming process in a physical sense, but also is a process with symbolic meaning.[43] In the latter sense, consumption is connected with people's identity.[44] The symbolic aspect of consumption gradually emerged after the reform and opening up. This is an important feature of modern consumerism, which did not exist during the period of the planned economy.

After the reform and opening up, consumer products and services produced for the market and sold a market prices have gradually undermined the dominance of the consumer sector by state's planned production. Since 1997, China has fundamentally eliminated shortages of consumer goods, and gradually moved into the era of the so-called "surplus economy". Consumer goods are not only physical products but also have become a kind of symbol embedded in people's social and cultural lives.

If consumers as defined by market economy did not exist during the period of the planned economy, then after the reform and opening up, consumers strictly defined (in sense of market economy) gradually appeared. In this sense, "consumers" refer to individuals and groups that have the feature of making free choices in the consumer goods market. They not only follow the economic logic but also the symbolic logic of consumption.

It is very obvious that the change in meanings of the key terms above reflects social change. This book uses the specific meanings of the above concepts corresponding to the period being discussed.

D. Labor, Labor Enthusiasm, Labor Efficiency

The concept of "labor", as used in this book, refers to professional activities or work. It includes not only physical work, but also mental work. In this book, "work" and "labor" are interchangeable.

Nevertheless, the meaning of "labor" (or "work") was different in the period of planned economy compared to the time of market economy. During the planned economy, work was considered part of cadre's and worker's "conduct", so it was not purely an economic activity. It had political overtones. In early 1960s when wage adjustments were frozen and in the mid 1960s when the bonus system was abolished, compensation according to work was not realized and working more did not mean getting paid more. In this situation, the economic reward of work is comparatively stable and predictable. To stimulate labor enthusiasm in a situation where working more does not mean more pay, political and ideological education and mobilization, as well as political honor (e.g., advanced workers) were major labor incentives. After the reform and opening up, the re-establishment of policies such as compensation according to work and getting more pay for more work, work has become a kind of wage activity, which does not have political overtones it did in planned economy. Labor stimulation is no longer done through political and ideological education and mobilization. It is done by economic means: wages, rewards, labor contracts, labor rules, etc. The main constraints on workers are no longer given by political and ideological education and criticism. Instead they are labor rules and professional ethics.

Labor enthusiasm refers to the strong motivation for work, willingness to work, willingness to devote full efforts and not being lazy and slack. During the period of the planned economy, the stimulation of labor enthusiasm mainly relied upon political and ideological mobilization, political reward and limited material reward. After the reform and opening up, stimulation of labor enthusiasm has relied mainly on economic measures (rewards, wages, labor discipline and professional ethics, etc.). Nevertheless, "labor enthusiasm" is not equal to "labor initiative". The former can be the result of subordinate's willingness to obey the orders of their superiors. The latter is not dependent upon superior's order but on workers being able to make their own choices independently. During the period of the planned economy, people may have been enthusiastic to work but may not have had much initiative to work. After the reform and opening up, as individuals, enterprises and local governments have acquired more responsibility, power, profits and more independence, the returns from labor and labor contributions are connected, so people not only have enthusiasm for work but also have initiative to work.

"Labor enthusiasm" and "labor efficiency" are two different concepts. Labor efficiency includes two components, one being macro labor efficiency and the other micro labor efficiency. Macro labor efficiency depends upon resource allocation, reasonable division of labor and the coordination of various departments. Labor initiative is a contributing element to macro labor efficiency, but is not the only element. If resources are not allocated properly, or various departments are not coordinated, labor initiative will likely be wasted and become inefficient. Micro labor efficiency is primarily dependent upon the calculation of input-output ratio by individuals and enterprises as well as worker's initiative and spirit of self-responsibility, which potentially maximizes output from a given labor input. Work which ignores costs and lacks awareness of the input-output ratio, even if it is positive, is still inefficient work. Therefore, labor enthusiasm is a necessary requirement of labor efficiency but not a sufficient condition. With labor enthusiasm, there could be comparatively high labor efficiency, or possibly ineffective work. It can be said, that during the period of Ma Zedong's planned economy, the national system plan used mainly positive labor incentives, but not in labor efficiency and in worker's self-responsibility and innovation. This explains why people seemed very active, but labor efficiency was still very low. The difference between the time of the planned economy and that of the market economy, is that the planned economy was oriented towards a purpose doctrine. Purpose determines everything but ignores costs, or at least many costs. Under such orientation control, people's work seems to be in full swing, but in fact is ineffective, even if often seems to creates all sorts of miracles. The market economy is instrumental in orientation, labor investment is recorded as a cost, and work processes maximize the output or return with least amount of input (costs). Such instrumental labor attitudes have greatly increased labor efficiency. However in the absence of standardized conditions, this can lead to the widespread occurrence of "unscrupulous" behaviors (e.g., proliferation of counterfeit products, low quality products, or adverse environmental effect), which in turn reduces macro labor efficiency.

E. Desire of Consumption and Labor Motivation

In this book, desire for consumption refers to a special form of desire. Labor motivation is a kind of psychodynamic or motivation engaged in work or commitment to work tasks. Desire for consumption (the following short as "desire") and labor motivation (the following short as "labor") are a pair in endless conflict. Through the ages, many people expect "to reap without sowing"; robbery, plunder, theft, war, exploitation, etc., are the product of this kind of psychological mindset. The history of human civilization, to certain extent, is the evolutionary history of the conflict between desire and labor. With the evolution of civilization, the psychological structure of human beings has undergone revolutionary changes: human beings are able to control their desire, to put the goal of immediate pleasure behind, and to achieve the deferred goal of pleasure[45] via labor. From the historical point of view, religion has played an irreplaceable role[46] in inhibiting desire and stimulating labor. People have learned in practice that the more they fantasize about "reaping without sowing", the less they would get in the end. Thus asceticism has is an ethic with a long history. People have learned to tolerate, and to benefit from the philosophy of "tasting the sweet after the first tasting the bitter". And the delayed pleasures of life have become people's objectives, something to look forward to and motivation for engaging in hard work. Even in capitalism, greedy desire is not encouraged. Hirschman believes that capitalism in fact uses some kinds of harmless, moderate desires such as money-making and participating in business as checks and balances to curb more dangerous and devastating desires (robbery, murder, theft, etc.).[47]

In modern society this kind of conflict between desire for pleasure and labor motivation persists. In fact, since 1949 in China, with regard to the conflict between desire for consumption and labor motivation, the state and individuals have formed different relationships. Through the state's adoption of methods to resolve the conflict between desire for consumption and labor motivation at different periods of time, we are able to uncover and interpret the inherent logic of the evolution and transformation of Chinese urban consumer system. In other words, the evolution of the consumer system has embedded in it the background pattern of institutional arrangement by which the state manages the conflict between desire for consumption and labor motivation. Countries manage differently the conflict between desire for consumption and labor motivation, which leads to different desires for personal consumption and different sources of motivation.

F. State

The "state", as used in this book, refers to government or governing mechanism in a specific territory, in this case to the central government of the People's Republic of China. It includes the central communist government, state council and the ministries. I agree with Levi that to study the state, we cannot but "bring people back to the state".[48]   Or in Chen Nabo's words, the state itself is not an active person. State action is nothing but group action in executing the state's power.[49] Therefore, in this book, so-called state action refers mainly to national leadership's or leader's action.

G. Legitimacy Resources

This book defines "legitimacy resources" as the popularity, prestige or reputation possessed by the state or an organization, as well as means available to obtaining these resources. Legitimacy resources are reflected to the degree (more or less) that the people accept, support, assist and follow the policy of the state or the organization.

Chapter Two

Institutional Arrangement of the Ascetic Society

From the early 1950s of the last century, through the reform and opening up, until today, Chinese society has experienced a deep transformation. One of the key transformations was in the social dimension that is related to the consumer system and consumer attitudes. I call the transformation of this dimension the transformation from an ascetic society to a consumer society. An ascetic society can also be called a producer society. The two are in fact are the same social form viewed from different sides. Therefore, when I call the period of Ma Zedong's planned economy an ascetic society, I do not deny it at the same time being a producer society, but focus on the aspect of people inhibiting their desire for consumption. Whether an ascetic or producer society, they are both opposed to consumer society. Of course, people in an ascetic society or producer society must consume, but society's objective at the institutional level or cultural level is to inhibit consumption.

The study of China's transformation from ascetic society to consumer society is a new topic. Research in this area is very significant to deepen our understanding of the transformation of contemporary Chinese society. In this chapter, I will start the analysis by considering the institutional arrangements of ascetic society and their systematic logic. The framework of the chapter is as the following (Figure 2-1):

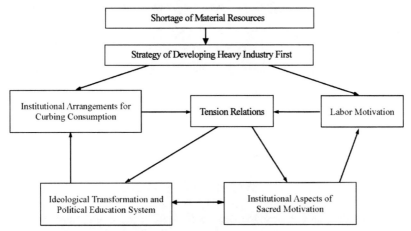

Figure 2-1   Institutional Arrangements of Ascetic Society: The System for Curbing
Consumption System and Its Derivative Systems

Institutional Arrangements and Their Logic in Curbing Consumption

After the founding of the country, the state imposed institutional arrangements to curb consumption in urban areas. It was not accidental that such institutional initiatives were implemented, as these arrangements had an internal logic. Such initiatives were far reaching and had strong influence on China's social development from that time, causing a chain reaction during the process of setting up the system. Therefore, it is consistent with the narrative that my analysis starts with the institutional arrangement of curbing consumption.

The main subject I discuss here are the institutional arrangements of the state, which is: the central communist government, state council and ministries, in particular the Party and state's leaders. The state's actions are nothing but human actions in exercising state power.[50]   In states with centralized power, to great extent, the state's actions are in fact the state leadership's actions, especially the core leadership's actions. These leaders are not normal action takers; they are macro action takers. They have the power of control the society through issuing orders and making top-down systemic arrangements. Rigby believes that there are three different activities in controlling society, in particular the coordination of social activities: custom, contract and command. "Custom-led society is called traditional society. Contract-led society is called market society. Command-led society is called organizational society."[51] Like the former Soviet Union, having centralized control and a planned economy, China is an organizational society. I am more inclined to call it a "command-led society". In this type of society, macro-system arrangements are mainly made and driven by the state leadership. It is without exception in the arrangement of the consumer system. Such a systemic arrangement constitutes the macro systemic constraint on the individual level of consumption. Therefore, during the time of the planned economy, what people consumed, how much and how they consumed were not determined by individuals. To a great extent, they are decided by the state. Consequently, in order to do research on Chinese citizen's consumption, we cannot but analyze the systemic arrangement made by the state for consumption.

A. Institutional Arrangements to Curb Consumption

Why should institutional arrangements be made to curb consumption? This is indeed a perplexing question. For a newly established state, it is surprising and may be unwise to take such initiative, because stability of the new state's power depends upon the people's support. Improving people's living standard is an important measure to win the people's endorsement. But this is only one aspect of the problem. Essentially, it is a rational choice for the state to take such initiatives. The drastic implementation of this kind of rational policy is intrinsically related to the rich "legitimacy resources" possessed by the state. Therefore, the above question has changed to: First of all, why was curbing consumption is a kind of rational institutional initiative? Secondly, what kind of legitimacy resources did the state have at the time?

Two aspects are related to why curbing consumption was a rational choice: First it was the state's goal. Second, was the availability of material resources at the time. The national goal and objective, at that time, was to lead the country's population to build socialist industry. This goal would lay the material foundation toward the final realization of communism. In this sense, China at the time was what Oakeshott's called a "business association-type" of state, but not "association of citizens type" of state,[52] which is to say, the party and state's goal is towards a common cause and mission: in the near term to realize socialist industrialization, in the long term, to realize communism. As Ma Zedong said, "We communist party members never hide our political opinions. Our future program or ultimate program is to push China to socialist society and communist society. This is determined and undoubted."[53] After the establishing the new China, the Chinese Communist Party expelled the imperialist forces, confiscated bureaucratic capital (to convert it to a state-run economy), and completed rural land reform. Based upon this foundation, the tasks of revolutionary socialism were put on the agenda. For this, the Chinese Communist central government in 1952 developed general guidelines for movement to socialism.[54] The guidelines were for the transitional period from the founding of the People's Republic to the basic completion of the implementation of socialism. The Party's general program was, over a considerably long period of time, to gradually realize the country's socialist industrialization, and gradually complete the socialist reform of agriculture, handicraft and capitalist industry and commerce."[55] This general program included two aspects. One was to achieve the socialist revolution in the ownership of the means of production, "to have socialist ownership of production become the only economic basis of our country and society".[56] The other was to establish socialist industrialization and to lay the material foundation for the socialist system. On the reform of the ownership, by 1956 the country completed the transformation to socialist ownership of agriculture, handcraft and capitalist industry and commerce. However, the socialist industrialization objectives were unlikely to be finished within a short period. It was a long-term process.

On industrialization, Mao Zedong pointed out explicitly in April 1945 when he gave his political report at the Seventh Chinese National Congress of the Communist Party: "Without industrialization, there would not be a strong national defense, would not be people's welfare, would not be national prosperity."[57] Therefore, "after New Democracy's political conditions are obtained, the Chinese people and their government must take practical steps to build up heavy industry and light industry within a number of years, and therefore to transform China from an agricultural country to an industrial country."[58] After the founding of the People's Republic, socialist industrialization became the consensus of the Communist Party's Central Committee.

The state's leaders realized that in order to create socialist industrialization, the emphasis should be on developing heavy industry. Zhou Enlai pointed out: "Heavy industry is a country's industrial foundation. Although we still have a tiny foundation of heavy industry, it is far from enough if we consider it as the base of industrialization. Therefore, we cannot but focus on developing heavy industry first. At the beginning of their first five-year construction plan, the Soviet Union still focused on developing heavy industry even though their base of heavy industry was bigger than ours. We need to primarily focus more on developing heavy industry, as our base is not as good."[59] It can be seen from this, that the policy of developing the country's heavy industry first, was inseparable from the model of the Soviet Union.

Obviously, the state leadership realized that in an economically backward country, to build socialist industrialization, it could not retrace the path of the capitalist industrialization, which started by developing light industry first. They must learn from the experience of the Soviet Union, to pursue an extraordinary development strategy putting heavy industry at the core and as the primary objective. Because heavy industry was undeveloped, light industry and agriculture could not be developed either. The intellectual route to making the development of heavy industry the priority is given in the first Five Year plan. Li Fuchun clearly pointed out in "The Report of the First Five Year National Economic Development", "Socialist industry is our country's core task during this transition period of time, and the center link of socialist industrialization is to primarily develop heavy industry."[60] Chen Yu also pointed out: "Our country's economy is backward. In order to catch up within a short period of time, the balances in the planned economy will have much tension. In the plan something must be given priority. In the near term, it is industry, especially heavy industry."[61] In his "Government Work Report" given at the first meeting of the First National People's Congress, Zhou Enlai pointed out, "It is known to all of us the policy of the first Five Year plan, which is: to focus mainly on developing heavy industry, to build up the foundation for the country's industrialization and the modernization of national defense; ... The reason that the first Five Year plan calls for focusing on developing heavy industry, which is metallurgical industry, dye industry, power industry, machinery manufacturing industry and chemical industry, is that only by relying upon heavy industry, can there be an assurance of the development of overall industrialization, assurance of development of modernization of agriculture and the modernization of transportation, and assurance of the development of modernization of national defense and power. And ultimately, only by relying upon heavy industry, can there be assurance of a continuous improvement in people's material life and cultural life."[62]

Heavy industry is capital-intensive industry. It consumes comparatively large material resources. But at the beginning, after the founding of the country, China was an extremely backward agricultural country. It had a very meager industrial base, and its people lived in poverty. The national statistical bureau's statistics give, before the liberation, annual production of steel up to 923,000 tons, coal production annually was only 6,188,000 tons, grain production annually was as much as 2,774,000,000,000 jin, and annual output of cotton was as much as 170,000,000 dan. Devastated after years of war, until the liberation in 1949, the annual output of grain and soybeans decreased 25 percent from the historical high and the output of cotton decreased 48 percent. In comparison, there was heavier loss in industrial production: output of production equipment decreased 53 percent and end-user goods dropped by 50 percent. Compared to the highest output before the liberation, the decrease in output of all kinds of industrial products were as follows: steel decreased 83 percent, raw iron decreased 86 percent, raw coal decreased 48 percent, electricity decreased 28 percent, cement decreased 71 percent, cotton cloth decreased 32 percent, sugar decreased 52 percent.[63] The war destroyed infrastructure as well, and seriously damaged transportation facilities led to difficulty in transporting materials. After the Communist Party took over in 1949, they faced a serious problem of inflation. Rising prices and increasing unemployment led to a sharp decline in people's standard of living. After two year's recovery, over which the government believed the economy was stabilizing, the Korean War broke out. The Chinese People's Volunteer Army went to Korea to join the war, which costs a large fraction of the nation's finances. The international environment in the early stage after founding of the country was not favorable to China. The western capitalist countries, represented by America, adopted a hostile attitude toward China. In the early days after the founding of the country, China could still trade with western capitalist countries. After the Korean War broke out, America imposed an embargo, blockade, and economic sanctions on us for a long time. Foreign trade channels were seriously blocked, therefore trade had to be conducted with the Soviet Union and Eastern European socialist countries. Until 1953, although the national economy recovered greatly, shortages of materials were still severe: food production was only 166,830,000 tons, cotton 1,175,000 tons, oil 3,856,000 tons, sugar 7,716,000 tons, raw coal 70,000,000 tons, crude oil 620,000 tons, power generation 920,000,000 KWh, raw iron 2,230,000 tons, steel 1,770,000 tons, processed steel 1,470,000 tons.[64]

Obviously, in the early fifties of the last century, the situation facing the country was quite grim. On one hand, the country's objective was to build up socialist industrialization. But in a very backward agricultural country, building up socialist industrialization meant the adoption of an extraordinary "catching up" strategy and developing primarily heavy industry. On the other hand, heavy industry is capital-intensive industry. And the problem faced by the state was the extremely poor availability of materials. With a limited total amount of material resources, the leadership of the country naturally made arrangements to rationally reduce consumption. They invested the limited capital resources into building up heavy industry in order to raise the ratio of proportional accumulation. Obviously implementing the policy of developing heavy industry first in an economically under-developed country such as China, meant sacrificing the people's consumption level. Zhou Enlai pointed out: "When the country needs to concentrate on developing heavy industry as priority to build the socialist foundation, all of us must focus our attention on the long-term benefits. We must not seek the immediate benefits but ignore the long-term benefits. For the well-being of our children and our grandchildren, we must face up to the many difficulties."[65]

Since the limited material resources were invested in projects for heavy industry, the development of light industry and agriculture had to temporarily be put on hold. At the same time, in order to reduce the cost of developing heavy industry, the cost of labor had be restricted to a reasonably low level, therefore a low salary policy had to be in place. This shows that an extraordinary industrial policy must be supplemented by an extraordinary consumer policy, which is the policy to curb consumption and to encourage people to save food and clothing. In the government working report made at the first meeting of the First National People's Congress, Zhou Enlai pointed out clearly the inevitability of curbing consumption:

"The heavy industry requires comparatively greater capital investment. The building time is longer and the return of profits takes place slowly. The majority of the products cannot directly feed people's consumption needs. So during the period when the country focuses on developing heavy industry, although there is level of development of light industry and agriculture, people still can not but tolerate certain difficulties and inconveniences in life. But shall we tolerate certain temporary difficulties and inconveniences for the return of long-term prosperity and happiness? Or shall we seek immediate small gains but consequently cannot break away forever from poverty and backwardness? We believe that all of us must think the first idea great but not the second one."[66]

Obviously, from state leadership's perspective, curbing consumption was people's temporary sacrifice of near-term benefits in exchange for long-term benefits for all the people. It was naturally necessary.

From the citizen' perspective, curbs on consumption were not necessarily a good thing. After years of wars and several years of economic recovery and rebuilding, people had just started improve their lives when the state began implementing the consumption curb system. This was apparently contradictory to people's expectations. So the state's implementation of the system to curb consumption was on the basis of a rational tradeoff. What was more important was the state's daring to implement the system of curbed consumption, which was closely related to its legitimacy resources. In the early days after the founding of the country, there is a sharp contrast in probity and corruption, between the ascendant communist party and its military versus Kuo-Min-Tang (KMT) and their military that had dominated before. The communist party's class line and policy objectives with regard to the poor people were very attractive to worker-peasant class that was the absolute majority of the population. Therefore, the establishment of the new political power was highly supported by the worker-peasant class. The party and the government, especially Ma Zedong, the highest leader of the party and the state, gained a very high reputation. This reputation comprised the state's political resource, which is a kind of legitimacy resource. In this book, we define "legitimacy resources" as the state's (or an organization's) popularity, its leadership's popularity, reputation and prestige, as well as the means and resources for gaining such popularity. The quantity of legitimacy resources is reflected in people's acceptance, support, and willingness to follow and obey the state (or other organization) and its leadership.[67]

Only because the state possesses rich legitimacy resources, can the state implement with free hand the institutional arrangements to curb consumption. In the mean time, the state induces the people to long for and yearn for the future socialist happy life. They persuade people to accept and support the system of curbs on consumption. Since curbed consumption is an arrangement made by a government supported by people, and curbed consumption is a kind of temporary stop-gap measure, and a "better life" is coming after some period of saving food and cloth as well as hard work, there is no reason that people would not accept such an institutional arrangement. With the worker-peasant clas's gratitude towards and trust in the party and the government, the country was able to implement this institutional arrangement at very low cost.

How does the state impose an institutional arrangement to curb consumption? After the establishment of a new political regime, followed by a short economic recovery (1949~1952), in 1953 the country started to implement the strategy of primarily developing heavy industry. In the first "Five Year Plan",[68] the state put forward a policy of investing in heavy industry, which was: the institutional arrangements of "high accumulation, low consumption". The basic tasks in the "first five" plan were: focus primarily on a core of 156 construction projects designed with help from the Soviet Union. Focus also on industrial construction with 694 large and medium sized construction projects. To make socialist industrialization as the preliminary basis for further developing collective ownership of agricultural cooperatives, and to develop handicraft co-operatives, so as to establish the socialist transformation of agricultural and handicrafts on a preliminary basis. Basically, to move away from capitalist industry and commerce toward various forms of state capitalism, and therefore to establish the foundation of socialist reform of privately owned business and commerce[69].

In his report about "the first five" plan, Li Fuchun explained the distribution of capital investment in basic construction: the total investment of the five year basic construction is 42,740,000,000 yuan, of which: industrial departments is 24,850,000,000 yuan or 58.2 percent; agriculture, water and forestry are 3,260,000,000 yuan or 7.6 percent, transportation and postal services are 8,210,000,000 yuan or 19.2 percent; trade, banking and material reserves are 1,280,000,000 yuan or 3 percent; culture, education and health sector are 3,080,000,000 yuan or 7.2 percent; construction of urban public facilities is 1,600,000,000 yuan or 3.7 percent; the others are 460,000,000 yuan or 1.1 percent. Obviously, the investment focus is industry.[70] In the "first five" plan, the investment in heavy industry construction as a fraction of overall industrial investment was 85 percent, and 72.9 percent of basic construction investment was in industry and agriculture.[71] After the first Five Year plan, accumulated reserve growth rate was much higher for quite some time than national income growth rate. The proportion of total consumption in the total use of national income decreased dramatically. High accumulation and low consumption became a long-term and increasingly strong trend (excluding the adjustment period 1963~1965) (see Table 2.1).

From the investment perspective, the country's capital investment significantly leans towards heavy industry. The investment in consumer goods industry is comparatively smaller. This trend continues for quite a long time (see Table 2-2).

Table 2-1 Chinese Consumption Calculated Based upon MPS, Reserve Ratio Moving Trend

Period	Consumption Level	Increase of Average Annual National Income Growth in Comparison to That of Previous Planning Period	Average Consumption Rate	Average Accumulation Rate	Increase of Average Annual Accumulation Total in Comparison to That of the Previous Planning Period
"First Five" Period	4.2		75.8	24.2	
"Second Five" Period	−3.3	35.8	70.6	29.4	73.5
1963~1965	8.6	8.1	77.3	22.7	−2.0
"Third Five" Period	2.1	35.6	74.2	25.8	51.5
"Fourth Five" Period	2.2	41.7	67.0	33.0	78.0
The First Three Years of "Fifth Five" Period	1.04		66.8	33.2	

(Source: Fang Anqin, ed., *Research on Our Country's Consumer Demand, Evolution and Consumption Policy* (Beijing: China Economic Publishing House, 2006), 4.)

Table 2-2 Proportion of Heavy Industry and Light Industry in Overall Basic Construction Capital Investment

Year	Light Industry of Overall Basic Construction Capital Investment (%)	Heavy Industry of Overall Basic Construction Capital Investment (%)
1953 — 1957	6.4	36.1
1958 — 1962	6.4	54
1963 — 1965	3.9	45.9
1966 — 1970	4.4	51.1
1971 — 1975	5.8	49.6

(Source: Hu Fangzhi: *The Studies on Wage Level During Chinese Economic Takeoff* (Beijing: China Economic Publishing House, 2005), 101.)

Li Yifu and others believe that once the strategy of developing heavy industry first was adopted, there "must be a whole set of macro-economic policies in place that are different from that of a market adjustment mechanism, so that resource allocation is beneficial to the development of heavy industry. In detail, it means to forcefully lower the costs of heavy industrial development."[72] One feasible way to reduce the cost of developing heavy industry is to reduce the costs of labor by implementing a low wage policy. Obviously a low wage policy is a double-edged sword. On one hand, the policy reduces the total amount of national consumption, reducing the consumer fund and increasing investment fund. On the other hand, it lowers the cost of heavy industry because it makes the costs of labor cheaper. Through unified revenue and expenditure, the state took overall control of total salary amounts and wage levels, which was: The central government issues their planned target for controlling the total wage amount. The adjustment of wage levels is done uniformly at the national level. Local governments, departments or enterprises have no ability to increase an individual salary. From 1957 to 1976, worker's wage levels did not increased at all. On the contrary, they actually dropped.

Regarding this wage policy, at the third plenary meeting of the eighth CPC Central Committee, Zhou Enlai explained again in "The Report on the Issue of Labor Wages and Labor Benefits":

"Our labor wage and labor benefits policy must integrate the people of the whole country, and first of all these policies should focus on improving the lives of the workers and peasants. We must properly arrange the basic starting point of urban-rural relationships, and implement a reasonable low wage system, so that everyone will have meals. And on the basis of developing production, there must be incremental improvement in the workers and peasant's lives. Implementing a low wage system is in fact arranging the salary level. We cannot start simply to increase industrial production and increase industrial labor productivity. We must start by developing the overall national economy and raising the whole of society's labor productivity. Only by implementing a reasonable low wage system, can it match the very low industrial and agricultural productivity level. ... Implementing a low wage system can guarantee as much as possible that everyone has food, which is what we often talked about as "three people's food to support five people."[73]

From an economic point of view, one of the prerequisites for a low wage policy is that the price of the living necessities that maintaining labor's capability to sustain itself cannot be too high. In Lin Yifu and other's words: to enable the urban working class to "face the pricing structure of life necessities determined by market, a comparatively low salary level may not be enough for them to purchase consumer goods and services to meet their basic needs. Labor may no t be able to sustain itself, therefore leading to social instability. It also affects the labor supply for heavy industry. To solve this problem, one way is to implement a low price policy for agricultural products, necessities and services. This will lower the costs to sustain labor to match the low remuneration."[74]

Based on such economic logic, the country implemented a system of centralized purchase and sale in 1953. The centralized control of purchase and sales was an effective way for country to control the prices of necessities, mainly food. On one hand, the centralized purchasing in rural areas excluded the market mechanism for adjusting the prices of food, cotton, oil and other products. It was rather done via administrative methods, artificially manipulating and stabilizing the prices of necessities at a level compatible (i.e., by the state's premium pricing) with the low wage policy. On the other hand, a centralized sale policy (ration system) in the urban areas achieved the goal of controlling urban and suburban resident's average per person consumption and prevented the rapid increase of consumer demands while at the same time, still able to maintain people's basic living standards. By allocating tickets to urban residents for the purchase of living necessities, the state was able to limit citizen's consumption of food, clothing, food oil and other basic consumer goods. After implementing this "ticket system", it had to be re-enforced, and the number of items covered by the system was increased as the lack of consumer goods intensified. The system lasted for quite some time after the reform and opening up.

Through the policy of centralized purchase and sale, the state artificially managed to keep prices low for major agricultural products. As a result, the cost of industrialization was transferred to great extent to the peasants. In "Central Government's Decision on Implementing Planned Purchase of Food and Planned Supplies", the CPC Central Committee requested clearly of the peasants: "the industrialization of the county is of the utmost benefit to all the people. It is also for the best interest of peasants … Helping the country's efforts in industrialization and supporting the country's policy of planned purchase and planned supply, are peasant's important obligations to the country. It is also peasant's patriotic duty."[75]

Saving food and clothes supported the nation's industrialization, not only because the savings were reflected in the capital accumulation required to develop of heavy industry, but also in freeing the capital needed to import machinery required by that industry. Because China was an agriculture country at the time, the technical equipment required for heavy industrial development had to be imported from overseas. But the only thing China could export was agricultural products. In exchange for the equipment required for industrialization, the state adopted the policy of giving the export of these agricultural products priority. In return, this policy intensified domestic shortages of agricultural products. Under this circumstance, it was inevitable to ask people to save food and clothing.

Chen Yu also elaborated with specific examples the meaning of the government's inhibiting consumption of agricultural products in favor of industrialization. For instance, he said: "Twenty thousand eggs can be exchanged for five tons of steel, so we should try to export more eggs."[76]   "In a condition that one ton of meat can be exchanged for five tons of steel, we should try to export more pork, which has a major effect in supporting the country's economic construction."[77] Therefore, Chen Yu advocates a foreign trade policy in which, "with exception of food and oil materials that have special regulations limiting exports, for all other materials and for a long period in future, domestic sales must submit to the needs of export. With some merchandise such as meat, sales in domestic market must be compressed in order to meet the demand of export. Some merchandise such as fruits, tea and varieties of small indigenous, should be given priority for export. The surplus can supply sales in domestic market. Only in this way, can necessary exports be guaranteed, in exchange obtaining industrial equipment for the country's construction."[78]

Such policy securing the export of agricultural products as priority was the last resort of the state under the circumstances. Chen Yu said: "Decreasing consumption is of course is not a comfortable thing to do, but we must choose one of the two: either temporarily reduce or much as possibly reduce consumption, in order to complete the country's industrialization, so as to build the foundation of our country to further develop agricultural or light-industry. It will allow us to rapidly increase the output of a variety of consumer products. Otherwise all consumption is made domestically, thus no industrialization can be achieved, which will cause a long period of backwardness for our economy. The whole country naturally should select the former but not the latter."[79] Thus "decreasing consumption" became a requirement and national choice.

B. Institutional Arrangements and Logic of Private Consumption: The Example of the Centralized Purchase and Sale System

In implementing the institutional arrangements for curbing consumption, different attitudes towards private consumption and group consumption were adopted. With respect to private consumption, the state adopted inhibitory initiatives. With respect to collective consumption, although it was curbed overall, it was still considered a form of social welfare, which reflected the state's "paternal love" and "generosity". Therefore, the state's institutional arrangements for private and collective consumption follow different logics – rational logic and legality logic.

In the early stage after the country's founding, one urgent problem the state faced was how to rapidly increase its capability to mobilize resources, so as to increase state's authority and power for controlling society. Since the Central People's Government had great financial difficulty in expenditure, the state's resource mobilization capability was limited, which enabled speculators to take advantage of the policy. According to Pang Song's description, in October 1949, speculators in Beijing started to hoard food, and engaged in price gouging. Capitalists in Shanghai were buying materials in short supply, leading to nation-wide price increases. This lasted over 40 days.[80] Within the central government, the finance committee chaired by Chen Yu led a fight to use economic means to combat speculators in order to keep prices under control. The finance committee quietly transported large quantities of materials in short supply (e.g. food, cotton etc.) to the cities. When prices rose to a peak on 25 November, a unified plan was put in to effect, with all merchandise being sold at state pricing, which led to rapid price drops. At the same time, banks in large cities shrank the money supply and additional taxes were levied. This forced speculators to sell their accumulated stocks at a very low price. Simultaneously, the government bought in large quantities.[81] These economic steps not only suppressed the inflationary trend but also were a heavy blow to the speculators who had hoarded merchandise. Afterwards, the well-known national capitalist Rong Yiren expressed, "The June silver wave was suppressed by the Central Communist Government. This time, only economic power was to enforce stabilization, which is unexpected by the Shanghai business community."[82]

Beginning from the early days of this economic "food cotton war", the state tasted the benefits of using the unified national administrative resources to mobilize economic resources. Clearly, improving administrative integration in order to enhance the mobilization of material resources, was a rational choice. In turn, because of the state's enhanced ability mobilize resources, its administrative authority was greatly increased. Thus, on 28 December 1949, Chen Yun, head of the Central Financial and Economic Committee proposed the "unified management of the financial economy".[83] In particular, he raised the importance of unified national allocation of food: "grain tax revenue, can be managed by the local administrations that are approved by the central government or a major administrative authority, the rest is to be allocated by the central or major administrative districts. ... The grain cannot be randomly allocated, allocation among major districts must be centrally determined, supplies among the cities must be adjusted, and it should become a major means for withdrawing currency from circulation in the future."[84] This illustrates that Chen Yun was clearly aware of the national mobilization of food and other resources. In a country with extreme poverty, only the concentrated application of national resources in a unified manner could improve resource mobilization enough to accomplish major tasks. He said: "In order to overcome temporary financial difficulties and move forward from a backward and poor economic base, we must focus as much as possible on the consistent use of material and financial resources. We do have difficulties, but we have hope as long as we put together our efforts to focus on the necessary areas, we can accomplish some major events."[85] The increased capability in national resource mobilization was also conducive to national leadership of the private economy. "For the private economy to follow, one condition is that state economy must have considerable power. If you have power, they will follow you. If you are not powerful, it will not listen to you. For instance, last year, we have power over such items as kerosene, food, and gauze that are important resources for living, thus we had command of the private merchants. This was also the case with industry."[86] The outbreak of the Korean War exacerbated the state's leader's concern for the mobilization of national resources, especially the ability to control the use of food resources. "... Food for our country has great political significance. Food is a strategic material, and we are often in control of one hundred tons of grain, regardless of threats from Truman. If famine hits the country and tens of millions of people have no food, though we have the whole country to feed, we will be able to get through."[87]

With the gradual stabilization of the economy, and the systemization of the financial and economic order, the state's role in resource mobilization was elevated to a higher status, which served the general goal of the transitional period, namely, to bring about the socialist transformation of agriculture, handicrafts and capitalist industry and commerce, and to have the transformed industry support state finance and economic development. In 1953, when production and economic order was restored and the state began preparing for the socialist transformation of agriculture, handicrafts and capitalist industry and commerce, shortages of food and other basic consumer commodities appeared again. The country's ability to mobilize its resources, especially food and other strategic resources, was once again put to the test.

Although China is an agricultural country, it has long been plagued by food issues. To solve the food problem, Mao asked the Finance Committee to take concrete measures. Chen Yun proposed the approach of levy and allocating, which is to acquire (levy) from rural areas, and to allocate in urban areas. The proposal immediately won support and praise from Zhou Enlai, Deng Xiaoping, Mao Zedong[88.] On 2 October 1953 the Political Bureau of CPC Central Committee held an enlarged meeting devoted to food issues, and decided to convene a national food emergency meeting. At the enlarged meeting of the Political Bureau, Chen Yun delivered a report on food problem. Mao Zedong summarized the discussion, saying, "Yes, we support Comrade Chen Yun's report. Detailed approach is to be discussed later. ... This is a battle to be fought, with one side being grain suppliers, the other side being the grain eaters. We cannot fight the battle unprepared. We must be fully prepared for emergency mobilization."[89] Mao also connected the unified purchase and sale with the state's socialist transformation of private capitalism and farmers.[90] Based on this position, "food acquisition, the consolidation of merchants and unified management, is imperative." As for allocation, he believes, "the issue of allocation can be considered. My observation is that it is imperative, because small-scale peasant production is very small, but the annual growth of urban food demand is great ... As for the name, we don't have to call it allocation, we can call it planned supply." Mao Zedong was also aware of the difficulty of carrying out unified purchase and sale, "by doing so, there might be problems. First the peasants may not be satisfied. Second, the public may not be happy. Third, there might be dissatisfaction reported in the foreign media. The problem is to see our work." He advocates, "strongly promoting the policy of unified purchase and sale of grain, but not in the newspapers."[91]

On 10 October 1953, the National Food Conference was held. On 16 October, the CPC Central Committee Political Bureau held an enlarged meeting again. With the passage of "A resolution to implement planned food acquisition and planned supply", it confirmed that by the end of November, preparation and mobilization are to be completed. By early December, unified purchase and sale of grain was to be carried out throughout the country (except Tibet and Taiwan). 19 November, at the Chief Administrative Council's 194th session, the CPC Central Committee adopted "The orders by Administrative Council on the implementation of planned purchase and planned supply".[92] Specific measures for grain purchase and sale were released on 23 November. It can be said that Chen Yun played the role of major architect in the process of forming the central government's policy on centralized purchase and sale. It is inseparable from his work for the central government's Finance Committee. Mao Zedong fully supported his policy design. Therefore, to understand the national decision-making process for this policy, we must understand Chen Yun's design ideas about it.

According to Chen Yun's speech on 10 October 1953 at the National Food Summit, the country's food problem was very serious. Unless appropriate measured were taken to resolve it, it would get worse. Specifically: first, the state was taking in less and selling more. Second, many places had begun to experience disorder. In the areas with no food stocks, grain traders in small cities and towns increased their activities, and many farmers have joined in food speculation by buying and hoarding food. This in turn contributes to the farmer's inclination to refuse to sell grain. The refusal of some regions to exchange food outside their borders has also caused panic buying of, and price increases for, food. Third, the important food producing area in northeast of suffered a serious disaster. Grain yield was reduced, and these areas were unable to fulfill their production requirements. The food gathered from the central northeast region, was reduced by sixteen billion kilograms, which is not a small number. Fourth, in Beijing and Tianjin, the supply of flour was not enough. Both needed sixteen billion kilograms of flour, but at the time the state only controlled only ten billion kilograms. With the difficulties in transporting grain from the fields, we could only implement quantitative placement, which in turn forced other cities to take similar measures. Fifth, the chaotic food situation, if not resolved, would cause the state's grain procurement plan of 1953 to fail. The sales targets would be greatly exceeded. Comparing purchase and sale, the difference would reach at least 4.35 billion kilograms. How to close this gap in the food supply? Chen Yun did not think it feasible by either reducing expenses, or reducing sale of food on the market, reducing grain exports and reducing the rations to the armed forces and agencies, or reducing food preparation or other methods.[93]

The food gap meant that the country's food resource mobilization capacity was insufficient. Dealers had the opportunity to buy and hoard food, disturb the grain market, and affect the stability of food prices. The increase in the price of grain inevitably led to increases in all food prices. Food prices would in turn led to increases in other product prices. Wage increases would be necessary to compensate, and labor costs would go up. The state would be over budget. Moreover, there was a danger of losing the price stability established by the People's government that was applauded by the common people. Chen Yun therefore believed that the food situation was serious, and that resolute measures must be taken to address it.[94] So, what measures should be taken to fundamentally solve the problem of the state's mobilization capacity in managing national strategic food resources? Chen Yun believes that "in the rural areas, take the food acquisition approach, in the cities use allocation in food sale. It can be named 'planned purchase', 'planned supply', simplified as 'unified purchase and sale'."[95]

From Chen Yun's view, food "acquisition" involves the relationship between the state and the farmers. It is one of the four relationships in which food is involved (between state and farmer, state and consumer, central and local government, and among local governments), and is the most difficult one to handle. Handling this first relationship well would make managing the rest easier.[96] Chen Yun said, "'requisition' the name itself is terrifying. What exactly to call it can be considered. But it is indeed of such a nature. Why do we propose compulsory purchase? The basic reason is that our demand increases day by day, but the supply of grain is lacking. There is contradiction between demand and source of supply. ... Given the tight food supply situation, the acquisition approach must be taken.

If we continue uncontrolled purchase, I think the Central People's Government will become "beggars", and spend everyday like the holiday on 'New Year's Eve'."[97] Clearly in Chen Yun's view, if the measure of requisition were not taken, and unregulated purchases continued, once the grain harvest fluctuated, there would be room for grain dealers to speculate. The farmers would therefore expect higher prices, or withhold grain, or refuse to sell grain to the state (at the below market state price). The central government's ability to mobilize resources would be severely affected. The government would be "beggars" (seeking farmers to sell them grain) everyday, and would meet the "debt collector" (the food requirements of urban residents) everyday. However, food requisition was bound to affect the interests of farmers, and affect the relationship between the state and farmers.

Since the requisition of grain runs the risk of farmers resisting, could alternative measures be taken? Chen Yun excludes these possibilities one by one, including "ration without requisition" (ration only in the cities, without using requisition in rural areas), "requisition without ration" (requisition in rural areas, no rationing in the cities), "maintain status quo" (following existing practice, free to sell, free to buy), "hasty" (use free purchase at first, imposing requisition when there is no other way), "mobilizing to subscribe" (country allocating requisition quota of grain to each local area, called primary subscription), "pre-contract" (pre-contracting, purchase based upon a pre-negotiated contract), "fragmentation" (adopting different approaches), and so on. Chen Yun believed that these approaches were not as good as "requisition and ration" (which is "unified purchase and sale").[98] But using this approach, they might run into resistance from the farmers, "There will be some small problems in the villages, or even big trouble."[99] However, even so, it was the only way forward for the national interest. "What would be the alternative if we do not do it this way? We would have to use all foreign exchange to import food. If we did that, we would have no money to buy equipment for construction or industrialization."[100] Between the national interests and the farmer's regional interests, the local farmer's interests had to yield to the country's overall interests. They must help to improve the country's resources capacity. Only once the national resource mobilization capacity is increased, can the country focus its finances, material and manpower on industrialization, which in turn supports rural development. It was clear that on the issue of dealing with rural resident's resistance, Chen Yun was somewhat prepared. But as the lesser of the two evils, Chen Yun still recommends the approach of unified purchase of grain. This practice of rational trade-offs reflects the high rationality (instrumental rationally) used during the process of implementing the policy of unified purchase and sale.

Chen Yun added, with regard to the difficulties in making food requisition work in rural areas, "This much more difficult than dealing with the capitalists."[101] Still, the state was able to gradually get the job done through its social mobilization mechanisms. "Who is to be relied upon to carry out requisition work? In rural areas we must rely on cadres and Party members. Now in many rural areas cadres have risen to be new middle peasants. If these comrades were persuaded to take the lead, they would play very useful roles."[102] To accomplish food requisition, not only were many economic measures taken, but also extensive political mobilization had to be carried out. This was not only a huge economic task, but also a great political task.[103] Meanwhile, country needed to resolve the problem of the rural household's shortage of food. "If the household's food-deficit problem is not resolved, it will shake the people's confidence, which is very unfavorable to our requisition work."[104] As long as the amount of food requisition is reasonable and does impose an unreasonable burden on the farmers, and the price is fair, we will be able to do a good job in food requisition.[105]

Chen Yun advocates a policy in which food is basically controlled by the state, and merchants can only be distributors. To put an end to the activities of grain dealers, one way is to block their distribution channel, so that they cannot sell it. A second way is to mobilize the public, by punishing a few dealers as an example. Grain merchants must be restricted to their authorized tasks. Those hoarding food should be severely punished. Food processing factories should only be allowed to process food but not allowed to trade grain. Food retailers must become the state's distributors.[106] The state's food requisitions will cut off the market in the grain. The requisition policy, by monopolizing the market for grain, greatly improved the state's strategic mobilization capacity for the resource of food.

Chen Yun also believed that the rationing policy was complimentary to requisitioning, involving the relationship between the state and the consumer. He said: "The term 'rationing' is not too nice. It reminds people of similar situation during the time when the Japanese and their puppet reign were in power. Now the name is changed to 'planned supply' as suggested by Minister Chang Nai-chi. Our rationing is different from the rationing in Puppet era. Back then the rationing applied to cooking oil, salt, soy sauce, and vinegar. Now we only ration grain. The rationing back then could not satisfy the famished stomach. The amount we ration is sufficient. The rationed categories are different, the numbers of items rationed are different, and the nature of rationing is completely the opposite."[107] By rationing the sale of food to urban residents, the state was able to control the rapid increase in food consumption and to stabilize the demand for food. However, this is only the visible consequence of the rationing system. In other words, the visible consequences of the rationing system reflects distinctly on the state's capability to control and regulate food demand and demand structure when food supply is not sufficient. However, its hidden features go beyond what the designer of the system anticipated. This point we leave for later discussion.

Chen Yun's policy of unified purchase and sale, as well as its formation process, from personal perspective, reflect his superb intelligence. From the national standpoint, the introduction of the policy is in full compliance with the "instrumental rationality" principle. It is a realistic "masterpiece" created in a condition of severe scarcity of resources. It can be seen, following the founding of the country, that the formation of policies or institutional arrangements follow two different logics, one being rational logic, the other being legitimacy logic, including ideological logic. Despite the planned economic system following the logic of ideology (legitimacy logic), the introduction of many specific policies, followed the logic of instrumental rationality (rational logic), and in reality, it strengthened the planned economic system and the centralized system.

As the purchase and sale policy had important political significance, its scope was expanded from grain to cooking oil, cotton and other basic consumer items. According to the Central Finance Committee's report, on 15 November, the CPC Central Committee made a decision on planned purchase of fuel in the country, which stipulated the requisition of oil, including cooking oil. As for cotton, the planned requisition was already implemented as early as 1951.[108] However, since then, although the production of cotton increased, cotton supply had not kept pace with consumer demand for woven cotton. Because of this, on 13 July 1954, the CPC Central Committee approved the Finance Committee's proposal for changing the cotton sales mechanism. 9 September, at the 224th administrative meeting, the Administration Council adopted an order implementation of planned purchase and planned supply (and order of planned requisition of cotton). Starting 15 September 1954, the city began using coupons to limit the sale of cotton to residents. (Cloth ration coupons were in use until 1983. In November 1983, the State Council decided that starting 1 December, the purchase of cotton, cotton cloth, and related products would be open without limitation. Cloth ration coupons were abandoned). Chen Yun summarized that, "mastering the supply through planned requisition, controlling sales volume through planned supply, are the two essential steps in maintaining market stability during shortages of many commodities." He therefore warned that, "In the upcoming period, the state planned purchase and planned supply of many varieties of goods will not be reduced, but gradually increase. Therefore the whole Party should have a clear understanding and fully prepared."[109] After implementing planned purchase and sale of food, cotton, oil, etc. the state gradually added tobacco, hemp, tea, silkworm cocoons, wool, leather and other food and industrial raw materials as requisitionable products.

With food, despite the state allowing small merchants to sell food, Chen Yun advocated that state-owned commercial food businesses should take over the city's food supply and operate in an effective planned fashion. He said: "Along with future economic development and improved living standards, in addition to the continued emphasis on state-owned commercial business on grain, cloth and major department-store items, there must be planned operation of food distribution in the cities. ... Food supply affects the working people's daily lives. Therefore, the state-run food business operators must focus on the operation of food distribution. They should develop a close relationship with the co-operatives, and gradually increase their food wholesale and retail businesses and expand the variety of foods, sufficient to guarantee the supply of food in urban, industrial and mining areas. At the same time, we must provide for necessary exports, in exchange for industrial equipment, in order to support national economic construction." "The Central Department of Commerce should establish a national food company, responsible for coordinating the requisition of food, its distribution and export markets."[110] "Meat, eggs, fruit wholesale and export should be managed by the state-run commercial operations."[111] Nevertheless, in the 1950s after the introduction of unified purchase and marketing policy, the "meat and animal fats are not rationed."[112] But later on, as the country's economic situation worsened, the food supply became tight in some places. Meat and animal oil distribution also adopted the ration coupon plan.

After the introduction of the policy of grain purchase in rural areas, the policy was refined through practice. To address the shortcomings and mistakes identified in 1953 and 1954 when the food requisition process was introduced, in August 1955 the State Council passed "Interim Measures for Rural Food Purchase and Sale" which required the implementation in rural areas of "three orders" for the control of food: production quotas in order, purchase in order, and sales in order. This approach was intended to improve the farmer's production enthusiasm, by further systemizing and institutionalizing grain purchase and sale policies.

The planning of the urban food supply was started in haste, the government taking a crude approach at first and later refining it. The government's distribution of food was based on the resident card account book, with residents allowed buy food using coupons issued by the government. Residents made food plans by themselves and submitted them to relevant authorities for approval. But often the approval process was just formality, leading to many loopholes on the distribution side. Many residents bought more than they actually needed, and some sold what they could not use in rural areas. In some places farmers had come in to the city and purchase food. In the second half of 1954, loose management of national food distribution lead to an abnormal rise of food sales in urban and mining areas. In view of this situation, the CPC Central Committee and State Council in April 1955 issued an instruction strengthening and consolidating the work on planned food sales, calling for the saving of food, and rectifying the issues of food supply in urban areas, by changing the original certificate system for food purchase to one that verified household requirements. After four months of the new policy, which closed some loopholes of "certificate for food purchase" program, abnormal grain sales began to decline.[113]

After that, to further overcome the shortage in the food supply, the PRC State Council has made provisions for rationing food supplies to the cities. On 5 August 1955, at the seventeenth Plenary Meeting of the State Council, they passed "The Interim Measures on Food Rationing in Cities", which was promulgated on August 25 of the same year. The measures include general principles, resident's rations of food, the industrial and commercial use of grain and grain products, feed grains; a total of five chapters with twenty-four sections. The main provisions were: the food distribution to residents, industrial and commercial use of grain, and livestock feed grain distribution was to be according to an approved number of certificates issued to distributors. Supply certificates were divided into the food supply permits for city residents, the business and industry usage card, a feed supplies permit, a permit for he transfer of food stocks for city residents, national general food stamps, local food stamps, and seven kinds of local material tickets. People's Committees in provinces, autonomous regions, and municipalities, were to set rations taking into account city resident's differences in work, age, and the consumption habits of different regions. This was to be done according to the relevant regulations per diem by work level, establishing standard monthly rations for a household, and distributing food supply cards; residents of a collective followed their work unit's process to receive their food allocation. Special foods needed for ethnic festivals, were given priority if used with frugality. Foreign personnel of foreign affairs units and foreign affairs agencies were to receive their food supplies according to documents issued by their sponsoring authorities. Rural residents coming to cities and towns, were allowed bring their own food, or could get food certificates in accordance with regulations for food stamps. Grain for industrial and commercial use was allocated based upon ascertained needs after verifying using approved indicators. For livestock feed grain distribution, a quantitative grading system was to be implemented.[114] Food rations for residents in the cities (processed food products), were divided into two regional bases: one for rice-based food or grains, and another for flour-based food, with nine different ration levels in all. Specific supply criteria are shown in Table 2-3.

Table 2-3   Urban Food Ration Supply Level and Standard Unit: Jin per person/month

Level	Regions where rice is the main food		Regions where grain and flour are the main foods	
	Standard supply rate	Average control index	Standard supply rate	Average control index
1	45~55	50	50~60	55
2	35~44	40	40~49	44
3	26~34	32	29~39	35
4	24~29	28	27~32	31
5	26~33	32	29~36	35
6	22~26	25	24~28.5	27.5
7	16~21	20	18~23	22
8	11~15	13	12~17	14
9	5~10	7	6~11	8

(Note: numbers under "level" in the table represent the occupational level: 1. Special heavy manual workers; 2. Heavy manual workers; 3. Light manual workers; 4. Agency and organization working personnel, public and private enterprises staff, shopkeepers and other mental workers; 5. University and high school students; 6, General population and children above10 years of age; 7. Children six years to 10 years old; 8. Children three years to six years old; 9. Children less than three years old. Source: State Department: "Interim Measures of Rationing Food Supply in Cities", from *Selected Important Documents Since the Founding of China*, Volume 7, 116~117.)

In fact, the use of food stamps gradually began in 1953 when the policy of state purchase and sale was started. However, its wide use began in 1955 after the State Council enacted "Interim Measures on Rationing Food Supply in Cities". In accordance with this, ration coupons to purchase food were to be non-negotiable, and were not to be used as money or resold as securities. Nevertheless, later on food stamps actually were traded on the black market as securities. The use of food stamps lasted longer than cloth ration coupons.

In order to improve the food ration in cites, in 1956 the state established three grain management systems. First was the grain license management system. Based upon the per diem allowance for each household member, appropriate to their age, sex and work level, the household as a unit was issued a "resident food supply certificate." Second, a management system was implemented for standard changes in resident's food rations due to moves and transfers. Third was the food stamp management system. Local food departments, based upon the instruction issued by the ministry of Food in 1955, "General Notice of Interim Measures for National Food Ration", managed the distribution of food stamps, redemption, registration and statistics management. Control of consumption of grain-based basic consumer materials by the distribution by ration tickets was thereby established.[115]

How long should the policy of centralized purchase and sales be continued? Chen Yun believed that planned requisition should continue for the long-term, but that the planned distribution was a temporary measure. At the first session of the First National People's Congress meeting, Chen Yun pointed out in his speech that, "Planned requisition policy will continue, it won't change. Because on one hand, it is necessary for the state to control the supply of various kinds of material resources in order to ensure the country's planned construction. On the other hand, it is to ensure that our farmers road to prosperity life is not the development of rural capitalism, but through co-operative socialism." In comparison, " planned supply can only be a kind of temporary measure, as long as industrial and agricultural production increases, the production of consumer goods can grow to fully supply the market needs to the extent that rationing methods should be cancelled."[116] However, he warned," but it should be noted that the day when the planned supply of food, oil, cloth will end will not come quickly, because ... the rate of increase in agricultural production is relatively slow. ... On the contrary, in order to handle the tight supply and demand situation, there's possibility in the next few years to expand the scope of planned supply."[117] While Chen Yun envisioned planned supply as only a temporary measure, over time it tended to strengthen and expand. The number of consumer products rationed by the urban household registration certificate, increased from a few kinds to over one hundred. The policy of planned supply lasted more than thirty years. It lifespan has gone far beyond what the original designers of the policy planned. Thus, the planned purchase and sale system designed by Chen Yun in 1953 laid the foundation and framework for consumer nationalism. By reserving for the state's scarce resources like oil, food and cloth, it greatly enhanced the state's command capability. Thus, the institutional arrangements for planned purchase and sale laid a solid foundation to for the establishment of "command-oriented society," and the state's "command of power".

In 1958, China launched the unprecedented "Great Leap Forward" and the people's commune movement. Orders given without regard to consequences, unrealistically high targets, reliance on an overblown rhetorical style that concealed lax work habits ("communist wind") and rampant "leftist" mistakes, coupled with natural disasters and contract breaches by the Soviet government, all resulted in the Chinese economy suffering serious difficulties in three consecutive years from 1959 to 1961. Food production was significantly reduced, food reserves sharply declined, moving food from one district to another was difficult; overall the food supply was strained and as a result the consumption level declined significantly. Because of this serious food situation, the purchase and sale system was expanded and consolidated in the first half of 1960. During Cultural Revolution period, the food sector was again seriously affected. The food situation, which had been improving, became tenuous again. The planned purchase and sale system was further expanded. Not until the reform and opening up, was the purchase and sale system loosened.[118]

Considering the growth of the urban population, the policy of planned purchase and sale, allowed urban food consumption to increase (except for the period 1961~1969) and people's food consumption has long been controlled in a stable range (except for 1958, 1961, 1962, 1963 was below standard). In 1953, the food consumption of urban population was 17.865 million tons, and it reached 26.625 million tons in 1960. During 1961~1969, due to the reduced supply plan and the decentralization of urban population, urban food consumption declined, remaining between 21 million and 24 million tons. Total food consumption in 1970 rebounded to 26.935 million tons, followed by a steady increase year after year, reaching 47.015 million tons in 1984. However, the fluctuation in per capita food consumption by urban population was very large. Within the 31 years between 1953~1984, it remained at about 200 kg. In that time, it was comparatively higher in 1953 and 1954 and in the early 1980s and lowest in in 1961 (179.49 kg).[119] At the same time, the rural population exceeded the urban population and their total food consumption was always more than that of the urban population. However, per capita grain consumption in rural areas, except in the years 1956 to 1958 and after 1980, was lower than the per capita consumption of the urban population.[120]

From the national standpoint, the purchase and sale policy played a very important role in helping the new China get through situations of difficult food shortages, ensuring food supplies, and consolidating the new regime, supporting the program of socialist construction. According to the editors of "China's Grain Work", who summarized the policy of purchase and sale of food, the policy played several roles. First, through the requisition plan, it ensured the peasant's food rations, and their supplies of feed grain and seeds. Second, it ensured the military's food supply, while at the same time, in the urban areas, where food rationing was implemented and for those farming families without enough food, or in related agricultural pursuits in rural areas (non-food crops, fisheries, forestry, salt harvesting, animal husbandry) the government sought to supply a full or partial ration. This guaranteed a stable standard of living, and supported the development of industrial and agricultural production. This is particularly important when the nation faced natural disaster, in which the national economy experienced serious difficulties and setbacks. Third, by controlling the purchase and sale of grain at the same time, the state maintains long-term price stability by managing sales prices uniformly, which creates an important condition to enable the development of socialist construction. Fourth, at the time, the purchase and sale of grain policy played a role in promoting and protecting the implementation of the transitional program, to achieve the socialist transformation of agriculture, handicrafts and capitalist industry and commerce.[121]

After the establishment of the purchase and sale system, not only were grain, cotton, oil, and sugar, pork rationed but a growing number of other consumer goods were included in the ration ticket system: matches, watches, sewing machines, bicycles, transistor radios, etc. The original intent of the unified purchase and sale system was to enhance the country's resource mobilization capacity, but with its development, it gradually became the route by which the nationalistic consumption pattern was established. On one hand, the unified purchase and sale policy helps to form a macro consumption system consistent with the national planned economic system. Its function is reflected in the key role it plays in agriculture, handicrafts, and the socialist transformation of capitalist industry and commerce. This role is also reflected in that it upgrades the state's ability to mobilize resources and improves the state's ability to command. Through the policy of unified purchase and sale, the state eliminated market factors and the space where the law of value of goods works, thereby enhancing the national mobilization of resources, and its ability to focus and schedule resources. This laid the foundation for the system of totalitarian state power and the mandatory planned economic system. However, because of the low efficiency and the emergence of shortages caused by the planned economic system, the policy of unified purchase and sale (which itself became one of the reasons leading to low efficiency) became the tool that the country used to deal with shortages. Since shortages were a widespread, nationwide phenomenon, the state's impulse to control consumer data became even more intense. The state's control of and redistribution of resources in short supply greatly enhanced the state's social control of urban residents. Since the state eliminated the replaceable supply channel of consumer goods, it basically blocked the flow of resources from "outside the system," and increased urban resident's dependence on the national legitimate supply channels, and their independence and autonomy declined significantly. This further promoted the state's social and other mobilization capabilities. As a result, the nationalistic consumption system became an integral part of the state's means of social control.

The sociology of nationalism is essentially consumer system. The state eliminates social consumption (market) factors and monopolizes the distribution and supply of basic subsistence goods. The country incorporates almost all basic consumption into its planned economic system, putting an end to the flow of basic resources from "outside the system".

As a result, it secures the redistribution of subsistence goods in accordance to a relatively egalitarian principle, providing low levels of goods to urban residents under conditions of constrained resource, and it is also able to curb increasing levels of consumption through the "super-economic coercion"[122] in order to concentrate resources on socialist industrialization. In its economic function, because the nationalist consumption system enables the state to effectively limit the "excess" consumption increases, to curb and squeeze people's ability to consume, the state can focus all resources on building socialist industrialization, ultimately serving the goal of realizing the state ideology (communism). In its social function, the nationalist consumption system enables the state to limit the autonomy of members of the society in their own choices, resulting in individuals having no bargaining power when facing the state, because the most important subsistence goods are controlled by the state. Therefore, the nationalist consumption system not only caused urban residents to depend structurally upon the state, but also led to a structure of obedience to the state. Although the planned supply of consumption ensured that under difficult conditions all urban residents would have food to eat and access to basic social security, the nationalist consumption system (together with the household registration system and the employee record system) severely restricted the freedom of the residents in migration, travel, change of work and occupation, marriages between non-agricultural and farming households, lifestyle, etc. It brought economic order and social order and stability, but at the same time, people paid a price of individual freedom of choice and autonomy in consumption. This is the price that an economically backward country with a "catching up and surpassing" policy pays, in its pursuit of concentrating the whole nation's strength on economic modernization.

In the state's economic difficulties, the policy of unified purchase and sale, together with the household registration policy, played a role of preventing peasants from moving to the cities.

The policy of unified purchase and sale system is the most important institutional arrangement the state made in urban areas. This institutional arrangement was not accidental, it follows a certain logic, which is "rational logic." The national goal was to achieve socialist industrialization. Given the extreme shortages of materials, to achieve this goal, the state needed to improve its resource mobilization capacity, which not only improved the government's authority and command capabilities, but also focused its resources on socialist industrialization. The unified purchase and sale system helped to improve the country's resource mobilization capacity, and thus improved the state's authority and command capabilities. Although such a system may be harmful, to some extent, to the state's reputation and legitimacy resources (such as Chen Yun's worry about farmer's resistance), the national leadership resolutely and unswervingly implemented this system. Obviously, the implementation of the system follows rational logic.

The state's ability to implement the centralized purchase and sale system stemmed from the state's administrative resources and power. The system led to different consequences farmers and urban residents. For farmers, the system deprived the farmers of the bargaining power they had under the market mechanism to negotiating farm prices, thus damaging the interests of farmers, which is why it was most difficult for the state to manage the relationship with the farmers during the implementation of purchase and sale system according to Chen Yun. As for urban residents, the negative effect of the purchase and sale system is that it limited their per capita consumption and freedom of choice in consumption. But at the same time, it also brought a significant benefits – it secured a stable supply of subsistence goods. Therefore, in implementing the unified marketing system, states are not very concerned about their relationship with urban residents. This is partially because states have rich legitimacy resources that can be used.

C. Institutional Arrangements of Collective Consumption and Their Logic

In the fifties, the state made different institutional arrangements for collective consumption and private consumption. As mentioned earlier, with regard to private consumption, the state took systematic measures to curb consumption based on rational choice. Therefore, its institutional arrangements follow "rational logic". By contrast, in collective consumption, the state made a "high welfare" type of institutional arrangement based upon the relative level of economic development. This "high welfare" did not mean the level of collective consumption was "high" (in fact, total collective consumption was restricted), it refers to the collective consumption of the "welfare" being high, as they were free of charge, covering a wide range of products. Despite these benefits offering some compensation to low-wage urban workers, the institutional arrangements made by the country in collective consumption cannot be explained rationally. In fact, this "high-welfare" policy is inconsistent to the level of welfare supportable by the level economic development. Clearly, the state's institutional arrangements for collective consumption cannot be explained by "rational logic". It in fact complies with another kind of logic — "logical legitimacy." In other words, the institutional arrangement of collective consumption is subject to the logic of ideology. Its purpose is to reflect the working people being emancipated, the party and the state's care for the common people's interest and well-being, and the superiority of the socialist system. From the nation's perspective, in this arrangement for collective consumption, there are more political considerations than economic considerations.

On 29 September 1949, at the first session of the Chinese People's plenary, the "Common Program of Chinese People's Political Committee" (hereafter, the "Common Program") was adopted.[123] It played the role of an interim constitution until the Constitution of the PRC was written in 1954. First of all, the "Common Program" in its first article affirmed the political status of workers and peasants, and that the new China would realize the people's democratic dictatorship. "Under the leadership of the working class, based on the alliance of workers and peasants, unite all democratic classes and all ethnic groups." It defines the working class leadership and farmers as the main object to rely on. Article 12 provisions the nature of political power, creation of political regime and the exercise of political powers. Here, the class with mainly workers and peasants became the main basis of the new regime. Workers and peasants (poor peasants) become major political force that the party and the country rely upon respectively in urban and rural areas. As to the city, the institutional arrangements for collective consumption must reflect the political position of the working class, and consumer welfare is a "gift" from the state to urban workers.

A year after the "Common Program" was announced, the Government Administration Council on 26 February 1951 promulgated the "Labor Insurance Regulations",[124] which established and implemented social security rights for workers. After amendments in March[125] 1953 and in 1956, China established comprehensive labor insurance (including health insurance) and social security systems for urban enterprise workers. On 27 June 1952, the Government Administration Council promulgated the "Instructions for Implementation of Public Health Prevention At Public Expense to the People's Governments At All Levels, Political Parties, Organizations and Affiliated Institutions of the National Staff", which started a public health system at public expense for government agencies and institutions. After that, by the end of 1955, a system for retirement and resignation was established for workers at the state organizations and institutions. At the same time, for urban workers and their children's education, employee housing and living services (e.g., cafeterias, bathing facilities, nurseries, clinics, hairdressing, etc.) associated with employment units, cultural services (clubs, reading rooms, elderly loyal, theaters, sports venues, etc.), maternity insurance, welfare system, women are starting to build up too.[126.] Social citizenship's right for urban residents was guaranteed.

Overall, the "Common Program", the constitution and the relevant social security legislation and provisions for collective welfare, are expressions of the "liberation effect". It declared a historical change of status for the workers and peasants, free from exploitation and oppression, in which they could stand up and assume power. It greatly enhanced the rights, benefits and status of common people — mainly workers, peasants and women. It established a system that affirmed these changes. The social status of workers, peasants and women changed dramatically.

Here we find a paradox. On one hand, in order to accumulate for industrialization, countries are stingy with regard to personal consumption. On the other hand, collective consumption and the welfare state (public health, universal primary education, public housing allocation) had become relatively more generous. I have already discussed the first point. Then what of the second point? First of all, the state offering of a variety of free collective welfare is a compensation for its low-wage policy. It constitutes real income for workers. Secondly, to implement a high coverage of welfare system in a poor country is a requirement of the socialist ideology. Collective welfare is responsible for a kind of production "legitimacy". It reflects the working people being emancipated, their rights, and also reflects state "paternalism".[127.] In fact, in the later official propaganda, social security and collective well-being were proving "the superiority of the socialist system". Obviously, the system implemented by the state in the area of collective consumption follows the "logic of legitimacy".

The role of collective consumption and collective welfare in manufacturing "legitimacy", in large part offset the negative effects of the state policy suppressing personal consumption. Moreover, collective consumption and collective welfare plays a more important role. It positions the party and the state as savior, liberator, dispenser of benevolence. Thus it enables the state to control the discourse in order to occupy the moral high ground. At the same time, it places workers, peasants and other beneficiaries in the "human debtor" position. In traditional Confucian culture, beneficiaries are to be grateful to their benefactors, and a favor must be reciprocated. Thus, even if the state must curb private consumption, one must understand the country's difficulties, and make a temporary sacrifice for the nation's industrialization objectives. In the mean time, one must work hard, dedicate oneself to the public good and pay back the favor provided by the party and the state.

Thus, by supplying collective consumption and collective welfare, the state receives a "gift effect." Collective consumption and collective welfare become the "state present" given to workers and peasants, which includes life-long job security, free housing, education, health care, work injury insurance and so on. In the present society, the gift exchange is mutually beneficial. Gift giving means that those who carry a "debt of gratitude" must offset this debt by reciprocating. So the state and individual have a certain kind of gift exchange relationship on collective consumption and collective welfare. The state is the giver, while the individual is the recipient. Here, the state has been personified into an entity with moral sentiments, incarnated in the party and government leadership.

Institutional Arrangements of Labor Incentives

In stark contract to its extreme shortage of material, China's labor resources are very rich. It can be said that labor resources is the most important resources that a country can rely on. Therefore, to fully mobilize the enthusiasm of workers and stimulate their productivity has become the key for the country to utilize its abundant labor resources. To motivate worker's enthusiasm and to stimulate their productivity, involves the institutional arrangement of labor incentives.

In general, material incentives are often the form of labor incentives. The more material rewards workers get, the more workers are motivated. However, as stated earlier, due to the extreme shortage of material in China, the country rationally chose a system to curb consumption, including adopting a low-wage system. Obviously, this low wage system created some tension with regard to labor incentives. But the realization of national goal (of socialist industrialization), relies upon sufficient incentive for workers. Therefore, how to solve the tension between curbing consumption and labor incentives is one major problem the country faces.

In theory, if worker's compensation is lower than their expectations, it may cause frustration and hurt labor enthusiasm, which becomes lazy, slowing down, careless and perfunctory. Therefore, how to lower worker's expectations of return, has become a key problem. Conditions for reducing the labor return are diverse. For example, with an excess of labor resources, there is a large army of the unemployed. In order to get a job, out of fear of unemployment, people will accept lower compensation, even a wage reduction. However, this condition never existed after the founding of the People's Republic of China, as the country adopted a policy of full urban employment. At the same time, once an individual is hired, unless that individual breaks the law, neither the enterprise nor unit can dismiss him or her. Job security under the "iron rice bowl" system eliminates people's concerns of being dismissed. Of course, the reason for the state's low wage policy is to guarantee the full employment of urban residents. It can be said, under certain conditions, the "iron rice bowl" system could become the "idle" system. Ensuring that the "iron rice bowl" does not become "idle" troubled the country during the planned economic era.

In fact, in the early stages of liberation, due to people's anticipation of liberation effects, there was a certain level of expectation of increasing consumption and wages. Taking food consumption as an example, per capita urban food consumption in 1953 and 1954 was the highest until 1984, respectively 242 and 236 jin (or 121 kg and 118 kg equivalent) annually. Later on, only because the state tightened the control of per capita food consumption, did food consumption come down (about 200 pounds per year) (see Table 2-4). Therefore, lowering the consumption level, and controlling the rate of increase in the consumption level, is a result of the state's human control. So if the state reduced the proportion of consumption and increased the proportion of accumulation, can people's motivation to work be affected? Objectively speaking, during the first Five Year Plan period and the "Great Leap Forward" afterward, when the country implemented the policy of centralized purchase and sale, people's motivation to work was not affected negatively by the state's curbing consumption. Or we can say that there was no obvious impact. A major labor motivation crisis took place later on, especially in the latter part of Cultural Revolution.

Of course, high labor motivation does not necessarily mean higher labor productivity (cf. chapter 1). Because many factors affect labor efficiency, including the failure of macro-economic policy that is not controlled by individual workers (e.g., the "Great Leap Forward's" devastating effects on national economy) and imbalances in the industrial structure. During the first Five Year Plan period, China's urban labor productivity was quite high, and except for macroeconomic policy, nothing went wrong. This was mainly because of the comparatively high labor enthusiasm. Although the state implemented its policy of centralized purchase and sale and aimed to curb consumption during this period, there was no significant blow to labor enthusiasm. Therefore, an open question remains, under such conditions where return to labor is low and consumption levels are artificially controlled and suppressed by the state, why was worker's motivation still rising? What is the reason?

By 1956, China had completed the socialist transformation of agriculture, handicrafts, capitalist industry and commerce. The planned economy was formed and the state's command of power greatly increased. Since China built its socialist society on an extremely poor economic foundation, the country urgently needed to focus all its resources on building the basis for socialist industry. To achieve this goal, the country required people to save food and clothing and "to tighten their belts" for the duration. This pushed worker's attitude and motivation to a more prominent position. The relationship between the state's policy of curbing consumption and labor motivation had become a problem that could not be ignored.

Taking workers as an example, their employers are no longer particular private owners.

They are in the public sector or the state, or an "imagined employer". Their agents are cadres at all levels of government and enterprises. Workers under this system virtually have no bargaining power in wages and benefits. This is because wages and benefits are determined by the common top agent – the central government. But workers have another right that is guaranteed by the Constitution: life-long employment without random dismissal. The workers won the right to make another deal with low-wage and low-consumption strategy, i.e., withholding their contribution of labor. So, the solution of the problem of reproducing of labor motivation is logically related to a country's industrial policy and public ownership.

In more general terms, the state's sacrifice of the consumer to facilitate industrialization and the policy of suppressing self-interest to facilitate public policy objectively rejected the most common mechanisms in labor history for labor motivation reproduction, which is material stimulation. At the Eight Meeting, the central government affirmed the role of monetary rewards, but material incentives were still severely limited and had a limited role. Furthermore, shortly after (i.e., after the "The Cleaning of Four Types of People" Movement), this policy was criticized as revisionist ("money is king"), and eventually abolished. Therefore, in general, before the reform and opening up, the state limited the active role of material incentives in stimulating labor motivation.

Excluding or limiting material incentives, the remaining mechanism for state to motivate workers would only be spiritual incentives. So, how does the state use spiritual incentives to motivate workers? What is the mechanism of spiritual incentives? How do they work? These are the questions to be answered below.

A. Sacred Incentives

In the industrialization of China, resource constraints were a serious problem. Therefore, under a condition of resources shortages, a weak economic foundation as well as other inferior elements, human resources constitute the country's most important and most dependable strengths. As Zhou Enlai pointed out: "China has a very large manpower. As workers, the creators and users of tools, human beings are the most decisive factor in social forces of production and are the most valuable 'capital'."[128]

However, human resources must be in an active state, rather than idle or inert. In other words, we must fully mobilize the enthusiasm of labor. Zhou said: "Of course, 650 million people's enthusiasm, such a great power in creation, as previously mentioned, would be impossible to be played out without socialist revolution. But even after the realization of the socialist revolution, without paying attention and mobilization by proper methods, this great power cannot fully play out, making it still impossible to achieve the goal of building socialism in a better and more economical way."[129] In the state's leader's view, because the country was poor, it was necessary to develop greatly. To greatly develop, we must aim high and get going fast, and we must mobilize the people's labor enthusiasm. During the revolutionary war, by desperately relying on team spirit and revolutionary enthusiasm, the Chinese Communist Party achieved victory in the war. Now, in the period of socialist construction, we equally need to rely on cadre's and worker's strong mental spirits and work enthusiasm. Mao Zedong pointed out:

"We want to keep up the efforts we had during revolutionary war, the surge of revolutionary zeal at that time, the hardy spirit back then, in order to carry the revolutionary work to the end. What is hard?" In "Water Margin", there is a diligent character called san-lang-shi-xu (literally, "working hard"). We used to have that kind of desperate spirit in pursuit of revolution. Everyone has a life, some 60 years, some 70 years, some 80 years, or 90 years, however long your life is. As long as you can work, you should work more or less. And when working, we should have revolutionary enthusiasm and a hardy spirit."[130]

This hardy spirit comes from the beliefs and consciousness of the revolutionary elite. The state's leaders believed that after the victory of the revolution, not only the revolutionary elite (party members and cadres) should maintain this kind of hardy spirit, but also workers, peasants and the populace should be called upon to carry this spirit forward. As was stated in a "People's Daily" editorial: "We should know: the working class demonstrating the greatest enthusiasm and creativity, with great perseverance to complete and surpass the industrial production and capital construction plan, is the decisive factor in ensuring the realization of our nation's building program and achieve the goals of the transition stage."[131] Zhou Enlai also said: in order to build socialism in a better and more economical way, "We must lead every enterprise to carry out large-scale mass movement, to develop the consciousness, enthusiasm, creativity of the masses, and lead them to strive for the best with all that they have."[132]

In fact, from the early days to the "Great Leap Forward", the people showed an upsurge in labor motivation. This is proven from the successful completion of the first Five Year Plan. The CPC Central Committee believed that "under the leadership of the party and the government, the broad masses of the country in various classes played a significant role during the socialist transformation and socialist construction. They expressed satisfaction for their victory."[133] In early 1958 Mao Zedong also believed that with the completion of socialist transformation in 1956 and in 1957 with the completion of the first Five Year program, as well as the completion of rectification campaign against rightists in 1957, "We are seeing the people's high enthusiasm and creativity in production which we have never seen before. The nation's people were encouraged by the slogan that within fifteen years or less the country would catch up with or exceed Britain in steel and other major industrial products. A new production peak has already being reached."[134] It can be said that, to certain extent, that because of the estimation correctly made by the country's leaders about the masse's enthusiasm, it prompted state leaders to launch the Great Leap Forward.

Thus, we find an interesting phenomenon - the country's policy of consumption suppression did not dampen the people's labor motivation, on the contrary, it stimulated labor's motivation to work. So, what was the cause that activated the people's rising labor motivation? What was the mechanism of incentives? In my opinion, the state, by using sacred incentives solved the problem of tension between consumer suppression policies and labor motivation. The so-called sacred incentives refer to linking the worker's labor to certain sacred or holy emotions, thus stimulating some kind of sacred feelings in workers (e.g., giving thanks, positive anticipation, a sense of being personally touched or called, a sense of honor, a sense of sublimity and mission), as the institutional basis for the enthusiasm of workers in production. Sacred incentives can be further divided into macro- and micro-incentives. Let us analyze from the perspective of a macro actors, how the national leaders use certain institutional arrangements to stimulate labor motivation.

B. The Macro Incentive System

As to why people have rising labor motivation, state leaders have a systematic point of view. First, they believe that people have high labor enthusiasm, because the victory of the revolution made the people the masters of the country. After completion of the socialist transformation, people became the owners of the means of production. They no longer worked for the exploiting class, but worked for themselves. Mao Zedong said: "Does the Chinese working class have that kind of slavery like they had in the past? No. They have become their own masters. The people living in the 9.6 million square kilometers of the People's Republic of China, are beginning to rule this place."[135] Liu Shaoqi gave a more detailed description of the people's controlling social status in a report at the Eighth political bureau meeting: "With the founding of the PRC, hundreds of millions of the hungry working class people who were insulted and damaged, rose to be the masters from being slaves. Their lives and freedom are protected. Labor is honorable. Women received equal status. A large number of workers, peasants, women, and youth take part in the national administration. They contributed to building our state agencies into hard-working, honest, people-serving governmental authorities."[136] Zhou Enlai also pointed out at the tenth anniversary of the state founding: "While we are celebrating the tenth anniversary, regardless of the political views of people in the world, we have to admit that China has undergone tremendous changes. The Chinese people became the fearless masters, from being slaves in hell, in control of their own destiny."[137]

From the national leader's point of view, because the people became masters of the country and participated in the construction and management of the nation, they naturally demonstrated great labor enthusiasm. An editorial in the "People's Daily" on 1 October 1953 said: "The rapid recovery of the national economy comes directly from the creative work of workers and peasants. The people's democratic system encourages them to work with high enthusiasm."[138] On New Year's Day 1955, the "People's Daily" editorial pointed out again that: "Under the leadership of the Chinese Communist Party and the government, our people have already become the masters of the country, the masters of society, the masters of history. We are able to follow the laws of social development, through our own creative work, to start the implementation of planned development, to build China into a prosperous and happy socialist society."[139] In 1960 Li Fuchun also pointed out:" People are liberated from the old society. They have become the masters under the socialist system. Therefore they are able to demonstrate fully their creativity and enthusiasm. The development of production and construction is at full speed."[140]

Clearly in the view of country's leaders, as the early days of the Great Leap Forward demonstrated, the enthusiasm of workers comes from the macro-system of incentives, which are the institutional arrangements that have the working people in control. Such macro work incentives can also be called legitimacy incentives. It is the macro form of sacred encouragement. The so-called legitimacy refers to people's recognition, support and respect for the state leaders, the new regime, and the new system. Legitimacy of incentive is endorsed by the natural formation of labor enthusiasm due to the recognition and support for the new regime and new system. As the new China is led by the working class and built upon the alliance of workers and peasants, the main body of labor - workers and peasants – see their political and economic status has been improved significantly. For example, economically, farmers gained access to land (after the introduction of co-operatives in 1956) and workers received job security, labor insurance and other benefits. Politically, the workers and peasants have been defined as the masters of the country. Thus, in the eyes of national leaders, it is very natural to have the worker's and peasant's supporting and backing the new regime. Thus, labor's enthusiasm to work, in a sense, is part of the "liberation effect". It can be said, from the early days to the period of Great Leap Forward, the working class of people and the State were in the "honeymoon period" of their partnership. Because of this "honeymoon period", when the state issued a call, the masses of the working class would actively respond. Seeing this "spontaneous" labor enthusiasm, the leaders did not perceive any issues in worker's labor motivation. At least during the "honeymoon period", national leaders were not worried about the motivation of workers in the cities. In fact, the national leaders were excited and encouraged by laborer's spirit and energy in their work. For example, in 1958, Mao Zedong wrote in "Introducing a Co-operative", "Based upon this, for production to catch up with the capitalist countries in industrialization and agriculture, China may not need as much time as we initially thought. In addition to the party's leadership, the population of 600 million people is a decisive factor. The more people there are, the more discussions there are, the higher the spirit is, the stronger the drive is. We have never seen people like this with high energy, high morale, high spirits."[141] It was this kind of belief in legitimacy incentives that encouraged state leaders to launch the Great Leap Forward campaign.[142]

The legitimacy incentive system is a macro incentive mechanism. In this mechanism, the stimulation of labor motivation is not based on specific micro labor discipline and labor regulation. It is based upon the worker's recognition, support and endorsement of the country's basic system and its charismatic leaders. It is based on the state's legitimacy resources. More specifically, from the early days to the time of Great Leap Forward, Chinese worker's motivation was built upon the foundation of their respect, love and support for Mao Zedong and the party. It was just these pure and simple class feelings and attitudes that prompted the working people's "spontaneous" labor enthusiasm.

Legitimacy incentives have different types. Specifically, there are several as follows.

1. Mercy – Gratefulness Mechanism

The so-called gratefulness mechanism refers to the parties being given the grace of help or interest, thereby having psychological appreciation and an attitude of gratitude toward the benefactor. The thanks-giving mechanism refers to the system that under the traditional cultural norms (the "reciprocity" concept), by doing favors for the beneficiary, the benefactor acquires the beneficiary's gratitude and desire of reciprocity. The thanks-giving mechanism in fact describes the relationship between the beneficiary and the benefactor. It can also be used to describe the relationship between individuals and the state. After the Communist Party led the people to take power, what specific favors and benefits did they bring to the workers and the peasants? This was discussed previously under the institutional arrangements of collective consumption.

Overall, the "Common Platform", the constitution and the relevant legislation on social security and collective welfare are reflections of the "liberation effect", which declared the workers and peasants (of middling, lower and impoverished status) released from their historical condition of exploitation and oppression, and recognized their control of the government. It greatly enhanced the rights, interests and social status of women, workers and peasants of main masses. And it was consolidated via a systematic establishment. The earth-shaking changes in the social status of workers, peasants and women, highlighted the Communist Party's role of being "liberators" and "mercy"-givers; however, the CPC Central Committee leaders themselves did not think themselves so. In fact, Mao Zedong as early as March 1949 when the party held the Second Session of the Seventh Plenary Meeting, foresaw people's paying-back psychology. He said: "Because of the victory, people would thank us. The bourgeoisie will come out to join."[143] In a country with a long, continuous Confucian tradition and culture, such national mercy-giving behavior will inevitably lead to the beneficiarie's psychological attitude of "gratitude". Constantly in media propaganda terms like, "Chairman Mao is the people's great savior", "I compare the Party more than mother", "the Party's mercy is deeper than the sea", "drinking water from the well, we should not forget digging the well, being able to stand up, we should not forget the Communist Party", are just the psychological manifestation of such thanks-giving (of course, one can not deny the constructional function of the official media). Being the beneficiaries, workers and peasants can reciprocate, by their loyalty to the party, their positive response to the call of the party and the country, their hard work and high labor enthusiasm. As stipulated in Article 16 of the constitution such work enthusiasm and creativity are exactly what the country encourages and expects.

In a poor country, implementing a high coverage welfare system satisfies the needs of the socialist ideology. Collective welfare has certain role in producing "legitimacy". It reflects the working people's rights after emancipation, their now being masters. It also reflects the state's care for its workers. In fact, in the later official propaganda, social security and collective welfare were used as a manifestation of the socialist system's superiority. The role of collective consumption and collective welfare in manufacturing "legitimacy", mostly offsets the negative consumer policy effects from government's suppression of individual consumption. Moreover, collective consumption and collective welfare play a more important role. It placed the party and the state in the position of being a benefactor, enabling the state to control the discourse, in order to occupy the moral high ground. At the same time, it placed the workers and peasants in the position of being beneficiaries.

Thus, providing for collective consumption and collective welfare enables the nation to receive the "gift effect". The state and individuals form a gift-exchanging type of relationship in collective consumption and collective welfare. Gift exchange is in fact a contract, but it is a hidden, non-mandatory contract. What is the contract? Schlicht believes that contract is a commitment to exchange. Contract has a binding function on both sides of the exchange.[144.] There are two types of contracts, compulsory and non-mandatory. A mandatory contract refers to the contracts bound by external forces (e.g., legal) and internal forces (e.g., mutual interests of both parties).[145] A non-mandatory contract refers to a contract bound by the customary exchange of behavior, for instance: daily interaction.[146.] Gift exchange is primarily a non-mandatory contract. Although there is no third party to force the recipient to reciprocate, the recipient who feels obligated by moral consciousness will always find a way to pay back the favor or debt. Since there are no written records of the exchange of as evidence, gift exchange can only rely on customs and moral self-discipline to work. Therefore, it can also be called an implicit contract. It is characterized by oral agreement (no written evidence), predictability and ambiguity, and being negotiated out of the public eye. The mechanism binding people to perform the implicit contract is customs and culture. Tearing up a contract would be subject to public condemnation. The individual's reputation, integrity and other symbols of capital would be lost. For example, raising children so that one can get help when getting old is an implicit inter-generation contract. A son avoiding the obligation to care for his aging parents would be reprimanded for "lack of filial piety" and being "outrageous." Gift exchange is also a hidden contract. As an implicit contract, the state can obtain from individuals the reciprocation (gratitude, loyalty, work motivation) through collective consumption and collective welfare.

However, the gift relationship between individual workers and the state in collective consumption and collective welfare, is actually an open contract: publicly, it is a gift but it contains an implicit contract of reciprocation. In other words, the state's delivery of he "welfare gift" is mandatory (specified by law), but labor's reciprocation (work motivation) is not mandatory. It is determined by custom. This means that, under certain conditions, workers may likely "take for granted" the social welfare provided by the country. And whether they are willing to work actively and reciprocate depends on whether they have thanks-giving psychology. One defect in the thanks-giving mechanism is that with aging of the older generation, the new generation may not have the same thanks-giving psychology to country's gift of welfare. Because they cannot compare the old and new society, and because of their upbringing, they may easily take for granted the gift of collective consumption and collective welfare.

2. Commitment - Vision Mechanism

The way the thanks-giving mechanism works is on the basis of the "past tense". It means that mercy and gifts come first, thanks-giving and reciprocal gifting take place afterwards. The recipient of a gift (the beneficiary) reciprocates based upon the past action of the benefactor and gift-giver. The way the commitment-vision mechanism works is in the "future tense". That is to say, people take appropriate efforts to realize some kind of commitment to the government, or to achieve certain vision of an ideal goal. In the so-called commitment-vision mechanism, through its described vision of an ideal blueprint for and a promise of a future happy life, the state tries to mobilize people's expectations for the future and their anticipation of a better life. The state calls on people to work hard to achieve this ideal vision and goal.

A prerequisite for a commitment-vision system to work is that, after the socialist transformation, market mechanism must be basically eliminated by the state. It was very difficult for individuals to realize their dreams of personal enrichment through the market. In the case that almost all economic activities are included in the country's planned economic management system, the market mechanism, leading to social stratification, does not exist anymore. At the same time, through the control of redistribution, the state artificially reduces the gaps among individual incomes (although gaps still exists, but relative to the era when the KMT ruled, stratification is narrower), which generally reflects a relatively egalitarian pattern. This situation led to a relationship of close interdependency between individuals and the collective. It is easy for the state to convince the masses to believe that the state's goal is also a personal goal, and to adopt national goals as their own beliefs.[147]   Thus, the planned economic system and egalitarian pattern of income distribution are the conditions for the commitment-vision mechanism to work. However, the risk run by such a mechanism is that over time, if the national commitment is not met, it is difficult to keep in force.

Clearly, the vision system is built on the basis of collective ideals, rather than on the basis of individualism. The state continues to strengthen the propaganda for its overall target, continues to commit to an idealized national blueprint and improved future well-being,[148] and continues to connect personal ideals with the collective ideals to stimulate labor motivation for the achievement of national goals. For example, the "People's Daily" editorial page on 1 October 1953, said: "In celebrating the fourth anniversary of the founding of the PRC, we feel the deep resentment for the previous age and we are so grateful to and treasure the new era! Seeing the possibility of a future happy life before our eyes, we are willing to work hard towards the realization of this hope!"[149] Zhou Enlai said more specifically:" The Communist Party's unswerving policy is to lead the Chinese people to build the communist society without exploitation, without classes, with prosperity and happiness. This is the one world that the Chinese people have always envisioned."[150] State leaders tried to convince people that all of the state's efforts were to achieve this "one world." On one hand, everyone is equal in this one world. There is no exploitation or oppression. This was achieved after the socialist transformation in 1956. On the other hand, part of the one world is the common prosperity. To achieve this depends on the people's striving and hard work. Through its portrayal of future well-being and its commitment to this, the state was able to mobilize successfully the people's enthusiasm for work for quite some time after the founding of the country. The most typical evidence is the high labor enthusiasm shown in the Great Leap Forward.

A natural defect of commitment - vision mechanism is that if the national leaders fall into a utopian state of mind (e.g., the Great Leap Forward), and take an unrealistic ideal as a "practical" blueprint of their goal, their commitment to future happiness and other ideals is likely to be broken. Should this utopian ideal be broken, it is bound to be a serious a blow to worker's labor motivation. Therefore, it is a big risk to take as the foundation of labor motivation the pursuit of a utopian dream for society, regardless of immediate return to the interests of individual workers. On this subject, we will have more detailed discussion later.

3. Appeal Mechanism

The appeal mechanism emphasizes the nature of state power, the charisma and style of the leading cadres at all levels, their closeness to the people and how they appeal to the masses. It refers to the assurance of cadre's maintaining integrity, their close contact with the masses and service for the people, so as to ensure the institutional measures of state power and the cadre's moral appeal. In the "Common Program" passed on 29 September 1949, Article 18 states: "All state organization of the People's Republic of China, must rigorously enforce a revolutionary work style by being clean, simple, and serving the people, punishing corruption, prohibiting waste, fighting against the bureaucracy of being detached from the masses." This provision is intended to protect the new regime's nature of being clear, clean and close to the people so as to put forth a good image and appeal morally to people. In essence, the appeal mechanism is the requirements for the leading cadres and Party members to measure their behavior according to a saintly moral standard, in order to inspire the cadres and the elite Party members to play a leading role in the appeal mechanism.

The Constitution passed on 20 September 1954 states: "All power in the People's Republic of China belongs to the people. Power is exercised by the National People's Congress and the local people's congresses at all levels." (Article II). The Constitution also states: "All state organizations must rely on the masses, keep close ties to the masses, listen to their views, accept the supervision of the masses" (Article 17). "All state organizations must be devoted to the people's democratic system, to obey the Constitution and laws, to serve the people" (Article 18). These two provisions set the required work style for state organizations and their staff. They became important provisions in ensuring the appeal mechanism of state political power and cadres worked on the masses.

In fact, it has been considered by the Communist Party of China as "good tradition" and "the key to success" to have close ties with the masses, to rely on the masses and join them in sharing joys and pain, enduring hardship together, and serving the people wholeheartedly. Mao Zedong summarized this traditional "mass line." Mao Zedong pointed out in his "On Coalition Government" that: three new Chinese Communist Party's work ethics are created: "The ethic of combining theory and practice, the ethic of closely connecting with the people and the ethic of self-criticism."[151] Closely connecting with people is one of the three new ethics of the Party's.

In the view of the state's leaders, that everything begins from the people's interests, and the need to have close ties to the masses, were important sources of the Chinese Communist Party's moral appeal during the revolutionary war. Mao Zedong said: "One of significant mark that made communists different from any other political party was our closest connection to the overwhelming majority of people. We served the people wholeheartedly and never divorced ourselves from the masses; everything starts from the people's interests rather than from the individual's or small group's interests; maintaining consistently to be responsible to the people and to the party's leading body; these are our starting points."[152] The reason the party did this is because the Communist Party's goal is the people's well-being, and not their own interests. Mao Zedong and the Communist Party of China set very high moral standards. He said: "The Communist Party is a political party seeking interests of the nation, for the people. It has no selfish interests. It is subject to the people's supervision. It should never violate the people's intention. And its members must stand among the people, and should never stand above the people."[153] Mao realized that, during the revolutionary war, the moral appeal of the Communist Party is very important. In "The Chinese Communist Party's Position in The National War", Mao Zedong said:

"The exemplary role of vanguard role very important. The communist party members in the Eighth Route Army and New Fourth Army should become a model for heroic combat, a model of carrying out command, a model of discipline, a model of good political work and fostering internal unity. ... Communist party members, working in the government, should be models of being clean, not selfish, doing more work, getting paid less. The communist party member, in the mass movement, should be the people's friend but not the people's boss, an indefatigable teacher but not a bureaucratic politician. No matter where and when, communists should not consider their personal interests first. They should make their personal interests subordinate to national and the people's interests. Therefore, selfishness, slacking, corruption, limelight seeking, and so, are the most contemptible; and it is most respected to be selfless, to strive positively and actively, to exercise self-restraint and devotion to the public, and to show a hard-working spirit."[154]

Mao Zedong believed that, as long as the Communists were role models, they would be able to appeal to the masses, to inspire and unite the masses and win the support of the masses, ultimately winning victory for the revolution. To maintain the moral appeal of the Communist Party, requires the Communists to look after the people's utmost interests at all times, relying on the masses and making themselves part of the masses. Mao Zedong said: "It should be clear to every comrade that the communist's words and deeds must be in line with the best interests of the masses, and must live up to the highest standards of the common people. All comrades should know, as long as we rely on the people and firmly believe that people's creativity is endless, therefore trusting the people and mixing with them, we can overcome any difficulty and not be overwhelmed by any enemy. On the contrary we will overcome all difficulties and overwhelm all enemies."[155]

The communist's moral appeal is not only reflected in their altruism and selfless spirits in their managing their relationship to the people, but also in a series of rule-based principles for strict moral discipline. A typical example is the "Three Rules of Discipline - Eight Points for Attention." Mao Zedong re-established the three disciplines and the eight notes for attention for the Chinese Red Army during the second interior revolutionary war. The specific content is slightly different at different times and for different forces. On 10 October 1947, when the liberation war was in full swing, Mao Zedong re-enacted the three disciplines - eight notes instruction. First, the three disciplines: (a) direct all our actions to follow command; (b) does not take needle or thread from the masses; (c) all captured goods belong to the public. Second, the Eight Points for Attention: (1) speak mildly and politely; (2) trade fairly; (3) return what has been borrowed; (4) pay for what is damaged; (5) do not hit or swear; (6) do not damage crops; (7) do not take advantage of women; (8) do not abuse prisoners.[156] The moral self-discipline of the communist troops made them seem virtuous and ensured their moral appeal to the people.

Since having close ties to the masses affects the party's appeal to the people, after the founding of China, Mao Zedong opposed the bureaucracy and command doctrine within the state cadres. Not long after the founding of China, Mao Zedong proposed to fight against bureaucracy and authoritarianism. Mao Zedong said: "The bureaucracy and command doctrine, in our party and the government, is not only a big problem at present but will also be big problem for a very long period of time. In terms of its social roots, we see the problem being a reflection of the reactionary style of the reactionary ruling class in dealing with the people (an anti-people style, the style of the Kuomintang), and the reflection of its remnants left within our party and our government."[157]

Mao also criticized a number of party cadre's growing arrogance, showing off their position, resting on their laurels, and their bureaucratic style:

"Some of our cadres think that they are the number one in the world. They look down on people, banking on their seniority. Once they become a government official, especially a higher rank official, they do not want to be perceived as being ordinary working class. This is a very bad phenomenon. ... Therefore, to get rid of bureaucracy, to eliminate bureaucracy, we must sweep away the bureaucracy among the cadres. We must follow the ones holding to the truth, regardless of whether they are the ones picking dung or digging coal or sweeping the streets, or are poor farmers. Whoever has the truth in his hands, we must obey them. Even if you are a high ranking official but you do not have the truth in your hand, we can not obey you."[158]

Bureaucracy detaches the cadres from the masses, which was criticized harshly by Ma Zedong. To eliminate bureaucracy, the system must ensure an equitable relationship between the cadres and the masses. For example, in enterprises, we must urge the cadres to participate in work, to treat people equally, and that workers participate in management, and so on.

National leaders believed that during difficult economic times, material incentives could inspire the worker's enthusiasm, but could not be the primary means of labor incentive. On the contrary, the primary means to stimulate labor motivation should be spiritual incentives, for example: strengthening ideological and political education, and increasing the percentage of collective welfare (which demonstrates the party and government's care for the people). The emphasis on equality between cadres and the masses, and the cadres and people's equitable treatment of each other, the cadre's participation in labor, and reducing the privileges of cadres, were all systematic initiatives intended to enhance the appeal and charisma of cadres. Mao Zedong attempted to define for the cadres a "self-cleaning" system outside the western "two-party" and democratic system. He believed that as long as ideological and moral purification worked effectively on the cadres, the cadres could be the external model which inspires the people by their appeal. And labor's enthusiasm to work can be great stimulated. However, it is worth mentioning that due the failure of the "self-cleaning" system, he had to resort to a more drastic measure, which was the "Cultural Revolution", to reform the cadres. On this issue, we will have more to say later.

C. Micro-incentive System

The macro-incentive system plays an indirect rather than a direct role in stimulating labor motivation. It is done through people's spiritual changes (the sanctity of grace and gratitude, the sanctity of commitment and vision, the sanctity of the moral appeal) to indirectly achieve the result of increasing labor enthusiasm. Nevertheless, it is not enough to have only indirect, macro incentives to stimulate labor motivation. The system of egalitarian economic distribution and life-long employment cause the objective existence of "social laziness" (i.e., a free rider psychology). Therefore, to avoid "social laziness", the state also needs to strengthen incentives for labor motivation from a micro perspective.

1. Mechanism of Labor Competition

As part of the change of the working class's status — from being oppressed to governing — in state-owned enterprises the Communist Party eliminated the old factory labor disciplines, the aim of which was to exploit workers and press them for increases in surplus value. Worker's labor motivation was stimulated more through ideological and political education as well as a variety of other methods. One was the system to win honor and gain a feeling of fulfilling a sacred obligation through competition in labor and production. This competition is actually one kind of social mobilization in production. It can be traced back to the days of the war against Japan, when the Communist Party instituted the policy of competition in production. To deal with difficulties of insufficient supply caused by the blockade by Chiang Kai-shek's government during the war, the Communist Party implemented a policy of self-reliance and hard work. In the communist base, the communist party launched a large-scale program among the military and civilian populations to establish organized labor competition in order to gain experience in promoting labor motivation in production through social mobilization. For example, in 1943, Mao Zedong said: "Our comrades learned to organize the masses of labor, ... organize labor competition, reward heroes of labor, organize exhibitions of production, mobilize the creativity and enthusiasm of the masses."[159]   This kind of social mobilization approach to encouraging labor motivation was applied to state-owned enterprises after the founding of the country.

This type of labor management is different from Taylor-style management. Taylor-style management relies upon scientific analysis work tasks and the design of procedures to achieve the scientific management of labor. In social mobilization, labor management relies on people's sense of honor and pursuit of sacred obligations to stimulate their motivation. At the time, winning the title of "advanced producer" or of "advanced production team" was a sacred honor. However, the effectiveness of this type of management of social mobilization is limited in scope. Why?   Because those who feel that the struggle to become an advanced worker is hopeless, due to the expected results of failing to win the competition, may "rationally" opt out of the competition, and accept a middle or last place status.

2. The Mechanism of Ideological and Political Work

Thus, to the state, it is not enough to encourage labor motivation only through labor competition. It also needs to stimulate labor's work enthusiasm through direct management of labor motivation. The direct management of motivation is ideological and political work. The purpose of ideological and political work is not only the transformation of people's general ideas and concepts, but also to change people's attitudes and work motivation.

Ideological and political work is an integral part of social mobilization. During the revolutionary war, by relying on ideological and political work by organizations at all levels, the Communist Party led the people to win the revolution. Since the victory of the revolution, the party's ideological and political work, being a tool of social mobilization, has been further carried forward. In the rebuilding period following the revolution, it was very natural to apply the traditional ideological and political methods to mining, workshops and the fields. Obviously, the Communist Party that won the military victory through social mobilization naturally wanted to achieve the victory of socialist construction through social mobilization. Therefore, not surprisingly, the leaders often habitually directed and mobilized economic development the same way as they directed and mobilized a military campaign. A typical example is the "Great Leap Forward". Besides being on a large scale, a kind of large formation economic construction "campaign", each specific task of the enterprise was treated as a "battle" or movement, with ideological and political work as necessary components to carry out the campaign. The task it undertook was to solve the issue of participant's morale and motivation for the "battle".

Having established a grass-roots organizations, the Communist Party was not only able to influence the masses with its members being exemplary role models, but also able to mobilize the masses using ideas and persuasion, to resolve the people's ideological and motivational issues. Therefore, the state leaders looked to ideological and political work with great expectations. Ideological and political work was institutionalized, and their functions sacralized and continuously enhanced. Especially after the failure of the "Great Leap Forward", the people's enthusiasm and labor energy suffered a large setback, and morale was seriously affected. The state thus re-emphasized the role of ideological and political work, trying to re-mobilize the enthusiasm of the people through ideological and political work. For example, it is pointed out in the 1964 New Year's Day editorial of the "People's Daily": "Further improving and finishing basic ideological and political work has significant meaning for the successful completion of the socialist revolution and socialist construction. Experience has shown that for those organizations that pay close attention to ideological and political work, hold high the red flag of Mao Zedong's political thoughts, the cadres and masses political passion and enthusiasm are greatly increased, and work is done very well."[160] Why? The editorial pointed out,

"Ideological and political work is the work to revolutionize people. It uses ideas of socialism and communism to arm people's minds. It is the work to arm the people minds with Ma Zedong's thoughts that apply the universal truth of Marxism-Leninism to concrete reality in China. Politics is the commander and the soul. By doing ideological and political work well, by doing ideological and political work flexibly, focusing on each individual's specifics, people's mental outlook would change, and a noble communist moral and social atmosphere would gradually be nurtured."[161]

It is obvious that from a national view, with changes in the people's mental outlook and the establishment of a high communist morality, labor enthusiasm would surges naturally. In the government's official discourse, ideological and political work links worker's specific labor motivation with the broader scope of socialist and communist ideas. By instilling thoughts of socialism and communism, inhibiting the concepts of selfishness and individualism, ideological and political work mobilizes the people's work enthusiasm and spirits of dedication to socialist construction. In essence, ideological and political work is intended to "overcome the erroneous ideas in some workers that they only care about the existence of personal interests but completely ignore politics, and do not care about national interests. Ideological and political work intends to solve the fundamental problem of whom to work for. The work intends to improve their sense of ownership of socialist construction and therefore to revolutionize cadres and the masses."[162] In fact, ideological and political work is a spiritual project. The socialist factory not only creates products by molding, but also shapes worker's souls through ideological and political work. Only after such shaping, is the human soul able to care less about remuneration, exercise restraint and abide, and to work unselfishly.

Whether ideological and political work has the function of stimulating labor motivation is different from whether the state believes that it has such a function. Let us discuss only the latter. It is clear that the national leaders believed in the role of ideological and political work and its power. Ideological and political work became a most critical institutional measure used by the state to address labor motivation under the system of public ownership and the planned economy. Therefore, the national leaders continued to emphasize and strengthen the party's efforts in the economy, especially to strengthen the ideological and political work in the field of economy. Li Fuchun said:

"All of our economic work is subject to political governance. Our mass movement is under the party's leadership. The party and the government called on the masses to get rid of superstition, emancipate the mind, and carry forward a spirit of bold vision and courage. In distribution of consumer goods the party and the government follow the principal of distribution according to work, while at the same time, educating the masses to work hard towards ambitious goals, without caring much about personal rewards. In the agencies, organizations, schools, businesses and institutions, in the communes, through speaking out and vigorous debate, posters in the form of criticism and self-criticism, the people are encouraged to educate themselves. This ensures that every worker has constant enthusiasm and high energy, to tenaciously overcome difficulties, to boldly create."[163]

In the view of the state's leaders the main purpose of ideological and political work is to convince the masses to work hard toward the country's ambitious goals, "not to care about personal reward," and ensure "that every worker keeps constant enthusiasm and high energy." Thus, "without remuneration" and the mobilization of labor enthusiasm are problems that ideological and political work needs to solve. Ideological and political work is the embodiment of the state's "persuasive power", influencing people's attitudes and behavior from the depths of the human's heart and soul. The implementation of such persuasive power at the grassroots level constitutes a micro sacred incentive.

State leaders hope that using ideological and political work as a means of social mobilization, will not only mobilize the enthusiasm of workers, but also induces the masses to innovate technologically. For example, in 1960, the central government forwarded the Anshan Municipal Party Committee's report on technological innovation on the industrial front and the progress of the technological revolution. The spirit of this report is summarized as the "Anshan Constitution".[164.] This report summarizes the experiences of the mass movement at Anshan Iron and Steel Plant, under the party leadership, in technological innovation and technological revolution.[165.] The main point is that through ideological and political work and social mobilization, labor enthusiasm is mobilized along with the creativity of the masses in technical innovation and invention.

Since 1963, the state leaders frequently issued directions to strengthen ideological and political work in the economic field.

The effectiveness of ideological and political work depends on two premises, one being that national goals and personal goals over the long term should be the same, the second being that ideological and political work follows a realistic discourse, with a sense of realism and internal logic. In the early days, the state's ideological and political work basically met these preconditions. However, as time went by, with poverty situation worsened and bureaucratic privileges rose, it became difficult for the country's ideological and political work to meet these two premises. Not only that, the words became more and more rigid, impractically dogmatic. They drifted further away from these two prerequisites. Therefore it became less effective as a labor incentive. In turn it forced the state to further strengthen its ideological and political work. On this issue, we will have further analysis in chapter four.

The essence of sacred motivation is the state's ability to use ideological discourse to achieve the result of replacing personal goals. In other words, replacing individual goals with national goals, requiring individuals to dedicate themselves to the national goals without pay but still working hard. In the process of implementing this incentive, on the one hand, the state aims to arouse the worker's labor enthusiasm by traditional moral ideals and moral resources, by creating "legitimacy incentives" through the national "gift" (the liberation effect), by outlining a grand blueprint and promising a better life, and by employing the power elite's personal appeal. On the other hand, the state directly attempts by its administrative resources to stimulate labor enthusiasm in workers (by labor competition and ideological and political work), and urges workers to work conscientiously through social and organizational mobilization. Such behavior by the state, for a period of time, achieved the desired results, but at the cost off a huge amount of ideological and political work. The premise of legitimacy incentives is that legitimacy must be reproducible. Should there by crisis in legitimacy resources, labor motivation under the low-consumption policy would be problematic. This is the problem the country faced during the late stage of Cultural Revolution.

Derivative system: The Institutional Arrangements of Revolutionary Ideology

As mentioned above, the state, on one hand, wants the people to work hard, but on the other hand, limits the forms of material incentives that can be used to motivate people to work. So the state can only use non-material incentives to stimulate labor motivation. The sacred incentive is such a systemic arrangement. What is derived from the system of curbing consumption system and the sacred incentive system is the institutional arrangement of "revolutionary ideology". It complements the previous two systems. As it has an inherent functional connection to the sacred incentive system and system of curbing consumption, revolutionary ideology is in fact, part of a "system chain". The essence of revolutionary ideology is establishing national goals as an ethical criterion, a test whether an individual's motives, attitudes and behavior are consistent with the national goals, and to treat any inconsistent personal motivation or ideas as taboos, therefore ensuring that personal motivation, attitudes and behavior are consistent with national objectives. It is the mechanism to unify people's thinking and promote consistent behavior across the country.

A. Plan of Transformation of Human Nature

Although in 1956 China completed the socialist transformation of the ownership of production, because of the fact that socialist public and collective ownership originated in private ownership, the people's ideological thinking may have not kept up with the change in ownership. Private property, self-seeking, hedonism, and other concepts still have a certain market. Therefore, to cope with changes in the social structure, the state launched an unprecedented ideological structural reform to match the various institutional arrangements made by the state in order to achieve its historical mission to realize socialist industrialization, and thus to realize communism. Obviously, to the leaders of the state, to make people to accept the institutional arrangements of curbing consumption, living frugally, working hard and living a simple life, while at the same time still playing the role of active productive labor, there must be transformation of human nature to realize the national ideological revolution; and that human nature can be thus modified. From the national leader's standpoint, in order to build socialism, a number of the bourgeoisie or exploitative class's mercenary and pleasure-seeking ideas had to be removed and an mindset of frugality be established.

In order to transform human nature and people's ideology, the state made the institutional arrangement of revolutionary ideology, including the system of ideological and political education, criticism and self-criticism, and the political purge (i.e., "class struggle") system. The goal was, first of all, between the ascetic and pleasurable, to make pleasure a stigma and set up asceticism as normal; secondly, between selfless dedication and the self-serving, stigmatizing selfishness and making selfless devotion normal; thirdly, between the privileged and spartan styles in the cadres, stigmatizing the privileged style and making the spartan style normal. Specifically, the transformation of human nature involves three levels: the first level involves the relationship between the individual and his material desires. The second level involves the relationship between the individual and the public (nation). And the third level involves the relationship between cadres and the masses.

Human transformation at the first level involves the relationship between the individual and his material desires. In this relationship, there is an opposition between the personal pursuit of "worldly pleasures" and adherence to the "sacred religion". The former pursues material desires, especially the maximum satisfaction of sensual desire, despising the ideal and spiritual, focusing rather on material comforts. The latter sees the dedication to a belief and the pursuit of an ideal as the highest goal, ignoring material and sensual enjoyment, and even sacrificing some material comfort for a sacred ideal. In the state's leaders view, during China's socialist industrialization process, pleasure-seeking activities were in conflict with the goal of building socialism. Transforming human nature away from a focus on the material toward one focused on the spiritual and ideal, disregarding enjoyment of material comforts, was therefore a necessary component of socialist industrialization. To this end, it was necessary to stigmatize motivation and behavior that pursued pleasure, and to make the "pursuit of material enjoyment," "hedonism," "luxury" and so on, moral labels associated with shame. National leadership pointed out that "We must strongly promote the spirit of diligence and thrift among the cadres and the masses, and further develop a social atmosphere that is proud of plain living, and ashamed of extravagance and waste."[166] From a functional point of view, once having inculcated a sense that the desire for material consumption is shameful, implementing a policy of curbing consumption will not frustrate the people's labor enthusiasm.

It appears to the designer of the system that in order to make people willing to sacrifice their personal material interests for the state's goals and to endure materially poor life, we must enrich the people's spiritual world, raise their awareness of the state, and establish the country's mission as a noble personal faith. In the words of Mao Zedong, during the revolutionary war, the Chinese Communist Party's collective mission and overall goal was to seek the interests of the Chinese people. "The Chinese people are suffering, we have the duty to save them. We have to work hard."[167] This noble and sacred mission enabled the elite revolutionary groups to endure hardship and poverty. After the founding of China, the country's leadership did not believe that their historical mission ended. The Communist Party continued to lead the people all across the country by looking after their long-term interests. The first goal was to realize socialist industrialization, and build a solid material foundation towards the goal of communism. The state leaders called for party members, cadres and the army to continue to maintain the spirit of arduous struggle. "We want to promote hard work, hard work is our political character. ... People should have passion."[168] The party's goal is the country's goal, and is also the common goal for people across the country. Therefore, the national goals have become the criteria for evaluating personal thoughts, words and deeds. The state naturally uses the standards of the Communists and the revolutionary armed forces to evaluate the people, asking them to accept an ascetic lifestyle of "hard work". In the view of the state's leaders, with ideological and political mobilization, individuals are willing and able to endure poor material conditions to achieve the state goals, by living an ascetic life style.

The second level of transformation of human nature involves the relationship between the individual and the public (or overall national interest). At this level, the state's goal is to eliminate the selfishness that originated in the society of private ownership, so as to make people accept communist beliefs and a collective spirit of selfless dedication. Clearly, in the eyes of the national leaders, selfishness is in conflict with the goal of building socialism. It becomes a barrier to the national policy of curbing consumption, because the system of consumption curbs requires individual interests to be subordinated to collective interests while selfishness places personal interests first, contrary to the state's goal. Mao Zedong said: "We always promote hard work, opposing placing personal material interests above everything else."[169] In Zhou Enlai's words: "We are opposed to all views and behaviors that only care for individuals but not society, care for the local but disregard the overall, care for the immediate future regardless of the long-term, care for privilege while disregarding obligations, care for consumption while disregarding producing."[170]

It can be said promoting the abandonment of personal selfish thinking, emphasizing that individual interests must to be subordinated to collective or the interests of the revolution, were continuous measures adopted during Mao's early years during his revolutionary transformation of the Communist Party, in order to improve its combat effectiveness. As early as 1937, Mao Zedong in "Anti-Liberalism" explicitly opposed individualism, opposing "placing personal interests first, and placing the interests of the revolution second".[171] He said: "A Communist should have largeness of mind, be loyal, active, seeing revolution as his very life and subordinating his personal interests to the interest of revolution; ... concerned about the party and the masses more than about any individual, concerned about others more than himself. He will thereby be considered a Communist."[172] In his view, as a party member, he or she must take the interests of the revolution (the overall collective interest) above personal interests, abandoning selfish thinking. In 1938, in "Chinese Communist Party's Position in the National War", he also pointed out: "The Communists should not put their interest first regardless of where and when they are. Their personal interests should be subordinated to the nation's and to the people's interest. Therefore, selfishness, slacking, corruption, limelight seeking, and so on, is most contemptible; selfless, positive efforts to exercise restraint and abide, a hardy spirit, is to be respected."[173] Opposing selfishness, advocating selflessness, has become a requirement for party members. In 1939, in the paper "Commemorating Norman Bethune," Mao Zedong proposed once again that communists must learn from Bethune's "willingness to benefit others instead of himself," the altruistic spirit of communism. Mao Zedong elevated Bethune's "serving others but not oneself" to "the spirit of Communism," setting up Bethune as a perfect model of the practice of the spirit of Communism, and called on everyone to learn from him: "We must all learn from him his spirit of selflessness. From this standpoint, we can make ourselves useful to the people. Regardless a person's capability, as long as he or she has such spirit, he or she is a noble person, a pure human being, a person who is moral, a person without vulgarity, a person who can benefit the people."[174]

After the founding of China, the state promoted party member's selflessness and self-sacrificing Communist spirit to the people across the country. Clearly, establishing selfless dedication among the people, with personal interests subordinated to the collective spirit, are without doubt conducive to the operation of the planned socialist economy. In order to adapt for the construction of a socialist society, we must develop a new structure of human nature that is compatible with socialist objectives, namely: suppressing the private and sacralizing a public, selfless, collective humanity with a willingness to sacrifice.

The third level of human transformation involves the relationship between the cadres and the masses. Whether in the case of the cadres or of the masses, the transformation of human nature must be carried out. However, in view of the state's leaders, the transformation of cadres is particularly critical. Why? After socialist system was established and the state eliminated the exploiting classes, the means of production belonged to the whole people under their collective ownership. Management of such means of production was taken over by cadres appointed by the state. Could the powerful elite group use their authority for personal gain and privilege? Will they degenerate to become the new bourgeois element? In Mao's view, this was an important symbol as to whether the state has changed the nature of its governance. Therefore, in order to ensure that state power does not change its nature, we must maintain the purity of the cadres. We must have strict requirements in their thinking and mode of living. We will have to ask them to be a role model during the ideological transformation. Therefore, we must require cadres to follow the mass line, to become part of the masses, sharing hardship and happiness, suffering or enjoying together. They cannot be superior, or engage in bureaucracy, let alone engage in specialization.

More specifically, the implementation of a universal policy to curb consumption is an important political premise. It is the way the power elite (party members and cadres) demonstrate their exemplary role. Whether the power elite abuses their power, or acts selflessly and served the people wholeheartedly, not only has a key impact on people's attitudes towards national policy (including the policy of curbing consumption), but also affects people's views and attitudes of the nature of the new regime. It affects party member's and cadre's power of appeal. So, paying close attention to the education and supervision of party members and cadres, and strictly dealing with cadres who became corrupted, became a significant political task for the state.

Regarding the degeneration of cadres, Mao Zedong was deeply concerned. On the eve of victory of the revolution, at the second meeting of the seventh plenary held by the party, Mao Zedong pointed out: "Because of the victory, the proud mood within the party, the mood of showing off as a hero, the mood of pausing and not making progress, the mood of pleasure-seeking and not wanting to live through hardship again, are likely to grow." As a result, he stressed that, "Comrades must be taught to remain modest, prudent and free from arrogance and rashness of attitude, comrades must be taught to maintain the attitude of striving hard."[175] Out of the concern for the degeneration of the cadres, Mao Zedong repeatedly emphasized that cadres must work to become part of the masses, share weal and woe with the masses, and not detach themselves from the masses in order to feel superior to the masses. In a conversation, Mao Zedong proposed that cadres present themselves in the way, "ordinary workers would appear."[176] The Central Communist Government pointed out in a special instruction, when forwarding Qi Yanming's report on the supply of special needs for senior cadres and intellectuals in Beijing: "We must repeatedly warn the party cadres that they must appear with the attitudes of ordinary laborers and as the people's servants. They must share weal and woe with the masses, promote the communist style of hardship first and enjoyment later, and constantly fight the temptation of privilege and the tendency to believe that they deserve special treatment."[177] Liu also pointed out: "All party members, regardless of how high their positions, are the people's servants. They should see themselves as ordinary workers, without any privileges. They must be concerned about the life of the masses, sharing their weal and woe. Every party member should be proud of plain living, and be ashamed of extravagance."[178] It is out of concern for the degeneration of party members and the cadres, that the party and state implemented a strict cadre system to monitor trends within the cadres and to ensure their impartiality and integrity.

B. System of Revolutionary Ideology

To elucidate the plan to reconstruct human nature to meet national objectives, we must understand exactly what system the state created to ensure the realization of those plans. In fact, it was already difficult to ask the people who joined the revolution to be "absolute selfless", let alone to ask the same of the general public. Self-interest and satisfying personal desires were traditional habits in the peasant economy. Even those who received their ideological education during the communist revolution were not able to overcome "selfishness" entirely. After the founding of the People's Republic, people very naturally expected a "liberation" effect (that is, liberation would lead to personal benefit). People who fought in the revolution believed that with victory, it was time to ask for compensation, to receive a better standard of living and material comforts. For the general public as well, after the liberation and the establishment of the dictatorship of the proletariat, there was the opinion that liberation should be reflected in the improvement and enhancement of people's living standards. Therefore, the state's insistence on frugal living and hard work, no doubt was inconsistent with people's social expectations of the "liberation" effect. Unable to meet the people's high expectations of the liberation effect, the state could only postpone delivering on the social expectations indefinitely. The state took advantage of this postponement of social expectations to encourage people to "temporarily" relinquish the pursuit of their immediate interests and an improved material life. Before the final advent of a future utopia, the people not only needed to struggle, but also to change their thinking, curb their desires, and promote the spirits of altruism, collectivism and communism. The state artificially overstated a person's capability to discipline himself or herself, in order to establish self-denial as the default position, precisely in order to reduce the individual's expectation of immediate improvements material living standards.

The self-discipline and rising ideological standards imposed by the state on the individuals to control their materialistic impulses, required that the state pay a cost to maintain those standards. Needless to say, the state's capacity to mobilizing resources enables it to make the nation to act according to its will. At the same time, states must have

-90-

the ability to make their populace obey willingly the command of the government. In other words, just as the system of control of basic units of consumption and the redistribution of resources enhanced the state's command authority, it may not have been able to make people to obey willingly the command of the state. Therefore, to make concerted efforts with the national populace, the state must have the ability to change people's thoughts, ideas, attitudes and motivation. In other words, the state must have persuasive powers in addition to the authority to command. If we say that the authority to command is "hard" power, the persuasive power would be "soft" power. The system of ideological and political work is an embodiment of the state's persuasive powers.

C. Persuasive System

If the state's ability to command power is a consequence of its highly centralized capacity for resource mobilization (including material, administrative and military resources), the state's persuasive power is related to its highly concentrated ability to mobilize words, which is obtained on the basis of its resource mobilization capability. In a state with a planned economy, not only is the economy within national control and management, but also are people's thoughts, ideas and desires. Through monopolizing and controlling people's words, the state shapes their minds, influences their attitudes, and can change people's motivations, including curbing people's desires. The system of ideological and political work is a mobilization mechanism employing a discourse created by the state, echoing and compatible with the planned economic system. It reflects state's ability to mobilize discourse.

A high degree of reliance on ideological and political work is a fundamental feature of the state's planned economic system. In countries with this type of system, people's ideas tend to be aligned with the state's mission and objectives. Therefore, ideological consistency and homogeneity have become state goals. The implementation of institutional initiatives to promote consistent ideology reflects the high degree of the control of mass media by the state and the primacy of the system of basic ideological and political work. In the early days of the People's Republic, Liu advocated the importance of political education for people. In his summary report at the first Chinese Communist Party propaganda meeting, he reviewed the party's propaganda in the past and pointed out important measures to be adopted to strengthen the Party's publicity. He said: "What should we do to educate the people? The idea is to adopt the principles of Marxism-Leninism. Within the ideological principles of Marxism-Leninism, educating the people across the country at all levels is the most basic political work of our party. To advance to socialism and communism we must first lay a foundation ideologically, educate ourselves and the people in the Marxist-Leninist perspective and methods. This is the task of the party's political work today under the new situation and new conditions."[179] The goal is to "educate the people in Marxism-Leninism, to raise the people's class consciousness and ideological level, so as to lay the ideological foundation to build socialism and to realize communism in our country."[180]

In addition to the education of the general public, the ideological education of young people to became a focus of political and ideological work. For example, 16 September 1955, the CPC Central Committee approved and transmitted to the Youth League Central Committee "The Final Task Force Report on Carrying Out The Training of Young Communist Morality and Resisting the Erosion of Bourgeois Ideology", in which the regional party committees were instructed to improve the communist education of youth, and to nurture young people's communist morality."[181] Ever since, the Central Committee has repeatedly issued documents calling for reform of the education system and strengthening political and ideological work in the universities, high schools and primary schools.

In order to strengthen ideological and political education, simply using mass communication is inadequate. It also requires the establishment of a special ideological and political work system, through which ideological and political work can penetrate deeply into all areas society on regular and routine basis. On 22 February 1964, the CPC Central Committee pointed out in forwarding the instruction, "Northern China Bureau Striving to Complete the Task of 'Fighting Against Five Evil's in Industrial Enterprises in 1964": "In order to achieve the goal of re-educating and transforming the people, at each step of the movement, we must put great emphasis on strengthening ideological and political work. We must also conduct the ideological and political work on regular basis, applying it to manufacturing, production and scientific research, to have it become part of everyday life."[182]

Thus, before the Cultural Revolution, the state authorities in the country had established a regular and routine political learning system. Later, this system was extended to other enterprises. This regular political learning system became important mechanism for carrying out state commands, persuading people to accept ideology advocated by the state, promoting uniformity of thought, encouraging obedience and transforming people's ideas.

Ideological and political education is diverse. In addition to the propaganda by the propaganda departments, political studies by the units and so on, the state also continues to promote heroes and role models, in order to set an example of communist spirit to the people of the country. For example, Lei Feng is a typical hero set up by the state during peacetime. It can be said that since the founding of new China, Lei Feng was the most influential moral role model for the people. Before the media found Lei Feng, he was just an ordinary soldier. Lei Feng's story was first publicized by military writer Chen Guangsheng, who once was morale officer of the regiment in which Lei Feng served before his death. In 1963 he co-wrote a book called "The Story of Lei Feng", the first book describing the Lei Feng phenomenon. Shenyang Li Jianyu and Tong Xi-wen of Shenyang province were the first correspondents first publicizing the Lei Feng stories in newspapers. After interviewing Lei Feng, they published the article "Chairman Mao's Good Soldier" in the newspaper "Forward Report". The story caused a stir. Later, the story was also published in the "Liberation Army Daily" the Xinhua News Agency also republished the story. The military quickly launched activities to learn from Lei Feng.[183]

On 1 March 1963, Mao Zedong wrote an article: "Learn from Comrade Lei Feng", and had it published in "China Youth" on 2 March and reproduced on 5 March in "The People's Daily". On 6 March, Liu Shaoqi, Zhou Enlai, Zhu De, Deng Xiaoping all wrote encomiums for the "Liberation Army Daily". Liu Shaoqi's reads: "Learn from Comrade Lei Feng's ordinary and great communist spirit." Zhou Enlai's reads: "Learn from Comrade Lei Feng's clear love-and-hate class position, his revolutionary spirit of consistently practicing what he preaches, selfless communist style, and selfless proletarian fighting spirit." Zhu De's reads: "Learn from Lei Feng, be a good soldier of Chairman." Deng Xiaoping's reads:" Whoever is willing to become a real communist, learn from Comrade Lei Feng's character and manner." The collective encomiums of the leaders of the CPC Central Committee soon triggered a boom across the country in learning from Lei Feng. Lei Feng was established as the model of communist spirit and the most representative exemplar in China of "doing good but not seeking fame," "enjoying helping the others," "living plainly and being thrifty," and being "selfless". He influenced several generations of the Chinese people.

Another form of political education was contrasting the bitter past with the good life of the present (Yi Ku Si Tian). This form of the socialist education movement originated in the countryside after the "three difficult years". In 1963, in the instruction "The Report on the Two Issues in Rural Socialist Education" submitted by Song Renqiong, the CPC Central Committee pointed out, that "Comrade Song Renqiong's idea of talking about village history, family history, community history, and factory history can be a good method of educating young people, which should be generally feasible."[184] Song Renqiong said in the report:

"Today's youth grew up after the liberation. Educated under the party, the majority have a certain consciousness and are very active in socialist construction. But because most of them did not personally suffer or witness the landlords and rich peasant's exploitation of the peasants, even being the children of poor peasants, they generally a lack of sense of class and class struggle. They do not understand the darkness of the old society. They do not understand the difficulty of revolution and construction. Many people have a rather vague class concept. They lack a firm class position, are vulnerable to bourgeois ideology and erosion. When things get rough, they are easily shaken. Many old farmers feel that the young farmers are "difficult" to manage. They criticize the young farmers 'not appreciating their fortune when they are the fortunate.' ... The socialist education experience proves that the method of recalling and contrasting is effective in educating the youth about the history of class struggle."[185]

This method was soon extended to the urban socialist education movement. For example, "relying on older workers and advanced elements, recall and compare the new and old societies, the causes of class struggle in the two historical periods of democratic and socialist revolution, recalling the bitter past and reflect on the current good (Yi Ku Si Tian), to improve people's socialist consciousness, and to re-classify the revolutionary class heirarchy."[186] Mao confirmed this method of education. For example, in 1965, during a conversation with Edgar Snow, Mao Zedong said: "Young people have not seen the landlord's exploitation, capitalist exploitation, nor have they fought, nor see what is imperialism. The ones in their twenties now, were only in their teens at that time. They do not know about the old society. So it is necessary to have their parents or the old generation talk about the past. Otherwise, they would know nothing about that part of history."[187] Through the mobilization of discourse, the state guides the people's perspective. The "Yi Ku Si Tian" approach guides the people in their comparison of the new society with the old one, highlighting the benefits of the new and thereby increasing the acceptance of the policies of curbing consumption and controlling individual desire.

D. The System of Criticism and Self-criticism

Criticism and self-criticism is a methodology of ideological education, reform and unification that was adopted by Chinese Communist Party in Yan'an Rectification Movement. In April 1945, at the Seventh National Congress held by the Communist Party of China in Yan'an, Mao Zedong delivered the "Report On Coalition Government". In the report, Mao Zedong summarized the methodology of criticism and self-criticism. According to Mao's summary, there are three types of working methods in the Chinese

Communist Party: "The major method is a combination of theory and practice, the method of closely connecting with the people and the method of self-criticism."[188] In a sense, "self-criticism" advocates   self-confession, self-inspection, self-correction of people's own mistakes and faults.

Self-criticism is an important method for party members to achieve self-reflection, education, reform, unity and the "purity" of the party's ideology. In the early days of the People's Republic, in his publications,   Mao Zedong added "self-criticism" in front of "criticism", which made it "criticism and self-criticism". Criticism and self-criticism is the practice of comrades criticizing each other, supervising each other, helping each other, and exposing each other's "inadequacies" and "shortcomings". At the same time, through self-criticism, it is reflection on one's own "inadequacies" and "shortcomings." In Mao's view, the criticism between comrades was neither personal attack, nor verbal abuse and retaliation. All comrades should not be afraid of criticism others, should correctly deal with criticism from others, while daring to criticize the shortcomings of others and be willing to criticize themselves.

This earnest style of criticism and self-criticism is but in reality a ceremony of ideological "purification". It is an ideological "repentance" and "redemption." In this conception of the "purification" ceremony, any beliefs, ideas, concepts or habits not conforming to the CPC Central Committee's doctrine would be overcome through non-violent punishment. Criticism and self-criticism is the persuasive power over the soul. The instrumentality of this power is discourse, the object being the soul. Through collectively mobilizing a legitimacy dialog by members of the organization, people purify each other's words that may have deviated from legitimate ideas and concepts. Therefore, the exercise of criticism and self-criticism to a certain extent, results in a reinforcement of legitimate of words and ideas, and consequently has the effect of purifying the thoughts of members of the organization.

After the founding of the People's Republic, Mao Zedong strongly recommended this method to all classes and all democratic parties outside the Communist Party. At the second session of the CPPCC National Committee meeting, he said in the closing statement: "Criticism and self-criticism is the basic method of self-education. I hope people of all nationalities, democratic classes, democratic parties, people's organizations and all patriotic democrats will adopt this approach."[189] In the opening statement of the third meeting of the CPPCC National Committee, he said:

"In the second meeting of the National Committee concluded, I have put forward the method of criticism and self-criticism as self-education and reform. Now, this proposal has gradually become a reality. Ideological transformation is first of all the reform of all manner of intellectuals. It is one of the important preconditions for our country to realize democratic reform and gradual industrialization. Therefore, we wish this self-education and self-reform movement make steady and increasing progress."[190]

Later, Mao Zedong recommended to all provincial and municipal colleagues the method of criticism and self-criticism. He said: "One doctrine of Marxism is called the criticism and self-criticism. ... Regular meetings, criticism and self-criticism, is a good way of mutual supervision among the comrades to promote the cause of the party and the rapid progress of the country. I suggest that provincial and municipal governments consider this. Can you do this too? Aren't you studying the central government? I think this is the thing to learn."[191] He advocated regular meetings and conducting criticism and self-criticism, and over the time building it into a regular and routine ideological monitoring and transformation system.

Subsequently, Mao expanded criticism and self-criticism as a common method to resolve conflicts among the people. He pointed out that:

"Self-criticism is our Communist Party's method. Later on, we want to try it out in the democratic parties. Now the democratic parties are widely engaged. At a most recent meeting of democratic construction committee, this approach was adopted and criticism and self-criticism started. This is the way to resolve issues among the people themselves. The Communist Party, government, democratic parties, workers, farmers, businessmen, landlords whose voting right was restored, all belong to the category of people. When there are shortcomings, problems, we must start with the objective of uniting people, using the method of criticism and self-criticism, put forward comments and requests, solving problems and achieving unity."[192]

Here, he distinguishes the method of criticism and self-criticism from that of class struggle. The former seeks to resolve conflicts among the people, and its starting point and goal is to achieve unity through non-violent resolution. Class struggle relies upon conflict, aiming to resolve the contradiction between enemy and us self.

Criticism and self-criticism gradually became institutionalized. The main institutional form is the regular meeting of the Communist Party, of state organs and institutions, businesses, people's organizations, democratic parties and other organizations. At meetings, people criticize each other while also criticizing themselves. These became institutional venues for the national mobilization of discourse, to perform conceptual "purification", to transform human nature, and promote intellectual hegemony. At such venues, individualism, hedonism, selfishness are regularly condemned by the mainstream discourse and criticism.

Individualistic ideas and behaviors are thus exposed and may therefore be rectified.

E. The System of Political Oppression (Movement of Class Struggle)

Criticism and self-criticism is an effective method of ideological reform. However, some organizations and departments may develop a small-group mentality or factionalism by forming alliances for their own interest. Because within a small group, to protect their own interests, people may alliances, covering for each other, being sympathetic towards each other, and only praising each other without criticism. Even if there is criticism, it may be irrelevant or evasive. In addition, some leading cadres may abuse their own power to retaliate against subordinates that criticize them by having the subordinates "wear small shoes". The fear of possible retaliation makes subordinates afraid of criticizing their superiors. Also, because of "selfishness", even between comrades at the same rank, one may hold a grudge, or become disgruntled, when criticized and seek an opportunity to retaliate. This led to failures in carrying out criticism and self-criticism. For these various reasons, criticism and self-criticism was likely to become "mere formality", practiced in name but not actuality. So when problems between leading cadres and workers accumulated beyond what the central government could tolerate, the problem-solving approach could no longer be "sweet and light" criticism and self-criticism. It required a more intense effort of mass political oppression (political movement and class struggle). From this perspective, we can understand why Mao Zedong repeatedly stressed the necessity for class struggle, even after the socialist transformation is completed. In his view, a political movements and class struggle is the last resort to rescue the cadres and workers, especially leading cadres, from corruption and degeneracy, and to prevent the ruling party and state regime from changing their political color. In fact, it is a method used by the state's highest leaders, in addition to the separation of powers and the Western "multi-party system", to prevent the corruption of the state. Of course, it also planted the seeds for a new kind of corruption in which leaders at various levels used "class struggle" and political movements to purge and extirpate their rivals for power.

According to Mao Zedong, after the completion of the socialist transformation, the so-called class struggle is no longer the struggle between classes, as the exploiting class as an entity has been eliminated. Instead, class struggle is an ideological struggle, i.e., the ideological struggle between the exploiting class and the proletarians. Here, the reservoir of bourgeois ideology may be the bourgeoisie of the past or the new bourgeois elements existing within the government. This is why during the Cultural Revolution, Mao Zedong stressed that, "The bourgeoisie reside inside the Communist Party". He repeatedly mentioned, that the proletariat having gained power, does not guarantee victory in the ideological field. It remains a contested issue who wins in that arena. He pointed out that:

"The socialist system has been basically established in China. We have had initial victory in transforming the ownership of the means of production. There is no real resolution as to who will win in the ideological field between the proletariat and the bourgeoisie. We still have a long-term struggle with the bourgeois and petty-bourgeois ideology. Without understanding this situation, it is wrong to give up ideological struggle. Any erroneous ideas, any poisonous weeds, any ghosts and monsters should all be criticized, and never be allowed to spread freely."[193]

National leaders worried that "bourgeois ideology" and "petty-bourgeois ideology" were bound to infect party members, cadres and workers, causing "erosion" and therefore, with help of the state's ideological apparatus, the state must criticize and purify the people's ideology through its capacity for the mobilization of discourse. However, in Mao's view, despite the state's control of the mechanisms of public opinion and propaganda, does not mean that the state will win certain victory on the ideological front. The reason is simple. Curbing desire is definitely more difficult than indulging desire. Therefore, Mao Zedong fully anticipated the sharpness of the ideological struggle between the bourgeois and the proletarians (e.g., the pursuit of selfish desires and hedonism), and asked party leaders personally to attend to this. He said: "The large-scale blizzard kind of domestic revolution, of mass class struggle, is almost over, but there is class struggle, mainly class struggle on the political and ideological front, which is really sharp. Ideological problems now have become a very important issue. The first secretary of each regional party committee should be personally at the front to run the ideological work."[194] Mao Zedong's theory of class struggle under socialist conditions, was systematically summarized at the Tenth Session of the Eighth Central Committee Plenary:

"The Tenth plenary of the Eighth national congress pointed out that in the whole historical period of the proletarian revolution and dictatorship of the proletariat, in the transition from capitalism to communism and throughout the historical period (this period will take decades, or even more time), there is class struggle between the bourgeoisie and the proletarians, and there is a two-route struggle between socialism and capitalism. The reactionary ruling class being overthrown is not willing to die. They always attempt to come back. At the same time, there is still bourgeoi's influence and the force of habit of the old society. Some small producers still have spontaneous capitalist tendencies. There are some people, not too many, who have not been transformed by socialism. They only amount to a few percent of the population. But once given opportunities, they always attempt to leave the socialist road to take capitalist path. In these circumstances, class struggle is inevitable. It is Marxism-Leninism's law that has long been clear. We must not forget. This class struggle is complex and tortuous, having ups and downs, and is sometimes very intense. This class struggle is inevitably reflected inside the party."[195]

Through this paragraph, we can actually see that the so-called "proletariat" and "bourgeois" or "socialist road" and "capitalist road" and other terms, have not been clearly defined. In fact, this ambiguity is the fundamental issue. The key is, by means of the categories "proletarian" and "bourgeois", "socialist" and "capitalist" and the class struggle with the opposition, the state gained a new tool to solve the problem of hedonism, corruption, theft, breach of the public trust, self-dealing and "degeneration" among the cadres and workers in their pursuit of self-interest. "Bourgeois", "capitalist" and other qualitative terms, are nothing but political labels, labels serving to mark behaviors as corrupt or irregular in nature. In essence, the class struggle aimed at curbing the spread of selfish desires and in consequence, preventing cadres and workers from degenerating. In its mode of operation, class struggle operates by clearing out an "alien class", achieving a deterrent effect on all staff, thereby preventing selfish desires and self-interest from spreading, as well as maintaining party members and cadre's purity of thought.

One objective of the class struggle was to curb selfish desires and interests, which is exemplified by the "four clean" campaign. The "Four Clean" (clean politics, clean economy, clean organization, clean thinking) movement included originally the so-called the "Five Anti-" campaign of urban and rural socialist education.[196.] "Five Anti-" movement is a shorthand for "opposing corruption and theft, against speculation, against extravagance and waste, against decentralization, against bureaucracy". It began in 1963. The CPC Central Committee pointed out:

"In recent years, in some of our cadres, the bourgeois style of thinking has indeed been growing. This is shown mainly in taking advantage of governmental positions, bureaucratic empire building, ambushes, game playing, pursuing parochial interests instead of national interests, excessive compartmentalization and departmental isolationism, all of which increase. Seeking personal enjoyment, pomp, extravagance, sacrificing the public interest to personal benefit, using 'back door' methods, undermining the system, taking advantage of people, squandering public assets, misuse of national resources, waste of the people's effort, all these symptoms are growing. What is especially serious is corruption and the theft of national assets, speculation, smuggling, the establishment of secret underground factories, illicit profit-making and other activities to undermine the socialist planned economy, all these capitalist activities have become rampant. Also in addition, there is an expanding class of new capitalists with growing influence. These have become a serious obstacle to moving our cause forward. All practices and phenomena incompatible with the interests of socialism must be resolutely corrected. All behavior damaging the socialist cause must be resolutely opposed. All the corruption, theft, speculation and other criminal activities that undermine the socialism, must be resolutely fought against."[197]

We can say that class struggle is the mass purge and political movement taken by the state cadres and workers in order to maintain the "purity" of the leaders and cadres. It is the state's last line of defense against the spread of self-interest and selfish desire. In fact, Mao Zedong's theory of class struggle after the completion of socialist transformation was a means of fighting against selfish desire in peacetime. After the victory of the revolution, people entered a period of reconstruction, with no enemy, the economy began to develop, people had the means to pursue personal interests and material enjoyment. Some cadres in powerful positions and even some workers took advantage of their positions to pursue privilege and leisure. This is exactly what Ma Zedong worried about, and was what he could not tolerate. To overcome this phenomenon, he tried "self-purifying" measures, one of which is "class struggle", in addition to the Western methods of "separation of powers" and "universal suffrage". Mao's class struggle theory became the measure used to resolve the problem of rising materialism and pursuit of self-interest during peacetime. Because of the persistence of materialistic desire and self-interest, although they may be temporarily curbed during the class struggle campaign, they are likely to make a comeback. This is why Mao Zedong tried to make the class struggle movement a regular and routine exercise.

In a sense, ideological and political education, criticism and self-criticism, political oppression and the class struggle movement are national measures undertaken by the state under conditions of extreme poverty, in order to curb consumption by focusing all possible resources on carrying out socialist construction and realizing ideal communism. In line with the national policy of curbing consumption, and to maintain the character of political cadres and workers, the state overstated the standards and requirements for the suppression of people's self-interest and material desires. It is through this that the state attempted to substitute an ascetic (or asceticism) for desire. To this end, the state monopolized the power of discourse and improved its capacity to mobilize that discourse so it could carry out the ideological reform of the people in accordance with the state's agenda. The state asked people to establish a communist outlook toward the world and life, to eradicate egoism, individualism, hedonism and other "bourgeois" worldviews. However, due to the limitations of the mechanisms for monitoring the exercise of power, some people inevitably find a variety of channels to satisfy their own desires, even breaching the public trust and enriching themselves. For example, during the country's difficult economic times, people used their positions to conduct "nepotism, or going through back door". They may have leveraged their positions to obtain privilege, or engaged in corruption, theft, self-dealing, and so on. Therefore, the state's struggle against the individual's pursuit of materialism and self-interest often ends in only superficial victory through repeated cycles of the class struggle and mass political movement.

In summary, under conditions of extreme scarcity of economic resources, in order to achieve its ideological objectives, the state is forced to take measures to address the problems of social mobilization (work motivation) and resource mobilization (curbing consumption). In order to improve its resource mobilization capacity, the state will rationally choose institutional arrangements to suppress consumption. However, such a policy of suppressing consumption is potentially in tension with labor incentives. The reason is simple. Material incentives are the most conventional labor incentives. However, in order to concentrate limited resources, the state restricted the range of material incentives. To ease the tension between the policy of curbing consumption and the need for work incentives, the state had to adopt "non-material incentives". This leads the state to direct its attention to measures that act on people ideologically, such as establishing a sacred, spiritual motivation mechanism, using spiritual incentives to replace material incentives, so as to mobilize people's enthusiasm for productive labor within the institutional framework of curbing consumption. This partially explains why the state made huge efforts to carry out ideological and political work, in order to maintain intellectual control, by continuously implementing various political movements. The ideological transformation of people is an inverse operation to their "natural instinct", and therefore its systemic cost is huge, and its result an artificial ideological uniformity.

In a country with a backward agricultural sector, to implement a rapid "catch-up" industrialization strategy the state must employ comparably powerful ideological campaign. The reason is simple. To reach the goal of socialist industrialization, the state must suppress people's consumption and improve resource mobilization, increasing the portion of resources reserved to accelerate industrialization. But by doing this, it creates a tension between the state's consumption policy and its ability to motivate labor. To resolve this contradiction, the state on one hand seeks to employ sacred incentives by defining national goals as personal goals, making these goals sacred. On the other hand, the state uses ideological pressure to suppress any words, deeds or desires contradicting national goals and ideology. Therefore, before the reform and opening up, "soul work" and ideological and political projects such as criticism and self-criticism were actually an integral part of the industrialization strategy. As a result, industrial production and the "ideology of production" constitute a dialectical unity. Industrial production must be based on people's "ideas of production" (e.g., curbing desire, austerity and self-discipline), and this mindset in return, reduced the cost of industrial production (by, for instance, low wages and low personal consumption). Thus, there is a specific form of social structure in Chinese cities and towns adapted to the ascetic society. This is what I want to analyze next.

Chapter Three

Asceticism in the Main Structure of Society

In the last chapter, I discussed the institutional arrangements made by the state to structure the ascetic society. Since any system must be constructed and implemented by people, this entails relations between the system and the humans inside of it. On one hand, a specific system of people's attitudes and behavior will give rise to constraints, thereby affecting people's attitudes and behavior. On the other hand, a specific system is always implemented by people having a specific ideology, that is, the system is always reproduced or modified by the behavior of these actors. System and human relations, Giddens said, in essence, are the relationships between structure and action, the relationships between the two are not one of "dualism", but a "duality of structure": the structure is the result of action, but also this action mediates the formation of the structure. On the one hand, the structure (inherent in the system) is the precondition for certain actions; any action is always constrained by the structure in which it occurs. On the other hand, the reproduction or modification of the structure can only be achieved through human action[198.] Therefore, to understand the reproduction or transformation of a social system, we must examine how the system (structure) and the people (subjects) relate to each other. After studying the institutional arrangements of the ascetic community, we must research the social structure of such an institutional framework.

From a sociological point of view, the so-called social structure, refers both to the architecture of the structure, and population that lives within the constructed system. The main, or social, structure refers to the elements that make people follow certain logical thought paths or have certain emotional reactions, and influences their actions. Different social structures have different logical thought models, emotional reactions and behavior patterns, because they create different psychological structures, personalities and habits. Elias believes that "civilized" behavior is different from "savage" behavior and that this difference is rooted in a different psychological structure, a psychological structure that is an adaptation to a different social structure.[199] Bourdieu pointed out that the people under similar objective structural conditions (e.g., of similar class status) will accumulate relatively consistent and persistent habits. These habits are the initiating force behind certain actions, but at the same time, they are also restrained and constricted by structural conditions and as a result, form a link between subjectivity and objectivity.[200.] With different psychological structures or habits a different social structure would arise.

As mentioned earlier, in order for the Chinese state to give priority to the strategic objectives of the development of heavy industry and socialist industrialization, it was necessary to make specific institutional arrangements to restrict the level of consumption, while fully mobilizing the enthusiasm and initiative of the workers. However, in the view of the national leaders, an institutional arrangement alone is not enough, because the system is constructed and implemented by people. In order to secure the national goals, people's ideas must also be transformed, reshaped to match the new national goal. The object of this transformation is to forget about personal self-interest, to become selfless, not expect remuneration, in short, become a being dedicated (or obligated) to the goal. In other words, with respect to the relationship between the rights and obligations of an individual, individuals have an obligation to accept the national requirements and dedicate themselves to these, and not try to assert their rights. In fact, often the state desired to portray the rights of individuals (e.g., welfare) as government-given personal gifts or favors, requiring individuals to reciprocate (e.g., to be grateful). Therefore, this social structure is not only a kind of dedication-type body, but also a thanks-giving-type body.

The previous chapter discussed the implementation of state's ideological and political work, which was one of the principal means used to shape this new body of thought. The purpose of this chapter is to reveal how the state, through ideological indoctrination or soul projects (including ideological and political work) shaped this body of thought, how it relates to the social structure and how it is embedded in an institutional framework .

The Main Goal of Shaping National Objectives

"Subject" was originally a philosophical term, used to refer to people, the opposite of an object (i.e., the external world). The subject has subjective and reflective sense the subject can also understand or change the object. With the rise of phenomenology and its expansion to the various branches of social sciences, the concepts of "subject" and "subjectivity" were also employed by subsidiary fields of social science. In sociology, with the rise of the Schultz school of social phenomena, the concept of subject and subjectivity were introduced. But here, I do not intend to follow the social phenomenology of "subject" or "subjectivity" as it is defined, on the contrary, I take a structural sociological perspective to explain the "subject" and, more specifically, I will use Althusser's approach to explain the sociological structure of "subject."

From Althusser's perspective of structural sociology, the subject is superficially the main initiator of his or her behavior, but in practice, the motivation of the subject is constrained and framed by the social structure, and therefore, individual initiative, motivation and justification are all framed by the social structure, which is a reflection of the social structure's influence on the individual's subjectivity. In the terminology of the story "Journey to the West", even though the individual may show "Monkey-like" activity and initiative, in the end it is impossible to escape the "Buddha's hand", the controls imposed by the social structure. Therefore, the so-called subject is not the abstract, capitalized, one-dimensional subject (Subject), but the concrete, lowercase, plural subject (subjects), which is created by a specific social structure and environment. In turn, these subjects through their own initiative and maintenance of the social structure shape their own social environment. Different systems (social structures) create different subjects; these subjects become the subjective condition for the reproduction of the institutional environment. Thus the system and the main body of subects are interdependent, and even mutually reinforcing. A rupture between the two will lead to institutional change or transformation. Thus, at different times, and linked to different institutional environments, there are different types of social structures.

Since the system and its subjects are social processes with interdependent aspects, the transformation of Chinese society is also took place at two levels, one being the institutional framework, the second being the social structure. The two are intrinsically linked. In the study of how the reform and opening up followed the earlier institutional arrangements, we will need to analyze the social structure of the institutional environment, and how the relationship between this institutional environment and its social structure was ruptured, leading to institutional reform. However, before this, we need to recall Althusser's ideas on the how the conditions of production reproduce themselves, and the state's ideological apparatus and its relationship to the social structure.

A. Althusser on the reproduction of production conditions, the ideological state apparatus and the social structure

Althusser begins from Marx's thesis that each community exists not only to produce, but also able to reproduce (or maintain) the conditions of its economic production. The reproduction of production conditions includes two aspects: the reproduction of productive forces and of production relations. The reproduction of productive forces has two aspects: the reproduction of production itself (e.g., the raw materials supplied by other companies to "my" company constitute the necessary conditions for "my" company to reproduce its production) and the reproduction of labor.[201] I discuss here only the problem of reproducing labor.

Althusser believes that unlike reproducing the physical conditions of production, the reproduction of labor occurs outside of the factory or company. Reproducing the labor force requires three things. First, there is the physiological maintenance of the laborers. It is reflected in the wages earned by workers to cover their cost of consumption (e.g., the cost of housing, food, clothing, child rearing, etc.). That is to say, wages must be sufficient to provide labor with enough consumer goods to meet their basic needs. These are not the essential or minimum needs required to sustain life in a biological sense, but, as Marx said, they are the historic minimum living standards, determined by traditional needs. For example, British workers need beer, French workers need wine, and so on. The establishment of these traditional standards was the product of class struggle.[202] Secondly there is the reproduction of labor skills. Reproducing the labor force requires not only the material conditions for its reproduction, but a technological division of labor in various occupations and the reproduction of job skills. It is achieved mainly through the educational system[203.] Third, there is maintaining the attitude of the workers. The reproduction of labor is not only its physiological reproduction, it is not only the reproduction of labor skills, but it is the reproduction of labor's obedience to the existing political order and the dominant ideology[204.] According to my understanding of Althusser, worker attitudes and skills are not reproduced separately, but together. People are trained to learn skills, but also learn how to live correctly, to correctly to fulfill their roles, how to "properly" behave and so on.

According to my further understanding of Althusser, the attitude of labor not only determines its level of motivation and enthusiasm, but it also affects the reproduction of existing individual roles, positions and relationships. In the latter sense, the reproduction of labor attitudes in fact relates to the reproduction of existing production relationships (including the ownership of production materials and therefore the relationship between labor roles and compensation). Therefore, how the attitudes of workers are maintained affects not only the reproduction of productivity, but also involves the reproduction of production relations. How to shape and change the attitude of the workers is a very important part of the reproduction of production conditions.

How is the reproduction of the worker's attitude to be achieved? Althusser believes that the reproduction of the required conditions relies upon the ideological superstructure. He divides the ideological superstructure into two parts: one is the repressive state apparatus (including the government, administrative agencies, the military, police, courts, prisons, etc.), it is backed by violence; second is the ideological state apparatus, which is the collection of specialized and unique institutions, including religion, the education system, the family, the legal system, trade unions, political parties, mass media, culture, etc., with ideological foundations. Of course, the repressive state apparatus utilizes ideological means, but it mainly depends on violence. Similarly, the ideological state apparatus will be supported by means of violence, but it mainly depends on ideology.[205]

State power is created by the state's use and control of these two apparatus. Through the ideological state apparatus, the state seeks to convince people to accept the existing relations of production and the corresponding social divisions given by labor, technology, personal roles, social status and codes of conduct, in other words, to create people who meet the requirements of the ruling government, and who are loyal to the existing political order. Thus, by the means of the state ideological apparatus, the ideology of the governing class is diffused throughout society, which is beneficial to the reproduction of production relationships, and in return it is conducive to reproduction of the workforce. The role of the ideological state apparatus in influencing the reproduction of production relationships can be seen as a superstructure built on the foundation of economics. Althusser believes that in a traditional society, the church is the primary ideological state apparatus, but in the modern state, the machinery of education is the primary ideological state apparatus.[206]

Clearly, the reproduction of the means of the production is not only the reproduction of physical production plant, but also is also the reproduction of the labor force. And the reproduction of labor is not only physical sustenance of the workers and transfer of their skills to new workers, but it is the maintenance of the attitude of the workers. The attitude of workers plays a crucial role in the reproduction of production conditions. Why? On the one hand, it involves relations within the processes of production that can either promote or hinder productivity. When labor is unhappy with the ownership of the means of production, or unhappy with the arrangements for distribution, they may develop negative attitudes, which leads to slack and reduced productivity, which is an obvious effect of production relations hindering productivity. Conversely, if the workers are satisfied by the nature of production relations, and they see an acceptable distribution of the ownership of production materials, then the attitude of labor will not be adversely affected, labor productivity can be maintained, and production relations will not hinder the development of productivity[207.] On the other hand, the attitudes of workers directly affect their motivation, including enthusiasm, initiative and creativity. Positive attitude, often leads to higher enthusiasm, initiative and creativity, and the corresponding higher labor productivity. It is clear that worker's attitudes are at the intersection of intersection productivity and production relationships, it also means that their reproduction is the reproduction of productivity and production relationships. At the same time, labor's attitude is also the starting point for the social superstructure to influence the economic foundation.

According to my interpretation of Althusser, how the workers perceive of the nature of production and distribution relationships, which is, under a specific production relationship, how the worker's attitudes are formed, is closely related to the worker's belief system (values, world view, attitude toward life, etc.). For example, if workers believe in living day-by-day, living for the moment, taking a fatalistic worldview and outlook on life, then they will not complain about exploitation, and labor can be exploited because of its enthusiasm will not be lowered. Conversely, if the workers recognize exploitation as an evil, they will not tolerate it and will avoid it, using a variety of methods: slacking off, striking or taking other action to improve their treatment. Thus, the formation of worker attitudes is closely linked to their belief system.

Therefore, how one can shape the belief system of workers (beliefs, values, attitude toward life, etc.), will become the key issue for the reproduction of production conditions. From this perspective, the counterbalancing role of the ideological superstructure of productivity becomes clear. In Althusser's words, the ruling party often needs to resort to the ideological state apparatus, to shape the concepts and attitudes (for example, professional ethics) of the working class to meet the ruling party's requirements and need for control, and therefore maintain the reproduction of production conditions, which includes the reproduction of the main work force.

No country allows the workers to freely arrange the social structure, instead relying on the ideological state apparatus to shape the main body of workers, teaching a particular belief system, which in turn affects their work attitudes and motivation. Therefore, the attitudes and work motivation of labor, is not only the product of individual rationality (e.g., evaluation of labor's efforts and rewards, the comparison with a reference group, etc.), but is also shaped by the state ideology. By implanting a certain ideology and corresponding belief system into worker's minds, the state shapes a specific type of labor force and establishes a certain labor belief system as the norm expected by state. Consequently, labor attitudes are maintained and labor motivation is reproduced.

From the standpoint of Althusser, the task of the ideological state apparatus is to shape the body of the workforce according to the requirements of the ruling order, and to persuade the workers to adopt these requirements "freely", and in accordance with this concept, to act "freely".[208] Althusser believes ideology is reflected in the main body of society, and only exists because of it. The function of ideology is to convert individuals into the main body,[209] in other words, 'recruiting' among individuals and to reform them into the main body. In fact, ideology always looks at individuals as it has the main body.[210] Althusser therefore concludes that individuals are always and already "subjects".[211] In other words, any individual is always and already a particular ideological subject as anticipated by a particular ideology (such as: a gender subject). The individual being perceived as a subject, is to have the individual voluntarily and "freely" obey the orders of a particular "Subject" (e.g., the ruling state government), also it is to have individual voluntarily accept the subordinate position. Therefore, the subject exists through its subordination, and its subordination is its reason to exist.[212]   Clearly, the magic of the ideological state apparatus lies in its ability to impress the will of the state onto the personal free will, and to make specific individuals (subjects) voluntarily implement the state's actions. Thus, in Althusser, an individual's subjectivity is a hidden national will, reflected in the individual's "free" will, but in reality subject to the control of the ideological state apparatus. If through the state apparatus of violence it obtains what Weber called "command power", then through the ideological state apparatus, the state obtains another power - "persuasive power." While the latter is realized by shaping individuals into a certain type of autonomous and "free" subjects that the meet the ruling party's requirements.

One contribution of Althusser's theory of ideology is that he points out the artificial aspect of a subject's "free will", the subject's "free will" is nothing but a manifestation of the state's will. However, his theory is inadequate. For example, he denies the individual's autonomy and initiative, ignoring differences between individuals in the same ideological environment. Nevertheless, his perspective on the subject's free being the reflection of the state's ideology, has been an important inspiration for our research.

B. Subject Model and Shaping the Subject

In a certain sense, the subject referred to is an ideological subject. A human being is a subject, but this subject is not abstract. It is instead a concrete entity that has been shaped by specific ideologies (e.g., religion) during a particular period of time. That an individual is part of this but not that social structure is a characteristic of the time and place in which the individual exists. To be more precise, it has social and cultural representations. And a specific social structure determines a specific pattern of logical thought and behavior. Therefore, different interest groups always want to individuals to adopt the social structure they desire. Shaping the social structure becomes a battlefield for opposing interest groups. The result is often that a state with a strong ideological apparatus has autonomy and initiative in shaping the social structure.

In control of ideological apparatus, the state is able to follow it desire to shape individuals into subjects that meet the requirements of the ruling party. To this end, the state must establish a specific type of subject model and to shape individuals based upon this model. For example, religion, as a part of the ideological state apparatus, teaches people to be patient and obedient. The subject with patience and obedience is what the state needs, in order to fulfill the requirement of maintaining the existing ruling order. Thus, regardless whether one is in a traditional society (working mainly through religion), or in a modern society (working mainly through education), the subject model is established in accordance with national objectives and requirements of ruling order, expressing the full scope of the state ideology. In this subject model, the state's objectives are perceived as the ultimate goal (belief), in which obedience and patience are glorified as virtues.

However, despite the state's autonomy and control in the shaping the subject (e.g., through religion and education), the ultimate formation of people's social structure is not entirely consistent with the subject model. The reason is that people are not entirely passive. Personality characteristics, class differences, local and external culture are all likely to have some degree of influence on the formation of the social structure of local residents. Therefore, the subject model of the residents established by the state has a degree of separation from the actual social structures of the residents. Nevertheless, the two have an overlapping relationship. In general, the more closed a society is, the bigger the overlapping area between the ideological subject model established by the state and the resident's actual social structure. Conversely, the more open a society is, the smaller the overlapping area between the ideological subject model established by the state and the actual social structure of the residents (Figure 3-1). In other words, the subject model of the residents in a closed society is a stronger ideological subject while the subject model of residents in an open society is a weaker ideological subject. Of course, the "strong" and "weak" here are used in a relative sense.

In general, states intervene in shaping the people's social structure. With two different types of states, the degree of involvement is different. Why is this so? To answer this question, we need a brief introduction to Oakeshott's theory of the distinctions between states. Oakeshott believes that in Europe, there are two types of states, one being a citizen-based national association, the other being a cause-based national association. The former refers to a state as an association between people organized by laws or rules, rather than around a common goal. The main role of the state is to develop and maintain laws to ensure that people co-exist peacefully and may conduct trade and exchanges in an orderly way, therefore promoting the pursuit of goals by the people on their own, rather than targeting

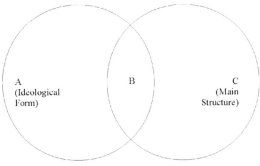

(1) The Subject of A Closed Society

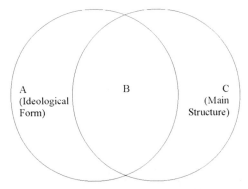

(2) The Subject of An Open Society

Figure 3-1   Different Forms of Subject Models

(Note: In the above graphs, A represents the content of the ideological model that is not integrated into the actual social structure. C represents the subject content that is not shaped by the ideological subject; B represents the subject content that is shaped into the actual social structure. A + B = the ideological subject model establish by the state; C + B = resident's actual social structure. In these two graphs, the larger the B area, the greater the scope for the state's shaping the subject model, which means that the subject is a stronger ideological subject. Conversely, the smaller the range for the state's shaping of the subject model, means that the subject is a weaker ideological subject.)

a specific mission to impose upon the people from the top down. In contrast, the cause-oriented state refers to an association formed to achieve a particular common goal, mission or target, for example: the communism of the Soviet Union, national socialism, Roosevelt's New Deal, mixed economies, French Unionism and welfare capitalism. In this type of state, the state establishes certain common causes or goals, and organizes the people to achieve this goal. Although such goals can be tempting, pursuing them often leads to violation of people's individual freedoms.[213] Undoubtedly, Oakeshott's view given above is far too simplistic. For example, he ignores market failures that cause crises in the delivery of public goods and the consequent impact this has on the collective goals and choices of organizations or groups. Nevertheless, his point of view in describing the state's involvement in shaping social structure has important implications and inspiring significance.

Clearly, comparing the citizen-based state and the cause-based state, the latter has greater ability to employ the ideological state apparatus to shape the people's social structure. The reason is very simple. Because the so-called common cause or goal has often been imposed upon people from the outside. In order to obtain the people's obedience and cooperation, the most effective way has been to change people's internal beliefs and ideas, so as to create a type of subject that meets the state's objectives. Therefore, compared with a citizen-based state, a cause-based state places more emphasis on organizing people around national goals and ensuring unified movement toward those goals, and it wishes to create a subject matching these national objectives. To this end, cause-based states are more dependent on the ideological state apparatus to shape social structure.

C. National Objectives and Social Structure

After 1956, with the introduction of socialist public ownership to China, the country faced two tasks: on the one hand, in order to get out of poverty and to achieve the state's goals for socialist modernization and the establishment of a strong industrial base, the state asked people to live frugally and curb consumption, so as to free resources for industrial construction. But at the same time, the state needed to ensure that labor enthusiasm was not dampened. On the other hand, the state had implemented a socialist system and established national public ownership of production materials and national collective ownership. In this public ownership system, the worker's pay and compensation, to a large extent was egalitarian-oriented, wherein the role of material incentives was limited. Objectively this could lead to "social laziness" (i.e., the "free rider" problem as defined economics). Therefore, the state had to provide, while implementing socialist public ownership, a means for preventing workers from becoming slack and lazy. Obviously, regardless of the country's modernization system ("curbing consumption" to achieve industrialization), or its public ownership system (eliminating exploitation and oppression and establishment of social equality), the state objectively faced the issue of how labor motivation was to be reproduced.

Thus, the issue of labor reproduction considered by Althusser, especially the reproduction of worker attitudes and labor motivation, also existed for socialist China. More importantly, since China built its socialism on an economic base of extreme poverty, focusing all possible resources on building a socialist industrial base, was a way to accelerate the realization of socialist industrialization. To this end, the state required people to save clothing and food to achieve this goal: "Tightening their belts". However, by doing this, a tension is created between the goals of curbing consumption and motivating labor, which pushes the worker's attitudes and motivation to a prominent position. Managing the relationship between the state's policy of curbing consumption and the reproduction of labor motivation, became a very important issue.

Workers, for example, are no longer employed by a private owner, instead their employer is the public sector or the state, or an "imagined employer" whose agents are government and enterprise cadres at all levels. The workers under such a system have virtually no bargaining power over wages and benefits, as these are set by the "public's" top agent: the central government. However, workers have another type of right, which their right of life-long employment guaranteed under the Constitution. Nobody has the right to dismiss workers. With such a right, the workers developed a strategy to deal with the low-wage and low-consumption policy, which is "showing up at work but not contributing." Thus the problem of reproducing labor motivation is logically connected to the state's industrial policy, public ownership policy, and the consumer policy of curbing consumption.

In more general terms, the state's policy of curbing consumption to ensure the progress of industrialization and its policy of sacrificing individual interests to benefit publically owned enterprises, objectively rejected the most common mechanism historically of reproducing labor, which is material incentives. Although at the Eighth Congress of the party, the central government affirmed the role of the bonus, the magnitude of material incentives was severely limited, with little scope for being effective. And not too long afterwards, this policy was determined to be "revisionist" ("money being the king"), and was eventually abolished. Therefore, in general, before the reform, the state limited the situations in which material incentives could be used.

By limiting the use of material incentives, the state had to rely upon spiritual motivation. As Hayek said, "many socialists have this idea of using extensive farmernon-economic stimulus ' to replace farmermonetary incentive's, which is a common phenomenon."[214] So, how is spiritual motivation achieved? How does it function? Obviously, spiritual motivation only works for certain types of workers, not all types of workers. The reason is simple: spiritual motivation works only when the workers see the value of the spiritual incentives and appreciate the spiritual reward. Otherwise spiritual motivation has no audience. Clearly one precondition of labor motivation is each individual's particular subject model. A specific motivation mechanism is only effective for a certain type of subject model. Even the mechanism of material incentives is not universal, because not all labor subjects see the importance of material rewards. Material incentives are a labor motivation mechanism not because of the incentive itself; it is because a particular labor subject gives positive confirmation to such material motivation. Worker's reaction to material incentives is based on their positive interpretation of material rewards, which is based upon a specific social structure. In contrast, in the primitive communist society, tribal member's respect (i.e., spiritual motivation) is a much greater force than material incentives. Although tribal leaders use material incentives as rewards, the award is perceived more as a symbol and representation (i.e., honor), and not simply as its material value. Regardless whether in the form of material incentives or spiritual motivation, for the labor motivation mechanism to be effective it must act on elements within the worker's social structure. For a particular incentive mechanism to function, a corresponding social structure must be created.

Since the state implemented policies to curb consumption and keep wages low, it must rely on spiritual incentives to motivate worker enthusiasm. Naturally, the state must transform people's thinking and shape its subjects to be consistent with the national goals. Not until the workers see the value of spiritual rewards (e.g., praise or honor), can spiritual motivation be effective. This is one of the reasons that during the time of the planned economy, the state paid so much attention to ideological and political education. The nature of ideological and political work is to transform the legacy social structure left over from the old society, based upon private ownership (and therefore focusing on self-interest and material return), by creating a new type socialist subject (able to suppress personal desire and self-interest).

To this end, the state fully mobilized the ideological state apparatus to carry out a sustained and extensive soul-reforming project, instilling workers with collectivist values and utopian ideals, in an attempt to create a new kind of social structure by downplaying the significance of material reward and emphasizing ideals and spiritual values. In this new social structure, the state's goals have become the worker's personal goals, and the state's will has become the individual's personal beliefs. Regarding countries with planned economies, Hayek made the following statement about their "goal substitution" process:

"The goal under social planning is a single target system. The most effective way to have everyone adhere to this single target system is to make people believe in it. To make a system based upon this general doctrine to play its role effectively, it is not enough just to force people to work toward the same goal. It is important that people should treat the goal as their own. Although the state must choose beliefs for people and impose these beliefs upon them, they must make these beliefs to become people's own, and therefore to become a creed widely accepted, so that the individual acts voluntarily as much as they can, according to the requirement set by the planner.[215]

The reasons that countries with planned economies are able to successfully shape the subject to requirements of the state are mainly their ideological propaganda and information shielding strategies. Hayek said,

"All propaganda works toward the same goals. All promotional tools are coordinated towards the same direction with the impact upon individuals so as to create unique farmerintegration' of the thinking of all people. ... If all media sources are controlled by a single governor, the issue is no longer convincing people this way or that way. So smart propagandists have the power to shape people's ideological thinking at their own choice. Even the smartest and most independent individuals cannot completely escape this influence if they are isolated from information sources for a long time."[216]

Obviously since the ideological state apparatus monopolizes information sources and distribution channels, they are able to use the propaganda machine in the way that they desire, permitting the state to effectively push people to accept the value system, standards and ideology it is promoting. Thus the state created a new labor force that is uniform and meets the nation's requirements. On the surface, individuals seem to have independent thoughts. In fact they have lost the ability to think independently. They think in the way the state wants them to. This includes believing "the government's every action must be holy and free from criticism".[217]

The labor subject in the socialist planned economy must be the subject matching national objectives, and is shaped and influenced by the ideological state machinery. Therefore we will need to look at the subject created by the state. The subject includes both physiological subject (body, skills and ability to act) and conceptual subject (ideology), with the latter being the core. In other words, the subject is mainly constituted by its ideas. Different ideas determine subjects with different modes of thinking, emotional reactions and physical actions. And ideological thinking has its own structure, in which ideas and thoughts are organized in a particular way. This particular model has a structure of ideas, which I call the main structure. In different subjects the main structure is different, meaning that people have different modes of thinking, and thus have different logical processes, emotional reactions and behavior.

In social structure, the most important part is the ultimate faith and belief, which is at the core or the highest level. This part also determines the rest of the social structure. Other parts of the social structure have many aspects, such as: gender, the concept of marriage, courtship rituals, and so on. However, to the state, the most important part was nothing more than the concept of labor and consumer attitudes, because the context of these two aspects related directly to the state's socialist industrialization strategy and policy of curbing consumption. Consequently both are objects for the state to influence and shape. Therefore, next to be analyzed in this chapter, are the three interrelated areas of the social structure shaped by the state during planned economy period: faith, the concept of labor and the concept of consumption (Figure 3-2).

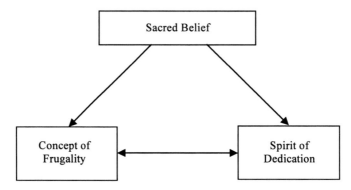

Figure 3-2   In Planned Economy Period, the Social Structure of the Ascetic

From the state's point of view, in order to shape a labor and consumption subject that meets national requirements, it must first create political subjectivity, so that the citizens accept the state's goals and mission, and see them as their own. To this end, the state must instill the concept of ideology and beliefs among individuals, creating a political subject that shares "the same fate and breaths together". During the planned economy period, it was inevitable to have conflicts between the national objectives and individual's personal goals (e.g., curbing consumption), yet the state had to create a new type of labor subject that downplayed material rewards and was willing to sacrifice. Because of this, the state needed to have people understand the necessity of curbing consumption and showing a willingness to sacrifice. To accomplish this, the state had to have the people understand and believe in a "common mission" and "common goals", which was the reason for the state to create a political subject. It is also why the state made great efforts in ideological and political work.

The next three sections will explain the social structure of asceticism during the planned economy period. Section II discusses political subjectivity of the ascetic citizen. Section III analyzes consumer subjectivity of the ascetic citizen. Section IV interprets labor subjectivity of the ascetic citizen. Finally, section V explores the spiritual crisis of the ascetic. Such a crisis prepared the subsequent reform and opening up.

Data used in this chapter comes from the in-depth interviews. A total of 39 people who joined the workforce before the reform and opening up were interviewed, representing different occupations and seniority (for the list of respondents and the interview outline see the Appendix). Step-by-step coding and classification were made using transcripts of the recordings, which conclude with the conceptual classification the ascetic social structure. The subject of the ascetic discussed in this chapter is but an ideal type. In real life, many individuals as subjects deviate from this. Nevertheless, such ideal type represents the social of the mainstream.

Holy Faith

Certain beliefs are always linked with certain socio-economic conditions. Under different socio-economic conditions, beliefs are different. A society short of material resources has great need to restrain the consumption of those resources. But for people to live continuously under conditions of abstinence, they must have some spiritual support that transcends material conditions. Historically, this support often comes from beyond the earthly realm or from the imagined conditions in an afterlife. It can be said that during times when there are more physical constraints, religion is more popular. It constitutes people's spiritual sustenance when they must survive under conditions of extreme material poverty.

At the same time, the greater the constraints on material resources, the greater the hardships that people must endure to obtain those resources. Therefore, the material constraints require not only that people must curb their consumption, but they must also give their labor unstintingly. In circumstances under which the material rewards of labor are very limited, labor needs the support of faith to maintain its motivation. For example, as Weber pointed out in his book "The Protestant Ethic and the Spirit of Capitalism", Protestant's strive in their work because it is their belief and faith that they will become God's chosen citizens in the next life. It is this belief in the spiritual realm that makes hard work tolerable and meaningful.

Both consumption and labor involve certain aspects of human nature. Consumption involves physical desire and labor involves overcoming physical inertia. Freud pointed out in his book "Civilization and Its Discontents" that the characteristic of civilization is that people can make use of the strength of ego and superego to conquer the nature, and thus have access to social progress. And faith is a spiritual force[218] that allows people to conquer their natural desire. Obviously, religion is part of culture and indeed to some extent, affected the advancement of society.

In the early days after the founding of the People's Republic of China, the country faced problems of material shortages and labor incentives. Material constraints required limiting consumption, but this policy was bound to cause tension to a certain degree with labor incentives. How to make people not only accept the policy of curbing consumption, but also summon their energy for work? Obviously, resorting to the power of faith, and thus to establishing a kind sacred calling, became a natural choice for the state. However, because of the official ideology of materialism and atheism, the state could not seek the help of religion to influence people's faith. It could only create another non-religious belief with similar power and extent.

A. Formation of Faith

Under certain conditions, belief is a product of social contact. For example, frequent contact with religious people or missionaries is one of the conditions for forming religious faith. After the founding of the People's Republic, the state was capable of monopolizing access to all channels to faith, by what Althusser calls of the monopoly of the "ideological state apparatus."[219] At the same time, by shielding society from information it considered threatening, it built a public access channel to faith. A retired army cadre from the war of liberation, described this very well:

People like us at that time were very simple, very pure. Moreover, from today's view, it was really blocked, the door closed without any interactions with foreign countries, which made us think very little. Our only firm belief is communism, the Communist Party and Chairman Mao. (A01-M-75 retired party cadre, provincial government level)

Under such circumstances, the state has great power to shape people's beliefs. The reason is that object of faith has a certain ambiguity. Just by describing a better life than the status quo, that life can become the object of desire and longing and the object of faith. As the retired cadre said:

Before The Cultural Revolution, we all think that socialism is good and the Communist Party is good. With such an idea it is all just material not being enough or poor. Isn't it something if you have a bicycle? But we have had strong faith in socialism, communism faith. But what exactly socialism and communism are, we do not know. Ah. At that time there are people's communes. Mao said that now people have three meals. Everyone works together, eats together, and no one will go hungry, and that is counted as communism achieved. Oh, there is not a standard to measure the objectives. In short, whatever they say, we would accept it. Our thinking was very simple. (A01-M-75 retired party cadre, provincial government level)

Specifically, there are two channels to beliefs. One is the organic channel to belief.

-118-

The other is mechanical exposure to religion. The organic access channel to belief refers to those people who joined the revolution because of their dissatisfaction with the status quo before the liberation, and who gradually accepted communist beliefs during the revolutionary process. A retired veteran's experience is a typical example:

Interviewer: Could you talk about the situation when you started to work for the first time? For example, when, what kind of work did you do?

Respondent: At the beginning, I was a soldier.

Interviewer: In the army? The Anti-Japanese War or the Liberation War?

Respondent: I did not join the army until 1949. That was almost the end of the Liberation War. I remember that I was only sixteen when I joined the army. At that time our hometown was still under the rule of Kuomintang. My mother died when I was three years old. When I was 5, my father died. Then my brother and I were both brought up by my stepmother.

Interviewer: Did you join the Communist Party's army?

Respondent: Of course. How could we join the Kuomintang's army? Moreover, we really had suffered enough back then. Our native parents died. We had to live with our stepmother. It was difficult time to live a life. I still remember the days when we suffered from no food. The KMT army was very bad at that time. We are hated them.

Interviewer: So, life's difficulties prompted you to join the Communist Party's armed forces, isn't the case?

Respondent: You could say that. Remember, I was only sixteen at the time. Life was so hard. We were just thinking to join the army to earn a living. ... We were very young at the time, very naïve. We would not have the ideas of liberating all mankind, let alone communism. I just wanted to have bowls of rice to eat. I would be very happy. At the same time we were politically protected too.

Because of dissatisfaction with the KMT, along with another a very simple motive (being fed), he took part in the revolution. In the course of the revolution, he was gradually educated by the party and formed communist beliefs.

At first, I went to become a so-called "little devil" (bodyguard). Although at the time I did not know what a communist society was. For that same very simple reason, to have things to eat, we would go to the battlefield to kill the enemy whenever we were asked by our superiors. ... After a while, we got quite some education by our superiors. Later, I participated in training and learning, and joined the Communist Youth League. I was very encouraged, felt very proud. After a few more years of tests, I joined the party, and took the oath. I really wanted to fight for the communist cause. At that time many of us comrades had these ideas, not just I myself. We all felt this from the heart, after so many years of education by the party and the people, and fighting so many battles. (A01-M-75 retired party cadre, provincial government level)

It can be said the elite who participated in the revolution before the founding of the People's Republic, largely formed their communist faith through the organic access channels of belief. Dissatisfaction with reality forced them onto the road of revolution. The revolutionary journey gradually deepened their understanding of the ideal of communism, thereby forming and consolidating their communist beliefs.

Distinct from the organic access channels to belief, the mechanical access and contact channel were established after the founding of the People's Republic. They were formed through the state's monopoly of propaganda, education and other "ideological state apparatus". In other words, for many people, especially the generation that was born and grew up after the founding of the People's Republic, belief was the result of the state's systems of education, propaganda and dissemination of information. The result of this kind of instilling of belief is a new type of social structure. A worker described this process:

Interviewer: So how did you see the ideal communist promoted at the time?

Respondent: In the past say, when we talked about the whole ideal of communism, we actually had no real idea what it really is. It is already a natural reaction. The slogan is this way, we follow and resonate the slogan.

Interviewer: At that time did people all reverently believe in this ideal?

Respondent: At that time, it should be the case.

Interviewer: How did you personally think of it?

Respondent: At that time I thought that communism would soon arrive, and then it would be one world. Later the situation kept changing. It gradually began to be far-fetched and distant.

Interviewer: Do you think there was anyone questioning the ideal?

Respondent: when we were young we never doubted it. We thought it would soon be realized.

(A24-F-52, pharmaceutical worker)

Needless to say, not everyone believed in communism. But for a considerable period of time before and after the founding of the People's Republic, communist ideals attracted a large number of devout and faithful believers. This is an incontrovertible fact. Obviously, as orthodox indoctrination was promoted and instilled by the state, communist beliefs spread rapidly. For many people, their communist beliefs brought their life into a sacred realm, giving them a sense of sacred significance. Whether the old revolutionary generation, or the new generation born after the founding of the People's Republic, they all had a reverent and faithful belief in communism. The following quotation is a statement of this faith:

I felt there were no other ideas at the time but only one belief, which was the communist's goal to realize communism and the ultimate struggle for communism in the end. To make positive progress politically, I have to join the party and become a communist party member. I just have to follow the Communist Party, fight hard for communism, having no other beliefs. (A04-F-67, cadre)

For the firmest believers, faith in Communism was a solid core. In the event of information or facts threatening those beliefs, for example, during the "Cultural Revolution", they could often disarm the threat through external attribution, maintaining the stability of the "core". For example, when the interviewer asked one older worker his opinion about the frequent political campaigns, he replied:

I think that the Communist Party does things as they planned. It is not impractical. The leadership has a plan, but the "gang of four" ruined things. The "Cultural Revolution" is the screw-up by the "gang of four". It is not Chairman Mao's fault. The "gang of four" has caused us having nothing to eat, no meat, no vegetables. My view is to follow the party. (A07-M-78 worker)

Andrew Walder said the Chinese Communist Party's ideological and moral education of the citizenry was the only effective way to arouse people's dedication and obedience.[220] During the process of mobilizing the working classes, the Party actually effectively extended its member's behavior and thinking standards to the entire population. Application of the Chinese Communist Party's standards of action and thinking to everyone has constituted a distinctive feature of China.[221] In the face of the state's high moral requirements, some residents could not express deviation from the mainstream even if they were reluctant to fully embrace certain ideals. Therefore, some of the respondents we interviewed noted that they had doubts about the communist ideal, but were unable to speak out about such doubts.

Even though some people had doubts, they could not express them. They had to obey unconditionally the state's institutional arrangements based on these beliefs. Obviously, under the conditions of the system at the time, because of rational choice by individuals, few dared to openly challenge the mainstream of society, its ideals and beliefs. Therefore, despite the failure of the communist ideals to win the hearts of some people (they were skeptical of the belief), society successfully eliminated the space for the existence of alternative belief (non-communist belief). Therefore, the skeptics of communist belief were still superficially allegiant, or at least did not behave in conflict with the established order. As a retired worker said: "We did not care about whether it was communism. In short, it would be fine so long that there are meals that can live on." (cf. A29-F-81 Knitting Factory worker). If their active work motivation was not because of this belief, they obviously show the traditional work ethic and philosophy of life (i.e., traditional culture) persisted in the absence of alternative faith. There was an intrinsic fit between the traditional culture (work ethic and life philosophy) and the mainstream ideology of the time, both being "honest", "conservative", "hard working" and so on. To some extent, these traditional cultural elements are the objective goals the communist state wants to achieve through the education. Therefore, onto the communist ideal can be "grafted" certain traditional cultural elements (values and ethics). This is the case in real life. Being "conservative", many workers perform diligently, which was often attributed to political reasons by the government or their work unit. They believed that diligent work was the result of the unit's ideological instruction (the communist ideal of education).

B. The Sacred Party

Belief in communism was also reflected in the desire to join the Communist Party. After the founding of the People' Republic, as the ruling party, the Communist Party enjoyed high prestige in people's minds. The sanctity of religion was also reflected in the party's sacred and noble nature. The party had an enormous magnetic effect in its attractiveness to people. Joining the party meant becoming part of mainstream and elite society.

According to the "rational man" model, joining the party must have been out of a self-interested motive. This assumption is not completely consistent with the prevailing social reality. According to our interviews, at least a subgroup of people joined the party out of a spirit of dedication to the realization of communism. This group held devout loyalty and faith in communism. However, we cannot rule out that some people joined the party for their own utilitarian purpose. They saw it as a rational choice to maximize personal gain, because to these people joining the party meant improving their career prospects and accumulating political capital for their personal development. The former had what can be called "super-personal utility" motives, the latter "utilitarian motives." In between are "mixed motives."

Super-personal utility refers to a motive for joining the party based upon devout faith in communism. For those joining the party with this motive, becoming a party member is for career advancement or to make a fortune or to maximize individual interests. Their reason is to use the party's higher standards to discipline themselves, and to make a contribution to the party and the country. Although objectively, joining the party benefited individual's career prospects, subjectively these people did not join the party for those benefits. The following is an excerpt from the interview with a retired veteran:

Interviewer: Do you think that joining the party helps you move up at work?

Respondent: I joined party not because I wanted to get moved up (a little bit excited - the interviewer's note).

Interviewer: I'm sorry, do not misunderstand, I mean, objectively speaking, did your promotion later have something to do with your joining the party? Or was it helpful?

Respondent: I did not think much at the time. I only know that since the organization accepted me, it means the party trusts me, trust my people. Then I would work harder to live up to the party and the people. Indeed I really tried hard to do so. It should be said, many times, by joining the party, we would better transform our thinking. We can often learn together. This helps to improve my knowledge and ideology.

Interviewer: In other words, having joined helps to improve your personal ability right?

Respondent: Something like that. But fundamentally, it is the issue of thinking. Joining the Party is not an end, not the ceiling. It should be interpreted as an increased requirement. Our joining the party is just the beginning.

Interviewer: Let me ask again. Was joining the party at the time a very glorious thing? How did the people around see and treat joining the party?

Respondent: You should not say it was a glory. It should be said that joining the party is a very honorable thing.

Interviewer: Why?

Respondents: The meaning of glory is a little show off. Real party members would not do that. (Spoke very seriously. – Note by the Interviewer.)

(A01-M-75, party cadre, retired)

For many people, joining the party meant "suffering first, enjoying later", paying more than others but not thinking of more in return. There were higher and stricter requirements for work, political and ideological performance. Therefore, from a rational perspective, this was not a "rational" or "worthwhile" choice. Although joining the party may objectively helps to advance a person's career, it was not the case for all members. For example, a retired university cadre replied to "whether joining the party helped to obtain a future raise in the office?" "No, no, no help at all, not to mention wage increase. No. The only feeling is more responsibilities after joining the party, and more social activities. That's all." (A36-F-70, assistant deputy dean) Thus, from the rational choice perspective, joining the party did not always "pay off". However, there were many like this one seeking to join the party, because their motives derived from sincere beliefs rather than the rational choice of someone with self-interest.

In addition to these pious motives, there were some people joining the party because they saw it could bring honor to individuals. Thus, while these people joined the party primarily due to their faith in communism, their motive was also mixed with some personal utilitarian purpose. For example, the pursuit of personal political honor, the pursuit of "progress" and career advancement, and so on. Nevertheless, these people joined the party not to speculate, to some extent, but because they also believed in communist ideals, and were willing to live up to the standards and requirements of the constitution. In other words, their behavior in joining the party's was consistent with their beliefs. They joined the party not for personal gain and "against their will". They tried to reach a unity of self-interest and public interest.

For soldiers, the promotion to be cadres was the goal desired. But the probability of getting promoted to cadre rank was relatively low, while the chance of becoming a party member was comparatively higher. So it became the goal soldiers would strive for. Similarly, the soldiers joining the party were not speculative, since more or less they believed in communism. But their joining the party was not entirely super-utilitarian, because for them party membership obtained political capital. This capital had substantial benefits for their work arrangements after the war.

After the Communist Party became the ruling party and the center of power and honor, those who did not necessarily posses a deep belief in communism also wanted to join the organization, since the party brought political capital to individuals for personal development and career advancement. Obvious advantages were an official raise or job promotion. Despite the ideal of the pious party applicant who does not seek to join the party for promotion to a cadre or for other promotion, objectively there were benefits from joining the party. It was bound to attract some who pursued those benefits by joining the party. Whether they really believed in communism, is a doubtful question.

Despite the utilitarian party applicants "impure" motive, it did not mean that the party to them was not sacred and noble in nature. On the contrary, the party of the noble and sacred can co-exist with utilitarian motives. For utilitarian party applicants, despite joining the party out of a hidden self-interest, they still had to accept the constraints given by the party's constitution. The constitution could play a role in binding them, indicating that they acknowledged the constitution's authority, and that such authority had an inherent relationship with the party's nobility.

Clearly, regardless of motivation, the party was regarded as a sacred organization. Becoming a party member, there was naturally a sense of sacred honor and a sense of mission. This feeling was most prominent at the party's swearing-in ceremony.

Interviews indicate that people felt excited to join the party, because they valued the party's position, and they valued themselves for becoming a member of the party vanguard. At the same time, it was a new beginning for his or her pursuit. If the behavior of joining the party were to some extent driven by faith, after joining the party, this belief would be a way to continue to enhance and strengthen the faith, as the party organizations have their own sets of procedures and rituals to strengthen the party's ideological consciousness and beliefs.

However, not all people can join the party. After all, party members account for only a small part of the population, although the absolute number is increasing. Most people are outside the party. So, does it mean the party lacks appeal among the masses or loses its sacred nature if the majority of the masses are not party members? It is not the case. People did not join the party for a variety of practical reasons. Some were beyond their own control, while other reasons lay in their own character or active decision.

A considerable number of people did not join the party because they had some "tainted" spots, for instance, family composition was not good, or they had overseas relations. One respondent said that her husband opened a small factory in the past (in 1957 converted to joint public-private ownership), so she did not have a good background and dare not join the party: "Because joining the party one needs to be possessionless. We dare not think about this. We only look for being average, not too good not too bad, we do not need to be too advanced." (A29-F-81, knitting factory worker). Another engineer had never seen her father's face, because her father went abroad before she was born. She was considered to have "overseas relations". She repeatedly submitted fifty to seventy applications to the party. Despite her resolute attitude and work enthusiasm, she was still unable to join the party. "(The Party) is not what you want to join, you may join. Nor is it that if you behave well you will naturally be accepted. Sometimes things are just like this." (A03-F-67, engineer)

For people not having such "tainted" spots, the reasons for not joining may be vastly different. But it boils down to personal ambition, a sense of distance, cost calculations and other reasons. First of all, some people did not choose to join the party because they did not have much ambition. For example, one respondent attributed his not joining the party to "sense of inferiority": "I am not a party member and I did not intend to join the party, because I was a little inferior in culture, although I read in high school, was admitted technical school. I originally intended to attend the university, but my family conditions did not allow me. Plus my personality, my language capability, the expression skills being poor, I can not move closer to the party." (A14A-M-58, mechanic) Another reason cited by respondents was bleak career prospects: "We work just as a security guard. We do not have much political potential. To put it plainly, we just want to seek a meal and never thought about a wage raise that sort of thing." (A27-M-52, security personnel) Secondly, some people did not join the party because their "conditions" were not enough. There is disparity between the requirements of the party. One respondent voiced this situation: "I think we should be a good Communist Party members, worthy of this title if we choose to become a party member. We should make a lot of effort. I'm afraid I can not do, so I did not join the party." (A24-F-52, pharmaceutical worker) Next, some people did not join the party because of a cost calculation. On the one hand, to join the party one needs to go through rigorous tests, to expend a lot of energy and time to "demonstrate" positively: "After a year of tests, you will not join if you are not qualified. The major standard is to see whether you are active not. If you are not active, you would certainly be out." (A07-M-78, worker) "Joining (the party) is difficult. One must sincerely work to contribute to the revolution, which it is all hard work. One has to pay attention to his impression in all aspects, which is true." (A04-F-67, cadre) " In the 1972, 1973 years, especially within our army forces, people compare with each other what they do. They compare everything they do. Because only by working actively, actively gets close to the party organizations, he or she would be able to become a Communist party member sooner." (A22-M-53, procuratorate cadre) This relatively high "upfront cost" made some people giving up their attempt to join the party. On the other hand, after joining the party, they will have to play an exemplary role, setting an example for the people, and applying higher standards to themselves. This "after costs" also made some people give up the idea of joining the party.

Despite the variety of reasons for people not joining the party, over a considerable period of time, the party and the party leaders were revered. At the least, people were obedient to them. The Communist Party had higher moral standards for its members (e.g., "suffer first, enjoy later", "play an exemplary role in work"), which objectively helped influence the masses and obtained public support and trust. During the revolutionary war, the "party culture" created by the Chinese Communist Party greatly enhanced the army's combat effectiveness. After the founding of the People's Republic, the Chinese Communist Party again spread this culture cross the country. The demonstrated effect of high ethical standards by the party members has played a very important role in enhancing the country's moral standards, or at least in inhibiting the decline of moral standards. Therefore, some people did not join the party not because they thought that the party was not good, but because they felt that the party's moral standards were too high. It exceeded the level that they could achieve. We can say that most of them respected the party even if they did not join the party.

C. Obedience and Submissiveness

Before the reform and opening up, at least before the Cultural Revolution, an important feature of social psychology was the population's unconditional trust and obedience to Chairman Mao and the party. "Before the reform and opening up, we listen to the central government for everything. Ah, the people back then were very naïve and innocent. We would do whatever the central government tells us to do. Whether we are able to do it or not, is another matter. We do our best to respond to the central government." (A02-M-71, retired military cadre) "Anyway, I would believe what the central government says. People are so simple, thinking nothing else. Ha, now we think of it very interesting, very funny! (laughs) People have no personal views." (A03-F-67, engineer) Even during times of national setbacks, such as the "three difficult years," people's trust of the party and the state remained unwavering: "Well tough times, once this period is over, things will be good. It would be over once we pay off the debt! We believed, firmly believed in the CPC Central Committee. It is just the way never doubted. We have natural disasters, three years of natural disasters, as well as the Soviet Union forcing us to pay off the debt." (A03-F-67, engineer) A security guard who came from a rural area also recalled: "In fact, in the countryside, farmers get up and just see each other, look down and only see the land. We have no political attitude of our society. We are not even clear what is happening in the world. How would you expect a farmer to have any political attitude? Anyway, we would support whatever is broadcast by the radio, oppose to whatever is broadcast to be opposed to. But in fact what we support or oppose is not clear to us at all. One thing is clear and recognized though, so long as the Communist Party is in charge, we would do whatever the Communist Party say." (A27-M-52, security personnel)

Trust in the party and the state leads to the populace's positive response and sincere obedience to the call of the party. To party members, responding to the call of the CPC Central Committee is unconditional: "I just follow the party, and do whatever the party asked me to do. Since I am a party member, what do I have to bargain about? I would go to wherever the Party told me to go. It was my attitude at that time." (A07-M-78, worker) Other people had same attitude, especially young activists. They always responded positively to the call of the CPC Central Committee, "We would do whatever the Party called upon us to do."

Such an enthusiastic response, as well as the obedience to the party and state, reflected people's belief in communist ideals, and their trust and worship of the party and the state's leaders. This attitude and behavior cannot be explained by a rational choice by narrow-minded and self-interested people, because from the perspective of the self-interested person, it is obviously not rational. Therefore, the interpretation of this type of mentality and behavior can only come from the realm of sacred faith and belief. Since people are in a non-secular, sacred realm, their behavior cannot be interpreted from a secular perspective. It must be understood from a sacred perspective. The sacred social psychology resolved many problems that secular methods could not solve, for instance, the issue of labor cost control during the process of industrialization. Therefore, the sacred beliefs stemmed from secular roots (industrial needs), and in return influenced the secular world (reductions in labor cost). Placing people into the realm of sacred belief is precisely a kind of political subjectivity. It is the result of the state's political propaganda, and ideological and political education.

Of course, not all obedience to the CPC Central Committee originates in the people's trust and worship. Obviously, there are two types obedience, one being voluntary, and the other being involuntary. The latter applies to those who did not enter the sacred realm. Their obedience is due to their "conservativeness" (i.e., the connection between traditional culture and state ideology), or because of their "helplessness." In fact, in environments where the country normalizes the ideological and political education movements in order to purify the people's thoughts, no one can or will dare to confront the state. Thus, it is rational to "flow with the tide", "to be silent", to obey passively in order to "protect oneself."

Passive obedience is complicated and diverse. The above quotations show specific cases. These individual cases prove that frequent political movements and an environment of political and ideological uniformity, applies invisible pressure to people. Such pressure made people obey the call of the CPC Central Committee passively and against their will, when clearly the call of the party and the state was contrary to economic laws (such as during the "Great Leap Forward"), contrary to traditional ethical arrangements (e.g., "disclose and criticize") or institutional arrangements (e.g., "The Cultural Revolution"). Therefore, "going against one's will" is essentially based on an individual's situation and a rational choice made for self-protection. In addition to the prevailing situation of political movements and political pressure, there were also other system conditions, for example, the work unit system, the ration ticket for "eating oil and grain", the file system for personnel management, and so on. It was also a type of control mechanism, which largely restricted people's alternatives. In real life, most people have conscious obedience and passive obedience. Those pious believers are more likely to consciously obey. But those with lower strength of faith or lack of belief demonstrate more passive obedience. Regardless active or passive, once people were accustomed to obeying, it became a part of the mainstream culture.

The Concept of Frugality

As faith and vision turn people's anticipation toward the future, the poverty and hardship of present-day reality become relatively easier to bear. Historically, the ascetic and religious beliefs have always been married (e.g., as in Protestantism). Asceticism often becomes a means of practicing certain religious beliefs. Just because of the association of religious beliefs with asceticism, asceticism is not only acceptable, but in some cases is takes on sacred meaning. From this perspective, the reason that the People's Republic was able to successfully implement the policy of curbing consumption is intrinsically linked to the state's promotion of ideological beliefs. As these beliefs direct people's attention toward the future, they make the ascetic life a necessary stage and a gateway to the future condition of well-being. Therefore people could accept the ascetic life, as a necessary price to pay for the future ideal. Thus, the faith and ethic of traditional thrift produced a "bonding" effect. People with imbued with the divine faith carried forward the traditional ethic of frugality. Consequently, a new consumption structure was created with a spiritual core of idealism and the external character of asceticism.

A. Low Wages, Shortages of Consumer Goods and Monotonous Experience

I have discussed in the previous chapter, that in order to implement its strategy of prioritizing the development of heavy industry, the state implemented the "low wage" policy (which was popularly described by Zhou Enlai as, "meals for three to be shared by five"). According to Hu Fangzhi's research, this policy began in 1956 when the monetary and wage system was established (prior to this there was a transitional wage system). The national wage reform unified national wage standards, and implemented an eight-level system for the production workers (as part of the package, the state also established a standard level of skills for workers). Most enterprise administrative staff was paid using a graded wage system. One position has several grades, upper and lower grades overlapping each other. State organizations and institutions were classified by function. Moreover, to account for varying regional prices, the state also provided 11 regional adjustments.

Because of the different regional adjustments, the same wage level resulted in different actual pay. Bu even after the wage system was established, the detailed system of wage levels was not really up and running. Wage increases were mainly based upon years of work and how many times a worker participated in the unified national wage adjustment. Only four times from 1956 to 1976, were worker's wages increased: in 1959, 1961, 1963 and 1971. Superficially, the total increase was 90 percent. Because to the limited number of wage increases, wages for many workers were not increased for a long time. Overall, for the two decades from 1957 to 1976, there were almost no wage increases for workers in state-owned enterprises, and the wages for some of them were even reduced. During this period, egalitarianism was very severe[222] (Table 3-1):

Table 3-1   Average Annual Wages of Formal Employees of State-Owned Units
in Various National Economic Sectors (Yuan)

Year	Total	Industry	Architectural exploration	Agriculture, forestry, hydro-meteorological	Transportation, Postal	Business Services Marketing	City Utilities	Cultural and educational science, health	Finance and insurance	State Organizations
1967	665	746	760	426	784	599	702	604	641	706
1968	661	732	741	430	766	598	699	602	653	706
1969	657	726	751	418	761	596	696	589	630	706
1970	626	666	737	458	729	555	607	560	643	706
1971	611	651	683	422	695	560	704	561	619	691
1972	640	671	736	435	728	615	605	615	601	669
1973	622	650	717	435	716	584	672	592	612	663
1974	633	660	719	488	722	585	676	590	632	670
1975	630	660	722	463	720	595	661	588	625	662
1976	621	651	712	457	705	579	653	582	618	657

The wages for urban workers across the country were generally low. Length of service, type of job, level of skill and position also determined wage differences. In this time period, because of differences in family size and the amount of support needed by rural relatives, the personal experience of low wages varied. But almost all respondents felt the constraints caused by the wage level at the time. Respondents not only remembered the low wages, but also the lack of wage increases over a long time made a deep impression.

Along with low wages there was a shortage of consumer goods. All of the respondents had fresh memories of the introduction of ration ticket supply system for grain, cooking oil, clothing and other basic consumer necessities. They also recollected the shortage of consumer goods in general. In the following excerpt the shortage of consumer goods described by a respondent:

Interviewer: So how do you see the ticket supply system such as clothing and food stamps?

Respondent: With less material, it is the only way. Otherwise, would we all try to rob? Impossible thing. Once there is robbery, the whole society would be in chaos, wouldn't it? To ensure that we all will not starve to death, none of us can eat fully. With this much, you can only give this much. You are issued a ticket, it doesn't mean that you can buy and get them all the time. There is no guarantee of supply, but provide much as possible. It is quite difficult thing without materials. A goose at the time cost fifty or sixty yuan. Think about it, fifty or sixty yuan at that time, is an incredible amount. There are no pigs. Well nobody raises them. People have no food for themselves. There is food to feed the pigs. Pork is hard to come across. Raising chickens and selling them, would be called engaging in capitalism. You just cannot just sell randomly.

(A01-M-75, party cadre, retired)

Respondents not only described in a variety of examples shortages of material goods at the time, but also recalled spiritual and cultural life being poor and monotonous. The following is an excerpt from one of the respondents:

At the time it was comparatively - how should I say? - Monotonous! Not that what you want, would you get. At that time, we don't know what TV is, what sound system is, quite confused and very isolated. That's all. At that time life is monotonous, where to go for fun, no places. No such ideas. All places I have been are places I traveled to on business. It is not that I go there only for fun. Life is monotonous, quite boring, no entertainment at all. Watching movie is fantastic, and I am always enthusiastic for movie. I live in Mei-Hua village. The restaurants inside provincial government quarter do not require money. Carrying a stool, I would go there with my work permit. I felt very good, very positive. (A03-F-67, engineer)

Generally speaking, people who lived through the era before the reform and opening up, all have a deep memory of low wages and shortages of consumer goods. This collective memory is a criterion for evaluating the state of today's consumer life. In turn, today's prosperous material consumption becomes a reference point for evaluating consumer life in the past. Thus, there could be discrepancy between the actual feelings at the time and the memories and recalled feelings based on this reference point. However, poverty had a very real existence at that time. Such poverty only can be felt deeply in today's context.

The monotony of life showed itself not only in the poor spiritual and cultural life, but also in the uniformity of people's lives. People sought commonality in life style with others. They did not dare highlight their own personality, or differentiate themselves; otherwise they would have been criticized, perhaps even by their work unit leaders. One respondent who was never married because of emotional problems and therefore a little poorly off economically said:

At that time, it is not proper to dress up decently. You can't wear something fitted, let alone wearing something better than the others. That is bourgeois ideology to be criticized. It is safe to wear something with patches on. If you wear a Dacron dress, people would call your having bourgeois ideology. At that time I was one of the worst in having bourgeois ideology, just because I was wearing clothes very fit, relatively fashionable, made of Dacron. My second aunt made it for me. They are even close to what today's young people wear, ah, like a low-cut or something. Now the principal's daughter of our kindergarten wears the clothes with her navel exposed, but not considered a bourgeois ideology. At that time because I dress a little more fit, I was told to have serious bourgeois ideology. I was given political criticism three times, which really scared me. Alas! I dared not speak out again, dared not talk about eating, talk about wearing or playing. There is nothing anyway. I only care of my own work, look after my own things. At that time being single is really very hard. And I am afraid of talking to others. (A09B-F-64, elementary school teacher)

In addition to clothing and food, jewelry, lipstick, hairstyles were all monitored and controlled. For example, "In the past, people dare not wear a necklace. But now even if your whole body completely is covered by jewelry, no one will say a thing to you." (A09A-F-68, worker) With the discipline of uniformity, the result was that people were stereotyped, thousands of people having the same appearance without differentiation. Take clothing as an example: "Indeed people did not pay attention to what they put on, from color to style. But you cannot say there was no change at all. There was a change, which was wearing black or blue, basically like this style, relatively old-fashioned."(A04-F-67, cadre) "What choices did people have at the time? All of them are dressed the same, same type of fabric: Jian-Gu-Ni. There was no care of fashion at all. People wore the same at work and off work. The color is gray or dark gray" (A07-M-78, worker). "Clothing was very simple. Everyone wears about the same. Sometimes it is hard to tell men from women for what they wear. We all wore the tunic or navy-style uniform. Each person only gets one coat of cloth coupon annually. If someone wore fancy clothes, he would be criticized or even ridiculed politically by the organization. He can be even excluded from the rest."(A35-M-72, state-owned enterprises leading cadre)

B. Welfare and Experience of Egalitarianism

Despite the low wages and constraints caused by the shortage of consumer goods, people still felt that life was stable and worry-free, because of the state's policy of full employment and welfare, along with the policy of keeping prices low. To compensate for low wages, the state in the 1950s introduced a wide range of non-monetary forms of welfare and service benefits, including pensions, health care, children's education, employment security, housing and so on. An old retired worker recalled the situation:

There were subsidies for the difficulties. At that time there were union benefits. If you really have difficulties in life, the union will give a grant to you. It started when I joined in 1958, 59. ... The housing was very cheap, a yuan or so for a place to live. The medical insurance is 100 percent coverage, simply by filling out a form. If you see a doctor and spend 100 yuan, just take the note (receipt) to the unit for reimbursement. This is so-called seeing doctor with a simple note. ... ... There is also public health coverage for the family, children younger than age 16 have medical care coverage with the family.[223] When they are 16, they will be on their own. And if you have children at school but have financial difficulties, you can apply for grants. In the past, there was a school run by our own unit. If you have financial difficulty, so long as you write a note to explain to the school, you can get remission of the tuition. (A07-M-78, worker)

Despite the relatively low level of benefits, in addition to acting as hidden income to workers, these benefits helped form the worker's "sense of security" and reinforced their dependency upon the state and the work unit. They provided employees with a personal experience of the state's "paternal care" and "asylum". They also experienced an emotional realization of government's official propaganda of the superiority of socialism:

Before we had a sense of security. With the Communist Party, what are we afraid of? We had fear of nothing, not illness or death. We just need to do our job properly. We never had complaints about places of work! Living in this society, we feel that socialism is good! In another word, we have nothing to worry about. (A03-F-67, engineer)

This sense of stability and security to a large extent offset the negative effects of the low wage and the low consumption policy. More importantly, full employment and comprehensive welfare were used by the state to prove that "working class had indeed become the masters". They were evidence to show the superiority of the socialist system. Therefore, the more strongly people believed in communism, the more they would trust the party, and the more they would be able to endure poverty. In fact, the Party Central Committee asked everyone in the country to "tighten their belts". Premier Zhou Enlai said during the period of the three difficult years: "Working hard and saving to build up the country means everyone must save clothes and food, accept lower wages and lower living standards, also everyone must work to build socialist services. Therefore our country can be built faster."[224] In this sense, thrift receives a different meaning from what it had in the past, because it is connected with the state's ambitious goals for socialist construction.

Another way to offset the negative effects of the low-wage, low-consumption policy was an egalitarian distribution of income. Since everyone was more or less equally well off economically, there was hardly social stratification and less need to compare and compete. We all were poor like each other, so there was no social polarization. There were no wealthy families to serve as a reference group and foil the egalitarian ideal. People had no sense of deprivation relatively. Poverty became easier to accept.

At that time the wages were very low, the material condition were very poor, standard of living was very low. There was no corruption. Everyone's economic situation is more or less the same, unlike today's situation where the poor are really poor and the rich are extremely rich. The wealth gap is getting larger. ... People back then did not feel poor, as individual income is not much different. ... ... People do not compare with each other in material living. At that time, each person's income has less than one hundred yuan difference. It is not the case now. Just thinking about the time picking up children at primary school. The children would comment about which family has a beautiful car. They proudly talked about how beautiful their father's cars were. Such comparison is severe. (A14A-M-58 technicians)

Even on the subject of food coupons and clothing tickets, people were of two minds. On the one hand, it limited people's basic consumption to a certain share, inhibiting people's consumption level. On the other hand, it also provided a guarantee of basic livelihood for urban residents. A retired old man commented: "That (ticket) system was in place very early on. When I started working, it was there already. These tickets could be fair. Everyone has a certain amount. No one would get anything more to eat. ... ... The level of consumption is certainly low, but there are food stamps, oil and other items rationing. People will not be too poor to eat." (A29-F-81, knitting factory worker)

C. Concept of Frugality and Strategies

Despite the low wages, the lack of consumer goods, and life being monotonous, very few people desired "extra" in consumer life. This is not only because of low wages and the shortages of consumer goods, or the political climate of uniformity not allowing for personalization and differentiation, but also because of the mainstream society had formed a deeply rooted concept of frugality. This concept of thrift is in fact a traditional ideal. But in the new social environment, it dovetails with the state's ideology. In fact, the concept of thrift was considered by the state as the spiritual embodiment of "hard work" towards communism, because "thrifty" behavior, in addition to being supported by tradition, is a communist ideal and belief. When the party and the country ask people to work hard and live plainly, they are likely to get a positive response. First, it is because people had a vision of the future and a belief in communism. And second, among workers and peasants or cadres from the same background, thrift was always a tradition. Since frugal behavior was given a new political meaning, it made the ascetic life acceptable. Thrift was a way to resolve the problem of shortages of basic consumer goods under conditions of poverty. Ascetic ideas, supported by lofty ideals and sacred beliefs, were part of the ascetic social structure shaped by the state, consistent with its national goals.

Once thrift is given political significance, people with faith in communism, and who follow the communist party and the government, naturally would practice frugality not only out of habit and tradition, but also because of their political conviction. It is this political conviction that glorifies thrift and makes the pursuit of pleasure a "shameful" thing. A retired veteran cadre expressed this belief: "Those of us, the older people who came from the war and experienced the revolution, always lived a simple life and tried to save, after so much suffering and so many movements. It is impossible for us to pursue enjoyment, because there is very little substance. It is a very shameful act, a shady (behavior)." (A01-M-75, party cadre, retired)

In a certain sense, frugality is a knowledge or strategy. In another sense, frugality is a moral belief and habit. Frugality as a knowledge involves how the household budgets, how it makes purchases in order to maintain a combination of disposable income and expenditure balance. In daily life people gradually accumulate knowledge of how to reduce costs while obtaining the food and clothing needed for survival. Frugality being a moral belief refers to the fact that thrift and austerity became deep-rooted beliefs and habits. Its typical reflection is that, assuming two products A and B, if A and B offer same features and exactly the same quality, and A is cheaper than B, but B has more non-functional attributes than A (e.g., a better appearance), then people tend to purchase A rather than B. In other words, under the condition where other products are an "economical alternative" (i.e., cheaper), people tend to buy cheaper products to replace more expensive products. Moreover, before the reform and opening up, when prices were very low, consumers had no choices at all.

In the cases in which disposable income is very limited, people pay more attention to cost saving rather than increased enjoyment. Therefore, people will not hesitate to spend more time on searching for information about cheaper products. This is the so-called "shopping around". On the one hand, this "economical alternative" is a rational choice; on the other hand, it is also the result of accumulated beliefs and moral values. When no additional revenue opportunities exist for people and their wage income is basically fixed, people receiving low wages will naturally direct their attention and wisdom toward optimizing their use of existing revenue. Oriented by survival, they would reduce "unnecessary" or "extra" expenditures and seek the most value from each yuan. Therefore, as a deep-rooted belief, thrift, in fact, is a kind of supporting consumer subjectivity derived from the institutional arrangements of prioritizing the development of heavy industry. National institutional arrangements led to a corresponding formation of consumption subjectivity. It in turn consolidates the state's institutional arrangements for curbing consumption.

In our interviews, respondents spoke often about frugal strategies and beliefs. Frugal behavior has both components of rational choice (strategy) and cultural elements (beliefs). It is difficult to separate the rational elements from the cultural elements. In fact, once rational ideas or accumulated beliefs become habit, they are transformed into cultural or emotional entities. Events contrary to this belief, it will lead to negative emotional reactions. Described below are several consumption strategies and beliefs systems that are commonly seen.

1. Live Within Our Means

Living within our means is a traditional concept of consumption. It is also the most common concept of consumption before the reform and opening up. In a situation of low income and a lack of consumer goods, a reasonable family budget is based on the amount of income and prioritizes consumption, so as to make expenditure and income balance. By implementing the national policies to curb consumption, this traditional concept has been reaffirmed by the residents. It became "of course." This "of course" mindset has both rational component and acquired component. People never questioned the phenomenon of "low income and lack of consumer goods" itself. They treated this situation as "natural" and therefore coped with it by a strategy of living within their means. Therefore, living within our means was part of the main consumption structure.

2. On A Budget

A limited income requires that each spending decision be planned carefully. Otherwise one may exhaust one's available financial resources. Therefore, after the founding of the People's Republic, the popularity of the saying, "breaking a penny into half to spend," reflected the prevailing consciousness of frugality at the time. Expenditure of very penny was carefully weighed.

3. Making The Best Use Of Things

Low wages and limited consumer goods forced people to find ways to extend lifespan of consumer products. Taking clothing as an example, the popular tradition of "the new for three years, old for three years, sewing for another three years" is a typical example. This means not only mending to extend the useful life of clothing, but also through "hand-me-downs" between the siblings to extract the maximum value from these consumer goods.

In addition to doing everything possible to extend the life of a product, people also looked for alternatives that could be processed into consumer goods. For example, many workers in a factory split their white safety cotton gloves and wove them into vests.

4. Live Frugally

Because of straightened economic circumstances, in order to balance their budgets, many families also reduced their consumption of the most basic goods. For example, in dining they were frugal, in order to save food. Also, because of the limited number of ration tickets and limited supply of food, people had to meticulously plan their food use, so that they could strike a balance among food consumption, their income and the availability of rationed goods.

5. Accumulation of Surplus

Although people's income was very low, with hardly any savings and occasionally indebtedness, nevertheless many families were still able to live frugally enough to have something left over. Over the long term they accumulated savings through toward the purchase of one of the "Big Three" (a bicycle, watch, or sewing machine) or other "valuable" products.

Long-term shortages and poverty fostered a sense of saving in order to "be prepared" and provide a psychological buffer against the possibility of hard times. Savings were an attempt to improve security in addition to the desire to save enough for the purchase of a "big-ticket" item.

In summary, although the concept of thrift is a traditional concept of consumption, because it dovetailed with the national ideology and the state's call for "tightening one's belt", it acquired a new meaning and formed an ascetic subjectivity consistent with the national goals. In this consumer subjectivity, thrift was not only "naturalized", but also was glorified as a "virtue". In contrast to frugality, "pleasure-seeking" was stigmatized. Since people believed in the ideal future vision promoted by the party and its state propaganda, thrifty behavior was not only a continuation of traditional values, but also a means to realize socialist industrialization and achieving communism. At the same time, the nations that have established general welfare systems and an egalitarian income distribution, have made being poor not only tolerable, but also manageable, because people formed frugal strategies and beliefs. Dominated by the holy faith, frugality is not only a kind of rationality, but also a culture, which is: a consumer culture (ascetic culture) in convergence with the goal of socialist industrialization.

Dedication

Low wages and the policy of curbing consumption inevitably came into conflict with labor incentives. Since inhibition of consumption was the state's basic economic policy, implementing both the low-wage and low-consumption policies without adversely affecting labor enthusiasm, was a problem. Obviously, the state could not transform people into the ascetics and at the same time accept their becoming lazy. How did the state resolve the tension between curbing consumption and incentivizing labor? In the previous chapter, I discussed the institutional arrangements of sacred incentives implemented by the state. Here, we will discuss the impact of institutional arrangements on the labor subjectivity.

From the state's standpoint, under conditions of low wages and low consumption, the problem of labor motivation can still be addressed. This is because the workers have become their own masters, the masters of the country. They are working for themselves, not for the exploiting class. An editorial of the "People's Daily" on the New Year's Day 1955, said: "Under the leadership of the Chinese Communist Party and government, our people have become the masters of the country, the masters of society, the masters of history. We can follow the laws of social development, through our creative work, to implement development and to build China into a prosperous and happy socialist society."[225] In 1960, Vice Premier Li Fuchun pointed out in his report that: "The general line of socialist construction in China has a very rich content. Its starting point is: people are the creators of history. They are the most active factor in productive forces. People are liberated from the old society. Under the socialist system, they have become masters and will be able to give full play to their enthusiasm and creativity, to achieve rapid development of production and construction."[226] However, to stimulate labor's enthusiasm for work, it was necessary to make people aware of their ownership status, aware of their personal relationship with the state. Thus, the national leaders believed that the masses must be educated. "We are opposed to all ideas and behavior caring for individuals but not for society, considering the local but not overall, seeing the immediate but not the future, asserting the right but not fulfilling the responsibility, spending but not producing."[227] Ideological and political education were to encourage people to think "for whom" they work, and to establish a route towards a fundamental solution of the problem of labor motivation under the state's policy of curbing consumption. Its purpose was to create a kind of labor subjectivity matching national objectives. From the viewpoint of the state, the country's development objectives (the short-term goal of socialist industrialization and the longer term goal of communism) were the individual worker's personal goals. The two are the identical. Individuals were to work towards the country's overall objectives rather than for their own self-interest. It is not difficult to understand why the state promoted and advocated a labor subjectivity of selfless spirit and dedication. Obviously, the main way to mobilize labor enthusiasm under the policy of curbed consumption was to transform people through ideological education and to establish sacred ideals. It was a question of how to shape a new kind of labor subjectivity. Once people considered national goals to be sacred, they would become the objects of their personal dedication and devotion. Then the issue of labor motivation would be fundamentally resolved. This is why, in the 1950s and 1960s, under the national policy of curbing consumption, people demonstrated high morale and work enthusiasm. Even those with selfish desires were swept up by this overwhelming trend.

Before the reform and opening up, especially in the 1950s and 1960s, urban workers in China formed a culture of dedication (the manifestation of new labor subjectivity). They would not muddle through at work because of low wages in a half-hearted way, or show slack or laziness. They were willing to sacrifice to establish this as a cultural norm. The formation of this culture was largely the result of ideological and political education. The macro-social norm was to praise the dedicated and selfless spirit, and to condemn selfishness. In this atmosphere, a spirit of dedication was established at work:

Back then, the idea of serving the people was really good. Since at the time, it was the education of Mao Zedong's era. Being one of the older people, I still miss that forms of education. Education at that time is not for themselves, their interests, but how to contribute to the country, the people. Then there was the "four clean" campaign, I did quite some work and performed quite well. (A14B-F-tx, SOE cadres)

For many people, the reason they were willing to demonstrate their devotion, was their lofty ideals and beliefs. They were willing to work wholeheartedly for the cause of the party and the people. Sacred beliefs became the incentive for them to work wholeheartedly:

Those of us work genuinely for the revolution. We work to serve the people wholeheartedly. Just as when we were taking the oath in joining the party, we would follow the party wholeheartedly, striving to liberate the whole China, even the whole humanity. I did not think about what to do, or where to go to work. In short, wherever the party and the people need me, I would go there. A person working for a cause, loves the work, invests energy and pays a very high price. He or she may even die. But he would work desperately hard for the career he loves. (A01-M-75, retired party cadre, provincial level)

The pursuit of belief even became a criterion used in performance evaluation. Work achievement had to be combined with political and ideological performance. Therefore, someone with good performance not only demonstrates positive work efforts, but also is actively "progressive". In the case of intellectuals engaged in technology, they needed to be "red and expert."

However, not all workers work diligently because of their belief in communism or the selfless dedication advocated by the state. In fact, many workers work hard out of a traditional work ethic. In other words, they work hard because of their "conservatism". According to the traditional work ethic, if you are paid, you should work hard, not be lazy or slack off, or cut corners. Thus, the state's ideological and political mobilization is linked or connected with traditional ethics.

I just did not think we should make a big deal out of our work. At very minimum, you should fulfill your obligation for your wage. This is very basic. We should be responsible for our own conscience, which is also a man's bottom line. ... I think regardless if you are a Communist party member or not, we should get our job done well. This is the most important. (A31-M-62, water conservancy bureau cadre)

Speaking of learning from advanced characters at the time, I am not saying that I resisted or I was against it. But then I know from my heart that, even if you do not call upon me, I would have done the same. So I did not present myself as being particularly active, because I think I have done what I should already. But then you will certainly be criticized if you behave this way. However, a man is supposedly to be this way regardless. Anyway, your sitting there and doing nothing is a waste of time. When we are young and at the prime of life, it does not matter much we do it well, not finding it too hard. So those people were bustling, also attending night school or some sort, although I am not against it on the surface or whatever, I don't think it necessary to make such big publicity. Because this is actually part of things that people should do. (A28-M-76 plant accountant)

Although this type of positive work behavior has its origin in traditional professional ethics, the country's ideological and political education intended to praise the active and criticize the backward, objectively played an important role in establishing the spirit of dedication (the new labor subjectivity). Ideological and political education might not have formed sacred belief for all workers, but it promoted traditional professional ethics that were consistent with the communist working spirit. It facilitated the "bonding" of the two.

The state's ideological and political education had three effects. The first was to make the workers accept communist beliefs, to work tirelessly for the faith with selfless dedication. The second was to make workers adopt enthusiastically traditional professional ethics so that traditional professional ethics and communist laboring spirit were "bonded" together. The third was to prevent laziness from spreading widely among workforce. The result is that by following this education, workers who cannot or do not want to become the activists, will not become "backward elements", but instead maintain "being in the middle".

On the whole, the country's sacred incentive system, at least before the Cultural Revolution, was effective in mobilizing labor enthusiasm. First of all, it made the national cause to be a noble cause for which individuals would fight. It therefore stimulated worker's enthusiasm and dedication. Secondly, it praised the "advanced producer", promoting "bonding" between the spirit of communism and traditional professional ethics. Thirdly, its criticism and education of the backward elements, by making people afraid to lag behind, herded them toward the mainstream. It further prevented the spread of laziness and slack. Thus, despite state's institutional arrangements of low wages and low consumption, people's enthusiasm for work was not compromised.

So, being one of the norms, in which areas is the spirit of dedication (the new labor subjectivity) reflected? The following discussion will analyze its main content.

A. Selfless Dedication

An important aspect of the people's dedication was its selflessness. People only saw the public or national interest rather than their own self-interest; they threw themselves into work, without fear of hardship and despite tiredness, and even without regard to their personal safety; when conflicts arose between family obligations and work, they placed work ahead of their family.

B. Not Asking for Remuneration

Under the state's low wage policy, it was necessary to eliminate within the worker's psychology of the balanced bargain: "how much money, how much work". The state and employees had to engage in an "unbalanced bargain", in order to reduce the cost of socialist industrialization. To this end, the state successfully established among the workers the ideal of dedication of "without remuneration". People were to work diligently and sacrifice, not for material reward, but out of belief or a professional work ethic.

C. Not Seeking Fame

In order to mobilize production and labor enthusiasm, the state introduced a system of selection and recognition of "advanced producers" and "model workers". Workers granted those titles were given some material reward (e.g., a basin, cups, towels, etc.) or opportunities (e.g., party membership, etc.). But these were mainly honorary titles. They were a kind of spiritual reward. It is easy to understand that most people would not bother to contend for these honors, as the number granted were quite limited and therefore the probability of being selected was relatively low. But it is interesting that even those employees winning the titles said that they did not deliberately pursue these honors. This was either out of their genuine belief or their conservativeness. Winning honors was a recognition and affirmation of their work performance and motivation, and afterward a spur to continue their efforts.

D. Serious Attitude and Being Responsible

In addition to selfless dedication without seeking fame or remuneration, the state also required employees to adopt a serious and responsible work attitude, and to complete tasks in the specified quality and quantity. Contributing to this attitude were both professional ethics and the specific aspect of dedication that is linked to the sacred faith and belief.

Finally, it is necessary to point out that in addition to the ideological and political education implemented by the state, before the reform and opening up an important social factor promoting the spirit of dedication was the egalitarian income distribution. We can say that egalitarianism objectively acted as an effective means for resolving the contradiction between the low-wage system and the need for labor incentives. Many respondents in the interviews mentioned the impact of egalitarianism. The following is an excerpt from an interview with a respondent:

I feel, because in that situation, it is not just for us, we are also in this situation. There is not much impact. Because how do you explain this? Take 21 yuan, or take the allowance in the troops, we all are in this situation, it has no impact on their work enthusiasm. (A22-M-53, procuratorate cadre)

In summary, at least until the middle of the Cultural Revolution, through the ideological and political work, egalitarianism and other institutional arrangements, the state resolved the tension between the low-wage, low consumption system and labor incentives.

On the one hand, people accepted the institutional arrangements for curbing consumption, and adapting to the policy of austerity and evolving their beliefs to compensate for the hardship caused by material shortages. On the other hand, people did not become lazy and slack, or cut corners because of the low pay and lack of consumer goods. Instead they worked to promote the spirit of dedication, not seeking personal fame or fortune, and working tirelessly. The ideal of thrift and the concept of dedication were joined in a kind of marriage. But in the main reason for wedding these ideas was the state's ambitious goals, and associated with these sacred beliefs were promoted across the nation by ideological education and indoctrination. Thus, whether the subject is the understanding of the nature of the people's consumption (consumer attitudes), or the understanding of the subject of people's work (the concept of labor), we cannot study it in isolation. Instead, we must place it within the overall cultural system that we seek to analyze. We must consider it in the background of state's formation of its ideological strategy.

Spiritual Crisis

The continuity of the ascetic subject is based on the stability of its social structure. Its social structure is the stable relationship between the desire to control spending (frugality) and the altruistic motives of labor (dedication). In this structure, faith is a core and key element. Its main function is to internalize the state's goal into a personal belief, and drive people to work toward this goal from deep within their heart. The practice of the faith is manifested in two ways, hardship and struggle: hardship, aspect of suppressing the desire to consume (thrift), and struggle, the aspect of labor contribution (dedication). "Building the country with thrift and hard work" expresses the relationship of three things: "Building the country" is building socialist industrialization, and ultimately the ideal of communism; hard work, meaning selfless dedication; "thrift" is self-denial, limiting consumption. Under the influence of the sacred faith, people made both positive and negative efforts: the positive, increasing their intensity of devotion to hard work, and the negative, minimizing their desire for consumption.

Obviously, if there are doubts about the faith, ascetic subjectivity will be shaken, because faith is key to stability of social structure of asceticism. Faith, at the same time, affects labor motivation and consumer ideology, enabling the co-existence of worker enthusiasm with curbs on consumption. Once a crisis of faith occurs, tension will form between labor incentives and consumption curbs. The main structural balance of asceticism will be broken.

Indeed, this crisis of faith occurred during the Cultural Revolution, especially in its later phases. Although it can be traced back even earlier (e.g., the "three difficult years"), the crisis of faith became a common phenomenon, in the late Cultural Revolution. The Cultural Revolution was a strange episode in the historical evolution of the People's Republic of China. It was ultimately the logical result of a particular path in history. But it was also a divergence from other logically possible historical paths. In short, the Cultural Revolution was foreshadowed by the historical transformations the occurred since the founding of the People's Republic. And the historical changes afterwards are reverberations of the Cultural Revolution. So without understanding the Cultural Revolution, it is difficult to understand the process of reform and opening up later. As the chief architect of reform and opening up and its standard bearer, Deng Xiaoping, said: "That our opinions are all the same on the policy of implementing reform and opening up is because we all have learned a disastrous lesson from the ten years of 'Cultural Revolution'."[228] He added: "Without the lessons of the farmerCultural Revolution', it would be impossible to develop the ideological, political, organizational guidelines and policy priorities since the Third Plenum. It was determined by the Third Plenum to move the focus of the work program from class struggle to the development of productive forces, to focus on building the four modernizations, which has support of the whole Party and people. Why? Because there is the farmerCultural Revolution ' to compare against, the farmerCultural Revolution' has become an asset."[229]

On the Cultural Revolution itself, there are too many issues beyond the scope of this book to discuss. Here I can only discuss how the people's crisis of faith happened during the Cultural Revolution, which led to a further crisis of labor motivation. This labor crisis was one of the seeds that grew into economic reform.

A. The "Cultural Revolution" Experience

Different people certainly had different experiences of the Cultural Revolution. For example, most of the leading cadres experienced "being denounced". And many of the Red Guards experienced fighting against the civilian populace. Therefore, our interviewees included people from various categories. Respondents basically spoke about their own experiences. These experiences had a profound impact on their beliefs and motives later on.

1. Partisanism and Resorting to Violence

Factionalism and the resort to violence during the Cultural Revolution left a deep impression, and were central to shaking the established faith of the people. Factionalism and violence sent the society into disorder and chaos. For people who cherished the state's sacred faith and beliefs, it caused confusion and agitation.

2. Violence and Persecution

Another phenomenon during the Cultural Revolution was the psychological shock to people caused by the use of violence as a means of political persecution. The collapse of the rule of law, violence, the abuse of and lack of protection for human rights, led to fear and resentment in many. Cultural "revolution" in name of fighting the capitalism establishment, released people's hatred and brought out sadistic desires to treat "capitalist roaders" and "active counterrevolutionaries" with violence and abuse. Those who were singled out, classified as deviant or had been denounced, lost even minimum protection of their personal safety. The rule of law was trampled on, human rights were insulted, and individuals publicly humiliated.

3. Watching Each Other, Competing to Sing "High Profile"

Because of limitless exaggerations by for partisan and political advantage, people were trapped in a "revolutionary" contest, competing to improve revolutionary standards, and exaggerating tainted opponents infinitely, promoting them to "counter-revolutionary" or "capitalist roader." At this time the personality cult of Mao reached its zenith. In this cult of political fanaticism, any disloyalty to Mao Zedong, or disrespectful remark, was not tolerated, even if the speaker's intended no disrespect.

Not only that, by encouraging informants to report on their neighbors, the Cultural Revolution created opportunities to settle scores or play for personal gain. This led to insecurity and plunged interpersonal trust into an unprecedented crisis. People watched each other in order to protect themselves. To protect themselves, people dared not say the truth, but in publicly, they "sing high profile", quoting the official language latest People's Daily editorial as their "linguistic armor". During the Cultural Revolution, people who dared to assert themselves and speak the truth had to pay a high price.

Such a political atmosphere created a conflict between people's conscience and conservativeness. Before the Cultural Revolution, even those who did not believe in communism were "bound" and "connected" with communist belief by their conscience and conservativeness. However, the evil and ugly parts of human nature was revealed by the Cultural Revolution in a unique way, causing tremendous damage to people's moral standards and consciences. Therefore, regardless of the depth of their sacred belief, people were inevitably thrown into an anxious and puzzled state.

4. Shock of "Nine One Three" Incident

This confusion and shock peaked with the "Nine One Three" Incident. On 13 September 1971, when CPC Central Committee Vice Chairman and Mao's presumed successor, Lin Biao fled by plane. The plane crashed in Mongolia near Öndörkhaan, and Lin Biao and his party died. The news caused a huge psychological shock. If the denunciation of many state leaders like Liu Shaoqi had already stirred people's doubts, the Lin Biao incident has caused people to ask: Lin Biao was Chairman Mao's chosen successor. Chairman Mao is so great, he is always correct. How could he assess the person incorrectly? Since then, the seeds of doubt began to develop. The original faith began to lose its sacred aura.

B. Spiritual Crisis

The impact of Cultural Revolution to people's faith and belief was fatal. In the middle to late Cultural Revolution (or even earlier), people gradually began to doubt the nation's grand goals. The originally established belief was shaken. It can be said, that the Cultural Revolution caused a spiritual crisis. One respondent described it:

At the time, the Cultural Revolution activists were still very positive, because it was the party's calling, and a revolutionary thing. But after being back and forth several times, they formed into two groups. There was nobody right and nobody wrong. All believed that they were to defend Chairman Mao. The revolutionary enthusiasm was very high. People were not afraid of death. "The revolutionists are not afraid of death. Fear of death is not revolution." The momentum was still very fun (laughs), Oh now think of it: in the middle of the night, it is said that there is a supreme instruction of Chairman Mao. We then went to the procession. When the highest order is read, was often at night. We all got up and went without sleep. We would not care for the children, just leaving them with mother or nanny. (Laughs) Oh, I tell you, before the "Cultural Revolution", people listened to the words of the CPC Central Committee wholeheartedly. No one would question anything. Why did so many people questioning with different views? It was because after the resort to violence during the "Cultural Revolution", people started to have more views, more thinking of their own. Sometimes they would ask why things are this way, not that way? The more questions there are, more selfishness there is. Before the "Cultural Revolution, people were very simple, did not expect something else. Like your being assigned to Tibet after the "Cultural Revolution," no one would go, it was not the case previously. Being in the northeast so many years, I have never thought to be transferred back. (A03-F-67, engineer)

It can be said that the "Cultural Revolution" in China led to a comprehensive spiritual crisis, including a crisis of faith, a moral crisis and a motivational crisis.

1. Crisis of Faith

Before the Cultural Revolution, people had hope for the nation's future in general. They still had dreams and visions, believing in socialism and communism. However, the Cultural Revolution to a certain extent, crushed people's dreams, leading to a crisis of faith. Disillusionment was created in society: people felt uncertain about future, without hope for the country. There was nothing to look forward to in life. Life had no meaning.

In the latter part of the Cultural Revolution, people lost their confidence in life. There is a saying: "Socialism is infinitely good, communism would like to know" [Guangzhou dialect], which is an irony, meaning that people lost faith in communism. (A35-M-72, state-owned enterprises leading cadre)

2. The Moral Crisis

The moral crisis was derived from the crisis of faith. People's sense of self-interest began to rise. For example, because of the shortage of basic consumer goods, the abuse of authority, "taking advantage of the relationship" and "back door" procedures became quite common.[230] In the competition of job promotions or other interests, people began to write anonymous letters denouncing their rivals, or "snitched" on their competitors. Some even fabricated scandals or used hearsay evidence (e.g., suggesting improper romantic relationships, etc.). But the most profound moral crisis came out of guardedness and self-censorship. People were less honest. Telling lies became popular. A respondent had deep feelings about this:

After the "Cultural Revolution," people's social views ... what exactly is true and what is false, what is right and what is wrong, it's like is a great education to ourselves. ... No matter who he or she is, to say things wholeheartedly without reservation, is almost impossible. After the "Cultural Revolution," it is unlikely! This is such a huge lesson to me. ... People's ideology is intangible and you cannot feel it. What can you do about it? When you were studying, you learned how to sing the high-pitched tones, and how to make sarcastic comments. But in fact what did you really think in your heart? How is your the inner world like? Who knows? All was messy! So I think the "Cultural Revolution" did not bring good results. (A04-F-67, cadre)

3. Motivational Crisis

Crises of faith and morals inevitably lead to motivational crisis. Before the Cultural Revolution, since people had a strong faith and belief, the poverty of material life did not pose a threat to the people's work motivation. However, once their belief was in crisis, the poor material life was bound to adversely affect their work motivation.

In the "Cultural Revolution", we were not diligent. It should be said that before the "Cultural Revolution," worker's attitudes were still very positive. Everyone worked hard. After the "Cultural Revolution", there was great confusion of who was right and who was wrong. The society itself was very chaotic, which is difficult to adjust to. At that time people talked about "fighting selfishness and criticizing revisionism". People would rather go home to make furniture [Guangzhou dialect: furniture] than coming to work. Pi-Xiu refers to criticizing the revisionism. At that time the working attitude was very bad. If not for reform, there would not be vitality of enterprises. (A14B-F-tx, SOE cadre)

More seriously, the commitment made by the state to a happy life for the people had not materialized after twenty years of hard work. In fact, people's living standard had declined. From 1957 through the Cultural Revolution, almost all wages were stagnant (only slight adjustments made by the state in 1962 and 1972 respectively). And people experienced the difficult period of 1959~1961. Still in the early 1960s, because of the state's rectification of and adjustments to the economy, on the eve of the Cultural Revolution, living standards had begun to increase. However, after the start of Cultural Revolution, with the abolition of the bonus system in 1965 and the long-term wage freeze (1963~1977), the living standards of most workers actually declined. Workers employed during the period of the wage freeze experienced many life difficulties. Simultaneous with the wage freeze, the housing problem worsened. The ration ticket system for food and consumer goods was unable to meet people's basic needs. At the same time, the distribution of goods was deteriorating. Even with money and coupons, you might not be able to buy things. In order to obtain consumer necessities, people began to use their network of acquaintances and relations. "Back door" procedures became widespread. It can be said that the mechanism by which the state promised an idealized future in order to motivate people to work hard, started to malfunction. In other words, the sacred incentive mechanism became ineffective.

Once sacred incentives lost their effectiveness, a different type of relationship formed between consumption curbs and labor motivation. As it had always been difficult to raise one's living standard, people were not willing to work as hard as they had been in the past.

Chronic poverty in life and the perceived inequality of wage income (e.g., workers were in eight-tier wage system), made certain specific age groups of workers start to be slack at work. Labor enthusiasm decreased.[231.] In Walder's words, labor became "demoralized."[232] Particularly in 1971~1972 and the years thereafter, labor discipline relaxed. Because of the political impact of the Cultural Revolution the authority of work unit leaders declined. Since increased labor discipline would bring upon management political risks, unit leaders were unwilling to enforce it. Management indulgenced in looser labor discipline.[233.] They could only attempt to mobilize the enthusiasm of labor through the use political education and cyclical industrial movements, which relied on political slogans, e.g., "grasping revolution, promoting production", etc.[234.] However, such sacred incentives were no longer effective, as people were paid the same whether they do a good job or not. It decreased the sense of responsibility in both the workers and their leadership. Such micro-scale changes in work attitudes led to macro-scale reductions in labor productivity. As a result, people felt on the one hand, that they were "busy" and working very hard. On the other hand, it was difficult to solve the shortage of consumer goods. The shortage of consumer goods, in return, made it hard to raise work enthusiasm. More insidiously, it encouraged people to seek satisfy their material desires using their personal "network and relationships" as well as "back door" procedures (e.g., for the purpose of obtaining a housing allocation, taking extended sick leave, etc.). This unequal competition for resources further depressed the effectiveness of sacred incentives, causing the labor force "to moralize." At the same time, the constant criticism directed at workers from political movements led to grievances and resentment. Tensions increased between cadres and the public. Activists were isolated. Factory workers frequently stole things from their work and took long-term leaves of absence by using faked notes from doctors.[235] Clearly, the intense political education and mobilization during the Cultural Revolution did not further the goal of labor motivation. It was a failure.[236]

In summary, during the socialist planned economy period, the state's ideology not only dominated the institutional arrangements, but also shaped the social structure of asceticism. During that time, the core of ascetic social structure was a holy faith and the corresponding labor subjectivity (dedication) and consumer subjectivity (frugality). The holy faith is the core of asceticism, wedding the concepts of frugality (consumer subjectivity) and dedication (labor subjectivity). Therefore, in the socialist planned economy period, maintaining the sanctity of people's faith is crucial. This also partially explains why the state had to implement ideological and political education, whatever the cost. However, the Cultural Revolution and related events forced the social structure of asceticism into a crisis of faith. The crisis of faith led to an increasing conflict between the original goals of curbing consumption and stimulating of labor motivation. The linkage between thrift (consumer subjectivity) and dedication (labor subjectivity) became vulnerable. Dissatisfaction and resentment grew. As described, the state not only ran into a crisis of social mobilization, but also faced a crisis of legitimacy resources. It was just these crises of social mobilization and legitimacy that forced the new generation of leaders to launch the systemic reform movement. This is what we will discuss in the next chapter.

Chapter Four

Transformation Towards a Consumer Society

In this chapter we return to the study of national institutional arrangements, namely, macro-level actors. However, the protagonist has changed. This change objectively directly contributed to the historical and social transformation. In fact, it is precisely because of this change, that reform and opening up occurred. Marx believed that people create history. And Marxists believe that individuals play an important role in history.[237] The individuals mentioned here are the macro-actors, rather than micro-actors. Because of the structural position of macro-actors, he or she can, to certain extent, hinder or advance the pace of history. The role of individuals is determined by the social structure. In other words, the structural location of macro-actors determines to a certain extent the progress of history. The role of the individual has been particularly evident in countries with totalitarian systems. Because of the centralized system, macro-actors, especially the most highly placed macro-actors, can to a large extent determine the will of the state, its policies and institutional arrangements. Therefore, when the macro-actors change, changes in historical trajectory will follow.

After the Cultural Revolution, and especially after the Third Session of the Eleventh Plenary Meeting of CPC, Deng Xiaoping became the head of China's second generation of collective leadership. Deng Xiaoping himself said: "Any collective leadership must have a core ... the core of the first generation of collective leadership is Chairman Mao. ... I was actually the core of the second generation. Because there is a core, even if there is a change of two leaders, it does not affect our party's leadership. The party's leadership has always been stable."[238] Deng Xiaoping's statement was recognized in the official party literature. In his report to the 14th Party Congress, Jiang Zeming first affirmed the historical achievements of the first-generation collective leadership under Comrade Mao. Then he pointed out: "The second-generation collective leadership with Comrade Deng Xiaoping being the core, has led the whole party and the country in beginning another great people's revolution. It is to further emancipate and develop productive forces, so that after a long struggle, China is transformed into a prosperous, democratic and civilized modern socialist country from a undeveloped socialist country. This fully reflects the superiority of socialism in

China."[239] Thus, Deng Xiaoping was in fact the most critical and most important macro-actors of the reform and opening up. In the official wording, he was the "chief architect" of the reform and opening up. Therefore, to understand the state's decision-making and actions, we must first understand Deng Xiaoping's thinking and actions. We can say that Deng Xiaoping's thinking directly affected the major decision-making and institutional arrangements of the party and the state since the Third Plenary Session of the Eleventh CPC Meeting. The study of Deng Xiaoping's thinking is the gateway to the study the state's actions during this time.

The basic structure of this chapter is as follows:

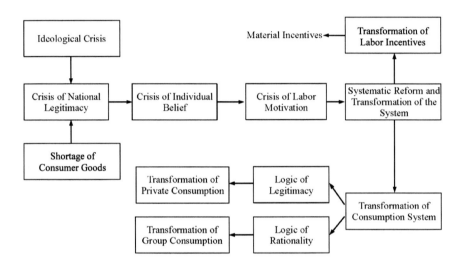

Institutional Arrangements of Consumption After Reform and Opening Up

Fang Aiqing and the others believe that national consumer policy (i.e., the official consumer system) after the reform and opening up has gone through three distinct phases: the phase of the subsidized consumption policy (1979~1988), the phase of the moderate consumption policy (1989~1997) and the phase of a policy that encouraged consumption (1998~2004).[240] In my view, this description is in line with historical facts. Considering the moderate consumption policy to be just an intermediate stage between the subsidized consumption policy and policy of encouraging consumption, it is omitted from this chapter's discussion. Here I only discuss the subsidized stage and the final policy stage of encouraging consumer spending.

A. The Institutional Arrangements of Compensation for Consumption

1. Legitimacy Crisis and Rejection of "Socialist Poverty"

Deng Xiaoping's thinking on reform and opening-up, to a certain extent, is the product of his reflection on the Cultural Revolution. And what made the deepest impression upon him was how the Cultural Revolution caused the depletion of the legitimacy resources of the party and state. Deng Xiaoping said when he met with Jim Bruni, Vice Chairman of the U.S. Encyclopedia Britannica Publishing Editorial Board, Lin Daguang, Director of East Asian Institute at McGill University and others: "If you came in the fifties and sixties, you would see China's social climate being very good. In difficult times, people were very disciplined, taking care of the overall situation, connecting their personal interests with the collective interest, with the national interests and the interests of all society. People voluntarily went though difficulties along with the country. The difficult three-year period beginning in 1959 went this way. Lin Biao, the farmerGang of Four', completely destroyed this social atmosphere."[241] Clearly Deng Xiaoping realized that after the Cultural Revolution, the party and state's legitimacy resources had been depleted to no useful end. The party and state's prestige was seriously damaged, and their power to persuade was greatly decreased:

"Lin Biao and the farmergang of four' caused great damage to our party. It should be said that our party's prestige among the people is not like what it was before. In the past, to overcome the difficulties, a call from the party, a saying by the CPC Central Committee, moved the country to follow and do so. It was very effective. The serious difficulties in 1959, 1960, 1961, were quickly overcome under the unified leadership of the party. It was very memorable. More than twenty million workers were sent to the countryside, to follow the mass line. With truth being told clearly, people did not complain. Now it is not as easy."[242]

Decline in the prestige of the party meant that the party and the state faced a crisis of legitimacy resources. While the central leadership could blame the decline in the party's prestige on the Cultural Revolution, and in particular, blame Lin Biao and the "Gang of Four" for the damage they caused, the party and the state's top priority was still to quickly marshal the people and rebuild their legitimacy resources. So, what was the starting point? The central government authorities adopted various measures, including disclosing and criticizing the "Gang of Four", disciplining party members, and so on. One of the most far-reaching actions was to reject the "poverty of socialism."

While the crisis of legitimacy resources had a direct relationship with the Cultural

Revolution, another critical factor was the party and the state's failed commitment to the people. For a long time, people respond positively to calls from the party. They worked hard and lived frugally, because they had hope. They believed that because of their hard work today, they would have a happy life tomorrow. But after many years of struggle, they were still poor, which could not but make them feel frustrated. They began to doubt the superiority of socialism promoted by the party and state. Obviously, Deng Xiaoping deeply experienced this crisis. In 1978, he said bluntly: "How could socialism demonstrate its superiority like this? After twenty years we are still so poor, why do we need to build up socialism at all? We want a revolution technically and in management, to develop production and increase worker's incomes."[243]

Deng Xiaoping disdained the "Gang of Four's" theory of "Preferring Socialist Poverty". He criticized it many times. In 1979 he said: the "'Gang of Four' prefers poor socialism, not rich capitalism. Socialism cannot stand on its own feet if it is always poor."[244] Deng Xiaoping also said: "The goal of our revolution is to liberate and develop productive forces. Without the development of productive forces, making the country prosperous, improving people's lives, the revolution is meaningless. We were opposed to the old society, the old system, because it oppressed the people. It prevented production capacity from developing. Now the problem is quite clear. In the past the 'Gang of Four' proposed to have poor socialism rather than rich capitalism. It is absurd."[245] Deng Xiaoping proposed that the purpose of the revolution was the "development of productivity, the country's prosperity and improvement of people's lives." (This is also the earliest representation of the "three 'benefits'" given by Deng Xiaoping during his "southern tour" speech in 1992. Among them, improving people's lives is, in fact, to increase their consumption. Here, the improvement of consumer life has become one of the goals of the revolution, and is a criterion to evaluate the success of the revolution. Thus, in Deng Xiaoping's view, improving people's consumer life should be an important route to restoring the legitimacy resources of the party and state. Socialism should not be impoverished. "We do not want capitalism, but we do not want an impoverished socialism either. We want the kind of socialism that develops production capacity and empowers the country."[246]

Deng Xiaoping thought that to reach consensus, the party and state had taken many detours. "We completed the socialist transformation in the past. Still we were engaged in this movement, that movement. Each campaign delayed a number of things and hurt many people. To demonstrate the superiority of socialism, the bottom-line is to significantly develop production capacity, to gradually improve and enhance people's material and spiritual lives."[247] In Deng Xiaoping's view, the superiority of the socialist system should be proved by a higher economic growth rate than that of the capitalism. It must be reflected in the gradual improvement of the people's material and spiritual life. If, over the long term, people's consumer life did not improve, the superiority of socialism could not be asserted. People would start to question the superiority of socialism. The party and state's legitimacy resources would inevitably be affected. The reason that the superiority of socialism was not manifest was the state's long-standing focus on political movements, ignoring the development of productivity and improving people's consumer life. So after so many years of socialist construction but with the country still impoverished, the top priority became rapid economic development. The party and the state shifted their focus to economic construction.

The reason why the state should shift its focus to economic development was that the criterion for the superiority of socialism was the development of productivity and improvement of living standards. Only once production developed and living standards improved would people believe the superiority of socialism. As Deng Xiaoping pointed out: "According to our own experience, talking about socialism, we must first develop production. It is the top priority. The superiority of socialism can only be demonstrated this way. Whether socialist economic policies are right, the bottom-line analysis is to see whether there is development of production, whether people's income is increased. This is the overriding criterion. Simply talking about socialism without content, people will not believe it."[248] He later added: "The task of socialism is to develop production capacity, to strengthen the power of socialist countries so that people's living will gradually improve, to prepare the foundation for moving onto communism later."[249] However, many years of practical experience proved that in order to develop production and improve people's lives, it would not be enough to relying upon the system of the past. There had to be economic reform and opening up to the outside world.

The purpose of the reform and opening up was to develop production capacity and to improve consumer's living standards, thereby demonstrating the superiority of socialism and rebuilding the legitimacy resources needed to consolidate the socialist system and the party's leadership. In Deng Xiaoping's words: "What is the target objective of our reform? The overall objective is to help consolidate the socialist system, consolidate the party's leadership and to help develop production capacity under the party's leadership."[250] It was also pointed out in the bulletin of the Third Meeting of The Eleventh Party Plenary Session: "Whether we can achieve the general task of the new period, whether we can accelerate the construction of socialist modernization, whether we can greatly improve people's lives on the basis of rapid development of production, whether we can strengthen national defense, all these are major concerns to people across the country."[251] Clearly, Deng Xiaoping realized that focusing on the issue people were most concerned with, which was the improvement of consumer living standards, was a major way to gain positive public support and to rebuild legitimacy resources.

Socialism requires the development of productive capacity and the improvement of people's lives. This is a lesson of the Cultural Revolution. Deng Xiaoping pointed out: "The Chinese suffered great bitterness from the ten-year catastrophe of the 'Cultural Revolution'. China's suffering was not only these ten years. Previously, starting from the second half of 1957, we made "leftist" mistakes. Generally speaking, we were closed to the outside. Internally we followed the path of class struggle, ignoring the development of production. The policies went beyond the primary stage of socialism." It was to correct the ways of the past, especially the "leftist" path during the Cultural Revolution that led to the subsequent reform and opening up: "At the Third Meeting of the Eleventh Plenary Session in 1978, the party made a systematic summary of the past, and proposed a series of new policies. The central focus is to move the program from class struggle to the development of production, to move from being closed to opening up, and to move from sticking to conventions to reform in all aspects."[252] He added: "In the past there was too much delay. Especially during the ten years of the Cultural Revolution, we created troubles for ourselves and brought about our own calamity. But it is very beneficial to learn from this lesson. The current principles and policies are a result of the lessons learned from the Cultural Revolution."[253]

Correcting the "leftist" errors of the Cultural Revolution, the populace's attention and work program were shifted to socialist modernization. This helped to consolidate socialism and the party's leadership because it re-established a goal, ideal and belief among the people. This belief was in the socialist "four modernizations", which were to build China into a prosperous socialist country. Deng Xiaoping believed that with this ideal, the party and the state would be able to re-unite people of the country to rebuild legitimacy. Whether or not the people have faith is an important factor in determining the integration of society. In the past the reason that the party has appeal among the people is that the ideal advocated by the party has become the people's faith. However, this belief was destroyed during the Cultural Revolution. Reform and opening up established a new faith. Deng Xiaoping said:

"Based on my long-time experience in political and military activities, I think that the most important thing is human solidarity. To achieve unity, it is necessary to have a common vision and a firm belief. In our hard work over the past few decades, we united

people with a firm belief. People will fight their own interests. Without such a conviction, there is no cohesion. Without this conviction, there would be nothing at all. We communist's highest ideal is to achieve communism. In different historical periods, we had different programs representing the overwhelming majority of people's interest for the people to strive for, so that we could unite and mobilize the masses of the people, which is the so-called one mind. With this unity, we could overcome any difficulties and setbacks. In the past, with this one-mind, we defeated several millions of the Kuomingtang's army that was equipped with modernized U.S. equipment. Back then we had no planes, no artillery, mainly relying upon people. So I would say that human factor is very important. Here I am not referring to ordinary people. I refer to the people who recognize their own interests and strive to fulfill their firm conviction. To our military, a firm belief is still a principle that built the army, which cannot be lost. This is China's unique characteristic. We talk about faith in the army. Among the people, and young people, we should talk about faith too."[254]

We discussed the importance of belief in the previous chapter when we discussed the shaping of subjectivity. However, in Deng Xiaoping's view, unlike in the past, the ideals and beliefs to be established were not based on people's belief in self-sacrifice. Instead, they were based on faith in continuously improving material and cultural life. This kind of belief was more easily accepted and supported by the people, and was more conducive to rebuilding the legitimacy resources of the party and state. In fact, after just a few years of reform, the country's economic outlook had greatly improved, and people's living standards had improved remarkably. It helped stabilize the party and the state. Deng Xiaoping said:

"It is proven in real life that the reform is right and effective. If our foreign friends can see the changes, see that we have done quite well. Can't our own people see it? People have their own personal experience. Their eyes are sharp. In the past they were hungry, had no clothes to wear. Now they have not only food and clothes, but also modern household items. People are happy. This being the case, can our policy still be unstable? The stability of the policy reflects the party's stability."[255]

In the past, tortured by the "leftist" line and "utopian" ideal, the people's ideals, passion and enthusiasm were consumed to depletion. Now, the ideal of realism advocated by Deng Xiaoping rapidly mobilized people's passion and enthusiasm to participate in reform. In this reform, what inspired people's enthusiasm was no longer a "utopian" ideal. It was a tangible and achievable goal, which brought benefits to people and was aligned with their interests. Therefore, if during the early days of the People's Republic and prior to the reform, the party relied upon the legitimacy of idealism, the since the reform and opening up the party state regained legitimacy resources.

Deng Xiaoping later summarized this new legitimacy by giving three criteria during his "southern tour speech": the three "benefits": *"The pace of reform and opening up is small, too timid. All comes down to the fear of capitalism, and being afraid of taking the capitalist road. The crucial point is the 'capitalist' or 'socialist'. The judging criteria should be mainly to see whether it is beneficial to the development of production capacity, whether it helps strengthen comprehensive competitiveness of the socialist countries, whether it helps improve people's living standards."*[256] He added: *"It would be a dead end if we do not adhere to socialism, no reform and opening up, no economic development, or improving people's living. The basic line to follow should be for a hundred years, not to be shaken. Only by sticking to this route, people will believe you and support you. Whoever attempts to change the guideline, principles and policies since the Third Plenum, will be put down because the people do not agree."*[257] Here, Deng Xiaoping openly stated that the legitimacy of the party and the state (including its popular and legal legitimacy) can only be measured by the "three criteria". Among them, the criterion of improving consumer living standards is one source of the party's and state's legitimacy.

Increased consumption and improved living standards have the function of providing popular legitimacy. And enhancing and improving the people's consumption life depends on the development of production, on economic development, and on modernization. In this sense, the economic development to enrich the people's lives (not ascetic economic development) becomes the party and state's main political subject. Deng Xiaoping said: "The economic work is the main political issue. The economic issue is the overriding political issue. Not just at present, I am afraid that for a long time in future our focus should be economic work." He added: "The so-called policy is the Four Modernizations. We opened the big mouth (to promise), at the end of the century we will achieve the four modernizations. Later we changed our words, calling it Chinese-style modernization, which is to lower that standard, especially with GDP per capita not being high."[258] This strategic focus shift was reflected in the spirit of the party document. The bulletin of the party's Eleventh Meeting and Third Plenary Session notes, "The party's work focus should more than in 1979 on socialist modernization."[259] In another place, the bulletin also said: "The emphasis of the party's work and the attention of the people should be directed toward socialist modernization."[260]

Deng Xiaoping said that although the party and state's attention had shifted to economic development, it did not mean that political work was no longer needed. But the sort of empty political preaching used in the past was ineffective. We had engaged in political campaigns for so long, and had shouted political slogans so loudly. But it only increased the tensions between people. People were still very poor. Thus, Deng Xiaoping was well aware that the earlier style of political and ideological work had to be reformed. Political work had to be implemented in the context of economic work. It must use economic means. He said:

"Some of the movements we had in the past, such as studying theories, studying back and forth, is not connected with reality. Everyone becomes tired of it. Of course, this is not to say that we do not pursue the political work. Some people think that getting rid of the department of politics is to abolish the political work. The party is engaged in what? What is union supposed to do? What about the Communist Youth League? And what is Women's Federation engaged in? Aren't all these supposed to do political work? Political work is to be done, and to be done really well. However, political work needs to be integrated into the economic development, and the political issue is to be solved from the economic point of view. For instance, the issue of implementing policies, employment, the issue of moving the youth back to the city after their being sent to the countryside, all these are social and political issues, which need to be addressed primarily from the economic point of view. If economy is not developed, these problems will never be addressed. The so-called policy is mainly economic policy."[261]

Deng Xiaoping realized that many of the real social problems could not be solved only through political preaching. Solving these social problems meant using economic means and had to be backed up by economic development. If these social problems were solved, the people would support the party and the country. Thus, the economic development gained political significance. Deng Xiaoping pointed out: "For our country internally, what are China's biggest politic tasks? The four modernizations are China's biggest political task."[262] Therefore, "To achieve the four modernizations with one heart and one mind, will be the people's long-term overriding central task. It is generation's great cause to determine the fate of our motherland."[263] He emphasized: "We must grasp this tightly and hold onto it. We cannot delay it for one day."[264] He added again: "Departing from putting economic construction at the center, there will be risk of losing material foundation. All other tasks should be the subject to this center, around the center. Nothing shall interfere with it. In the past two decades, we learned saddening lessons this area."[265] What was that previous lesson? It was that we did not to focus on economic construction, instead on a political movement. In the future, unless there is a large-scale world war, we must grasp and hold on to the center of economic construction.

Deng Xiaoping set the minimum goal of the four modernizations, which was to achieve prosperity by the end of the 20th century: "We made the minimum target of the four modernizations is to achieve prosperity by the end of the century. In December 1979 when I met with former Japanese Prime Minister Masayoshi Ohira during his visit, I talked about this for the first time. The so-called prosperity from the standpoint of gross national product (GDP's) is to reach eight hundred U.S. dollars per capita."[266] On prosperity, Deng Xiaoping had a more specific explanation later on:

"We identified a political objective: economic development, to quadruple by the end of the century, GDP per capita reaching eight hundred U.S. dollars, a comfortable standard of living for people. This goal is insignificant for developed countries, but for China it is an ambitious and magnificent goal. More importantly, on this basis, with another 30 to 50 years of development, we will strive to get close to the world's developed countries. It is not very easy to achieve our goal. Lying and empty talk will not work. We must have a set of internal and external guidelines and policies. Since the Party's Eleventh Meeting's Third Plenary, we have identified the policy to invigorate domestic economy and to open it to foreign economic liberalization. We cannot succeed without such a policy."[267]

Deng Xiaoping learned from the previous lesson that not realizing national commitments actually causes damage to national prestige. The state's goal must be achievable, not a fabrication or empty words. Therefore he proposed a realistic standard of prosperity. The so-called prosperity, according to Deng Xiaoping, is in his words "not poor, not rich." He said: "We have struggled for decades in order to eliminate poverty. The first step, at the end of the century, is to reach prosperity, which is not poor, not rich, living a relatively better than average life. Second step, is to spend thirty-to-fifty years, to get close to the economic level of developed countries. People will have more affluent lives, which is the overall objective to achieve."[268] Such a staged program to achieving this goal is more realistic, more practical and more feasible. More importantly, it can bring tangible benefits directly to people's lives, therefore improving and enhancing people's living standards, eliminating the long-term dependency of poverty. Clearly, the goal of prosperity is actually the people's consumption goal. It is the goal to enhance and improve the people's living standards. Through the establishment of this goal, the party and state re-established their appeal to regain the people's support and endorsement, to reconstruct legitimacy. This source of legitimacy is from the condition of people's lives rather than political dogma and utopian ideals. A political party that cannot solve the issue of people's living conditions is bound to lose legitimacy. In countries with unresolved issues of living conditions, the biggest political task is resolving this question, which may potentially yield the largest source of legitimacy.

In addition to highlighting prominent economic development objectives, Deng

Xiaoping did not ignore the building of people's morale. He called the development of the economy material construction, while morale building was called spiritual and moral ideals. He said: "In a socialist country, once a true Marxist political party takes over, they must be committed to developing production capacity. On this basis, they shall gradually improve the people's living standards, which is the material construction. ... At the same time, the party must also build a socialist spiritual civilization. The fundamental thing is to make the majority of the people to believe in communist ideals, to have morality, culture, and discipline. Internationalism and patriotism are all areas of spiritual civilization."[269]

Deng Xiaoping's central idea of economic construction re-established what was confirmed at the party's Eighth Meeting, that the main contradiction after the basic transformation of a socialist society was no longer the contradiction between the proletariat and the bourgeoisie, instead it was the conflict between the people's growing demands for material good and backward production capacity. At the party's Eleventh Meeting Sixth Plenary Session, the party unanimously passed "The Resolution by The Central Committee of the Communist Party of China on A Number of the Party's Historical Issues Since the Founding of the Party". The resolution clearly reaffirmed this principal contradiction. It demanded that all the work must be subordinated to and serve economic construction.

Deng argued that in order to develop the economy, a market economy can also coexist with socialism. The market versus the plan is not a standard for distinguishing capitalism from socialism. They are means of economic development. As long that it is conducive to economic development and improving people's living standards, it can be used by socialism. As early as 1979, Deng Xiaoping expressed this idea:

"It is certainly not correct to say that a market economy exists only in capitalist society, and there is only capitalist market economy. Why cannot there be a socialist market economy? This cannot be called capitalism. We are the planned economy, but also combine it with market economy. But this is a socialist market economy. Although the method is basically similar to that of the capitalist society, there are also differences. The relationship is state-owned, and of course, it has collective ownership. It also has foreign capitalist relationship. But in the end, it is socialist and belongs to socialist society. Market economy cannot be said just for capitalism. ... Socialism can also practice market economy. Similarly, to learn good things from some capitalist countries, including business management, does not mean to implement capitalism. It is the socialist using this method to develop production capacity. Using it as a method will not affect the entire socialism, nor will it return to capitalism."[270]

Later, Deng Xiaoping repeatedly talked about this idea. For example, in 1985 he said:

"There is no fundamental contradiction between socialism and a market economy. The issue is to use which method that is more effective in developing production capacity. We have always had planned economy, but years of practice has proved that in certain ways, a totally planned economy hampers the development of production capacity. The planned economy and market economy combined is more powerful in liberating production capacity and accelerating economic development."[271] In 1987, he said: " Why do we always relate it to capitalism soon as we talk about the market? Why is only the planned being socialism? Planning and market are both methodology. As long as they benefit the development of production capacity, they can be used. As it serves socialism, it is socialist. It would be capitalism if it served capitalists. Just like talking about the plan must be socialism, it is not right. There is a Planning Agency of Japan, so is the case with the United States."[272] In his 1992 "southern tour speech", Deng Xiaoping said again: "The scheme with more market or less planned is not the essence of the difference of socialism and capitalism. Planned economy is not equivalent to socialism. There are plans with capitalism as well. Market economy is not equivalent to capitalism. Socialism also has market. Planning and market are both economic means. The nature of socialism is to liberate and develop production capacity, eliminate exploitation and polarization and eventually realize common prosperity."[273]

Deng Xiaoping' view that the market and the plan could both be used had tremendous impact on the policies of the party and state. The party's recognition and acceptance of market was a step-by-step process. At the party's Twelfth Meeting, a planned economy supplemented by a regulated market was proposed. At the Twelfth Meeting Third Plenum, it was proposed that the socialist commodity economy was an unavoidable stage of economic development. China's socialist economy was based on public ownership of the planned commodity economy. At the party's Thirteenth Meeting it was proposed that the system of the socialist planned commodity economy should be a unified system with integrated planning and a market. After the Thirteenth Meeting Fourth Plenary Session, the party proposed to establish an economic system and operating mechanism for a planned commodity economy, adapted to the development of a combined planned economy and regulated market. At the Fourteenth congress the party put forward China's economic reform goal as being the establishment of a socialist market economy system, in order to further emancipate and develop production capacity.[274.] This process clearly reflects the reciprocal relationship between ideological legitimacy and realistic legitimacy. In other words, ideological legitimacy gradually retreated, and realistic legitimacy took a dominant position (developing production capacity, improving people's consumption and living standards). The establishment of a market economy has greatly affected the people's consumption life. This point we will leave for later discussion.

2. Adjustment of Saving vs. Consumption Ratio

Improving people's living and consumption standards was a way to rebuild the legitimacy resources of the party and state, and this required adjusting the tendency toward encouraging saving and discouraging consumption that had existed since the founding of the People's Republic. By the beginning of the reform and opening up, the state also had the ability to increase the portion of consumption. This is principally because, after twenty years of hard work, China had built a relatively complete and independent industrial system. The crisis of legitimacy resources caused by the Cultural Revolution put on the agenda an adjustment of the saving to consumption ratio, and of the relative sizes of the agricultural, light industrial and heavy industrial sectors. Here we focus on the analysis of the policy literature on the adjustment of the sizes of agricultural, light industrial and heavy industrial sectors, as well as the ratio of saving to consumption, between the CPC Central Committee Eleventh Meeting Third Plenary Session, and September 1985. (In the 1985~1987 period, to control overheating consumption, the state resumed a policy of curbing consumption.) This period was not only a turning point in China's social transformation, but also an important turning point in the national consumer policy. Deng Xiaoping said:

"We used to engage in long-term planning. A big disadvantage is that we did not adjust well a variety of ratios. The ratio of Agriculture to industry is not balanced.—The proportion of farming, forestry, animal husbandry and fisheries, versus that of light and heavy industry is not balanced. Coal, electricity, gasoline and transportation versus other industries are not balanced. 'Bones' and 'meat' (which are industrial and residential construction, public transportation and other municipal construction, commerce and other business services) are imbalanced. Saving and consumption is not balanced. This year's plan is better. But to completely reverse this situation, it still requires great efforts. In addition to these proportions, there is another significant unbalanced ratio, which is economic development vs. education, science, culture, health development. The expenditure is still quite low for education, science and technology development, cultural and health development. It is out of proportion."[275]

Among all relationships, the imbalance between agriculture and industry was particularly prominent. In 1979, at the Central Government Work Conference Li Xiannian said that in the past two decades, agricultural development in our country was really slow. Although there was a level of development after smashing the "Gang of Four", it still lagged far behind what was needed by population growth, industrial development and the improvement of people's living. Total grain production exceeded the best level in history, but per capita supply of grain was only slightly higher than the level in 1957. Rations in many places were not enough to meet the farmer's needs. Total production of cotton, peanuts, sesame production had not yet returned to the best level in history. The per capita supply of cotton dropped to the current 2.3 kilograms from 2.55 kilograms in 1957. The per capita supply of oil dropped to 5.5 kilograms from 6.6 kilograms.[276]

The imbalance between agriculture and industry was not only harmful to rural economic development, but also detrimental to the state's legitimacy resources because such an imbalance hinders the improvement of people's basic consumption and living standards, which consequently affects people's confidence in the party and socialism. After the Cultural Revolution, there were still shortages of food and other basic consumer supplies. The issue of how to help the people out of poverty was still not fully resolved. Therefore, in order to improve consumer living standards, top priority was given to rapidly increasing agricultural productivity. And to develop agricultural productivity, we must begin at the policy level. We had to change the rigid policy of grain purchase that suppressed the enthusiasm of agricultural producers, further stimulate agricultural producer's enthusiasm, and to increase production and supply of food and other basic consumer goods. As a result, a decision was made by the party at the Eleventh Meeting Third Plenary Session to raise the price paid for grain and other agricultural products. At the same time the state, through financial subsidies, kept the selling prices of food and other agricultural products unchanged to ensure urban resident's consumption level would not decrease. The bulletin of the Eleventh Meeting Third Plenary Session mentioned that:

The meeting felt that throughout a comparatively long period of time in future, the national food acquisition indicator should be stabilized based on the "fixed five year plan" for the years from 1971 to 1975. It is absolutely not allowed to over-purchase grain. In order to reduce the pricing difference in the agricultural and industrial product exchange, the Plenary recommended that the State Council raise the grain procurement prices by 20 percent in summer 1979 when the crop hits the market. Additional procurement will be priced at additional 50 percent increase from that price. The purchase prices of cotton, oilseeds, sugar, livestock, aquatic products, forest products and other agricultural products should also be adjusted with gradual increases accordingly. Based upon cost reduction, the manufacturer prices and sales list prices for agricultural machinery, fertilizers, pesticides, agricultural plastics and other industrial products used in agriculture, should be reduced by ten to fifteen percent in 1979 and 1980. The benefits from the cost reduction should be basically transferred to farmers. After the procurement price increase for agricultural products, we must ensure that the living standards of urban workers will not drop. The selling price for grains shall be fixed; the selling prices of other agricultural products as people's life necessity shall remain stable; some essential price increases should be compensated with appropriate subsidies.[277]

After that, at the CPC Central Committee Eleventh Meeting Fourth Plenary Session, the discussion was especially focused on how to speed up agricultural development; how to develop agriculture on a large scale. Also, specific implementation was made of the proposal presented at the Third Plenary Session to increase the purchase price paid for grains and to stabilize their selling price.[278] The measures mobilized the enthusiasm of the majority of agricultural producers, promoted food and agricultural product development and greatly relieved the tension caused by the food supply situation. With the market being re-established, the supply of agricultural products greatly improved. This policy not only increased farmer's income, but along with the state's implementation of financial subsidies to keep the selling price of food and agricultural products unchanged, it also brought benefits to city residents. Food consumption levels were greatly improved.

In addition to the problem of imbalances between agriculture and industry, the ratio of light to heavy industry was seriously unbalanced too. In 1979 at the Central Work Conference, Li Xiannian gave a detailed description of this disorder: during the first Five Year Plan period, heavy industry accounted for 46.5 percent of the entire capital investment, while light industry accounted for only 5.9 percent. During the third Five Year Plan period, investment in heavy industry was 57.4 percent, and light industry was 4 percent. During the fourth Five Year Plan period, investment in heavy industry was 54.8 percent, and light industry was 5.4 percent. In 1978, investment in heavy industry was 55.7 percent and that in light industry was only 5.7 percent, which was even lower than during the "First Five" period. These figures above may have some level of incomparable factors, but they do reflect the disproportion between light and heavy industry. As light industry lagged behind, the market supply of major light industrial products could not meet people's needs. There was lack of competitiveness in exports too.[279] In addition, size of the fuel and power industries compared to other industries was severely unbalanced.[280]

After the Eleventh Meeting Third Plenary Session, the Communist Central Committee established the approach of "adjustment, reform, rectification and improvement."[281] Adjusting imbalances was one of the priorities of their work. For the imbalance situation between light and heavy industry, the central government proposed speeding up the development of the textile industry, bringing light and heavy industries into proportion, so that the supply of goods would satisfy domestic purchasing power and was accordingly adapted to the growth of exports. Investment in the textile industry was to be increased appropriately. It was also determined to appropriately increase the foreign exchange needed for the construction of light industry, to develop some light industry with less required investment, and would yield more profit quickly, to meet domestic and international market needs; and to develop less heavy industry with high investment and long construction time. We must give priority to ensure the coal, electricity and raw materials required for the production of light industry are available. Under this premise, re-arrange the production of steel and other heavy industries.[282] The policy reversed the strategy implemented over the years to develop heavy industry as the priority. Its purpose was to avoid the trend of developing heavy industry at the expense of basic necessities (i.e., consumer goods). The Central Government clarified that the supply of necessities was the priority. Developing them should have priority over the production of the means of production. Li Xiannian said: In the planned economy, we must first properly arrange, in line with current production levels, the people's needs of clothing, food, housing, usage, transportation, and then arrange infrastructure construction. When the supply of raw materials is limited, there must be a better distribution in sequence. First, we must ensure the minimum production needs to grow necessities. Second, we shall ensure the production needs for the growth of the means of production. The remainder will be used for capital construction. In his view, this order is for the purpose of maintaining basic living needs, and avoiding the undue expansion of infrastructure. Not doing this will fail to improve people's lives, and will not increase labor enthusiasm. The four modernizations will be difficult to achieve.[283]

Corresponding to the severe imbalance of agriculture, light industry and heavy industry, there was a serious imbalance between accumulation and consumption. Li Xiannian described the situation of the imbalance of accumulation vs. consumption: for more than a decade, the average income of farmers hardly increased; worker's employment opportunities had expanded, but average wages had not increased. There was a lack of investment in collective welfare, staff housing, utilities, environmental protection, culture and education. There were also some problems. The proportion national income being saved in the past two years was actually up, 31 percent in 1976, 36.5 percent in 1978, both higher than that of 1958, and much higher than the 24 percent in the "First Five" period and 26 percent in the "Third Five" period. In more than the past decade, a large number of factories were built with "skeleton" but no "meat". He admitted frankly that the saving rate was too high.[284] On one hand, the neglect of consumption led to the situation in which people with money had no goods to buy. And on the other hand, many people had no money to buy things because of the longtime low-wage policy, and can only maintain basic subsistence, and their purchasing power was very low. At the same time, due to the low investment in collective consumption, there was a serious shortage of housing, utilities, and cultural and educational development was stagnant. In response, on behalf of the State Council, Li Xiannian said that economic development must be based upon improving people's living standard. We must try to bring the saving rate down below 30 percent in two or three years.[285] Li Xiannian also pointed out that the saving rate in 1979 would decrease to about 32 percent (4.5 percentage points drop from 1978) and to 30 percent in 1980. Afterwards, depending upon the actual situation, there would be continuous adjustments. In addition, investment in collective consumption will gradually increase to solve some problems accumulated in areas of urban construction, staff housing, culture, education and health.[286]

However, despite the measures taken by the central authorities, due to a variety of problems in the process, after two years of adjustments, the issue of serious imbalances in the national economy was still fundamentally unresolved. Furthermore, the state encountered fiscal difficulties. At the end of 1980, Zhao Ziyang pointed out in a report that after the Party's Eleventh Meeting Third Plenary Session, the central government affirmed its policy to adjust, reform, rectify and improve the national economy, which should have brought about a fundamental change in economic development. However, over the past year, we did not recognize seriousness of the problem. The ideology within the party itself was also inconsistent. After raising rural and urban resident's consumption standards, the overall level of the basic construction was still not coming down. Twenty-two large import projects that should have stopped did not stop. Local and regional enterprises purposelessly built a number of duplicate construction projects. Capital expenditures by the state on basic construction and a variety of projects exceeded their budgets, resulting in financial difficulties. Consequently, the central government decided to conduct a major economic adjustment.[287]

The result of such severe imbalances in national economy made the CPC Central Committee further realize that the pursuit of high savings, along with aimless and excessive infrastructure building was not a path to success and had many flaws. He said that this old path was not to be repeated in future.[288.] By the end of 1981, at the fourth meeting of the National People's Congress, in his government work report, Zhao said that in future, in managing the relationship between people's living standard and construction, the principle the state adhere to is to ensure people's living standard first.[289.] On this, in his government work report, Zhao Jiyang emphasized the importance of giving priority to the consumer goods industry so as to accelerate its development.[290]

By the early 1980s, the series of measures taken by the CPCC and the state since the

Third Plenary Session of the Eleventh National Congress, on the proportions of agriculture, light and heavy industry, and the ratio of accumulation to consumption gradually showed results. Regarding the consumer goods industry, because the government set guidelines and took a series of specific measures to focus on producing consumer goods, light industry greatly advanced. Merchandise varieties increased, quality improved, and the market improved significantly in comparison to that of the previous years. Substantial manufacturing growth of consumer goods for several consecutive years played a significant role in meeting people's needs in urban and rural areas, enriching market with prosperity, stimulating economic activities, maintaining the entire industry growth at a steady rate in order to increase fiscal income.[291] On the consumption funds, Zhao pointed out that the distribution of national income has undergone a significant change. From 1979 to 1981, due to the rise procurement price of agricultural, government subsidiary and tax reduction efforts to release the burden in some of rural areas, the state lost a total fiscal income of 52 billion RMB yuan which correspondingly increased farmer's income. During these three years, over 20 million urban jobs were created. With wage increase and introduction of an incentive system, the increase of state capital expenditure and revenue income reduction totaled 40.5 billion yuan, which correspondingly translated to the increase of labor wage income. These two activities reduced the state fiscal income by a sum of 92.5 billion yuan, which is 54% more than the original budget of 60 billion yuan. With a variety of effective measures, problems left from many years ago were resolved, people's living in urban and rural areas were improved, the proportion of consumption in overall national income went up from 63.5% in 1978 to 70% in 1981; the proportion of accumulation came down to 30% from 36.5% correspondingly. It should be said that the situation of serious imbalance between accumulation and consumption has been greatly improved.[292] Zhao Ziyang also suggested that during the sixth "Five-Year-Plan" period, the country continue to reduce the proportion of accumulation funds, appropriately increase the proportion of consumption funds, therefore to continuously improve people's living.[293]

On September 23, 1985, the Chinese Communist Party National Conference adopted "The Proposal of The Seventh Five-Year Plan of National Economy and Social Development" The Proposal stated that:

"Efforts should be made to expand the production of consumer goods industry, to actively develop the civil engineering and construction industries." During the period of "Seventh-Five", China's consumption in urban and rural areas will develop into diversity. People will be more particular about food nutrition and improved clothing. The proportion of spending on housing, high-end and mid-range consumer goods and consumer durables

goods will be greatly increased. To adapt to this situation, we must continue to focus on the production of daily necessities, while at the same time, we must increase the production of brand names and quality products, develop new varieties and new products, as well as new categories. The priorities should be food industry, garment industry, durables goods industry, which act as a catalyst for the development of the overall consumer goods industry."[294]

The Proposal also pointed out that in order to ensure the accelerated development of the consumer goods industry, the state should give priority to making available lending, foreign exchange, supplies of energy and raw materials, transportation, etc.[295] "During the 'Seventh Five' period, we must continue to increase manufacturing the daily necessities and, at the same time, make efforts to increase the supply of meat, poultry, eggs, milk, aquatic products, fruits, instant food and drinks, all kinds of fabrics, high-end clothing and accessories. There should be increased supply of television sets, refrigerators, washing machines, bicycles, the supply of complete sets of furniture and other goods."[296] "While increasing people's consumption, we must open a large number of additional commercial and services outlets, expanding all kinds of services around living."[297] "During the 'Seventh Five' period, there should be further build-out of basic public utilities such as water, sewer, electricity, heating, gas, roads, public transport and telephone facilities, so as to make people's lives more convenient."[298]

It is obvious from the "Seventh Five" planning that the strategy shifted completed from heavy industrial development to the consumer goods industry having strategic priority. In addition to the fact that expanded consumption helps to satisfy the state's obligation to improve people's material lives, economic development adopted a new growth model, in which economic development was driven by consumer demand. Along with the increased supply by the state of consumer durable goods such as televisions, refrigerators and washing machines, this led to a tidal wave of consumer durables in the late 1980s, mainly home electronics, that lasted for many years.

3. Reform of Wage System: Wage Growth Since the Reform and Opening up

Increasing supply of consumer goods had to be supported by raising the level of resident's income. Therefore, since the reform and opening up, in addition to shifting the strategic priority from heavy industrial development and increasing investment in consumer goods industry proportionately, the state continued to take measures in wage reform, gradually raising urban resident's income level. On 7 May 1978, the State Council promulgated "The Notice on Implementation of Reward and Wage System", which restored the piece-rate based wage system and a bonus system. "For those enterprises introducing incentive system, under the premise of the comprehensive national plan, the extraction ratio of the total bonus money (including the existing base and additional salary, the same below), is tentatively scheduled at no more than 10 percent of a worker's total standard salary." "For enterprises implementing piece-work based wage system and for those business services using a commission wage system, the bonus for over quota (and the commission) should be capped at 20 percent or less of a worker's standard wage."[299] By the end of 1979, wage upgrades were no longer based upon "political performance", instead they were mainly based upon employee's work attitude, their technical capability and the level of contribution." State-owned large and medium enterprises adopted rewards based upon retained profits, with corporate bonuses linked to the corporation's operational profits.[300] In 1983, the State took the first step to implement "taxes based on profits" among the state-owned medium and large enterprises. The state gave up the control of capping total bonus money in the enterprises. Instead, for those companies with better efficiency and more bonus funds to give out, the state capped the highest bonus payout. In 1984 the state implemented the second phase of "taxes based on profits" where the corporate bonus was linked to enterprise economic efficiency (profit after tax), and abolished the bonus caps. Bonuses given by enterprises were limited to a percentage of wages but the total payout amount was not capped. A bonus tax would be imposed upon the portion exceeding bonus limits.[301] In January 1985, the State Council issued "The Notice of Wage Reform of State-owned Enterprises", which proposed a wage reform program "connecting wages to labor efficiency", namely: the total wages at a state-owned enterprise was to be linked to the economic efficiency of the enterprise, and was to fluctuate accordingly with its level of economic efficiency. This reform meant that the state's regulation and control of enterprise wage system moved from the level of individuals to a global level. Worker's wage increases were primarily tied to the improvement of economic efficiency of their enterprise. As a result, enterprises obtained unprecedented levels of autonomy in wage distribution, moving away from the state's "big food pot" policy and the enterprise's so-called "iron rice bowl". Enthusiasm within the enterprises was improved. Wages for labor also significantly increased.[302] In 1987, the state implemented a personal income tax. In 1988 the state increased "wage and enterprise efficiency linkage" to 70 percent for the state-owned enterprises, and continues to perfect it.[303]

At the Fourteenth National Congress (1992), the party set the goal of establishing a socialist market economic system, to further promote market-oriented wage reform. In 1994, the state implemented a new tax system that is intended to achieve the goal set at the Third Plenary Session of the Fourteenth National Congress of establishing a modern enterprise system. The new tax system stopped collecting adjusted payroll and bonus taxes from enterprises and institutions.[304] In 1996, the state began to establish macro-guiding principles for the enterprise wage system. Its main contents include: first, establishing a system of wage guidelines, namely: by issuing wage guidelines, the state indirectly guides enterprise worker's wages and the annual growth rate of their wages. Second, establishing a guiding price level for the labor market, to indirectly guide enterprises to set up different wages for different positions (jobs). Third, setting up a prediction and warning system for labor costs.[305] Jiang Zemin proposed at the party's fifteenth congress the "distribution systems dominantly based upon pay-by-contribution with coexistence of multiple distributions. Pay-by-contribution must be combined with allocation by production factors, giving priority to efficiency and fairness". "Allow and encourage capital, technology and other production factors to determine income distribution."[306] With the income distribution system moving towards the direction of "efficiency and fairness", worker's wages had gone up but at the same time the income gap between people also widened.

While the reform of wage system took place among the state-owned enterprises, the state reformed the wage system of administrative institutions. According to Hu Fangzhi's policy analysis, in 1985, state agencies and institutions began a structural wage system with job position being the main factor. The four components of the structural wage system are base salary, pay based on job type, seniority allowances and incentive pay, which decouples state institution's wage system from that of the enterprises. In 1993, the state conducted further wage system reform of state organizations and institutions. The reform follows four main principles: First, pay by contribution and manage by category. Set up wage systems for organizations and institutions accounting for their specific characteristics. Second, staff salary increases should be planned to be consistent national economic growth. Third, establish a wage level for government agency workers comparable to the wage level for state-owned enterprise's personnel. Fourth, adjust staff salaries with a cost of living index so that they are protected from price increases. Ever since, according to the provision of a position-based salary increase for every two years and a level-based promotion once every five years, most state-owned enterprise and institutional workers had their salaries increase in 1995, 1997, 2001 and 2003. In 1998 and 2003, state enterprises and institutions launched a level-based wage promotion mechanism. Also in 1997, the state adjusted the base salaries for government agency staff, which modified the state institution's salary standards accordingly. In addition, in 1999 and 2001, the state adjusted wage standards.[307]

Although there have been shortcomings of all sorts since the wage reform,[308] it is an undeniable fact that resident's income has been rising since the reform and opening up.

Although during the same period of time, the prices of consumer goods have risen, the adjusted gross wage has steadily improved. Table 4-1 shows the average wage increase since 1978.

Table 4-1   Average Wage Income Since Reform and Opening up
(with the previous year base at 100)

Year	Average wage currency (yuan)	Average wage currency index	Urban consumer price index	The actual average wage index
1978	615			
1979	668	108.6	101.9	106.7
1980	762	114.1	107.5	106.1
1981	772	101.3	102.5	89.9
1982	798	103.4	102.0	101.5
1983	826	103.5	102.0	101.4
1984	974	117.9	102.7	114.7
1985	1148	117.9	111.9	105.3
1986	1329	115.8	107.0	108.3
1987	1459	109.8	108.8	101.0
1988	1747	119.7	120.7	99.2
1989	1935	110.8	116.3	95.2
1990	2140	110.6	101.3	109.2
1991	2340	109.3	105.1	104.0
1992	2711	115.9	108.6	106.7
1993	3371	124.3	116.1	107.1
1994	4538	134.6	125.0	107.7
1995	5500	121.2	116.8	103.8
1996	6210	112.9	108.8	103.8
1997	6470	104.2	103.1	101.1
1998	7497	106.6	99.4	107.2
1999	8346	111.6	98.7	113.1
2000	9371	112.3	100.8	111.4
2001	10870	116.0	100.7	115.2
2002	12422	114.3	99.0	115.5
2003	14040	113.0	100.9	112.0
2004	16024	114.1	103.3	110.5
2005	18364	114.6	101.6	112.8

(Source: *China Labor Statistical Yearbook*, China Statistics Press, 2001.)

Overall, since the reform and opening up, urban resident's real wages have increased steadily (taking into account the income gap, the wage income of some industries, some companies and some officers must have ben higher than the average real income growth rate). Thus on the one hand, people's purchasing power has gone up. On the other hands, with more variety, improved quality and an increasing quantity of consumer goods, consumer enthusiasm keeps rising. Objectively speaking, at least in the early days of the reform and opening up, the improvement of living standards clearly played an important role in rebuilding the party and state's legitimacy resources.

In the era of the planned economy, the state's shift of policy focus from developing heavy industry to developing consumer goods manufacturing not only followed the logic of economic performance, but also is compliant to the logic of legitimacy. The long-term policy of suppressing consumption not only led to a lack of consumer goods, but also caused the state a crisis of legitimacy resources. This crisis reached its peak during the Cultural Revolution. To overcome the crisis and to rebuild the legitimacy resources of the party and state, Deng Xiaoping initiated economic reforms. One of the objectives of the reform was to improve and enhance people's material and cultural living standards, particularly, consumer's daily lives. To achieve this goal, the state increased the proportion of capital invested in the consumer goods industry and raised the wages of urban residents so that they would have more purchasing power, which subsequently raised consumer enthusiasm tremendously. This enthusiasm not only compensated for the lack of consumption during the planned economy era, but also restored the people's confidence in the party and the state, thereby increasing the party's and the state's popularity. Legitimacy was reconstructed. Clearly, during the social transformation period, especially in the early days of the social transformation, people's standards of living carried political significance. It was through the continuous improvement of people's material and cultural lives, through tangible experiences that they could touch and feel, that people benefited from the reform and opening up.

4. Ending the "Unified Purchase and Sale" System: the Example of the Abolition of Food Ration Tickets

Before the reform, the food problem was never resolved. The unified purchase and sale of food and other items ensured a stable supply of agricultural products in the city, but failed to overcome food shortages. This situation worsened during the Cultural Revolution. Farmers who had private plots of cropland and livestock, as a household sideline, were labeled the "tail of capitalism" and were to be eliminated by the state. The state canceled the trade fairs and operated a single agricultural policy of "taking grain as the key food supply", which caused either monotonous agricultural supplies or shortages. Meanwhile, with population growth and a stagnant consumer goods industry, people's daily lives became more impoverished. This situation led to people being increasingly dependent on their work unit. Urban residents, on the one hand, with the help of ration coupons for food, fuel and cloth, had the guarantee of basic survival. On the other they completely lost their autonomy. The state gained the control of urban residents through their monopoly and control of the basic means of survival. In this sense, the consumption pattern formed under the unified purchase and sale was not only a type of economics but also a type of politics.

One of the reasons for stagnant agricultural production was the unreasonable procurement pricing for food. National food procurement prices were set by the state unilaterally. Since the overall food purchase price increase in 1966, purchase prices had not changed until twelve years later in 1978. At the same time, in order to increase the production of food, local production teams increased their use of pesticides and fertilizer. Along with requiring more labor than basic farm practices, this caused the cost of agricultural products to rise. Food procurement prices became disproportionately low. According to a survey, in 1976 the production costs plus agricultural tax for 1296 production teams growing 6 major agricultural products, averaged 11.60 yuan per 100 jin (based upon 0.80 yuan per work day), while the average purchase price was only 10.75 yuan, lower than cost by 0.85 yuan.[309] In accordance with the CPC recommendation at the Eleventh Meeting Third Plenary Session, the State Council decided on 1 March 1979 that starting in the summer of 1979 when the summer grain crop was released, the state would raise grain procurement prices by 20 percent, with a 50 percent increase for purchases over the committed quantity. Procurement prices for cotton, oilseeds, sugar, animal products, aquatic products, forest products and other agricultural products were raised accordingly.

The shortage of food and agricultural products was also connected with the country's extreme left agricultural policy. During the ten years of the Cultural Revolution, most food and trade fairs were closed, and negotiated purchase and sale was also stopped. In December 1978, it was pointed out in the bulletin of the party's Eleventh Meeting Third Plenary Session that: "the commune member's private plots and household sideline production as well as trade fairs are all necessary components that are complimentary to the socialist economy. Nobody shall interfere."[310] It was stated more clearly in "Regulations on the Work of Rural People's Communes (Trial Draft)": "After completing the acquisition quota set by the state, the commune members should be allowed to trade through the market, a small amount of grain and oil. The food sector can participate in negotiated purchase and sale." Since then, food trade fairs and bargaining business were gradually restored and developed.[311]

On 30 March 1981, the CPC Central Committee, State Council issued the notice of the State Agricultural Committee's "Report on Positive Development of a Variety of Commercial Operations in Rural Areas". The notice called for correcting the practice of producing only grain, which "squeezed out a variety of businesses and family sidelines, resulting in imbalance of agriculture." The Report proposed, "farming more of herbivorous livestock and fish, producing more cooking oil, vegetables, sugar, starch, dried fruits and wild plants and other products to expand the variety of food, gradually improving the food structure."[312] The family-based responsibility system was introduced, increasing farmer's production autonomy. Farmer's enthusiasm was greatly enhanced by being able to pursue household sideline production and a variety of business initiatives.

After the Eleventh Meeting Third Plenary Session, a few regions took leading roles in implementing the various aspects of the agricultural production responsibility system. These practices were certainly reaffirmed by the leaders of the state. It was recognized in a national summary of the "household responsibility system", which was promoted in early 1980s in rural areas. It ensured that after farmers fulfilled the procurement quota assigned by the state and paid the agricultural tax due, they would own all remaining product. The implementation of the system greatly stimulated the farmer's enthusiasm to produce. Agricultural products increased rapidly. From 1978 to 1983, in addition to the increased year over year food production (5-year increase of 27.1 percent), cotton production increased 114 percent, oil production increased 102.2 percent, animal husbandry production value increased 100.4 percent and as a fraction of total agricultural output value increased from 13.6 percent to 15.3 percent, fisheries production increased by 30 percent and as a fraction of total agricultural output value increased from 1.4 percent to 1.8 percent, of which 87.5 percent was the growth of freshwater aquaculture with an average annual growth of 13.2 percent.[313]

Just a few years after the Eleventh Meeting Third Plenum, with the rapid growth of agricultural production, the situation of long-term agricultural shortages was fundamentally changed. After the government raised the purchase price of agricultural products in 1979, the output of economic crops grew rapidly, and for the first time there were oversupplies instead of the previous shortages. By 1982, crops other than sugar were close to or had reached market saturation. Oversupply in food production appeared slightly later. After the 1983 harvest, farmers for the first time ever encountered "Difficult Grain Sales". By 1984, "Difficult Grain Sales " became universal. There was excess food supply, with total amount of over-supply of as much as 300 billion kilograms, with grain supply exceeding demand by 5.4 times.[314]

On the basis of agricultural growth the State Council adjusted the procurement base and scope of the unified purchase and sale. Starting in 1983, the state gradually reclassified some second-class categories of products to the third-class, which allowed free buying and selling. At the end of 1984, there were only 38 products under the system of unified purchase and sale (of which 24 were kinds of Chinese herbal medicine). On the pretext of adjusting the range and scope of unified purchase, the state gradually expanded the scope of the market mechanism in agriculture, carried out negotiated purchase and sale of food, established trade centers and wholesale markets, and restored the traditional rice market.[315]

The policy of unified food purchase was terminated given the conditions of oversupply. In 1985, with the oversupply of food, the state canceled its unified grain purchases and started contract purchase, which was: before the planting season, the commerce department negotiates with farmers and signs a purchase contract. The state set food pricing using a "reverse three-seven" ratio: 30 percent of food intake is set at the original unified procurement purchase price, 70 percent is set at the original purchase price above the assigned quota. After entering the purchase contract, no unit was allowed to issue mandatory production orders to farmers. Farmers, upon satisfying the national food contract, owned the remaining grain and could trade in the market freely. Their business was not subject to the original division of labor restrictions. Agricultural management, processing, and consumption units could directly enter into purchase contracts with farmers. If the market price were below the unified purchase price under the original system, the state would purchase at the open market price to protect the interests of the farmers. However at this time, urban residents were still under cheap ration ticket system.[316]

With substantial production increases of food and agricultural products, shortages of food were gone. The longtime outstanding problem of shortages of food and agricultural products was fundamentally resolved. With more variety and increased quantity, the food situation in the urban environment underwent a fundamental change, with a decrease in direct grain consumption, for instance: in 1985, the average annual consumption of grain for an urban resident was 134.76 kg. In 1993, it dropped to 97.78 kg. At the same time, the consumption of meat, poultry, eggs, aquatic products, alcohol and other products increased (see Table 4-2). As the production of meat, poultry, eggs and other agricultural products requires grain products for animal feed, there has been an increase in indirect grain consumption.[317] (Table 9-1).

Table 4-2 1985 and 1996 Average per Person Annual Consumption of Agricultural and Subsidiary Products, and Indirect Food Consumption by Urban Households

Item	1985	Indirect Grain Consumption	1996	Indirect Grain Consumption	1996 vs. 1985 Increase in food consumption (percent)
Meat (kg)	16.75	58.63	39.20	137.20	
Poultry (kg)	3.24	9.40	3.97	11.51	
Fresh Eggs (kg)	6.84	23.94	9.64	33.74	95.86
Fish (kg)	6.71	13.42	23.10	46.20	
Liquor (kg)	7.80	31.20	9.72	38.88	
		136.59		267.53	

(Source: Pei-Gang Zhang, Liao Danqing, *Twentieth Century China's Grain Economy* (Huazhong University Press, 2002), 613.)

As mentioned above, in 1985 the state abolished unified grain procurement and replaced it with contract order, but at the same time the state maintained the unified sale of grain in the cities. As the grain purchase price and sale price had an inverse relationship (the purchase price was higher than the sale price), the state was burdened by the huge amount of subsidies. In the early stage of unified purchase and sale (1953~1960), when the price of the planned supply of grain was almost the same as the market price, the profit from the sale covered the cost of purchase and operating expenses. The state did not need to provide a subsidy. During the second phase of unified purchase and sale, from 1961 to 1978, the grain sale price was equal to or slightly higher than the purchase price. The state's subsidy was only needed to cover operating expenses. In 1966, the state raised food prices, but at the same time the state increased worker's salaries to compensate for the price increase. The third phase of the unified purchase and sale was from 1978 onward. The state not only needed to subsidize operating costs, but also needed to compensate for losses from buying high and selling low. Further, although unified purchase was canceled, unified sale still continued. The state's subsidies because of purchase prices being higher than sale prices in 1980 were 11.359 billion yuan, in 1985 increased to 20.248 billion yuan, and were 44 billion yuan in 1990.[318] Moreover, due to decreased direct grain consumption by urban residents, extra food coupons became negotiable securities in circulation, which led to speculation and arbitrage of the difference between coupon face value and the negotiated market price.[319]

Under these circumstances, the reform of "unified sale" was put on the agenda. In the spring of 1992, the Guangdong provincial government decided to abandon price control for food sales. Throughout the country, food sales in the cities were opened up. The system of "unified sale" was abolished. At the end of 1993, after being in effect for 40 years, the food ration system, whereby urban residents bought grain with food coupons from government owned grain stores, finally came to an end.[320] A legacy of the planned economy era, and tangible proof of the nation's control of the food supply to residents - food coupons - finally exited the stage of history. With the abolition of food coupons and the cancellation of clothing vouchers that had been announced earlier, urban resident's food and clothing consumption moved towards a market economy. In other words, basic living materials for urban residents were "de-nationalized" (i.e., the state no longer had a monopoly or control), and were no longer resources "within the system".

There were at least two kinds of dynamics in China's social transformation. One was a top-down reform, where the state advocated the reform. The purpose of this reform was to rebuild the legitimacy of the state. Another was the rise of resources "outside the system." With the formation of factors "outside the system" that were free from the power "within the system", the factors "outside the system" gradually became a factor in disintegrating the structure and elements of the "within the system." Overseas Chinese, foreign companies, foreign tourists, "the self-employed", international relations, etc., are all such "outside the system" resources. These "outside the system" factors continue to have an impact upon the factors of "within the system", and to some extent changing the factors that are "within system". In vast resources "outside the system", the impact of cancellation of food coupons and the adoption of market supply for grain on social change is particularly worthwhile mentioning.

Market supply for food helped break the monopoly and isolation of work unit system, which created an indispensable condition for the free flow of talent. When food supply is part of what the state controls, a major obstacle for the free flow of talent is the so-called "ownership of grain and oil." During that period, food was an element controlled "within the system". It was the power "within system". Loss of these "within system" resources meant the loss of life protection. When grain and oil is based upon market supply, people have the protection of resources "outside the system". People are no longer as dependent on their work unit with its ownership of grain and oil as they were in the past. Once people leave their work unit, whether because of conflicting interests or their own needs (e.g., "getting one's feet wet" in business), they were not as worried about survival as they were in the past. In this sense, the market supply of food reduced individual's reliance on their work units. Individual's independence and personal freedom were increased. Marketization of food supply creates the conditions for a labor and talent market.

The marketization of food supply is also indispensable for the creation of an environment in which people can move around and relocate freely. In the past, on business trips, people had to bring food coupons, because food in hotels and restaurants had to be purchased with them. When traveling out of province, people had to exchange their provincial food coupons for national food coupons. This coupon-based food supply system was one of the factors preventing large number of rural residents from moving out of rural areas. With the market supply of food, there were fewer obstacles for rural-to-urban migration. The end of food coupons created an environment for surplus rural labor to migrate to the cities. Abolition of food coupons was a necessary precondition for the free movement of labor across the country. Without labor moving freely, there would not have been the miracle of the economic boom in the southeast coastal areas in the 1990s.

Market-based food supply, along with market supply of other agricultural products, increased consumer autonomy. During the years when grain and other agricultural products are allocated by coupon system, consumers have no power to choose what they would eat. The question at that time was not "whether there is a choice?" Instead it was more a question of "whether there is food?" With the marketization of the supply of food and agricultural products, and the availability of more varieties of food, people began to have choices. They began to be able to satisfy their own needs for comfort and pleasure through consumption. People were no longer bound by the coupon allocation system. They could arrange their lives according to their own wills. Consumer life began to have a "private" meaning. "Private" social circles began to form that were gradually separated from the state. Individuals, being consumers, began to break away from the state's control, obtaining personal independence and autonomy. This shift laid the foundation of the upcoming rise of consumer culture.

B. Institutional Arrangements to Encourage Consumption

In the era of commodity shortages, consumer demand often had to be suppressed. That is to say, the country not only uses economic policy to curb consumption, but also use its propaganda machine and its ability to mobilize discourse to continue an attack on desire, pleasure, luxury and waste. However, near the end of the twentieth century, in the late 1990s, with excess production capacity and supply, the lack of demand became a constraint on economic development and the state had to adopt an economic policy to stimulate and encourage people to consume. Ideological condemnation and criticism of consumer desire gradually disappeared.

In the early days of reform and opening up, institutional arrangements by the state in the area of "consumption compensation" follow the "logic of legitimacy", because such a consumer policy has the function of restoring the popularity of the party and rebuilding its legitimacy resources. During that period, the improvement of the people's living standards had a strong political color. However, as the state gradually rebuilt its legitimacy resources, the Chinese economy moved toward a "buyer's market" economy, and as low domestic demand became an obstacle to economic development, the state began to establish institutional arrangements for encouraging consumption. Such institutional arrangements mainly follow "rational logic" rather than "legitimacy logic", because consumption returns to an economic role.

The reason why countries encourage consumption is because a lack of consumer demand has become one of the bottlenecks for economic development. The pace of economic development had become the main source of legitimacy in the new era. It is an overall problem. It is clear that, in a way, economic development is not only an economic issue but also a political issue. When lack of consumption drags on economic development, the state must take measures to intervene. This intervention subverted the national discourse of curbing consumption in the planned economy era and paved the path toward a consumer culture system.

Regarding the country's attitude toward consumption, 1998 can be seen as a turning point. First, during this period, the situation of goods shortages began to reverse. On 5 March 1998 at the first meeting of the Ninth National People's Congress, Li Peng pointed out in his government work report that by 1997, "the supply and demand of major means of production and consumer goods are either balanced or show a pattern of supply exceeding demand. The issue of shortages of goods that has been troubling the country is fundamentally resolved."[321] Moreover, there began to be "relative" product surpluses[322] during this period. According to the estimate by the former State Economic and Trade Commission, in the first half of 1998, there were zero shortages of the 601 kinds of major commodities. Before this, in 1996, only 7.6 percent of goods had an over-supply, and in 1997 the over-supply of goods rose to 31.8 percent, in 1998 it rose to 33.8 percent, and in 1999 it surged to 80 percent.[323] Secondly, after 1993, in order to control inflation, economic tightening measures were implemented in 1997 to achieve zero inflation. But this also led to deflation by 1998. The strategic restructuring of state-owned enterprises put a large number of workers 'out of work' (in 1997 the number of state-owned enterprise workers made redundant reached 12,750,000). Thirdly, housing system and social security system reform, in which the old government turnkey system was abolished, caused more uncertainty in people's expectations for the future. Individual savings were increasing and near-term consumption was decreasing. Fourthly, an unexpected international crisis — the Asian financial crisis — resulted in a decrease of China's exports to this region. At the same time, the direct foreign investment from this region to China was significantly reduced. Zhu Rongji said in March 1998: "Recently, the financial crisis in some Asian countries is a clear reflection of globalization of economic development. It has much stronger negative impact than expected. This financial crisis is not over yet. The outlook is still not clear. Negative impact and further potential impact on our country should not be underestimated."[324] A combination of all these factors caused an overall contraction of the Chinese economy.[325] Faced with these difficulties, the state had to take measures to ensure sustained and rapid economic development. Increasing domestic demand was the countermeasure.

At the party's Fifteenth Congress in 1997, Jiang Zemin pointed out in the congress report: "Improving people's lives, improving people's living standards, are the fundamental purpose of the reform and opening up and economic development. On the basis of economic development, people across the country will live a comfortable life and gradually progress to a higher level. We must make efforts to increase the real income of urban and rural residents, broaden the field of consumption, and guide rational consumption. While at the same time improving material life, we must enrich people's spiritual life, beautify the living environment, improve quality of life, especially improve housing, health, transportation and communication conditions, and expand service consumption."[326] Subsequently, in February 1998, regarding the financial crisis in the Southeast Asia, he specifically instructed: "To counter this financial crisis, the most fundamental thing is to secure our domestic economic work and to enhance our ability to withstand and resist risks." One job is to " maintain the sustained, rapid and healthy development of the national economy's momentum, under the premise of continuously improving and optimizing the economic structure. To maintain this growth momentum we must make efforts to increase domestic demand and to play the huge domestic market potential."[327]

One national policy to expand domestic demand was to adopt a proactive fiscal policy to expand the demand for domestic investment.[328] At the same time, consumer demand had to be increased as well.[329] On 5 March 1999, at the second meeting of the Ninth National People's Congress, in his government work report Premier Zhu Rongji admitted, "Clearly we still see many difficulties and problems in our progress. These mainly are: the market demand is not high, so it is difficult to jump start."[330] Therefore, he advocated expanding domestic demand and continuing to implement the proactive fiscal policy: "While we increase investment demand, we must also take effective measures to guide and expand consumption demand so as to form a double boost to economic growth. We must increase urban and rural resident's income through various channels, especially the low-income people's income. We must accelerate the development of consumer credit, promote urban housing reform and support the resident's ability to purchase big-ticket consumer durables items. We must actively guide the people to increase spending on cultural activities, entertainment, sports, fitness and tourism, expanding the service consumption areas. We must stimulate market liquidity and vigorously develop the domestic market, especially the rural market."[331]

Jumpstarting and expanding the consumer market became a strategic choice for future economic development. One policy to expand the consumer market was to increase farmer's income and to increase state aid to the poor, especially the efforts[332] to directly relieve poverty in the west central areas and develop the rural market.[333] Efforts had to be made to increase urban and rural incomes, especially of the low-to-middle income group.[334] We had to make arrangements for the livelihoods of workers who were laid-off by the state-owned enterprises and re-employ them,[335] increasing their employment opportunities. In August 1998, the state adjusted the income of low-income urban residents and increased the living assistance to workers laid off by state-owned enterprises and other low-income people. At the same time, the wages of government employees were raised. Since 1999, there have been three large wage increases for employees of government agencies and institutions.[336] By 2000, Zhu Rongji realized that one of the reasons why people reduced their immediate spending was their sense uncertainty about the future caused by the reform of the social security system. He proposed to, "Improve the transparency of the reform measures, to improve people's psychological comfort and encourage them to increase immediate consumption." Meanwhile, he said, "We must actively foster new consumption hot spots such as housing, to make housing construction truly to become an important industry. We must actively develop telecommunications, tourism, culture, entertainment, health, sports and the consumption of other services."[337] In October the same year, at the Fifth Session of the Party's Fifteenth Congress, "The CPC's Proposal for the Tenth Five-Plan for National Economic and Social Development" was passed. The Proposal points out: "To improve urban and rural people's lives and to continuously raise the standards of urban and rural resident's material and cultural living are both the starting points and destinations of economic development. They are also dynamics in increasing domestic demand to ensure sustained economic growth. To move towards a more affluent and comfortable life, we must further improve the urban and rural resident's consumption of food, clothing and durable goods, optimizing the consumption structure and increasing consumer services. We must increase urban and rural living space, improving housing and environmental quality; also we must develop public transport, encourage families to purchase computers and cars, and increase the telephone penetration rate. We must strengthen the construction of urban and rural public facilities to improve the consumer environment."[338] The state had already taken measures to encourage families to purchase cars and improve the penetration of telephones. In October 1998, the Bank of China promulgated the "The Scheme of Auto Loans" which allowed major banks offer consumer credit for automobile loans. After that, the state issued another series of policies to encourage families to buy cars. In addition, in 1999 the state took measures to improve telephone penetration. Starting 1 March1999, the Ministry of Information Industry made structural adjustments to the charges and rates of post and telecommunications services. Telephone installation and connection fees, Internet charges, long distance surcharges and other charges dropped significantly, which greatly improved the popularity and use of telephone and Internet services.[339]

In September 1999, the State Council revised the "Methods for Implementing Annual Leave and National Holiday Days Off". The national legal holidays were increased from 7 days to 10 days. And by adjusting workdays and weekends around May Day, National Day and the Spring Festival, three holidays with seven consecutive days off work were formed, the so-called "golden weeks", guaranteeing people's travel. Domestic tourism began to be popular. In April 2001, the State Council issued a notice on further accelerating the development of tourism, pointing out that "We must place the development of domestic tourism in an important position, by increasing products and services that meet the expectations of the domestic market, while at the same, moderately developing outbound tourism."[340]

In March 1999, the People's Bank of China issued a "Suggestion of Implementing Individual Consumer Credit Lending", calling on all localities to conduct consumer lending, and starting 1999, allowing financial institutions to offer consumer credit.[341] In 2001, the State Planning Commission proposed policies and measures to accelerate the development of the service industries. They also proposed "of improving the consumer service environment, complete the consumer policy, promote healthy and civilized consumption patterns, to guide urban and rural residents to increase consumption and therefore create a social atmosphere that helps expand consumer services." At the same time, China had to "establish an individual credit system, improve the process of consumer credit lending and raise the standards of credit services."[342] The development of consumer credit played a major role in stimulating consumption, especially the consumption of housing and automobiles.

In March 2002, at the fifth meeting of the Ninth National People's Congress, in his government work report, Zhu Rongji further reaffirmed and refined the policy of expanding domestic demand. He pointed out that:

"To increase domestic demand, we must first increase the income of urban and rural residents, especially low-income groups, to nurture and improve people's purchasing power. First, we shall take more effective measures, do everything possible to increase farmer's income and reduce their burdens. Secondly, we shall further improve the social security system in the urban environment. ... Thirdly, we shall continue to raise the basic wage of government employees appropriately, and increase the retiree's of agencies and institutions salaries accordingly. On the basis of improving economic efficiency, the income of workers at enterprises with various types of ownership shall be increased as well. ... Fourthly, we will actively expand employment and reemployment. ... Fifthly, we will expand consumption and improve the consumption environment. By deepening reform and adjusting policies, we will eliminate all barriers that limit consumption. We encourage resident's consumption on housing, tourism, automotive, telecommunications, culture, sports and other services, fostering new consumption hot spots."[343]

The statement above can be said to summarize the measures taken by the state to expand domestic consumption since 1998. These measures are not merely expedient or temporary. In fact, these policies define the era of the state's encouragement of consumption. The reason is because China's economic development has entered a different mode from the previous times, namely: consumption has become an essential driving force for economic growth ever since. This change is a structural change. Its socio-economic and cultural impact is immeasurable. At the least it means that the policy of controlling consumer desire set by Mao Zedong had become obsolete. Moreover, the policies to encourage consumption were in tension with the austere tone of the official discourse of plain and thrifty living.

In any case, the economic logic caused changes in official attitudes. Realizing that consumption had become the driving force behind economic development was a significant ideological change for national leaders. The state's attitude toward consumption, from discouraging it in the past to the present encouragement, had undergone a fundamental change. This change brought more a profound and objective understanding of consumption to national leaders. For example, Li Lanqing once said that large-scale production would inevitably bring about big spending, because without big consumption, there would be no need for large-scale production. And large-scale consumption requires large supply. Large supply encourages consumption, and large consumption further promotes large-scale production.[344] Obviously, Chinese leaders had realized that China was already in the consumer economy era, and that economic development is ultimately driven by consumption. The stimulating effect of consumption on the economy was consistent with the party's fundamental purpose of promoting socialist economic development in order to meet people's growing material and cultural needs. In this sense, consumption gets a double meaning: an economic meaning (stimulating economic growth) and a political significance (the fundamental purpose of the socialist modernization drive).

The marriage of the consumer economy and consumption politics was reflected dramatically when the Party proposed the goal of building a moderately prosperous society at its sixteenth congress. Building a moderately prosperous society is not only a political task, but also an economic development objective, in which consumption plays an important role. On the one hand, people's consumption is an objective indicator measuring how well-off society is. On the other hand, consumption is a means of achieving a well-off society. What does the goal of building a moderately prosperous society mean? Jiang Zemin pointed out in his report to the Party's Sixteenth Congress: "Based on optimizing structure and improving efficiency, we shall strive to quadruple gross domestic production in 2020 from that in 2000, strengthening overall national power and international competitiveness. Basically we shall accomplish industrialization, build a perfect socialist market economic system and a more dynamic, more open economic system. There is substantial population growth in the fraction in urban areas. The increasing trend of differences between workers and peasants, between urban and rural, and regional disparities shall gradually be reversed. The social security system will be more healthy, a relatively full employment society, a general increase in household assets, and the people will lead more affluent lives."[345] "The prevalent increase in family assets, and people's having more affluent lives," are obviously a reflection of consumption in a well-off society. The fundamental purpose of building a moderately prosperous society is to improve the nation's material and cultural level of consumption. Jiang Zemin said: "The fundamental purpose of economic development is to improve the living standards and quality of live of people across the country. Along with economic development, urban and rural resident's income must be increased. We must broaden the consumer field, optimize the consumption structure to meet the diverse material and cultural needs of the people."[346] Thus consumption is a means to achieve well-off society. Therefore, we must "implement policies to encourage consumption, to form the double pull of investment and consumption demand to help economic growth." [347] In his government work report at the second meeting of the Tenth National People's Congress, Wen Jiabao also pointed out:

"China's consumption share of GDP is low, is not conducive to the steady expansion of domestic demand, is not conducive to sustained and rapid growth and to forming a virtuous cycle. Efforts must be made to increase urban and rural incomes and to improve the resident's purchasing power; increase the income distribution regulation, improve low-to-medium income people's consumption capacity; develop consumer credit lending, perfect the consumption policy, and improve the consumption environment; meet changes in consumption structure, expand consumer services, and improve the structure of production supply; the reform measures should be conducive to enhancing consumer confidence and therefore, to create good consumer expectations and increase immediate consumption. Through continuous efforts to gradually change the situation of a high investment rate but a low spending rate."[348]

From the curbing consumption (pre-reform) to promoting appropriate consumption (1980s to late 1990s) and then to adopting policies to encourage consumption (since the late 1990s), not only means that the legitimacy of consumption has been restored, but also, along with economic development, the status and role of consumption has increased. Consumption, starting from logical legitimacy, gradually transformed itself to rational and instrumental logic. It is this institutional background that gave birth to China's urban consumer culture and consumerism. In other words, consumer culture and consumerism are embedded in the fabric of the system.

C. Transformation of the Collective Consumption System: The Example of Housing Reform

The policy of jumping-starting domestic consumption demand in the late 1990s had some not very satisfactory effects. This was partially related to the reform of the collective consumption system. In the late nineties the reform of collective consumption had negative effects to private consumption.

After reform and opening up, especially in the late nineties, the state gradually reformed the social welfare system left from the era of the planned economy (including education, health care, housing and other systems). The idea was to improve the efficiency of welfare, the supply of consumer information and consumption itself. To this end, the market factor was introduced into the collective welfare consumption pattern. The overall direction was to introduce of market forces, consumer products and services in order to improve the collective efficiency of supply, and to reduce the financial burden on the government in providing collective products and services. Therefore, the state's use of the "legitimacy logic" principle in the area of collective consumption, before the reform and opening up, was gradually replaced, especially after the late 1990s, by "rational logic". This logical replacement was not accidental but inherent. When the state had succeeded in raising the level of private consumption and thereby reconstructed its legitimacy resources, collective consumption's role in constructing legitimacy is naturally weakened. However, inability to supply collective consumer products and service may easily lead to a crisis of legitimacy. Therefore, improving the supply efficiency of collective consumer products and services, implementing a rational logic, became the state's choice.

Here, I only use collective welfare housing as an example to explain the supply of the collective welfare and the model for the reform of its consumption.

Before the reform and opening up, and for some time afterward, housing was a welfare benefit. Low-rent housing was provided by work units for their staff. State run enterprises, relying on retained profits to provide housing to workers gave, in a sense, additional compensation to low-wage workers. It was also a way to maintain the necessary conditions for the reproduction of labor. Workers accepted low wages, while at the same time, they looked forward to welfare provided by their work unit. This had become an implicit "social contract"[349] between the workers and their work unit or the state. We previously discussed that the state's provided workers with welfare (collective consumption resources), based on legal requirements (which was reflected in the idea that the common people had become their own masters and the state's paternalism). But, as Zheng Gongcheng and others also noted, state funding was the sole channel of resources to supply welfare, and there was serious shortage of funds. At the same time, since the cost of the welfare is free, this stimulates the expansion of the worker's desire for social welfare, leading to an increasingly prominent conflict between the supply and demand for social welfare benefits. The result was that long-term residents lived in poor housing conditions. In 1978, the average living space per capita for urban residents was only 3.6 square meters, in 1985 it was only 5.2 square meters, even by 1990 it was only 6.7 square meters.[350]

Zheng believed that the traditional welfare system led to serious alienation of employee benefits. It is mainly reflected in the following. First, the nature of alienation is that employee benefits are no longer governmental (or social) responsibilities, but are transferred to business enterprises. Second, the level of alienation is demonstrated in employee benefits being equally important as income. Third, the function of alienation is to counteract the earlier egalitarianism in the distribution of welfare, which was allocated equally regardless of labor performance, fostering laziness rather than stimulating labor enthusiasm. Fourth, the effect of alienation is for benefits to foster an employee's "personal attachment" to their working unit. As the benefits provided by the unit become a living necessity, it has become difficult for workers to give them up. Therefore, welfare provided by the work unit leads to the unit's control over worker's spiritual freedom and freedom of movement[351]. Lu Feng pointed out that the unit is a "patriarchal welfare community", having on behalf of the state employees an infinite responsibility for them in illness or death. "The low-wage policy, the principle of egalitarian distribution of consumer goods and personal property, and the denial of ownership rights, other than for daily necessities, can not but make important aspects of personal life depend on the work units for providing social welfare, such as housing."[352] This kind of dependence on the benefits provided by the unit not only hindered the freedom of workers, but also limited their movement, preventing a labor and talent market from establishing itself. As part of the economic reform, in 1980 Deng Xiaoping proposed the sale of public housing, rent adjustments, promoting the overall vision[353] of housing reform. The reform of the housing system started in the late 1980s.

On 23 September 1985, the Chinese Communist Party's National Conference adopted the "The Recommendations of the Seventh Five-Year Plan of National Economy and Social Development". The Recommendations included the following about commercialization of urban housing:

"Actively promote the commercialization of urban housing, speed up the civil construction industry, and make the construction industry to become a pillar of industry. For a long time, China's urban housing system was based on the policy to build collectively, allocate collectively and to collect low rents. This approach is not conducive to solving housing problems, and increased the state's financial burden, causing the civil construction industry to lose vigor and vitality, resulting in the urban resident's purchasing power focusing lopsidedly on consumer durables. A more mature approach must be made as soon as possible to gradually implement the major policy of housing commercialization."[354]

The central government was clearly aware, that in order to solve the housing shortage and reduce the financial burden on the state, the welfare housing benefit system had to be reformed, commercializing the housing market. Because this involved a wide range of complex issues, in the mid 1980s, the state first conducted a pilot reform of the housing system in a number of cities (Yantai, Tangshan, Bengbu, Changzhou, Jiangmen) to accumulate some experience. After several years of pilot testing, on 25 February 1988, the policy paper "The State Council on Implementing National Urban Housing System Reform in Stages" was published. In this document, the State Council approved the implementation plan of the Leading Committee on Housing System Reform, reforming the housing system by stages. The State Council also decided that starting 1988, within three to five years, housing system reform would be implemented in batches in urban areas. Taking into consideration different local conditions, the State Council suggested that reform of the housing system be conducted mainly by the provinces, autonomous regions and municipalities. In the future, the state would manage the macro-unified national policy, strengthen planning and guidance, and summarize and promote successful experiences. The State Council required local governments to follow the guidance of the unified national policy, to start from their own actual situation and local conditions, to chose right practices for their own situations, and demonstrate their full initiative and creativity.[355]

Issued by the State Council and drafted by the Leading Committee on Housing System, the "Implementation Plan of the National Urban Housing System Reform" (hereafter, "Implementation Plan") discussed in detail the housing system reform program and processes. The Implementation Plan pointed out that objectives of China's urban housing system reform were:

"According to the socialist planned economy, we must achieve the commercialization of the housing market. We will start with the reform of the low-rent public housing system, and will gradually change the current distribution of commodities to money allocation so that through purchase and sale, residents will have access to housing ownership or the right of use. Therefore, housing, being a large consumer item, will develop a healthy market, which formalizes the virtuous cycle of capital investment and return in housing. This is not only helps solve the urban housing problem, but also promotes real estate development as well as the development of the construction and building materials industries."[356]

Here, for the first time, the state proposed commoditizing housing in a policy paper. It also proposed to change the proportion of welfare provided by housing compared to that provided by cash. Meanwhile, for the first time in a policy document, the state put forward the issue of the privatization of residential property. Overall, the goal of housing reform was to change the nature of housing away from being a welfare benefit, and to change the original tangible housing benefit distributed by the work unit into housing subsidies in cash with free circulation in the market (becoming part of wages), so that the residents are able to obtain the ownership or the right to use through the commercial exchange.

The Implementation Plan stated that to achieve this goal, the reform of housing system included several elements: First, changing the structure of the allocation of funds. Gradually the funds that paid for housing would be moved into normal consumption channels so that the previously hidden costs of housing construction and repair would be apparent, and could be budgeted. Funds for housing would be incorporated into wages. Second, reforming the planning and administration system that has treated housing as a fixed capital investment and establish an advisory planning and administrative system that treats housing as a commodity product. Third, through a variety of reforms of the fiscal, taxation, wage, finance, pricing and real estate management systems, gradually establish a healthy source of capital for housing. Fourth, adjust the industrial structure, opening up the real estate market, real estate finance and real estate development. According to the above objectives and elements of reform, the Implementation Plan stated that the mission for the next three to five years was to adjust the rent of public housing, curb the "unreasonable" demand for housing, promote the ability of individual workers to buy a house, and lay the foundation for housing commercialization.[357]

The Implementation Plan put forward specific policies for housing reform. One was reasonable rent adjustment for public housing in order to curb "unreasonable" demands and to encourage workers to purchase housing. With rent increases in public housing, there was accordingly a need to issue housing vouchers to workers living in there (vouchers without cash value). Housing vouchers could be saved into a bank as an individual housing purchase fund. The Implementation Plan also proposed to rationalize the sources of funding for housing, building a three-level housing fund for cities (towns), enterprises and institutions, and individuals. Housing funds at these levels could only be used for housing production, management and consumption. They were not to be used for other purposes. They were centrally managed as segregated funds by the appropriate financial institutions of each city and their use was monitored.[358]

The Implementation Plan also proposed the sale of public housing to actively organize and promote the purchase of housing by individual workers. "With the purchase of housing, the individuals will own the property. They can use it, make it their inheritance or sell it. Upon sale, an individual is only entitled to retain the profit on the portion of the price paid for the property, less government subsidy."[359] Although such home ownership has limitations, it confirms the state's recognition of individual ownership of the property, which is of special significance. In the past, the state denied urban resident's property rights in all but everyday living necessities. It was the first time ever that the state encouraged workers to purchase public housing in which they would hold private property rights, promoting the privatization of public housing.

In 1991, the State Council issued a Notice to continue the reform of urban housing system actively and steadily. In addition to supplementing and refining the details of The Implementation Plan issued by the State Council in 1988, the Notice especially defines the property rights of workers who have purchased public housing. The Notice required that, "In the future, for public housing purchased at the market price, after the purchase the buyer has full property rights. Workers buying public housing shall follow the state's rules in the size of housing allowed for purchase, and will pay the standard price. They have the full ownership of the property after the purchase, and can inherit or sell; for the part of the housing that exceeds the national standard, the buyer will pay market price."[360] Here, the country distinguishes between partial property rights and full property rights. The State allowed workers with partial property rights to sell the property on the market five years after purchase. The sales proceeds, after deducting the applicable taxes, were distributed proportionally to the state, the collective and individual according to the allocated property rights.[361]

In 1994, at its fourteenth congress, the party declared the goal of economic reform was to establish a socialist market economic system. Especially after the Fourteenth Meeting Third Plenary Session, to carry out "The CPC Central Committee's Decision of A Number of Issues around Establishing Socialist Market Economic System", on 18 July 1994 the State Council issued "The Decision by the State Council on Deepening the Urban Housing System Reform" (hereafter, The Decision). The Decision pointed out that the fundamental objective of the urban housing system reform was: "to establish a new urban housing system that is adaptive to the socialist market economic system, to realize the socialization and commercialization of the housing market; to speed up housing construction, improve the living conditions and meet the growing urban demand for housing."[362]

The Decision provides the basic details of urban housing system reform: First, "change the investment in turnkey housing construction from solely by the state and unit to a system composed of three parties, being the state, units, and individuals." Here it clarifies that individuals should be responsible for the costs of housing construction. Second, change "the unit's construction, distribution, maintenance and management to a system of socialization and professional operation." Here, it clearly describes market-oriented housing supply and management, separating the housing supply and management system from the unit's management. Third, "Change the distribution of housing benefits to wage distribution based upon work performance." Here, it explicitly highlights the change from an allocated housing benefit to a monetary wage distribution. Fourth, "with the target being low-income families, establish a supply system for affordable housing with the nature of social security, and a supply system for luxury housing for high-income families." This clearly states that in parallel to housing commercialization, for low-income families, the state must implement a supply system for low-cost housing having the nature of social security (affordable housing). Fifth, "establish a housing provident fund system." The Decision for the first time proposed the concept and system of a "housing fund". Sixth, "develop housing finance and housing insurance, establish a housing credit system with co-existence of policy orientation and commercialization." Here, through financial support and insurance policies, the state established a housing credit system, promoting the commercialization of housing. Seventh, "establish a standardized model real estate exchange market and develop a social housing maintenance and management market. Progressively realize a virtuous cycle of capital input and output in housing, to promote the development of real estate and related industries." Orderly measures were presented above for the development of real estate.[363]

For the first time the Decision proposed a full implementation of a housing provident fund system. The Decision stated that employees of all types of enterprises should contribute to housing provident funds by following the principles of "personal savings, unit subsidies, unified management, special use." Thus the housing provident fund system was established. Money for housing was accumulated by individual workers and their units, by the monthly allocation of a percentage of wages. The workers owned the funds and their monthly contribution went into individual accounts. The fund could be used for the purchase, construction, or repair of housing. Retired workers would get the principal balance plus interest balance once the account closed. The Decision also stipulated that the current contribution from the individual and their work unit to the housing provident fund is specified to be 5 percent.[364]

The Decision reaffirmed the effort to reform housing rents, to steadily sell public housing, and promote the privatization of public housing. It also proposed a detailed discounting method for converting worker's length of service into part of the purchase price. The Decision further reaffirmed the need to clarify home equity. Workers buying housing at the market price possess full property rights and can legally put it on the market. They are required to pay taxes. After taxes, any balance from the sale of the property goes to the individual sellers. Workers who buy housing at its cost price, own the property rights. Generally, domestic law allows that after five years, they can put the property on the market for sale. After paying back "land right" fees and paying the required taxes, the individuals can sell the property and retain the balance. Workers buying the housing at the standard price own a partial property right, which includes possession, use, and priority in disposal of income and return. The property can be inherited. Ownership proportion is accounted by the ratio of the standard price paid to the cost price. Workers purchasing housing at the standard price can put it on market after five years.[365]

In 1997 Southeast Asian countries suffered a financial crisis, which gave the Chinese economy a severe shock. In response to this crisis, the state adopted a policy of expanding domestic demand. Speeding up housing construction was incorporated into the national strategy of expanding domestic demand. On 24 March 1998, Premier Zhu Rongji, suggested that "we must be determined to stop the allocation of housing so that the supply and demand of housing is market oriented. This way housing construction can truly become part of the new economic growth."[366] Following that, on 3 July 1998 the State Council issued "The Notice of Deepening the Urban Housing System Reform to Expedite Housing Construction" (Hereafter, Notice). The Notice pointed out that the guiding principal of deepening the urban housing system reform was: "Steadily promote the commercialization of the residential housing market, socializing it, and gradually establishing a socialist market economic system and a new system of urban housing; aligned with China's specific national conditions. We must speed up housing construction, to promote the housing industry to become a new source of economic advancement, to meet the constantly increasing housing needs of urban residents."[367] Here is a new formulation of the guiding principal of the housing industry, namely: the state should promote the housing industry to become a new economic growth center. Residential housing was to be included in the state's policy for jump-starting consumption and driving economic development.

The Notice stipulates the "objectives of deepening urban housing system reform are: to stop the physical allocation of housing. Progressively introduce a housing purchase system. Establish a multi-level housing supply system with its main focus on an affordable housing supply. Develop housing finance; train and regulate the real estate market."[368] Here, a new symbolic policy was to stop the physical allocation of housing and gradually implement its commercialization. The Notice also provides a specific timeframe to implement this policy: "Stop physical housing allocation during the second half of 1998. Progressively introduce a commoditized housing distribution system. Regarding the specific times and steps: they are to be decided and managed by the provinces, autonomous regions and municipalities based upon local conditions. After the allocation of housing is ended, newly-built housing is only for sale, not for rent."[369] This policy meant that urban residents in the future would no longer have a housing allocation as a form of welfare. The supply of housing began to move toward a fully market-oriented and socialized system.

In parallel with the commercialization and socialization of residential housing market, was the monetization of housing. The Notice stated that "worker's housing funding sources are: wages, the housing fund, individual housing loans, and in some places housing subsidies converted from the original construction funds owned by the original units."[370] In order to increase the worker's purchasing power for residential housing, The Notice decided that the state must broadly implement and continuously improve the system of housing funds and developing housing finance, "to expand the scope of individual housing loans. All commercial banks are available in all cities and towns to make housing loans.

Remove the restriction on the sizes of individual housing loans and appropriately relaxing the repayment time limits of individual housing loans."[371] The Notice also required accelerating the reform of the housing maintenance and management system, establishing a highly socialized, specialized, market-oriented property management system that combined owner's autonomous management and professional property management companies.[372]

Thus, a multi-leveled national institutional framework has been shaped around the commercialization of housing supply and distribution, and the commoditization of private home ownership. Under the mechanism of this framework, work units gradually phased out supplying residential housing as a benefit. Workers no longer had a relationship with their units for the supply and distribution of housing. In other words, urban resident's housing problem became their relationship with the housing market. The state was out of the direct supply of housing. Resident's dependence on the state and their work units for housing had changed into a relationship with the market for choosing and buying housing products. This shift had a profound impact on worker's relationship with the work unit and state. On the one hand, employee's dependence on the work unit and state was weakened. They became more independent. Workers began to appear in the role of a consumer in a market, pursuing the satisfaction of their desires. On the other hand, the state withdrew from directly supplying housing to reduce its financial burden, which has led the public to some extent lose the "dependency". It also planted the seeds for local governments to push up housing prices by "land finance" from 2003 and onwards. When the housing market soars and prices go up, affordable housing is no longer available or economical to build (local governments are unwilling to provide it or are reducing its supply). Many members of the lower-to-middle income classes cannot afford housing, and the residential housing has once again become a social problem.

From transformation of the residential housing system, we can see that the state gave up the "legitimacy logic" it possessed when it supplied housing as welfare, instead turning to "rational logic." Residential housing's commercialization, marketing, commoditization and privatization have greatly improved the efficiency of providing housing and significantly reduced the state's financial burden. Because of the adherence to "rational logic" during the residential housing transformation, it caused the system of housing as social insurance to lag far behind the marketing and commercialization processes in the residential housing industry. And in turn it has led to a series of social problems. This "rational logic" was also used in the reforms of health, education and other traditional areas of collective consumption. It led to dramatic changes in the model of redistribution, and to a series of negative economic, social and political consequences.

Transformation of Labor Incentive System: From Sacred Motives to Secular Incentives

As discussed in the previous chapter, workers originally had high motivation to work. However, due to the long period of low wages and the restrictive consumer policy, and especially because of the crisis of faith caused by the Cultural Revolution, there was a dramatic decline in worker's enthusiasm. However, we need to distinguish two cases here. One is the situation where workers are lazy or inert. The other case is where although workers have a very positive attitude but for various reasons, the overall labor efficiency is very low, and worker's enthusiasm for their work was wasted. The former can be called "motivationally inefficient labor". The latter can be called "consequentially inefficient labor." Both cases existed in the past.

Before the Cultural Revolution, under the influence of the idealism of the time, workers were generally more positive. "Motivationally inefficient labor" was not particularly obvious. At that time, the major issue with labor efficiency was "consequentially inefficient labor." It was principally caused by mistakes in macroeconomic policy. For example, the Great Leap Forward movement was typical of "consequentially inefficient labor." With regard to this, Liu Shaoqi, at the "Seven Thousand People's Congress" made extensive and lengthy comments. He said: "Some comrades, indulging in this kind of charade, or so-called 'mass movement', which in fact, was divorced from the masses and violated the people's interests. ... In our work there has been much ordering without thinking through, this is reckless performance. Many cadres are self-righteous, trying to be smart and not discussing with the people, arbitrarily forcing people to buckle down to some stupidity. People's energy is wasted in vain, and the masse's enthusiasm is dampened."[373]

In addition to macroeconomic policy mistakes, rigid structure was also one of the factors contributing to "consequentially inefficient labor". Under the constraints of the traditional planned economic system, people worked actively because of their personal beliefs. That is to say, this system solved the problem of labor enthusiasm through sacred stimulation. But it is hard to solve the problem of worker's initiative and creativity. People are willing to be the "screw", with their obedience to superior leadership. But it is difficult for them to take initiative and to be creative. The reason for lack of this initiative is due to the fact that they have been taught to obey the command of the leadership. As a result, people had the enthusiasm to obey authority, but not to exercise their own initiative and creativity.

During the late period of the Cultural Revolution, in addition to "consequentially inefficient labor" (e.g., the imbalance of agriculture and light industry, which caused a shortage of consumer goods) issue, "motivationally inefficient labor" became a prominent issue as well. The process of reform and opening up was not only to solve the "consequentially inefficient labor" issue, but also the problem of "motivationally inefficient labor". The very early stage of the reform started by changing "motivationally inefficient labor". During the Cultural Revolution, the state had also tried to solve this problem. But that solution was to use political campaigns and ideological and political work, such as the political campaign of "Grasping Revolution and Promoting Production". However the fact is that "Grasping Revolution" does not necessarily "Promote Production". Often it hinders the development of production.

"Motivationally inefficient labor" is caused by principally by labor's lack of enthusiasm. For instance: work does not contribute, soldiering, "taking faked sick leave", lazy, and so on. The Cultural Revolution especially impacted the management level, causing a decline in the work unit's management authority, making them afraid to strengthening labor discipline, with management in fact relaxing and loosening labor discipline.[374] We can say that "motivationally inefficient labor" is a product of a motivation crisis. It is also the crisis of the incentive system. In a country with persistent poverty, when worker's beliefs are in crisis, it is difficult for sacred stimulation to function effectively.

The sacred stimulation system mobilizes the enthusiasm of workers mainly through the ideological and political work to educate the people in idealism and collectivism. Material incentives were suppressed to the lowest level possible. For a long time, poverty persisted and economic conditions deteriorated (i.e., nearly two decades of hard work had not improved people's material life, and life was worse in certain ways), which meant that the blueprint with grand promises made by the state early on had come to nothing. This left a great sense of frustration. When the Cultural Revolution shook people's faith the party, the state faced a crisis of legitimacy. It was difficult to continue to rely on idealism and the spirit of collectivism as the main education methods to effectively mobilize labor enthusiasm. It was in this context that increasing people's income and improving consumer's living standard gained a positive meaning. On the one hand, it helps to restore the prestige of the party and to rebuild the state's legitimacy resources; on the other hand, it can mobilize people's enthusiasm to work. Along with the restructuring of the country's consumption system, the labor incentive system underwent a corresponding gradual transition from sacred to secular incentives.

Secular stimulation includes material incentives and systematic incentives. On the one hand, due to the strict implementation of a socialist distribution system according to work, material incentives played a strong role in motivating workers; the idea of working more and being paid correspondingly more greatly increased worker's enthusiasm. On the other hand, material reward only is not enough to mobilize labor enthusiasm. Changes had to be made to the traditionally highly centralized, rigid, system of economic management, to decentralize and to improve the autonomy of local governments, enterprises and production workers. It was necessary to take measures to improve production responsibility, labor discipline, labor contracts, and implement a modern management system to improve labor productivity, revitalize the economy, promote the development of productive forces, on this basis improving people's standard of living. The following analysis examines the evolution of the secular incentive system in the early days of the reform and opening up, and how it gradually replaced the sacred incentive system.

A. Material Incentives and Distribution According to Work System

As early as 1974~1975, when Deng Xiaoping presided over the State Department, he faced the issue of the decline in labor discipline and labor enthusiasm. In order to reverse the situation, he reorganized industry. One of the measures was the implementation of socialist principle of "Distribution According to Work; More Work, More Pay", in order to mobilize the enthusiasm of workers. He said:

"Sticking to the principle of distribution according to work is always a big problem during socialist construction. We have to think hard with our brain. The so-called material incentives in the past are not a lot. Shall different contributions get different treatment? Being workers, some of them are more technical than others. Should they be given raise or better treatment? Is the technical staff's treatment to be improved? If, regardless of contribution, technical level, capability, severity of work, wages are all forty or fifty yuan, which seems to be equal pay on the surface, but in fact it is not consistent with the principle of distribution according to work. How could we mobilize people's enthusiasm? I think people engaged in work with exposure to high-temperature, high altitude, underground, toxic types, should be treated differently from those engaged in normal types of work."[375]

When he was back again in 1977, Deng Xiaoping once again stressed the principle of distribution according to work:

"We must adhere to the socialist principle of distribution according to work. Distribution according to work is to be allocated based on the labor's quality and quantity of work. In accordance to this principal, we assess worker's levels of wages, mainly looking at the quality of his work, his technical level, and the amount of his contribution.

Political attitudes are also considered. But to make it clear, political attitudes should be reflected in a good performance for socialism, with great contributions. If looking at labor's political attitudes rather than his work determines his pay, it is not distribution according to work, but according to politics. In short, distribution should be based only on work, not on politics or government. Nor is it based on qualifications."[376]

Under the sacred incentive system, the state placed too much emphasis on spiritual stimulation while neglecting personal material interests. Therefore, when people started to doubt their faith, this kind of mental stimulation was no longer effective. So, recognizing individual interests not only helps restore the people's faith, but it also helps improve labor enthusiasm. Of course, recognizing individual interests is not to favor personal interests over national and collective interests. Instead, it is to acknowledge individual material interests on the premise of uniting them with national and collective interests. Deng Xiaoping said: "We advocate the distribution according to work, recognizing material interests, to fight for the material interests of all the people. Each one should have some level of his individual material interests. But by no means, shall one set aside national, collective and the other's interests, to promote only one's own material interest. We do not advocate everyone looking up for 'money'."[377] He proposed that we should not apply the requirement for the advanced workers to the masses. We cannot deny the people's material interest, we cannot merely emphasize self-sacrifice and ignore the common people's material interest. He pointed out that: "Not talking about 'more work, more pay', not emphasizing people's material interests, only works with a small number of advanced workers. It does not work with the masses. We can do this for a period of time but not for the long-term. Revolutionary spirit is very valuable. There is no revolutionary action without revolutionary spirit. But revolution is generated on the basis of material interests. If we only speak of the spirit of self-sacrifice, but ignore material interests, that is idealism."[378] The decline of labor initiative before the reform was the result of talking only about the mas's sacrifice while ignoring their material interests. Deng Xiaoping said: "We implemented a low-wage policy, a policy intended to last for a very long time. Currently the maximum wage for eighth level workers is one hundred and a few yuan. In the future with the development of production, wages will increase gradually at all levels."[379] Wage increases show the new focus on the masse's material interests. Obviously, the emergence of a secular incentive system with characteristics of material incentives is a result of the failure of sacred incentive system, with its focus on sacrifice.

In the low-wage environment, egalitarianism leads to harmony between people. However, egalitarianism in the Cultural Revolution led to a growing number of negative effects, one of which was to shelter the underperforming. Since there was no difference between doing much or little work, doing well was no different from doing badly, compensation being in all cases similar. Because of this, some people developed a "free rider" mentality, working half-heartedly, only muddling through and adopting slovenly habits. In turn, this hurt the initiative of "advanced elements". To change this situation, Deng Xiaoping advocated recognizing the material interests of individuals, and that personal income and benefits must be linked with individual labor contribution. He said: "Qualified management personnel, qualified workers, should enjoy a relatively high treatment that is truly according to work. This is not bourgeois. The average wages of one hundred twenty yuan will not make him a capitalist. Does this lead to a negative effect on other people's enthusiasm? There will be grumbling. But it stimulates people to go upward. Economic development increases worker's incomes, which in turn promotes economic development. So is the case with agriculture. It will increase farmer's incomes, which in turn will stimulate agricultural development and consolidate the worker-peasant alliance."[380] In Deng Xiaoping's view, only by implementing distribution according to work, and by linking together the state, collective and individual interests, can the state mobilize labor enthusiasm. As he stated: "Socialism is the first stage of communism. It is a very long historical period. We must implement the principal of distribution according to work. We must link together the state, collective and individual interests so as to mobilize labor enthusiasm to develop socialist production."[381]

Deng Xiaoping's views and ideas on distribution according to work, material incentives, recognition of personal material interests, directly influenced the policies of the party and state. For example, in the "The Decision of CPC Central Committee on Accelerating the Development of Agriculture", the CPC Central Committee asserted that material interests are one of necessary components of mobilizing enthusiasm: "Without some sort of the material interests and political rights, it is impossible to see any initiative naturally occurring within any class. Whether our policies meet the needs of developing productive forces, is to see whether such a policy can mobilize the enthusiasm of the production workers."[382] Vice Premier Li Xiannian also pointed out at the national planning meeting:

"We want to promote the development of production, we must adhere to socialist principle of doing our best individually, and of distribution according to work. We must link economic development with people's immediate interests so that workers often receive tangible material benefits. This further mobilizes the enthusiasm of the masses. In previous years, due to the interference and sabotage by Lin Biao and the 'Gang of Four', the

egalitarian tendency in distribution was severe. A lot of work was done in recent years and the situation has gotten a bit better. Still we must continue to implement the principle of distribution according to work conscientiously to overcome egalitarianism."[383]

In implementing the principal of "distribution according to work, more work, more pay", and breaking with egalitarianism, uneven distribution among the people must be allowed. In Deng Xiaoping's view, egalitarianism hampers worker's enthusiasm: "Practice of egalitarianism, eating from the 'iron rice bowl', will never improve people's lives. Labor enthusiasm is never up."[384] "The practice of egalitarianism in the past, and eating from the 'iron rice bowl', is actually common backwardness and common poverty. We are at a disadvantage because of this. The top priority of the reform is to get rid of egalitarianism and to break the 'iron rice bowl'.[385] In breaking egalitarianism, we must allow gaps between people's incomes, allowing some people to get rich first to demonstrate the result, so as to lead others to get rich together. Deng Xiaoping first proposed this view at the end of 1978 in one of his programmatic speeches:

"On economic policy, I think we should allow some areas, some enterprises, some workers and peasants, who work hard and score high, to get more income first and live a better life. Some people living better first will inevitably demonstrate and influence their neighbors and lead other regions and other work units to learn from them. This will continue to make waves to push the national economy to move forward, so that people of all nationalities can get rich relatively quickly."[386]

In the city, the principal of distribution according to work was reflected in the reinstatement of the bonus system. Companies retained part of the profits that had been paid to the state and used a portion to pay their staffs bonuses. In 1984, in their decision on the economic reform, the CPC Central Committee further noted that with the wide implementation of taxing excess bonuses, and the expansion of their various economic responsibilities, enterprises generally established employee bonus systems based on their operating conditions. The state only taxed the part of a bonus exceeding a limit. The Central Committee said that in the future they would take necessary measures to link worker's wages and bonuses to their institution's economic efficiency. Within an enterprise, there should be wage gaps and grade differentials, which help reward the hard working and punish the lazy, praising the excellent and punishing the laggard. This fully demonstrates 'more work, more pay, less work, less pay' and fully reflects the difference between mental and physical labor, between complicated labor and simple labor, between skilled labor and unskilled labor, and between heavy labor and non-heavy labor.[387] These practices aimed to break the earlier egalitarianism in distribution. In its decision on economic reform CPC

Central Committee consider that egalitarianism was a serious obstacle to the implementation of the principle of distribution according to work. Widespread egalitarianism inevitably destroys social productivity. Of course, socialist society will ultimately achieve the goal of common prosperity. However, common prosperity by no means the same as all being equal to the average. It is not the same as — and it cannot be the case — for all members of society to get rich at the same speed, and at the same time.[388] Clearly the central government's decision reflects Deng Xiaoping's thinking.

In Deng Xiaoping's view, allowing some people to get rich first is, in fact, only a means of development. The ultimate objective is the common prosperity of people across the country. However, in achieving this "common prosperity", we will have to allow certain time lag between the "first group of the rich" and "the group that gets rich later on". This time difference is necessary. The goal of socialism is to gradually make all the people rich, which is against polarization and against the emergence of a new bourgeoisie. Therefore, after some people get rich, certain measures must be taken (e.g., income tax, etc.) as necessary restrictions. Deng Xiaoping said:

"The purpose of socialism is the common prosperity of people across the country, not polarization. If our policy has led to polarization, we have failed; if a new bourgeoisie is created, we would really have gone astray. What we advocate is some regions getting rich first, to inspire and lead other regions to become wealthy. And the areas getting rich first can assist the backward areas to develop. For the same reason, we advocate some people getting rich first. Some restrictions should be imposed on the individuals who have got rich first, for instance, income tax. Also, we promote that those people getting rich first, to voluntarily contribute to education, road construction. Certainly, we don't engage in apportionment. And now is not the time to over-promote, but it should be encouraged."[389]

How shall we accomplish the goals of "some people getting rich" and ultimately "common prosperity" for all the people? Deng Xiaoping believed that we could use the taxes from the rich regions to support the development of poor areas. In other words, national tax policy would, through transfer payments and redistribution of wealth, stimulate the economic development of backward regions.[390]

However, it is important to point out that in the early stage of the reform and opening up, while recognizing the role of material incentives, Deng Xiaoping and other macro-actors did not forget the traditional ideal and teaching of self-sacrifice. Although sacred inspiration was not effective with many people, as it was a tradition, the country should continue to carry it forward. Deng Xiaoping said: "We must always educate our people, especially our youth, to have a dream. Why in the past could we struggle through very difficult conditions and overcome hardships to win revolutionary victory? We have a dream. We have belief in Marxism and communism. We work for the cause of socialism, with the ultimate goal of achieving communism. Of this, I hope the public will never forget or ignore."[391] Deng Xiaoping said that all party members should continue to promote fairness, integrity and spirit. Even in the environment of the reform and opening up, communist ideology and morality should continue to flourish.[392]

However, the ideals and morals advocated by Deng Xiaoping were only a requirement for party members and other advanced elements. For the majority of the people, they were an exhortation. More important, ideological and political work had to be combined with material interests. As Li Xiannian said: "It is wrong if we do not care for the masses, do not speak of their material interests. But it is also wrong if we rely only on bonuses rather than political and ideological work to mobilize the enthusiasm of the masses."[393] Practically, however, the effect of traditional sacred incentives was greatly reduced relative to that of secular incentives. Although during the whole period of reform and opening up, the CPC Central Committee never gave up ideological and political work, never gave up promoting communist ideals and moral education, objectively, material incentives and institutional incentives replaced spiritual motivation. They have become the most important driving forces in mobilizing labor enthusiasm. We can say that the foundation for secular incentives was laid at the beginning of the reform and opening up. In parallel with the progress of the reform and opening up, secular incentives became more institutionalized and became the core of mobilizing labor enthusiasm. Sacred incentives, if they still play a role, it is one of increasingly limited role extent and scope. Their role has been marginalized.

On 14 November 1993, at the Fourteenth Meeting Third Plenary Session, the CPC Central Committee passed "The Decision on A Number Issues by CPC Central Committee In Establishing A Socialist Market Economic System". It was proposed to "Establish an income distribution system with distribution according to work being the main factor, giving priority to efficiency, and considering fairness. It encourages some areas and some people to get rich first, taking the road towards common prosperity."[394] For the first time, the Decision proposed "giving priority to efficiency and consideration to fairness" in the area of distribution. Encouraged by this policy, labor enthusiasm was further activated. However this also led to rapidly widening income gaps among local areas, across departments of the government, across different industries, enterprises and classes, resulting in the polarization of income distribution. This was a departure from Deng Xiaoping's original suggestion that the goal was "common prosperity". The problem has attracted the attention of the new national leaders. Through the concept of the "harmonious society", they have tried to correct the negative effects of this policy.

B. System Incentives and Labor System

The traditional economic system was a highly centralized planned economy. Localities, enterprises and production workers produced according to the orders of higher authorities. They lacked production and management autonomy, which led to local governments, enterprises and workers lacking initiative, innovation, and creativity. Therefore, one of the goals of the reform and opening up was to reform the economic structure, changing the over-centralized management of the planned economy. This meant reducing the central government's authority and interests, increasing the autonomy of local enterprises and production workers in order to mobilize all aspects of their enthusiasm. On the eve of the Eleventh Meeting Third Plenary Session, the central government held a working meeting that set the tone for the Third Plenum. At the closing session, Deng Xiaoping delivered an important speech entitled "Emancipating the Mind, Be Realistic, United and Looking Ahead". The speech was actually the central theme of the Third Plenum. At the meeting, Deng Xiaoping said: "Now the management authority of the Chinese economy is too centralized. There should be a bold plan to delegate. Otherwise the enthusiasm of four areas, being the state, localities, enterprises and individual workers, cannot be demonstrated. It is not conducive to implementing a modern economic management system and improving labor productivity. We should allow local government, enterprises, production and management teams to have more autonomy."[395] The speech set the tone for economic reform. Devolution of power, expanding the autonomy of local enterprises and production workers and mobilizing their enthusiasm became a starting point for economic reform. After the market-oriented reforms, the state further proposed the goal of establishing a modern enterprise system. In the reform of economic system, the reform of incentive systems has two aspects. One is to reform the central government's incentives to local business and enterprises. The other is to reform enterprise's incentives to their workers. The discussion below is only focused on the latter aspect.

The reform of the incentives offered by enterprises to their workers was part of the country's overall economic reform. The implementation of material incentives, distribution according to work, "more work, more pay", were all part of the overall labor incentives reform. In addition to material incentives, the state also established system incentives. Although system incentives and material incentives are intertwined, here we will concentrate on analyzing the progress due by the state's system incentives.

In the view of the nation's leaders view, labor enthusiasm was not only to be stimulated in the positive sense (e.g., reward for exceptional labor contribution), but was also to be sanctioned in the negative sense (e.g., punishment for violation of labor discipline). To this end, it was necessary to set up a system through which workers become the main body and they are responsible for the consequences of their actions. Deng Xiaoping said that during the Cultural Revolution period, one reason for the decline in labor productivity was the destruction of reasonable business regulations and labor discipline. Deng Xiaoping said that Lin Biao and "Gang of Four", "Incited sectarianism in workers, incited protest, instigated production downtime, brutally persecuted the factories and enterprises of the revolutionary cadres, model workers and union activists. They destroyed manufacturing facilities and entire industries and brought the entire national economy into a state of anarchy. They are against the socialist planned economy, opposed to the principle of distribution according to work, against all reasonable rules and regulations, and disrupting labor discipline."[396] Therefore, economic reform was to restore the reasonable rules and regulations, to establish management accountability, necessary labor discipline, and to strengthen enterprise management.

Deng Xiaoping believed that in industrial reform, the first thing was to reform the management system of the enterprises, improving their efficiency.[397] One cause of management inefficiency was the lack of personal responsibility by management.[398] Lack of personal responsibility causes bureaucracy and inefficiency in business management. "A project was assigned, but nobody would ask whether it was carried through. Nobody cares whether the project is done well or badly. There is an urgent need to establish a strict responsibility system."[399] How was the situation to be changed? Deng Xiaoping proposed a system with a director or manager in charge must be put into place. He said: "Our enterprises must adopt a director or manager responsibility system under the leadership of the party. We must establish a strong production chain of command."[400] The establishment of a system with director or manager in charge was to prevent buck-passing and irresponsible bureaucracy. Therefore, "when we implement the system of the factory manager in charge under the party's leadership, we must clearly define roles and responsibilities."[401] To make the responsibility system really work, Deng Xiaoping also pointed out, that there must be measures taken in the following areas: "First, we must expand management's authority. Designate authority equally as responsibility is designated. Second, we must choose right person for the right job. Third, we must give them strict assessment, reward and punishment. ... The reward and punishment must be connected to material interests."[402] Deng Xiaoping also argued that in order to improve management efficiency, it was necessary to change the traditional practice of political and ideological work. China also had to learn from advanced foreign management methods.[403]

After establishing a system with a director or manager in charge, to clearly define management responsibilities and allot rewards and punishments, there must also a system in place to measure and appraise employee's performance, so that rewards, punishment and penalties assigned. As early as 1978 before the convening of the Third Plenum, commenting on the past management practices that depended on only spiritual encouragement, Deng Xiaoping stated that it was required to establish a performance appraisal system for penalties and rewards. While continuously encouraging spiritual motivation, material incentives had to be adopted and a bonus system reestablished. He said:

"We must implement the appraisal system. Assessment must be done rigorously, comprehensively, and often. All industries need to do this. There must be rewards, penalties and punishment. After being assessed for doing well or badly, there must be different compensation, rewarding the good and punishing the bad. We follow the principal of spiritual encouragement being the main incentive system with supplementary material incentives. Giving out medals and certificates is spiritual encouragement and a political honor, which is necessary. But there should not be less material incentives either. On this, all effective measures we used in the past should be restored. The bonus system must be restored. Inventors must be rewarded. People making special contributions will be given bonuses."[404]

Thus, after the Eleventh Meeting Third Plenary Session, the bonus system proposed at the "Eight National Congress", but criticized and banned later, was quickly restored. The responsibility system for employees of enterprises was also built up. In January 1982, the CPC Central Committee and State Council made a decision overhauling state-owned industrial enterprises (Hereafter, the Industrial Consolidation Decision). The Industry Consolidation Decision proposed to rectify and perfect the economic responsibility system, and to improve business management. The Industry Consolidation Decision also stated that the purpose of implementing the economic responsibility system was to link the economic interests of enterprises and workers with their economic responsibility and their economic effects, to mobilize the enthusiasm of enterprises and workers, to address the issue of uniform treatment among enterprises, and among the staff within an enterprise. In addition to establishing accountability between businesses and the state, in the implementation of the economic responsibility system within a single enterprise, the same principle should be followed linking responsibilities, rights, benefits and interests. From the department and workshop to the team, group, and individual, we must establish and perfect the system of personal responsibility, so that individual economic interests can be linked to the collective outcome, and the individual labor contribution can be connected to the principle of distribution according to work. We must improve the keeping of original records, measurement, statistics, accounting and other basic work. We must set up advanced quotas for average production and consumption, and strengthen quota management.[405]

The Industry Consolidation Decision also stated that besides establishing personal responsibility within the enterprise, there must be an overhaul and strengthening of labor discipline, in which the reward and punishment system is strictly enforced. "In order to strengthen labor discipline, we must establish a strict reward and punishment system. The employees with good work attitude, discipline, and a proven track record, should be recognized and rewarded; for serious violations of labor discipline, the enterprise has the right to impose financial or administrative actions in accordance with the relevant provisions. Punishment will increase if there are no corrections; dismissal and expulsion will be imposed as ultimate penalty."[406] The Industrial Consolidation Decision allowed companies to dismiss employees. It altered the life-long job security system that had existed in the past. From a system perspective, this changed the situation where "doing well" and "not well" were treated the same with lax discipline and labor conditions. The past system of relying upon ideological and political education and the practice of criticism and self-criticism was replaced by a system of clear penalties and rewards.

In May 1984, the State Council made interim provisions to further expand the autonomy of state-owned industrial enterprises. It states that "directors (managers) have the right to reward and punish the stuff, including giving promotions, incentives, or the sanction of expulsion." "Based upon their specific needs and their industry's characteristics, under the guidance of public sector labor recruitment, enterprises can hire employees publicly after examination. Enterprises have the right to resist any arbitrary personnel placement by any departments or individuals that violate state regulations."[407] These provisions greatly strengthened director's or manager's personnel management autonomy. The state no longer used an "all encompassing" approach to employment (i.e., a system of lifetime job security). The secure "iron rice bowl" enjoyed by employees in the past was taken away. The cost of labor motivation was greatly reduced when the "iron rice bowl" was taken away. Workers began to have a sense of crisis, and therefore formed self-awareness of their responsibility. Being the main labor entity, employees had to be responsible for the consequences of their actions. The color of sacred incentives had faded. The secular incentive system based upon reward and punishment had emerged.

On 12 July 1986, the State Council promulgated four provisions on the labor system:

The Interim Provisions for the State-owned Enterprises Adopting and Implementing the Labor Contract System,[408] The Interim Provisions of Worker Recruitment by the State-owned Enterprises,[409] The Interim Provisions of the State-owned Enterprises for Dismissal of Indisciplined Employees,[410] The Provisional Regulations for the State-owned Enterprises on Unemployment Insurance for Laid-off Workers.[411] These four provisions became effective on 1 October 1986. There are totally 36 articles in The Interim Provisions for the State-owned Enterprises Adopting and Implementing the Labor Contract System. It states that "Enterprises that intend to hire permanent waged workers within the country's planned labor and wage targets, unless specified otherwise, shall use the labor contract system uniformly. The form of employment, based on the company's needs in production, job characteristics, can be five-year long-term contract employment, or short-term, one to five years of work, with either regular or rotational workers. No matter what form of employment, it should be compliant with the provisions of labor contracts. Enterprises recruiting temporary, less-than-one-year workers, or seasonal workers, should have labor contracts too."(Article II)" Labor contract workers enjoy the same rights in work, study, participation in democratic management, access to political honor and material encouragement as the original permanent workers of the enterprise." (Article III) "Companies recruiting workers with the labor contract system should define a probationary period. The probationary period can be three to six months, determined by company with reference to different types of job." (Article VI)   There also specific provisions about the process of recruiting, the specific content of the labor contract, contract establishment, changes, termination and release, treatment during the period of work, unemployment and retirement.

The Interim Provisions of the State-owned Enterprises In Dismissal of Undisciplined Employees specifies the conditions of dismissing undisciplined employees of the enterprise: "Enterprises can dismiss the workers for the following acts, after education or administrative sanction is no longer ineffective. (1) Serious violation of labor discipline, affecting production or causing workplace disorder; (2) Violation of rules, damage to equipment or tools, waste of raw materials or energy, resulting in economic loss; (3) Poor service attitude, quarreling often with the customer or causing damage to the customer interest; (4) Not complying with normal relocation; (5) Corruption, theft, gambling, and fraud not criminally sanctionable; (6) Vexatiousness, assault, or adverse impact on social order; (7) Making other serious mistakes."   Workers considered for expulsion were to be dismissed according to "The Regulations of Enterprise Employee's Reward and Punishment System" This provision strengthened labor discipline, breaking the "iron rice bowl" of the planned economy era. The system promotes employee self-management, diligence, dedication and hard work. From a certain perspective, it eliminates the paternal warmness of the planned economic era, with which both the state and enterprises treated their employees. The sacred incentive mechanism therefore lost its foundation. The implementation of the labor contract formalized the secular incentive system.

In the 1990s, the reform of labor system was deepened. On 12 October 1992 Jiang Zemin, in his report to the Fourteenth Party's Congress, announced the establishment of a socialist market economy system. Labor market reform was also included on the agenda. The Third Plenary Session of 14th Party Congress passed "The Decision on A Number of Issues by the CPC Central Committee on Establishing the Socialist Market Economy System" (Hereafter, the "Decision on the Market Economy System"). It proposed converting the operations of the state-owned enterprises to establish a modern enterprise system. At the same time, "The Decision on the Market Economy System" suggested that the country foster and develop the market system, including the reforming the labor system, and gradually form a labor market, setting up open access to and reasonable allocation of human resources as a starting point, encouraging and guiding the shift of rural surplus labor to non-agricultural industries and regions in a gradual, orderly manner. It also suggested developing a variety of forms of employment and using economic measures to adjust the structure of employment so as to formulate a two-way choice between employers and workers, and a mechanism for the rational movement of labor.[412] Fostering the development of a labor market meant that labor had become a commodity. Workers themselves were the owners of production labor. They could trade and exchange freely in labor market. With a mechanism for the rational movement of labor, the price of labor can be maximized. However, because the institutional barriers to labor mobility were reduced, especially with the migration of rural labor to the cities, the competitive pressure on urban employment increased. The existence of such a large reserve labor pool forced workers with jobs to work harder in order to keep their "rice bowls."

The breaking of the "iron rice bowl", the elimination of guaranteed wages, and especially the commoditization of labor, meant that workers had less dependence on their work unit. Workers to a certain degree had become their own masters. The concepts of rights, individual consciousness and self-responsibility began to form. The concept of contract and exchange replaced the previous concept of sacrifice freely given. The sacred incentive system from the planned economy period largely lost the soil for its growth, since professional culture had undergone a fundamental transformation. Secular motivation, in the new era, became the major labor incentive mechanism. The labor contract system and the external labor market pressures changed worker's internal self-discipline and motivation. Within this institutionalized secular incentive system, human consciousness and ideology have evolved.

The transformation of sacred incentives and spiritual encouragement from the era of Mao Zedong, to the secular motivation system after the reform and opening up, was rooted in crisis of labor incentives that occurred during the time of the planned economy. Many reasons led to this crisis, one of which was the failure of idealistic discourse. When the prevalent and common values (idealism) used to organize society fell into crisis, motivation cannot continue to rely on such idealistic discourse. It had to rely instead on the introduction of immediate interests. It can be said that the emergence of secular motivation was a logical decision based on the failure of the sacred incentive system.

What are the consequences of secular motivation? First of all, during era of the planned economy and sacred incentives, because of the central role of the social ideal, the state emphasized equality and equity. Income distribution took the form of redistribution, excluding a role for the market. The result was a smaller income gap, and the country was in an egalitarian state. After sacred incentives shifted to secular incentives, especially after the Third Plenary Session of the 14th Party congress (the end of 1993), the state emphasized that in income distribution the principle of "giving priority to efficiency and considering fairness" must be followed. Market factors played a stronger role in determining the income distribution. Such a focus on efficiency and market factors in income distribution, coupled with corruption, monopolies and other factors, made income gaps expand rapidly among the various sectors of society. Meanwhile, because of lagging reforms of the supporting mechanisms of redistribution, the income gaps expanded more quickly. The total income of the community was tilted toward a fraction of the people. As a result, some people became "rich first" by taking advantage of restructuring opportunities. They took the lead and entered the ranks of consumerism forming, in the Western concept, the main body of consumer culture. To put it simply, the conversion of income distribution from prioritizing fairness to prioritizing efficiency sped up the divisions between social classes, rapidly creating a main body of consumer culture, i.e., the "rich first" class.

Secondarily, the replacement of sacred incentives by secular incentives meant that the "meaningful system" of the era of sacred incentive, in which the common people are motivated by the mechanism of idealistic belief, declined. Secular incentives focus people's motivation around "narrow" personal interests and materialism, motivation and meaningfulness being separated. People's motivation to work to an increasingly large extent, becomes instrumental (i.e., making money to make ends meet). In some cases, meaning does not exist in work or on the job, but exists outside. Moreover, people's beliefs no longer revolve around a common idealism as in the past, but around personal goals. For many people, the personal goal is often material, not spiritual. It is real rather than illusory, concrete rather than abstract, secular not sacred. The mechanism of significance is personalized, becoming materialistic and secular, in which consumer culture has replaced the meaning that the mechanism of sacredness provided in the past.

Sacred motivation being replaced by secular motivation also means that the state no longer needs to artificially suppress people's "natural instincts". Before the reform and opening up, in order to suppress the people's interests and nature in seeking pleasure, the state paid a huge price in its ideological and political work. After the reform and opening up, people's concept of self-interest and pleasure-seeking was no longer "evil" or a "plague", but the "natural" human condition that could be taken advantage of. Although after the reform and opening up, the national discourse of official propaganda still promoted hard work and the concept of collectivism, in economic practice, what the state adopted and relied upon in formulating it economic policies, was human nature pursuing self-interest and pleasure. Although this concept of self-interest and pleasure-seeking was still subject to certain constraints, the state did not require crushing it with great efforts, as it would have needed to do before the reform and opening up. The state ending its siege on the lifestyle associated with self-interest and ideas of enjoyment, laid the objective foundation for consumer culture or consumerism to rise.

In summary, the ideological crisis of the state grew during the "Cultural Revolution" (the contradiction between the ideal and reality, as in the spread of "back door" dealings) and the increase of poverty (the failure of national commitments), leading to a crisis in people's beliefs and in the state's legitimacy resources. These two crises led to the crisis of work motivation. Under the system of job security, the old incentives could no longer overcome the crisis of labor motivation. In order to fundamentally resolve the problem of labor motivation, a new generation of national leaders implemented new institutional arrangements. On the one hand, they denied an inherent "poverty of socialism", expanding the proportion of consumption, and improving people's material standard of living. On the other hand, they broke the "iron rice bowl" system, linking the contribution of labor with remuneration, implementing material incentives, strengthening labor discipline, implementing labor contracts, so as to replace the past sacred incentive system with a secular incentive system. Rising consumption and material living standards, as well as the implementation of the new incentive systems have stimulated labor enthusiasm and increased production and labor efficiency. In a way, this helps reconstruct national legitimacy resources.

However, in institutional arrangements, the country pursued different logics in private consumption and collective consumption. In private consumption, the state pursued a "logical legitimacy" because after the Cultural Revolution, the policy of improving people's lives helped to restore the prestige of the party and the state, and to rebuild its legitimacy resources (in late 1990s, the state's institutional arrangements for private consumption returned to "rational logic"). By contrast, in collective consumption, in the late 1990s, the state, eager to reduce its financial burden and to improve the efficiency of the supply of collective consumption, increased government investment. Therefore in its institutional arrangements, it pursued "rational logic", and reformed collective consumption in a liberal style, reducing the fraction of government supply of collective consumption, introducing market factors into the supply of products and services and increasing the cost to the individual of collective consumer goods and canceling free public welfare. In housing, for example, the state implemented a housing market, with a financial and commercial system, but delayed setting up a supporting social security system. This series of reform measures of collective consumption has caused many new problems. One is a new crisis of legitimacy resources. How will the system of collective consumption further evolve? It yet remains to be seen.

Chapter Five

Transformation of the Social Structure
and Rise of Consumerism

As mentioned earlier, in the process of reform and opening up, the state's institutional arrangements surrounding urban resident's consumption and living, and the incentive system, have undergone major transformations. Before the reform and opening up, the spiritual crisis caused by the Cultural Revolution and persistent material poverty, led to the failure of the sacred incentive system. In this context, the state turned to material incentives and systemic encouragement to mobilize labor enthusiasm. With the increase in private consumption and the improvement in people's living standards, the state tried to rebuild its legitimacy resources. So, whether from the national point of view, or from the cultural point of view, the people's spiritual and belief crises were major causes of the transformation of labor incentives and mainstream culture. The transformation of labor incentives, in turn, further accelerated changes in people's beliefs. After disillusionment with utopian schemes, people were no longer willing to believe in a grand, intangible collective ideal, but instead believed in tangible, practical, personal benefits. People abandoned their sacred beliefs and turned to secular pursuits. The realistic approach replaced the idealistic approach. This belief change led to changes in work motivation and consumer attitudes. On the one hand, people no longer upheld the spirit of dedication, with work only becoming a means or a tool for an individual to make a living or to develop a career. Self-sacrifice no longer had a sacred aura. On the other hand, although people no longer adhere to ascetic ideals, they continue to believe that thrift is a virtue. However, frugality in itself is no longer a goal. It is only a way of accumulating purchasing power when starting from the condition of small financial means. Enjoying life is the only purpose of life. However, it is necessary to point out that when we say that consumerism was on the rise in Chinese cities, it is not equivalent to say that concepts of frugality or ascetic culture have completely disappeared. In fact, due to China's two-track structure[413] of urban society, the concept of thrift still exists and persists in some sectors (e.g., among migrant or laid-off workers). However, from the perspective of change or transformation, consumerism reflects the substance of the cultural change. The concept of frugality is cultural continuity. The focus of this chapter is to explore cultural changes, rather than cultural continuity. Therefore, the concept of frugality adopted by those at the bottom of today's social classes will be discussed in the next chapter.

Transformation and Shaping of the Social System

As I suggested in the third chapter, prior to the reform and opening up, by means of the ideological state apparatus, the state shaped urban residents into a dedicated type (or obligation type) of main body, namely: with respect to the relationship between the individual rights and obligations, the state sees the individual rights as the state's "grace", which individuals need not and should not bargain over or argue against. At the same time, the state treats personal dedication and sacrifice for the country as a personal obligation. To create such a sense of dedication and sacrifice with the main body of society, citizens must be isolated from the outside capitalist world (because people in capitalist society particularly care about personal rights and interests). At that time, the shaping of the main body was done in a closed society, with the state monopolizing information and discourse resources. And with ideological propaganda and ideological and political education, the state succeeded in shaping a main body consistent with the national goals, transforming the individual's own free will into the state's will. First, individuals took the state's ideals and goals as their own personal beliefs. Second, individuals worked hard and selflessly for these personal beliefs (or did not oppose them); they were actively contributing. Again, with this faith, individuals understood the "difficulties" described by the state, accepted the national policy of suppressing consumption, and lived a frugal lifestyle to assist the state during the troubled time. Obviously, from the national standpoint, shaping the main body of society is a most effective means of social control. If we say that the nation's punishment mechanisms, backed by violence, are a rigid (external) means of implementing social control, the country's ideological apparatus would be a flexible (internal) approach of implementing social control, as it works on human mind and soul. Such national power exercised on the mind and soul works more effectively than the threat of punishment through violence.

After reform and opening up, due to the failure of the traditional spiritual incentives, the state had to establish material incentives, for which the state must grant individuals a certain awareness of their rights and interests. Accordingly, the dedicated type of main body gradually changed to the interest type of main body. Of course, an interest type of main body does not necessarily mean that no obligations are recognized, but rather that individual's awareness of their interests and rights, which had been suppressed in the past, recovered to a certain degree. People were no longer ashamed of talking about their personal interests. On the contrary, people could openly pursue and protect their personal interests and try to maintain their individual rights. Correspondingly, the available means for shaping the main body of society irrevocably changed.

The substance of the reform and opening up was not only in how it changed the existing system, but also how it changed the rigid ideological thinking behind the original system, changing people's relationship to the social structure. Ideological change is a precondition for system change, which is why in the early stage of the reform and opening up, national leaders launched the ideological liberation movement. In the view of the state's leaders, ideological change and institutional change were a process with two interdependent aspects. The process of changing the social structure was to change people's ideology. The ideological liberation movement was essentially a movement to remodel the social structure, which was to re-create a kind of main structure consistent with the objectives of the reform and opening up.

Reshaping the main body was not only the will of the state leaders who launched the reform, but was also the inevitable result of movement toward the reform and opening up. National leaders were eager to achieve their goal. But once the process was started, it was difficult to contain. On the one hand, many of the policies of economic reform were no longer built on the ascetic and dedication type of social structure, but on the basis of "people's self-interest". For example, the bonus system that reflects "distribution according to work and 'more work, more pay'" was based on the assumption that all people are motivated to pursue their self-interest. The implementation of economic reform policies no longer needed to rely heavily upon people's sacrifice of their personal interests, as they had during Mao Zedong's planned economy era (which is why the state needed a high degree of reliance on the ideological and political work). Instead, these economic policies are based upon the assumption and premise of "everyone pursues their own self-interest". Therefore replacing the planned economy with market economy inevitably leads to the change of social structure, because one assumption of the market economy is that people are selfish in market transactions and they do not need to be fair and impartial." On the other hand, the reform process is also a process of opening up to the international community. This process inevitably brings heterogeneous information and ideas from outside. The state's "information block" was eliminated. The closed society began its transition to an open society. The introduction of "heterogeneity" was bound to have impact on the original concept of "homogeneity", making it hard for the state to monopolize the process of shaping the main structure. And contact with outside systems, especially foreign information and discourse, was bound to influence people's ideas, and to a greater or lesser extent, change resident's social structure. This process was so rapid that national leaders worried that the changes were going beyond the range they had intended. They started the "removal of spiritual pollution" campaign (1983) and "anti-bourgeois liberalization" campaign (ca. 1986) to curb the excessive transformation of the main structure. But as long as the reform process was not stopped, the process of the transformation of the main structure was difficult to contain. Every time a conservative ideology rebounded, it invariably fostered more radical ideological changes.

From a historical point of view, the ideological transition and social structure change is often divided into two phases. The first phase was from 1978 to 1991, the second phase, 1992 to the present. The first stage is further subdivided into early and late parts by the "anti-bourgeois liberalization" campaign of 1986. In the early part of the first phase, to eliminate the constraint of dogmatism, the new generation of leaders initiated the ideological emancipation movement. Its landmark event occurred in 1978, the "great debate on the criterion of truth." This movement was initiated by the intellectuals from "within the system" and supported by national leaders. The movement eliminated the constraints of the "two whatevers", removing the dogmatism that had been a rigid ideological barrier to the process of reform and opening up. At the same time, the literary and artistic event of "scar literature" and the "big debate about life" initiated in "China Youth" magazine which in May 1980 published a letter from Pan Xiao "The Path to Life Becomes Narrower and Narrower".[414] The debate raged across the national media for over six months, promoting people's awareness and reflection of the damage done by the ultra-leftist line in the past. Through the ideological liberation movement people were gradually freed from ideological dogmatism and gradually developed more skeptical and independent thinking. Individual consciousness began to form. The introduction of the various economic reform measures (e.g., the "responsibility system", the breaking of the "big common rice pot" and the "iron rice bowl", the bonus system, etc.) encouraged people to break with their past beliefs of idealism, dedication and asceticism. The shaping of the social structure moved from one dimension to multiple dimensions. Reflective discourse and liberal influences from the intellectual elite began to affect the shaping of the main body. In order to prevent the influences on the main body from getting out of control, and to prevent the works of the intellectual elite from going beyond the limits set by the state (as they did in the movie "Bitter Love"), the state leaders launched the "anti-bourgeois liberalization" campaign in 1986.

The later phase of first part started after the "anti-bourgeois liberalization" campaign. With the state's permission, another wave of intellectual liberalization took place. Milestones include translations of Western academic works (e.g., the "Towards the Future" series), the academic "Great Culture Debate" and the political commentary television series "River Elegy", itself a reflection of traditional Chinese culture. This liberalization was terminated by the tragic Tiananmen Event that shocked the whole world in 1989, which led to a subsequent resurgence of conservative ideology, for example, the "anti-peaceful evolution" movement.

Overall, the first stage of ideological transformation was led by the state, which intended to break the shackles of leftist ideological dogmatism. Prior to the reforms, individuals who challenged the mainstream ideology often faced significant political risks, or even loss of their lives. In this environment, the original ideology was hardened and obdurate. Even two years after smashing of the "Gang of Four", incumbent party and state leader Hua Guofeng still adhered to the "two whatevers"[415] and rejected ideological transformation. Not until 1977, when Deng Xiaoping returned to office, did he launch the emancipation movement to eliminate the dogmatism that had imprisoned peoples minds.[416] It is clear that ideological transformation could only be implemented from top to bottom, being initiated by the state's leaders who promoted it to the grass-roots level. Otherwise, ideological change would be extremely difficult. Therefore, the reform and opening up of ideas could only be a state-led transformation. Meanwhile, there were advantages to the state leaders taking the lead: the state could control the ideological transformation within a specific scope, limiting it and preventing it from going beyond specified boundaries. This is why from 1978 to 1986, the ideological transformation process included repeated efforts to control its effects (for instance, the "removal of spiritual pollution" and "anti-bourgeois liberalization" campaigns).

The first phase of the transformation of the national ideological consciousness was initiated and led by the state, but this transformation was a controlled, rather than a liberal transformation. It was not a transformation of spiritual enlightenment. Nevertheless, this ideological transformation had far-reaching consequences. On the one hand, it completely broke the hold of the old ideological dogmatism, opening the door to emancipation, reflection and enlightenment. On the other hand, it caused a gradual transition of resident's social structure. The way of shaping resident's social structure underwent a major change. The ideological liberation movement promoted by the state led many people to gradually form self-awareness, self-concept and skepticism (new consciousness). The official ideology publicized by the state no long had as strong an influence on shaping resident's social structure, that it did in the past. For example, the "Shekou Storm" in Shenzhen in 1988 showed that people began to have ideas consistent with the new economic policy, and that traditional idealistic propaganda was not as effective as it had been.[417] Nevertheless, generally speaking, in the first phase, the spirit of idealism did not completely vanish, and the official ideology to some extent, shaped the social structure.

The second phase of the ideological transformation began in 1992 with Deng Xiaoping's "southern tour speech"[418] and continues until today. Deng Xiaoping addressed his speech mainly to the leftist ideological resurgence after the 1989 "Tiananmen Event", which was a departure from the basic line of reform and opening up. He complained: "The pace of reform and opening up is not big enough, not striking. This all comes down to the fear of capitalism, fear of taking the capitalist road. The crucial point is the question being 'capitalist' or 'socialist'.[419] He warned: "basic line should be for a hundred years, not wavering. Only by sticking to this route, people will believe you and support you. Whoever attempts to change the line, principles, policies since the Third Plenum, they will be down as people do not agree."[420] He pointed out that whether it is 'socialist' or 'capitalist', "The standard to judge by should be whether it benefits the development of the productive forces of socialist society, whether it helps to enhance the overall strength of socialist countries, and whether it helps to improve people's living standards."[421] Whether it is, "A bit more of planning or a bit more of market forces is not the essential difference between socialism and capitalism. The planned economy is not equivalent to socialism, and capitalism has plans too; the market economy is not equivalent to capitalism, and socialism has market planning as well. Both planning and the market are economic means."[422]

Promoted by macro-actors, the ideological transformation at this stage was mainly the legalization of the market economy, and the state's ideological recognition and affirmation of the market economy. It was reflected in the fading of dogmatism and utopianism in the state ideology and the concept of market ideology taking a preeminent position. If, in the first phase, between "breaking the old" and "establishing the new", "breaking the old" had the greater weight, then, in the second phase, between "breaking the old" and "establishing the new", "establishing the new" had the greater weight. The "new", was mainly affirming the role of the market, and including the legitimacy of the market into the socialist system. That the market economy was seen as an integral part of socialism was confirmed at the party's 'Fourteenth Congres's (October 1992), at which a new wave of ideological changes debuted. This wave was the market-oriented ideology associated with the market, but which went beyond it.

The market economy had been legalized. The state had introduced the institutional arrangements for the market economy. But the market is not actually controlled and operated by the state, but rather by civil society and market participants. The state's role is to set aside space for the market and the market ideology. It only provides policy support, an institutional framework and legal environment for the market and market ideology, and supervises it according to law. The state largely does not participate in the market itself and its ideological operation. Therefore, to some extent, the state steps back from civil society, giving civil society a degree of autonomy, and enabling a civil society discourse. The most social influence of the discourse is the market ideology. The most typical market ideology is commercial advertising.

In China, commercial advertising began to reestablish itself as early as the 1980s. But ideological advertising began in the 1990s. In the 1980s, the situation of product shortages was yet to be overcome, consequently advertising appears mainly in the form of messenger-type ads. After 1990, and especially in the late 1990s, the state has solved the problem of product shortages and there were even surpluses. This evolution corresponded to changes in advertising, namely: a shift toward advertising that seeks to persuade or stimulate desire. The process of persuading or stimulating desire was often achieved by means of ideological advocacy skills. Therefore, in China, advertising has gone through the transition from messenger-type to ideology-based advertising. For example, by analyzing 20 years of advertising content in the "Yangcheng Evening News" (1981~2000), Chen Sheng confirmed this hypothesis: "the advertisements reflecting the functional value of consumption decreased over time, and those reflecting the symbolic consumption value increased"[423] Here, the advertisements reflecting functional value are messenger-type, and those reflecting the symbolic value of consumption are of the type that persuade or mobilize people's desire, with the latter having the function of influencing people's sense of value, therefore having obvious ideological function (i.e., ideological advertising).

Advertising as a persuasive tool has the function of shaping the social structure. Its role in shaping the social structure is mainly to provoke the audience's desire for consumption, and to naturalize and legitimize such desire. On the one hand, advertising tries to arouse the audience's desire through an idealized image attached to the product.[424] On the other hand, advertising again naturalizes and legitimizes consumer desire to possess the product. Goldman and Papson pointed out: "Advertising is a cultural device for the symbolic construction of commodities. Through adding images of social and cultural value to brands of merchandise, advertising thereby increases the value of the brand: brand + image significance = product symbol."[425] Advertisements then invite the audience to consume the commodity symbol, affirming their good social position.[426] This type of advertising, which attaches a certain kind of ideal social and cultural image to goods so as to provoke the consumer's desire to buy them, has ideological characteristics. Why? Goldman and Papson defend the definition of advertising as ideology on the following grounds:

"(1) It is a world of discourse by way of social and cultural construction; (2) It covers up and conceals the unequal, unjust, irrational and contradictory nature of the discourse; (3) It is the discourse that examines our world and our relationship to it from a normative perspective; (4) It is the logical discourse reflecting capital. In this sense, ideology refers to 'the significance of our social conditions that must be manufactured, and at the same time to be made permanent.' As long as advertising builds necessary social illusion, and normalizes distorted communication, it is ideological."[427]

Being a representation of capital, advertising has become another type of ideology outside of the state's ideology - market ideology. Thus, in discourse on the market, the state and market society reach a consensus, and form a conspiracy. In late 1990s, and especially afterward, in order to start and stimulate consumption, expand the domestic consumer market, and deepen the institutional arrangements of the market economy, the state objectively needed cooperation from market society, and needed the cooperation of market ideology. Therefore, even if market ideology and orthodox values (e.g., plain living) were to some degree in tension, the state had a laissez-faire attitude toward market society so as to manipulate market ideology. Accordingly, following the logic of capital appreciation, the market society continuously produces market ideology as represented by mass media advertising.

Since advertising does not take a realistic approach to its narrative of goods, but constructs its commodity narrative ideologically, it plays a role in shaping resident's consciousness. This shaping is especially seen in the socialization of children and young people. Advertising shapes the value system of children and adolescents. Since advertising often uses the standard of living of a small number of the wealthy to describe the "average" standard of living, and normalizes such a standards of living, advertising overstates the "normal living" standard and raises the level of people's desire accordingly.[428] In a sense, by shaping the social processes of children and adolescents, advertising creates a new consumer body. When growing up in such an advertising environment, children and young people tend to have a different type of social structure from their elders. They debut on the historical stage with their own consumer identity. With their different social experience, the generation that grew up during the reform and opening up had a different consciousness and social structure from older generations. There were generation gaps. These gaps were caused by the rapid social transformation.

Since the state abandoned totalitarian ideological control, implemented limited alienation, civil society gradually formed its own discourse, which is public or civil discourse. In addition to advertising mentioned above, public discourse also includes private discourse (e.g., conversations at bars and restaurants), the market or quasi-market media discourse (e.g., publications such as "Shanghai Fashion", "Bazaar", "Concert", "Family", "Origin of People", "Phoenix Magazine", "Southern Urban News", "Yangcheng Evening News", etc.), network broadcasts and so on. Beyond them, the voice communication over the internet is a recent evolution in discourse. It already avoids state control to some extent (or at least has obtained a temporary reprieve from state supervision), and has become a relatively autonomous, independent discourse. Especially the appearance of online communication platforms (such as chat rooms, online forums, email, etc.) has allowed internet-based communication an unprecedented degree of freedom. For example, the QQ platform has created a network of private discourse. In addition, many scholar's independent commentary and writings are widely disseminated over the Internet, forming an independent discourse outside of the state ideology.

The emergence of public discourse had revolutionary significance. On the one hand, it heralded the end of the state's totalitarian control policy. The public gained, to a certain degree, space for freedom of speech. On the other hand, it meant a transformation in the way that the social structure was shaped. The state could no longer monopolize the process completely. There are diverse ways of shaping the social structure. Public discourse became another force able to shape it. Thus, the formation of the social structure was no longer completely under the control of the state. And the state no longer needed full control of shaping the social structure. For the state, a full ideological control is neither possible nor necessary to fulfill national goals. Along with the market economy, allowing a certain degree of freedom of speech, is necessary to release social energy and civil society's creativity. Therefore, the state conceding some space to uncontrolled thought and speech did not lead to social chaos, but instead to some extent improved social discourse. This was because the social market economy led to higher levels of system integration. The state could rely on system integration to maintain social order. It no longer needed to use ideological pressure to achieve the same result. What is particularly worth mentioning that because of the shift from spiritual to material labor incentives, the state no longer needed to shoulder the huge burden of ideological and political education in order to maintain labor motivation. Material incentives and labor discipline had become institutional arrangements. The system itself is sufficient to mobilize the labor motivation.

Because of the reduced role of the macro-system in shaping the social structure, the state partially weakened local control of the formation of social structure. The diversification of ways by which the social structure could be shaped led to a transformation in the ways of shaping it. Correspondingly, the social structure itself has also undergone a transformation. First, the sacred believers turned into secular utilitarians. Second, the devotee to the sacred cause has become a self-serving person. Third, asceticism became consumerism (Figure 5-1). The social structure includes a combination of many elements. But in order to correspond to the social structure during Mao Zedong's planned economy period, I will only discuss three key elements and their relationships: the position of faith (idealism or realism), consumer attitudes (asceticism or consumerism) and labor motivation (selfless dedication or interested self-discipline).

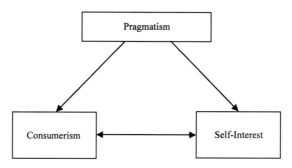

Figure 5-1   The Transformed Main Structure

In Figure 5-1, the formation of concept of consumption (consumerism), and the collapse of faith are intrinsically linked. That is, a belief vacuum makes consumer life an important alternative source for the "meaning of life". Consumer life therefore compensates for the loss of belief. Formation of self-awareness (self-interest doctrine) is also related to the collapse of faith. Because people no longer adopted a sacred belief as their supreme goal and aligned their behavior with this goal, they turned to the pursuit of self-interest, thus forming consciousness and awareness of the benefits of contract. At the same time, consumer attitudes (consumerism) and self-awareness (self-interest doctrine) interacted with each other.

The following sections elaborate on the relationships shown in the diagram. Data comes from semi-structured interviews with 78 residents living in Guangzhou (young adult group). Information on the respondents (e.g., occupation, income, age, education, etc.) and other interview details are included in the Appendix. In the remainder of this chapter, Section II describes the pragmatic attitude that developed after the weakening of faith.

Section III describes the transformation of labor motivation: from selfless dedication to a doctrine of self-interest. Section IV discusses the transformation of consumer attitudes: from asceticism to consumerism. As in the third chapter, the social structure described here is an ideal type.

Pragmatism

In a sense, the rise of pragmatism is the result of the crisis of traditional ideology and the collapse of faith. The loss of faith I am talking about is not that people do not have any faith, rather that they no longer believe in the traditional ideology and the propaganda of its ultimate goal. People are not willing to accept this ultimate goal as their individual goal. Instead, individuals give priority to obtaining tangible benefits in the real world. At the national level, although the state departed from its early leftist ideological dogma, it preserved the core of the traditional ideology. While the state made practical arrangements that permitted many things that were considered taboo under the traditional ideology (e.g., employees, the market, private enterprises, etc.), as an alternative to the traditional ideology the state's new ideological system was still not complete. In general, the state adopted a pragmatic approach towards the traditional ideology, not entirely giving up the old, but modifying it according to the immediate needs and making practical trade-offs. In addition to being pragmatic in their choice of content, the state's pragmatic attitude toward the traditional ideology is also reflected in the "speaking" (ideological declaration) and "doing" (specific policy) arrangements, which were not entirely consistent: sometimes, the state would "do what they say", sometimes it would "say but not do", sometimes "do without saying", and sometimes "doing but not saying" (i.e., first, testing whether the policy works, then cloaking it with additional ideological legitimacy). Because "saying" and "doing" were inconsistent, there was tension between traditional ideology and the policy of reform and opening up, as well as the state's "mix and match" towards the traditional ideology. Reflected in national policies and arrangements, when the policy arrangements of the reform and opening up clashed with traditional ideology, the state abandoned the traditional ideology, and followed a doctrine of trial and error ("feeling for the stepping stones when crossing the river", "trying hard, correcting the mistake later"), which, for example, was used when the Stock Exchange was established. Once reform went out of control (as it did in the political turmoil of 1989), the state partially returned to the traditional ideology.

With state practicing pragmatism, the people's ideological orientation was also changed. Pragmatism replaced idealism. The romantic orientation was replaced by the pursuit of self-interest. People were freed from the traditional constraints of the faith and its ultimate goals, and began to rationally pursue their individual practical interests. They became reality-oriented "pragmatists". The emergence of pragmatism was the inevitable result of the social transformation from a sacred society to a secular society.

Before the reform, the ideological and political education by the state continuously required individuals to take national goals as their personal goals, and place the state's interests above their own, even demanding people sacrifice their personal interests for the national interest. This ideological and political education cultivated a personal faith, in which people took the national objectives as sacred, while minimizing their own interests, even being willing to sacrifice personal interests for the national goals. However, during the Cultural Revolution this idealistic faith gradually weakened, and people began to pursue their own practical interests.

After the reform and opening up, in order to mobilize the labor enthusiasm, the state abandoned the institutional arrangements of sacred incentive system in favor of material incentives. After the transformation, the incentive system confirmed the legitimacy of pursuing of personal interests (as long as the public and national interests are not harmed). In this systemic environment, the orientation of people's behavior is no longer toward the ideals and sacred beliefs of the past, but is secular and utilitarian. People no longer believe that individuals should sacrifice their personal interests unconditionally for the national interests. People realize that national interests should not conflict with personal interests, and should not be achieved at the expense of personal interests. Only if the interests of citizens are protected, can the national interests be achieved.

Obviously, people no longer believed in the propaganda of "national goals above all else," because the so-called "national goals" or "national interests" may be the disguised self-interest of few interest groups. "There many types of interests " (B09-F-31, originally a salesperson, now retired), "We should not sacrifice personal interests in names of the community or the country. Sometimes what is called 'for the society or the national interest' is not a sure thing. It may even be some thoughts of hot-headed leaders, not validated by experts, without scientific evidence, without the vote of citizens. But the interests sacrificed by these people are very real, such as immigration, relocation. It is said that one family is given a million to relocate. In fact they may get less than one thousand each into their hands."(B36-M(1)-30, doctor)   Neither do people think that the standards used for Party members should be the same as applied to ordinary people. Party members should be held to a higher ethical standard.

Since it was not necessary to sacrifice personal interests for national goals, the pursuit of immediate material interests by individuals was naturally justified. It was also allowed by the state system. "If you can not fight for your own interests, how could you help the others with their benefits? How to fight for the collective interests?" (B02-M-23, private technology company's sales clerk) "Everyone would like to pursue some material benefits ... as long as it is not illegal, not harming other's interests, national interests, I think this is normal, and it should be."(B01-F-23, civil servant) "Everyone wants to live better, so the state also encourages this, encouraging people to pursue material interests, which there is nothing wrong with. People cannot live on spiritual beliefs to survive, so there is nothing wrong with their pursuit of personal interests. On the contrary, not pursuing material interests is improper."(B35-M (1)-28, owner of a small advertising company and advertising designer) From this perspective, the pursuit of money is a practical approach.

Obviously, the pragmatism spoken of here is that of individuals rationalizing personal interest as the basis of their behavior and standards. From the perspective of pragmatic ideology, national and individual interests are not antagonistic. We should not sacrifice the individual interests to achieve the national interests. Instead, individual interests and national interests are able, but also can be unified. Individuals can pursue personal interests within normal boundaries. The national interest is to protect everyone, without prejudicing one's ability to pursue his or her own interests, under the premise of not damaging the public interest.

Given this new pragmatic approach, joining the Party, which in the past had been considered a sacred calling, has become a utilitarian act. Although we cannot deny that some people still join the party out of their "pure" or "sacred" motives, we see an increasingly common phenomenon in which people join the party for the sake of individual advantage. For example, joining the party is one way to get a job or promotion. When asked why they joined the Party, many respondents said that their motives had practical, utilitarian considerations:

"*You entered the national institution ... ...you joined the party for your future ah. It will impact on all the things you have ... ... Like promotion to chief, deputy chief, unless you are a party member, you are not considered for a raise. Ah, only party members can participate in such competition, promotion and other aspects of things ... I do not think I am like some others that want to be so great, or saying that I am serving the people in whichever way, or how I am serving the people. I completely go with the trend of our society, the trend of the working units to join the party.*" (B29-M (1)-32, policeman)

From a practical point of view, since joining the party confers personal gain, for some people, especially the ones living "outside the system", choose not to join the party since it does not bring them benefits. During the era of Mao Zedong, people who were unable to join the party still saw party membership as being a very sacred thing. Now, being more practical and utilitarian, people would not consider joining the party if it did not bring material gain. When asked why they did not join the Party, respondents also gave utilitarian reasons. "There will be a lot of trouble if I join the party. All day long, I will have to write reports, attend meetings. Secondly I think there is no need, because I do not work at a government institution. It does not make differences whether I join the party or not." (B14-F-22, bank staff), "Not interested, all day long talking about things that do not even exist." (B16-F, 27-year-old insurance company clerk) "I do not think whether to the party ... I do not know why, anyway. I don't feel it matters. With the party or without the party, I feel the same way." (B10-F-30, cashier at a leisure center)" This party is not as worthwhile pursuing as before; I was prepared to join the party but gave up because of work." (B15-M-42, owner of a private business) Some people even do not know what joining the party is about.

We do not deny that in today's society there are still a number of people who join the Party out of sacred belief. But it is clear that in the era of the faith vacuum, the reasons for joining the party are very different than they were in the era of Mao Zedong. Some people joined the party, not primarily out of devotion to the sacred faith, but for pragmatic and utilitarian reasons. It is similar with people who do not join the party. Practical, utilitarian considerations dominate people's consciousness. The old idealistic passion has been replaced by today's cool realism. People have given up their pursuit of the "metaphysical", instead seeking the "physical" or utilitarian. In short, people have changed from "saints" into "mortals", from idealists into pragmatists. Many human actions have changed from being driven by the need to establish spiritual worthiness to calm and rational choices, and from being purely political acts to utilitarian pursuits.

The Doctrine of Self-interest

The faith vacuum and the weakening of idealism had an impact on people's working objectives, motivation and direction. In the era of Mao Zedong's planned economy, the state rhetorically exaggerated the citizenry's role as (Communist) "saints". The state applied a sacred ethical code to all residents. Therefore, the social norm of that era was that of "moral sainthood." With regard to work motivation, a sacred morality asks people to dedicate themselves and work selflessly. Once the populace changed from being "saints" to "mortal", "moral sainthood" has lost its social rooting. Labor motivation had changed.

Dedication was replaced by the concept of self-interest, embodied as self-awareness and a consciousness of obligation. In addition, professional ethics had become an important standard for guiding labor practices.

A. Self-awareness

For a more detailed understanding of people's consciousness, two aspects were including in designing interviews. Questions centered on how people dealt with what was popular in the past: "selfless dedication", "free overtime" and "left for other opportunities". The results presented below are based on data analysis.

1. Ending of "Selfless Dedication"

"Selfless dedication" was a mainstream discourse and commonsensical conduct before the reform and opening up, especially before the Cultural Revolution. With the reform and opening up, the state's incentive policies changed, encouraging the people to achieve the nations goals by pursuing their personal interests. The spirit of "Selfless Dedication", although it was still officially praised, was no longer a topic of general public awareness. On the contrary, it was replaced by "self" awareness. The contemporary view the previous popular attitude of "selfless dedication" can be divided into two categories: (1) contemporary society has lost the social environment required for "dedication" ("environmental theory"); (2) people are innately selfish and cannot be selflessly dedicated ("human nature").

When asked about the older generation's "selfless dedication", many people have expressed their admiration but also said that they would not be able to emulate it, primarily because they do not have that the kind of faith and social environment is also different. "They had pure faith, worthy of our admiration; their dedication deserves our recognition. And we lack faith, we will not be, and cannot be, that selfless." (B07-M-25, credit guarantee corporation account manager) "I admire them. But to be honest, I could not do that, mainly because of the overall environment. The older generation of revolutionists did not enjoy today's material sense."(B15-M-42, owner of a private business)   More specifically, in today's society the required social environment is lacking:

Interviewer: How do you assess older people's selfless dedication? Do you personally adopt this spirit?

Interviewee: I think this was determined partially by the social environment and the level of economic development at the time. With the development of today's society, the whole value system has changed. Speaking of dedication back then, we cannot divorce it from the social background at that time. It was the time that the country was just being founded. The whole country was being developed similarly without much gap between the rich and the poor. Although people had different jobs, total income was about the same, daily life was not very different. Therefore, everyone speaks of dedication. Certainly, individuals will do it unconditionally. Now the gap between rich and poor has widened, being divided into several different groups. That is a problem of the economic base determining behaviors. If I were still living in a very poor or suffering state, I would need to survive. And if I were still asked to dedicate, my life cannot be guaranteed. So I think that the individual will have his selfless dedication, but he will be more concerned about his personal life of at this stage. For example, how he feeds their family, or how he develops.

(B08-M-28, joint venture manager)

Market transformation destroys the necessity for and social basis of "selfless dedication". With the reform of social welfare and security system, people were faced with a sudden increase in risk and their sense of security was reduced. In such circumstances, people had to take care of themselves first. It was impossible for them to show "selfless dedication."

More importantly, for a person to have "selfless dedication", a precondition is that other people must be "selfless" too. If others are selfish under such conditions, individuals adhering to the spirit of "dedication" must carry along the "free riders". And many people in today's society have become selfish:

Older people had selfless dedication, it was produced in the context of society at that time, there was that kind of society. Now in the society we have now, people have become more selfish. If they still insist on this spirit, I believe that society will soon be eliminated. But if there is really a need for me to be dedicated, I will sacrifice. Only there are too many untrustworthy factors in today's society. Sometimes someone sacrificing can be "taken for a ride."

(B18-M-29, engineer at a private enterprise)

In Mao's planned economy era, the state leadership believed that human nature could be transformed. Therefore, there was a need for political campaigns, political learning, continuous criticism and self-criticism, and constantly "fighting selfishness and criticizing revisionism." After restructuring the economic system, human selfishness, in the eyes of the state, was no longer an "original sin". The ideological and political campaigns and political education were no longer needed. On the contrary, human selfishness was precisely the thing the state's economic policy took advantages of. In this environment, not only the state's view of human nature and its "main model" changed, but also people's view of human nature and consciousness. Under the default condition in which people are selfish, people adjust their behavior accordingly. Since other people are selfish, I must also be correspondingly selfish, and am not able to show "selfless dedication." "I think most people in today's society have no such selfless dedication. ... After all, there is selfishness, there is a conflict when both sides will think of themselves first, then think of others." (B14-F-22, bank staff). "People are selfish. It was the case before, the case for now and for future. Isn't 'benefiting others' under the premise of 'self-interest first' more practical, more sustainable?" (B12-F-23, customs employee) Some respondents pointed out that there should be distinctions among the objectives of "selfless dedication": If it is to help vulnerable and needy people, volunteering is appropriate. But this should not be the case with a privileged group:

I think the sacrifice is necessary, but "selfless," was debatable. I volunteer every month, because I think we need to help the weak groups. And you should have the time and the ability to sacrifice. But if this is because the boss wants you to make unnecessary contributions, I do not think this is worth it.

(B40-F-23, account manager at a bank)

2. Ending of "Free Overtime"

Whether people are willing to do overtime work for free is not a simple problem since it depends on their type of work. Depending upon the nature of work, the compensation landscape can be divided into three categories: "extrinsic rewards" (e.g., salary) and "intrinsic rewards" (e.g., happiness from the challenge of the work and the creativity it requires) and a mix of intrinsic and extrinsic rewards. Accordingly, the work can be divided into "extrinsic reward" work,[429] "intrinsic reward" work,[430] and "mixed extrinsic and intrinsic reward" work.[431] Viewed from the perspective of motivation, work can be divided into "pay plan" work (in which the purpose of work is the salary) and "career" work (in which work is a personal cause, to achieve personal career development and promotion, or to satisfy personal interests). The "extrinsic rewards" compensation belongs to the "pay plan" type work. The "intrinsic" and "mixed intrinsic-extrinsic" compensations apply to "career" type jobs. However, the distinction between the two is also related to a person's stage in their work life. People initially entering the workforce are satisfied with "salary" type of work. Later, they will enter the track of a "career" type job.

In general, people engaged in different types of work have different attitudes towards working overtime for free. People engaged in "extrinsic return", or "salary-seeking" type of work are often opposed to overtime for free. People engaged in "intrinsic return" and "mixed intrinsic-extrinsic return" work or who have a "career" type job, will have an attitude toward unpaid overtime that is often related to whether the unpaid overtime work will help their prospects for career development.

In addition, attitudes towards "free overtime" also involve the labor system. If the labor system is imperfect, the lacking protections for workers, the employer will be in a strong position, and may be able to force workers to accept unpaid overtime because of their weak bargaining position. So, there are two cases with unpaid overtime, either actively accepting or passively accepting overtime. Under certain conditions, whether people accept the unpaid overtime is related to their own conditions and capacity.

People aware of their self-interests are sensitive to the time boundaries governing their employer's use of their labor. Of course, with the increasing complexity of contemporary social tasks, the time boundaries of labor use get more complicated and increasingly blurry. The simpler a work task, the clearer the time boundary for labor to perform it. Conversely, for a more complex work task, the time boundaries for the necessary labor are blurrier. If the employee compensation is linked to the overall performance, the time borders of labor use are even fuzzier. Therefore, there are some difficulties in defining what is "unpaid overtime". In the case of simple labor tasks, you can clearly see unpaid overtime. In the case of complex work tasks, it is difficult to judge unpaid overtime, because remuneration is not linked with eight hours of work, but with the job performance or contribution over a longer time period (e.g., month, quarter, year). But no matter how defined, in our interviews, respondents said that their labor was not free and could not be used without compensation. Facing the use of unpaid overtime by employers, labor used three strategies. First, they could conditionally accept the unpaid overtime, but overtime must be "limited" and "conditional" and could not be "unlimited" and "unconditional". It had to be within the responsibility of the job and must be short and occasional. Second, there could be some other compensation for the unpaid overtime. Or the overtime is forced by the nature of the job or other pressure. Third, labor could completely oppose the unpaid overtime.

In many cases, the time boundaries of Chinese working people have not been very strict. Especially in the case of task-based or achievement-based employees, workers do not object to extending work hours because of the need to complete tasks on time. However, over the long term, they do not want to their own labor to be uncompensated. "Unpaid overtime" is conditional. The conditions include: whether the unpaid overtime is within the "scope of the job responsibilities", or is only "limited unpaid overtime."

In our interviews, respondents said that if a task falls within their work responsibility, and the work must be completed by a given time but has not yet been completed, then they would be willing to work unpaid overtime. Other than that, they would not. "With our own work, if not completed within work hours, we would work overtime." (B07-M-25, credit guarantee corporation account manager) "Overtime is counted for our own business, so I didn't quite care about it. It might have been the momentum when I just arrived in Guangzhou. If I were now still with the company, and the boss asked me to work overtime, I would probably turn it down. "(B35-M(1)-28, owner of a small advertising agency and advertising designer)

When employers need labor to work unpaid overtime, for the interests of the company and their own benefit, workers are willing to perform a limited amount of free work, for example, doing short or occasional overtime for tasks that are relatively simple, if it leads to more respect from the leadership of the enterprise. However, people do not want to do this if it lasts for too long. "It depends. Not a hundred percent, depending on the circumstances—two or three days overtime—it would not be problem for eight or ten days. ... If it becomes a long-term overtime, of course we cannot do this. Have to see how long the time is. If you do this for a long time, the company should give something back. They should compensate for the overtime. If this it is short-term, eight or ten days overtime for a company employee, it would be okay, as we want the company to do better, and everyone will benefit too."(B09-F-31, originally a salesperson, now retired)

Some workers see "unpaid overtime" as a disguised way to get additional compensation, or at least as a way to avoid certain adverse consequences. It is also concerned with job stress, job pressure, labor and management bargaining power higher or lower. Therefore, the compensation for unpaid overtime may not be financial, and may include the situation where the labor system is flawed and workers must make compromises to keep their jobs. "Nowadays, which companies do not work overtime? People should not get lazy from working at government institutions for long, unwilling to work unpaid overtime. Since the leadership requires us to do more, certainly they will see us doing this with their eyes, which can be intangible assets. I heard this year the employment rates of vocational school graduates vs. college graduates are 40% and 70% respectively, which is a severe unemployment situation. We should not be too picky."(B12-F-23, customs employee) "Not being willing to work unpaid overtime easily leads to making a bad impression on the leaders."(B17-F-31, printing computer operator) It can be seen that although there is no immediate compensation for unpaid overtime, there is delayed compensation. People are willing to work unpaid overtime, apparently not because of some grand ideal, but by their expectation of future compensation. Therefore, such an instrumental act of unpaid overtime, to a certain extent, is driven by human consciousness and self-interest.

In our interview about attitudes towards "unpaid overtime", there was a class of people explicitly opposing "unpaid overtime". This group of people held low paying jobs having poor career development prospects. Therefore they had the strongest sense of the need to insist on overtime pay:

Interviewer: If a leader or boss wants you to work overtime, but is not giving any overtime pay, would you be willing to do that?

Respondents: of course not!

Interviewer: Why?

Respondents: Of course not. Like you said, there is no pay increase, no overtime pay...

Interviewer: Why not willing to?

Respondents: Working hard without overtime pay, it is not worth it.

(B06-F-28, garment factory worker)

People's attitude towards unpaid overtime reveals the end of selfless dedication. One of the reasons leading to this was the economic restructuring caused by the diversification of employment. In the planned economy period, employers were state-owned or collective units. Under such ownership structure it is easier to establish an illusory "Public" (those who employ them), identifying the public interest with the individual interest, and therefore, induce workers to accept a spirit of selfless dedication. With the change in ownership structure and reform of the labor and personnel system, the identity of the employer became very specific. The divergence of interests of workers and employers was simple and clear. People had an increased self-awareness and a clear sense of the need to bargain with their employers. They saw unpaid overtime as a challenge to their bargaining power within the new system framework. Regardless of the one's attitude toward unpaid overtime, the starting point of this attitude is self-interest, and the defensive or compromise strategy was taken under the established condition of bargaining power.

3. "Quitting for Other Opportunities": Maximization of Labor Returns

In the planned economy era, urban residents had job security, but lost the freedom to choose their work unit freely. After the reforms, with the advancement of the labor market, individuals lost job security but gained freedom in selecting their career and workplace. It was because of this freedom, people no longer behaved as they did in the planned economy era, relying upon work unit "single-mindedness" and "compromises." Employees and employers had a contractual relationship. And the relationship is adversarial. From a personal point of view, people always want to maximize the return on their investment in the company or unit. Therefore, if they find that they would have done better, either a obtaining a higher position or greater compensation for given effort with another unit or company, they would tend to find another job, engaging in so-called "job hopping." "Job-hopping is common. You don't have to put up with any pressure that by moving to a different company, it is a "betrayal". This is a two-way street. Well, I jumped so many times and there is less and less emotional attachment with any companies." (B18-M-29, engineer at a private company)

If their contract does not expressly specify the distribution of certain benefits, but employees feel they have lost out in the distribution of rewards; or the employer does not perform what contract states, and the employees are unable to enforce it, they will often break off such an "uneconomical" employment relationship and select a different work unit, seeking to maximize their income. While individual rights have increased, in that they can select a career freely, their "loyalty" to their work units has correspondingly decreased.

Of course, at different times, and in different workplaces, the situations of "job hopping" or "quitting" are different. In the short term, at government agencies and state-owned monopolies, because of the variety of excellent benefits and protections, the competition for jobs was fierce. For workers in these sectors, the voluntary "quitting" rate was relatively low. In the market sector, which lacks the variety of benefits and protections that were provided by government agencies or state-owned enterprises, the "quitting" rate was relatively high. The most common reason for "quitting" is an employee's complaint of the low wage or salary at his original work unit. By changing jobs, an employee improves his wage. In this kind of job switch, employees are not satisfied with their wage, so by hopping around, they achieve higher incomes. "I hopped around many times, seven or eight times. Most recently I quit mainly because of the salary, also the job does not seem to allow me to play my full capability and to progress." (B18-M-29, engineer at a private company)   "I feel I am very unsatisfied with my current income, ready to change jobs." (C03-F-F-24, company staff)   "Before the first job in Guangzhou, I just wanted to get out. Before that I was an art teacher in a small village in Sand River, working for a little more than one thousand yuan. I felt that the pay was too low,... Suggested to me by my classmates, I found an advertising design job in Guangzhou. I found myself swimming like a duck."(B35-M(1)-28, owner of a small advertising agency and advertising designer)

The second common reason for quitting is that someone feels they are not being treated fairly by their original work unit. They quit to end the unfairness and secure fair treatment. Here are two examples: "I was at a school, worked one year. The school discussed my promotion to become one of the middle school leaders. I've gone through the procedure. But a new principal came. There were three positions when he came. I would have been one. But he just let his acquaintances take two. I am told to wait for another year. I did not, so unfair! "(B15-M-42, owner of a private business) "The main reason is unfair treatment, including the internal staff's attitudes towards us, as well as the superior's attitude towards us. At least for me, this is the primary problem and the most important issue causing me to change my job."(B12-F-23, contract worker for customs)

Third common reason to quit is to seek an environment where self-competence and talent can be fully demonstrated. After the reform and opening up, as a result of the reform of the work units and the labor and personnel system, people could move freely around the country. Many people from the inner mainland or the north (which are relatively conservative) moved to the south to seek personal development (the south being more socially open). This also led to lot of people from north abandoning their jobs to move south:

People from the Northeast are also more conservative in their thinking. I am a kind of "undisciplined thinker", a "hedonist." I do not like to deal with these leftists and believers in Marxism-Leninism. People in the Northeast are deeply influenced by the Soviet Union. I cannot accept the Soviet model. You do one thing in the Northeast, there will be so many eyes staring at you. You cannot do this, cannot do that. I like what Sun Yat-sen advocated: "independence of thought, freedom of spirit." Down here, I do my job well at work, after work, I am a free man. I love this. When I was leaving my original unit, they certainly hoped that I would stay! Because they feel that I am a person that can do something, capable of doing something. (B26-M (1)-34, Institutional cadre)

The normalization and liberalization of quitting one's job was both an assertion of the employee's rights and freedom and a means of negotiation between the employees and employers. By the threat or act of "quitting", employees gain a comparative advantage, and are able to improve their treatment and income, or fully demonstrate their ability. The commercialization of human labor enabled employees to learn how to manipulate the marketplace so as to maximize their own interests.

B. Sense of Contractual Obligations

With the reform of the labor and personnel system, the idea of the "work unit person", which existed in past planned economy era gradually went into decline and was replaced by the idea of the "contract person". A "work unit person" was protected by their working unit (the country's primary agent), and enjoyed the extensive benefits and lifetime job security (the "iron rice bowl"), with care in sickness to arrangement for burial all being provided by the work unit. In a sense, the unit is actually a "sanctuary" for a "work unit person". It can be said that the "unit person" has a strong sense of dependence and personal attachment. With the reform of the labor and personnel system, labor became a commodity. The contract system was widely deployed. The relationship between people and their work units underwent tremendous change. On the one hand, the employer has changed. Private enterprises, joint ventures, and foreign-funded enterprises have become employers "outside the system". People have diversified employment opportunities. On the other hand, personnel and labor are commoditized. People in the labor market have free choices, and freedom of movement. Worker's dependence on their work units has been reduced, and personal attachment has disappeared. The relationship between people and their employers is no longer, as it was in the past, being asylum seekers (people) and the asylum (the work unit). They now have a contractual relationship. The "contract person" gradually replaced the "unit person."   In this condition, the sentimental relationship between individuals and their work unit is weakened. Furthermore, the relationship of the interests of individuals and their employers has been made clear. People's self-awareness and sense of the contractual relationship were greatly enhanced. People have learned how to maximize the value of their own human capital through mobility in employment.

1. Labor Contract And "Contract Person"

How does a "Contract Person" define his relationship with the company or the work unit? In our interviews, most respondents are clear that their relationship with their employer is a contractual one: "In fact, many people are reluctant to admit it. I think it mostly a contractual relationship. "(B26-M (1)-34, cadre). "The relationship between individuals and companies may be a relationship of trade. ... I trade my knowledge and time for the company's pay to me. (B16-F-27, insurance company clerk) "We are in a complete contractual relationship. Every year we sign a contract. Between employees and the company is a relatively simple business relationship. When you sign the contract for the upcoming year, you are told how much you need to work. At end of the year, they evaluate your performance. Your performance will affect your next year's salary increase, promotion, year-end awards, and adjustment of your positions." (B08-M-28, joint venture manager) As the employees and the employer are in a contractual relationship, the employer is no longer a patron providing a full-range or protections. They are just one party transacting among many. "The company in my mind is where to make money, isn't it? Nothing more than that."(B10-F-30, leisure center cashier) "Now between my company and me myself, there is simply working relationship, not any strong emotion." (B18-M-29, engineer at a private company)   As one party in this transaction, employees should continue to improve their human capital, and increase their bargaining power with their employers, rather than showing loyalty to a company:

Since the two decades of the reform and opening up, this kind of thing, feelings and attitudes towards the work units, changed a lot. This concept of single-mindedness for the unit and sense of stability are very strong. Now there is a saying that I do not necessarily need to be loyal to the company. I must be loyal to my own profession. Because you do this type of work, you have to accumulate your professional background and your professional reputation. With this background and your professional reputation, you can go and work for whichever company you want. It can also be said of that it is a kind of loyalty to our own. It is a process of managing ourselves. What is often talked about is your reputation being a person in life, and your work in the industry. If you are good, any business needs such good people. (B08-M-28, joint venture manager)

The contractual relationship between individuals and work units may easily become adversarial, with individuals and their work units locked into defending their narrowly defined interests or benefits. Once individuals perceived this interest against themselves, they will inevitably have negative attitudes and emotions towards their work unit. A doctor at the hospital expressed his "general feeling of being exploited":

I feel that my relationship with the hospital is purely a working relationship, unlike the older people who had strong feelings for their working unit. Humanity inside the hospital is relatively weak. Staff is working, cooperating, similarly to a company's business operations. It is just a lifelong company. We are different from schools. There is not much pressure with schools, as they rely on administrative allocation of funding. We at the hospital are to make money to feed ourselves. Deep down we know how many surgeries we do. But we have worked and paid so much, only with limited return. Some people doing almost nothing still get similar treatment as we get. I created a hundred dollars of value. If he were in a good mood, he would give me thirty. If he were in a bad mood, he would give me ten. Thus I felt like being exploited. (B36-M (1)-30, doctor)

Because of this sense of contract, often people define their relationship with their employer from the perspective of a balance of interests. Once they feel interests are unbalanced and that they are at a disadvantage, people will argue and attempt to fight for their interests and benefits. In this situation, the contract becomes a useful weapon for defending individual rights. A kindergarten teacher said in an interview:

It is like a family property dispute. It does not belong to me anyway, or I barely had anything to do with it. If I also sought to fight the case, it is not necessary, isn't it? Because there are already so many qualified people, and all portions are divided and passed down.

It is hardly going to be your turn. Why go to war trying to steal it? But if it is something in my work, and it is written in the contact as a bonus, if you did not give me, I am going to fight. (B13-F-22, kindergarten teacher)

The formation of contractual awareness between employees and employers did not mean that their relationship was limited to a competition of interests. They could have common interests in the prosperity of the enterprise. Thus, although people's feelings and attitudes towards their employers are different now from those in the planned economy era, they are still aware that co-operation with their employers may be mutually beneficial.

2. Professional Ethics

A sense of obligation is not only reflected in the formal or explicit labor contract, but is also reflected in professional ethics codes, which act as an informal or implicit contract. In the planned economy era, the work ethic and sacred belief are the bond between the worker and the workplace. After the reform and opening up, with the decline of sacred belief, professional ethics and an official contract are the bonds. Thus, in the era of reform and opening up, although labor performance is increasingly dependent on supervision or labor discipline, traditional ethics has not disappeared. Today's "self-interested person" is not entirely mercenary and selfish, but is clearly aware of his own interests and rights. They may use legal means to fight for their own interests and rights. Self-interested people have a clear sense of exchange and contract. They believe that their personal interests must be realized through exchange. They believe that their work needs to be worth what they are paid. Therefore, "self-interested people" are not necessarily lazy, slacking off, or cutting corners. The rise of the market economy and the deepening social divisions within labor led to the development of professional ethics. Professional ethics are generally classified into three categories: role-model professional ethics, industrial professional ethics and behavioral professional ethics.

The role-model type of professional ethics refers to those provisions and codes of conduct for an occupation or industry. They are the expectations of employers, also the standard of self-discipline for employees. The following is a sample of relevant examples of the role-model professional ethics. "(Interviewer: Can you talk about your understanding of professional ethics?) Perhaps it is that if you get your share of wages, you ought to do the things you should do." (B16-F-27, insurance company clerk) "I think ethics are the necessary rules and regulations that each profession complies with. For example, secret agents cannot leak confidential information." (B17-F-31, printing computer operator) "Professional ethics? Whichever industry, I think the most important thing is that you should follow the rules of the industry, and do things you are supposed to do. That is sufficient." (B09-F-31, originally a salesperson, now retired) "I think from an individual point of view, you should get your own work done well. If the work is not complete, then hurry up. We don't need the boss to remind us. Overtime or burning the midnight oil, we will have to finish things. I think this is the kind of basic professional ethics. Taking initiative? I never take the initiative in asking for extra work. There are things at the company that suit us. We then shall make efforts to get it done right."(B18-M-29, engineer at a private company)

Industrial ethics refers to ethical codes associated with a specific industry. They have more specific content than the role-model type of professional ethics. The following are examples of industrial professional ethics. "I think that such professional ethics are important. First of all, let's talk about our police. If you do not have the work ethic, I can only give you a case, and you are careless and only do a so-so job. You will not be able to break this case. But if you engage it very carefully, you can break this case. What is it inside this? It is our work ethic "(B29-M (1)-32, policeman) "Here these are the basic ethics of kindergarten. At the least you care, not punishing children physically, not a bit. This is the most basic."(B13-F-22, kindergarten teacher) "(Interviewer: Do you work overtime because you want overtime pay?) It is professional ethics. The work requires it. We cannot say that in saving a patient's life, we stop treatment as soon as the hour is over. The nature of my work has a kind of unpredictability. There are calls at the hospital late at night. The nature of this occupation determines that I have this obligation. "(B36-M (1)-30, doctor)

Behavioral professional ethics relate to more general personality characteristics, referring to the moral characteristics which are the standards of the profession, such as loyalty, dedication, hard work, responsibility, care, meticulousness, enthusiasm, and so on. Such professional ethics rely more on individual initiative and self-discipline. Rules and regulations are not enough to guarantee that employees have these ethical characteristics. It belongs more to the cultural as a whole. In a market economy, as transactions between employers and employees repeatedly takes place, employees who have high professional ethics are more likely to be employed. And those who lack such professional ethics may find it hard to obtain work. Even if they are hired, they are more likely to be dismissed. Therefore, the code of professional ethics forms a professional culture between employer and employees from their repeated interaction. "(Interviewer: how to evaluate your work ethic?) To fulfill my duty, being diligent, responsible, working hard enough, it is just that simple. But this is not easy to do. These moral values are difficult to explain, but I know they are very important to workers." (B40-F-23, bank account manager) "Professional ethics should first be loyalty. Because the company pays you and treats you appropriately, you should care about the company's development, and should safeguard the interests of the company and its business image. Secondly you shall not do anything harmful to the interests of the company or to company's development, including things with negative impact on company's business image and causing bad social influence." (B08-M-28, joint venture manager)" (Interviewer: how do you evaluate professional ethics?) The first is dedication. At least we should fulfill our work obligation. The second is to be faithful, or loyalty. Otherwise the simple effect is the neglect of duty. If serious it can be a dereliction of duty. Also we shall not be afraid of hardship. We should have a sense of spirit." (B12-F-23, customs employee)

Clearly, self-interested people are not "wicked" or profit-seeking people. In contrast, during the process of market development, professional ethics have become a civic culture and means for professional self-discipline. Here, professional motivation is no longer the packaged grand slogan (e.g., "building blocks for the socialist cause"). It is no longer the lofty ideal or moral belief in the sanctity of saintly people. It came from the basic definition of a professional. In other words, professional ethics replaced sacred moral ethics. It has become a kind of self-discipline and norm in people's fulfillment of their professional obligations.

Of course, this does not mean that everyone in the process of market development complies with professional ethics. In fact, it is not uncommon to see violations of professional ethics. For example, doctors have refused to treat dying patients who cannot afford treatment. Police collude with thieves. Company employees sell the company's trade secrets. Food manufacturers add harmful ingredients to food in order to make it look appealing, etc. All of these are manifestations of a lack of professional ethics. They are the result of self-interest not being constrained by the system, which is an abuse of the principal of self-interest. These phenomena in turn prove that the concept of the people as moral saints is completely bankrupt today. Now self-interest has become the universal principle dominating human behavior. However, this principle has is subject to effective constraint by civic ethics. And the construction of civic virtue and ethics is closely related to the construction of the system.

Consumerism

The process of reform and opening up not only encouraged people to pursue personal material interests through a system designed to solve the problem of labor motivation, but was also a process of transforming people into "self" individuals. It was a process of unshackling people's desires and transforming them into consumers in the modern sense. It can be said that the process of reform and opening up not only led to the country's "economic take-off", but also led to urban resident's 'desires taking off.'[432.] One by-product of the Chinese social transformation was the rise of consumerism. Consumerism emerged as an important dimension of the new social structure produced by the social transformation. It is also one of the symbols of China's urban transformation from an ascetic society to a consumer society.

What is exactly consumerism?[433] Numerous scholars in China are often off track in defining consumerism from a derogatory moral point of view. They see consumerism as a disease. By doing this they seem to achieve the goal of criticizing consumerism, but the actual effect is opposite. Why? Consumerism has become a social force in modern society, and because of its public nature, "normal" (or constructed as the norm) and "being considered as inevitable". In view of this, Miles argued that scholars should not define consumerism from a moral position in order to condemn it. They should see it as a systematic fashion, a construction of the arena of social life, a way of lifestyle.[434] So here I define consumerism not from a derogatory moral point of view, but from a value-neutral point of view. Consumerism emerged in China after its market transformation as a "quasi-popular" lifestyle and a main source of consciousness.[435] Stearns believes that consumerism describes a society in which, to some extent, many people see obtaining items as a life goal, and while obtaining these items may not be necessary or traditional in people's daily lives, getting them is a way of confirming their identity.[436] Falk believes that the characteristics of modern consumerism are reflected in three aspects: first, the formation of desire goes beyond the "necessary" level; second, the desire is unlimited; third, people tend to have endless desire for new products.[437] Belk believes that consumer culture (or consumerism) refers to a culture in which most consumers strongly desire certain goods and services and some people seek, obtain and display them, and that these goods and services are valued by their non-functional features, such as demonstration of status, to provoke envy in others or for their novelty.[438] Gronow believes that the modern consumerism is caused by the desire of happiness; the modern consumer is essentially a hedonist.[439]

In summary, consumerism (or consumer culture) involves at least the following characteristics: First, the formation of consumer desire is no longer simply the consequence of biological factors or economic motivations, but also involves social, cultural and other complicating factors (e.g., identity, status, etc.).[440] Second, consumer desire continuously grows and expands.[441] Third, consumption involves the pursuit of experience and the value of pleasure and happiness. Such pleasure and happiness have the nature of being transient and easily deformed. This is evidenced in people's endless pursuit of new products and fashion.[442]

Obviously, regardless of one's point of view, the constant changes in and uncontrolled expansion of desire are fundamental characteristic of consumerism. As Huang Ping points out: "Consumerism is such a lifestyle: the goal of consumption is not to meet actual needs, but to constantly pursue the satisfaction of stimulated desire."[443] The major factors leading to expansion of desire are neither biological nor economic. On the one hand, the desires so formed go beyond the level given in the traditional biological sense of necessity. On the other hand, the desires so formed often go beyond the limits of the consumer's resources (i.e., are unaffordable). In fact, consumerism is a form of *ideological desire* in modern consumption. It is an important feature of the modern social structure taxonomy. If we say that the traditional form of the ideology of desire is relatively stable and fixed, reflected in strategy of "living within one's means," in the modern social structure, the ideology of desire is dynamic and constantly expanding[444]. And often with the help of the modern consumer lending system, people may adopt strategy of "living beyond one's means".

Consumerism, as the ideology of desire in the modern social structure has two different aspects. One is that as disposable income increases, desire increases and takes the form of gradually ratcheting up. The other aspect is not connected to the level of disposable income. The desire to spend is balloon-like, rising ever higher. Borrowing the words of Chen Xin, the former type reflected the gradual rise of "concrete high consumption", the latter type is reflected in discontinuous leaps and bounds: it is "conceptual high consumption".[445] Given China's reality as a "dual society", if we concentrate only on urban society, we can see that the standard of living that people perceive they "should have" is rapidly escalating. The upward movement is so fast that some people's desire has grown far beyond their disposable income to support. Therefore, the "amphibious" consumer is a by-product of the rise of consumerism.[446] It is a family budget strategy in response to the tension between conceptual consumerism and limited affordability. In urban society, whether from the "concrete high consumption" point of view, or from the "conceptual high consumption" point of view (i.e., the "should have" standard of living), a social structure characterized by consumerism has become popular in China.[447]

Needless to say, the economic foundation that has enabled society's desire to take off is the continuous rise of disposable income. This is the result of the reform and opening up, which has improved livelihoods and people's living standards. With rising disposable income, consumer spending has increased year after year. At the same time, the structure of consumption has changed as well. The Engel coefficient has declined in the urban environment, and per capita housing area is also growing (Table 5-1).

Table 5-1 Per Capita Annual Disposable Income of Urban Residents, Their Consumer Spending and Changes in Engel Coefficient

Years	1980	1985	1990	1995	2000	2001	2002	2003	2004	2005
Disposable income (yuan)	-	690	1510	4283	6280	7703	8472	9422	10493	11759
Per capita consumption expenditure (yuan)	412	673	1280	3538	4998	5309	6030	6511	7182	7943
Engel coefficient (%)	56.9	53.3	54.2	50.1	39.4	38.2	37.7	37.1	37.7	36.7
Urban per capita housing area	7.2	5.0	13.7	16.3	20.3	20.8	22.8	23.7		

(Source: *China Statistical Yearbook.*)

Table 5-1 only tells us the fact that consumption increases as disposable income grows. But it does not tell us the social and cultural changes hidden behind these facts. Nor does it provide any indication of how these changes affect the social structure. This change is the focus of this chapter. It can be said that income growth is the economic precondition for consumer desire to take off. Apart from this economic requirement, the contemporary explosion in consumer spending is closely related to the transformation of the system (the institutional arrangements have changed from curbing consumption to encouraging consumption) and the transformation of the social structure. "Physical" material life replaced "metaphysical" sacred beliefs, and has become the ultimate source of meaning in life. The pursuit of individual experiences in life has replaced the grand collective ideal. At the same time, this new ideal of personal consumption also constitutes part of labor motivation. Labor motivation and the pursuit of consumerism interact and promote each other. In more general terms, consumer attitudes came from a secular and self-interested cultural environment. They have an interactive relationship with that environment.

In Mao Zedong's planned economy era, people's consumption was strictly limited and constrained. In order to limit consumption while maintaining labor enthusiasm, the state not only took an egalitarian approach to distribution but also used idealism (sacred discourse) to motivate workers. During that period the main social structure was one of asceticism. On the one hand, through its systemic arrangements, the state limited people's desire for the consumption and enjoyment of goods to a great extent. On the other hand, by continuously portraying a grand idealized future (the national commitment), the state tried to mobilize and encourage people to make sacrifices toward this goal. This is a typical system design for delaying gratification. People (especially activists) who adopt an ascetic life are "full of energy" because they attribute a special significance to their actions - their efforts will realize the future "paradise"; they are called to and labor for the future ideal world.

We can see that before the reform and opening up, during the time of the planned economy, the state adopted a two-pronged approach to control people's desire. On the one hand, people's desire for consumption was limited and restricted to a very low level. On the other hand, human desires were diverted and sublimated in favor of the nation's goal, the national goal replacing individual goals. There was tension in the relationship between the state and individuals with regard to consumer desire. In other words, personal desire for consumption was strictly suppressed by the state. At that time, by controlling the supply of consumer goods, the state forced consumers to impose maximum self-restraint (so-called "moderation") on their desire to consume. In order to alleviate the tension in consumer desire and stimulate worker's enthusiasm, the state incurred a huge cost in ideological and political work, continually making commitments to the public promising a "happy future." However, by the late seventies, after more than twenty years of this approach, real life was far from the state's promised condition of happiness, and the goal was not getting closer, but receding. The stimulative effect of the state's promises and its ideological and political work was greatly reduced.

It was under these conditions that the state initiated economic reforms. By giving workers direct, tangible material benefits, enterprises compensated for the loss of labor enthusiasm caused by the state's failure to deliver on its promises. Such material benefits were intended to lead to urban residents increasing their consumption. One was to increase the worker's wages. A second, an adjustment of the ratio of savings to consumption, improved the supply of consumer goods. To a certain extent, these measures not only saved the state's credibility, which was damaged before the reform and opening up by its failure to provide the promised better life, but also helped rebuild the state's legitimacy resources. Simultaneously, with transformation of the incentive system from a reliance on sacred motivations to material incentives, and through the reform of the labor and personnel system, the crisis of labor motivation was fundamentally resolved. The state no longer needed to devote immense resources to ideological and political work in order to mobilize the worker's enthusiasm.

After solving the labor incentive problem from the system perspective, the state was able to focus more energy on further economic development and improving people's lives.

The improvement in people's lives is often reflected in the increasing supply of consumer goods. Therefore, increasing people's consumption not only helps rebuild the state's legitimacy resources, but it also relieves the tension over the desire for consumption that existed between the state and individuals in the planned economy era. The state did not suppress people's desire to consume; it encouraged people to consume. Such encouragement became particularly obvious after the Asian financial crisis in 1997. We can say that unrestricted consumption desire has become widespread and is the "common denominator" between the state and individuals. The increasing consumption level and availability of consumer goods have become evidence proving the legitimacy of the "reform and opening up" policy. In turn, the increase in consumer goods and consumption levels are an important reason for residents to support the reform and opening up. Clearly, the livelihood economy and politics implemented during the reform and opening up played a positive role in restoring the prestige of the party and the state, and rebuilt their legitimacy resources.

Clearly, in the planned economy era, the failure to meet national commitments had consequences for the spirit of idealism, and it was logically necessary to provide for timely material consumption by urban residents to compensate. It can be seen that the pursuit of consumerism existed not only within the personal realm, but also relied on national objectives - it was a national program implemented by the reform and opening up, one of the sources of legitimacy resources. After the crisis of the traditional value system, during the transformation process that established a new value system, consumerism and patriotism were important means for the state to maintain social integration. It was in this context that the evolution of people's desire occurred, gradually shifting from the asceticism of consumerism.

As previously mentioned, so-called consumerism refers to a form of modern desire. Consumption desire in the modern social structure is not built upon the basis of traditional absolute needs (natural needs), but upon perceived relative needs. And relative needs grow, leading to the continued expansion of people's desire. The so-called absolute necessity or natural need refers to a person's desire primarily by physical needs, as well as the traditional mode of production and lifestyle. In a traditional society, people's desires are often relatively simple and do not change much with time. For thousands of years people can have the same consumption desires, consume the same products, and spend in the same way.[448] In this case at least a few factors limit the non-physiological, non-traditional (especially hedonist) influences on people's desire. First, the lack of resources constrains the expansion of human desire. Correspondingly, people formed religious and ethical values to suppress the desire. Desire became the object that religion or ethics sought to attack. Second, the strict boundaries of social hierarchy prevented the lower classes from imitating the upper class. Fashion in a traditional society neither has an economic base, nor a social base. Third, people established a relatively stable, unchanging lifestyle for generations. Their desires were compatible with their way of life. Constrained by their traditional lifestyle, people do not easily change the way in which they live their lives. Therefore their desires remain stable and constant.

The so-called relative need refers to a person's desire that is established by comparison with the product standards and categories demonstrated by a reference group. Whether people form a desire or not depends on whether they sense that they lack something that a reference group or individual possesses. It is this sense of relative deprivation that causes their desire. So, what factors led to the continuous expansion of desire? First, the revolution in the means of production and the improvement of productivity have fundamentally changed the resource-poor conditions of the past and greatly reduced the constraints on resources, enabling people to expand their desires. At the same time, desire is no longer the object of moral condemnation or ideological criticism. Second, boundaries between social classes have been broken. Opportunity and social mobility have increased. People who desire to rise to a higher social position, begin to imitate upper class consumer behavior. Fashion and its culture began to take shape. Third, industrialization led people to change their lifestyles, and this rate of change is accelerating. One dynamic reason for lifestyle change is the variety of consumer goods, consumer services and consumer amenities provided by industrialization. People eager to participate in the modern way of life are bound to form consumption desires and consume products that are compatible with that lifestyle. The other driving force of industrialization is market competition. In order to gain an advantageous position in the market, companies need to continue technological and business innovation, to reduce the cost of production, and to constantly develop new products. The process of new product development and marketing is in fact the process of creating new desire. We can say that consumerism is the economic, social and cultural result of industrial development reaching a higher stage.

Among contemporary Chinese urban residents, the desire for consumption began to expand. Some people's desire to consume exceeded their purchasing power (their capability to satisfy their consumption desire). The reason they buy goods, is not simply because they require these goods to meet their physiological needs (i.e., are absolutely necessary), but it is more because other community groups - particularly the groups they chose to compare themselves to - are using those products. Meanwhile, material products are increasingly becoming the signifier of a certain lifestyle. Buying a product, in fact, expresses a desire to participate in a mainstream lifestyle. Increased social mobility and more openness with regard to self-definition, make people reference each other more when comparing consumer products and consumption models, forming consumer fashion and style. Social status in the current era has constantly fluctuated. People have generally felt that they are "relatively deprived" (i.e., they sense that they lack things that others have), and their expanding desire is a manifestation of this sense of relative deprivation.

Under conditions of relative scarcity, goods become a social symbol. When all of mainstream society uses a particular product or practices a certain lifestyle, if someone cannot afford the product or practice that way of life, he or she will inevitably have a sense of "relative deprivation." From this perspective, whether one has a particular item becomes a representation or symbol of "joining", "success" or "failure", which means it is a symbol of self-identity. Therefore, the desire for material objects is not simply built on the basis of natural need, but on relative need or on being a symbol, that is to say, on the basis of establishing self-identity and a symbolism of social identity - these are psychological needs. As a result, the grand collective idealism of the era of the planned economy was replaced by individual materialism and consumerism in the era of reform and opening up. In other words, in a sense, consumerism has become one of the new personal ideals which substitutes for the idealism of the era of the planned economy. It is because of this ideological desire change that ascetic individuals transformed themselves into consumers.

Consumerism as a form of desire is inseparable from the institutional arrangements of the consumer society. The institutional arrangements of consumer society include advertising, fashion, media, shopping malls and promotions, credit and credit cards, and national economic policy (tax rates, interest rates, tariffs, etc.). People's desire for consumption is formed through the effects of inducement, stimulation and mobilization in this institutional environment. Social interaction and demonstration effect of reference groups further affect people's desire for consumption.

At the national level, in a country that had implemented asceticism for a long period of time, making adjustments to the system to improve people's consumption level had huge social and cultural effects. In fact, as I said before, in the late seventies the state faced a legitimacy crisis, it was through the improvement of people's living standards that the state regained popularity, thereby rescuing itself from the crisis of legitimacy resources caused by its failure to fulfill the promises it made during the planned economy era.

The state's attention to the resident's consumption level followed different logics at different stages. In the eighties, by increasing wages, the state adjusted the ratio of accumulation to consumption, improving the supply of consumer goods, and greatly increasing the state's legitimacy resources. Thus, during this period national consumer policy followed "legitimacy logic". It led directly to the first consumer revolution after the reform and opening up, which was evidenced by the increasing popularity of home appliances and other durable goods. In the late 1990s, and especially after the Asian financial crisis in 1997, because of a shrinking export market, domestic demand took an increasing role in stimulating economic growth. The state began to adopt a policy of expanding domestic demand. In addition to the expansion of investment, it started to encourage consumption. We can say that during this period of time, national consumer policy followed "rational logic." This logic allowed the state escape the negative attitude toward consumption it had fostered during the era of the planned economy. At this stage, stimulating and expanding people's desire for consumption, was not only consistent with national goals (economic growth), but also became an objective managed and regulated by national economic policy (e.g., within a short number of years, interest rates on bank deposits were lowered eight times in a row). Individual consumer desires therefore obtained national support and encouragement. At the same time, the market (advertising and promotion) and culture (media and fashion) were also involved in inducing consumer desire. Obviously consumerism has become an ideological desire that constantly expands under these institutional arrangements.

It can be said that in the planned economy era, by "tightening their belts" people were actively involved in socialist industrialization. By doing this, they showed the spirit of idealism and forward vision. With the end of idealism in the late seventies, the state had to find new incentive mechanisms. The mechanism adopted was to link people's income levels to their economic contribution, which encouraged people to pursue their material interests. In this context, consumerism has replaced idealism and become the new impetus for work.

Specifically, consumerism can be divided into three dimensions: materialism (the consciousness of possession), hedonism (the ethic of pleasure) and expressionism (the will to perform). Now I will discuss all three dimensions in sequence.

A. Consciousness of Possession

Hedonism (the ethics of pleasure) and expressionism (the demonstration of will) will be discussed later. Here, I will concentrate on materialism (the consciousness of possession). So-called materialism means that driven by the need for such products, the possession of consumer durable goods (subsequently referred to as "objects") was incorporated into the social structure as a way of providing both self-identity and social identity. This has led to people to indulge continuously in the pursuit of consumer durable goods. These objects are symbolic. They are pursued not only because of their physical properties or value in meeting human needs, but because the object is defined as the means of achieving individual happiness in life and is the "raw material" for building self-identity and social identity.

As durable consumer goods are one of the most important personal material interests, there is significant motivation to possess them. We can say that possessiveness is one way in reflecting materialism. And possessiveness is one of the main features of the "self-interested" person, for whom possession and use of the object must be exclusive. Therefore, materialism and "self-interest" are in fact twins. "Self-interest" implies materialism, and materialism requires the existence of "self-interest" as a premise. To the "self-interested" person, even if he has a relationship with the state's ambitious goals and objectives, the state's goals appear to be far away. It is important to the "self-interested" person to satisfy his own desires and meet his own goals within his lifetime. Materialism is a manifestation of this consciousness.

Materialism is a form of desire, namely: the desire to possessing the object (consumer durable goods). It is people's desire to possess the object whether due to their needs and or their sense of deprivation if they lack it. And this desire continuously expands without limit. The state, market, society and culture, each from their own standpoint, prompt, encourage and stimulate the formation of the desire to possess material goods. For example, the state, through the reform of the housing system, promoted and stimulated the desire to purchase and own a home. How the state, through its series of reforms (e.g., housing reform) stimulated consumption was discussed earlier (Chapter 3). We will not discuss it further. The following analysis is only focused on the question of how the people's materialism revolved around consumer durable goods.

1. Ratio of Family Ownership Consumer Durables Goods and Their Consumption

A remarkable achievement of the reform and opening up was the rapid improvement in the supply of consumer durables. From the beginning of the reform into the mid-1980s, consumer durable goods experienced a double change. On the one hand, the traditional consumer durables most sought during the planned economy era (bicycles, sewing machines, radios, fans, etc.) were largely available. At the same time, some products become obsolete and new products emerged (e.g., radio, black and white television, etc.). By the late 1980s, ownership of these items was gradually decreasing. But the process of opening up introduced new technologies and imported products. New appliances (e.g., color television sets, washing machines, refrigerators, tape recorders, etc.) began to be available in urban China and entered into consumer households (cf. Table 5-2).

Table 5-2   Number of Durable Consumer Goods per Every Hundred Urban Households, 1981~1986

Name	Unit	1981	1983	1984	1985	1986
Bicycle	ea.	135.90	159.93	162.67	152.27	163.45
Sewing machine	ea.	70.41	76.21	77.52	70.82	73.85
Watch	ea.	240.76	268.24	282.95	274.76	298.96
Fans	ea.	42.62	63.61	66.41	73.91	90.01
Radio	ea.	100.52	104.55	103.11	74.52	68.71
Black and white TV	ea.	57.06	80.58	82.04	66.86	65.42
Color TV	ea.	0.59	2.57	5.38	17.21	27.41
Washing machine	ea.	6.03	29.08	40.13	48.29	59.70
Refrigerator	ea.	0.22	1.65	3.22	6.58	12.71
Recorder	ea.	12.97	27.11	34.17	41.16	51.66
Camera	ea.	4.29	7.28	8.92	8.52	11.91

(Source: *China Statistical Yearbook 1987.*)

The reform and opening up led to a first wave of consumer products becoming available from 1979 to the middle 1980s. The main durable goods were black-and-white TV, bicycles, sewing machines, watches and radios. Within this period, a second wave of consumer durables quietly landed, including color televisions, refrigerators, washing machines, tape recorders, cameras and other new appliances. The acquisition of these items by urban households greatly expanded by the late 1990s, with the washing machine being adopted fastest and color televisions having the highest adoption rate (Table 5-3).

Table 5-3   Number of Durable Consumer Goods per Every Hundred Urban Households, 1981~2005

Name	1981	1985	1990	1995	2000	2005
Bicycle (ea.)	135.90	152.27	188.59	194.26	162.72	120.04
Sew sewing machine (ea.)	70.41	70.82	70.14	63.67	51.46	-
Electric fan (ea.)	42.62	73.91	135.5	167.35	167.91	172.18
Washing machine (ea.)	6.03	48.29	78.41	88.97	90.52	95.51
Electric refrigerator (ea.)	0.22	6.58	42.33	66.22	80.13	90.72
Color TV (ea.)	0.59	17.21	59.04	89.79	116.56	134.80
DVD player (ea.)					37.53	68.07
Recorder (ea.)	12.97	41.16	69.75	72.83	47.93	39.26
Photo camera (ea.)	4.29	8.52	19.22	30.56	38.44	46.94

(Sources: *China Statistical Yearbook 1987, China Statistical Yearbook 2006.*)

For the older class of consumer durables, sewing machines, black and white televisions and radios, the ownership rate began declining from its peak in the mid-1980s. Bicycle ownership peaked in the mid to late 1990s, declining gradually afterward. Opposite to the drop in ownership of sewing machines and other small appliances, ownership of fans kept growing until the late 1990s. Then, due to increasing sales of air conditioners, the growth rate flattened (Table 5-3). Washing machines, refrigerators and color televisions are representative of the new generation of appliances available to urban households since the mid 1980s. By the late 1990s they had become widely popular. We can say that since 2000, in urban areas the ownership rates of washing machines, color televisions and refrigerators have been at or close to saturation. At the same time, due to the emergence of DVD players, the household ownership of tape recorders, which had replaced radios, reached its peak in the mid 1990s and then began to decline. By the late 1990s the ownership rate of camera reached more than a third, and has grown steadily (Table 5-3). Home appliances arriving in the second wave of the middle 1980s were considered "luxury" goods, making them enormously attractive to urban consumers. Color televisions, refrigerators and washing machines became known as the new "Big Three", replacing the old (bicycles, watches, radios). By 2000, when the ownership rate of the second wave of consumer durables was close to saturation, they lost their "luxury" status, and became necessities.

The third wave of consumer durables appeared in the mid and late 1990s. The ownership rate of these increased gradually after 2000, although some grew relatively fast (air conditioners, water heaters, cooking range hoods, microwave ovens, fixed-line and mobile telephones) (Table 5-4). This wave of consumer durables had two characteristics. First, they are products that rely on digital technologies: home computers, mobile phones and so on. The new generation of refrigerators, washing machines and color televisions also began to utilize more digital technologies (e.g., digital television). Second, the ownership rates of certain items — air conditioners, water heaters, cooking range hoods, microwave ovens, fixed-line phones, DVD players, motorcycles, home music centers, etc. – have grown even faster than in earlier waves. (The emergence of motorcycles can be traced back to the early 1990s, earlier than those consumer durables in the same wave. The ownership rate of motorcycles grew rapidly in the late 1990s. But after 2000, because of the emergence of private cars, and some cities banning the issue of new motorcycle licenses, the ownership rate did not grow as fast).

The ownership rate for consumer durables of the third wave has not yet reached its peak, and a fourth wave of consumer durables began to appear in the early 2000s, being gradually adopted by some urban families, such as the personal family car, camera, fitness equipment, etc. (Table 5-4). Also, because of technological development, television sets were being upgrading, with plasma television becoming available in cities and being purchased by a small number of families. As part of the housing system reform, the state stopped welfare housing in 1998. Housing has become the largest item in the fourth wave of consumer durables. Overall, this wave has just started. The rate of family ownership of these items is not high (excluding residential housing). The future trend in the adoption rates depends upon country's economic development and distribution of wealth and income.

Table 5-4   Durable Consumer Goods per Hundred Chinese Urban Residents: Year-End Statistics (1981 ~ 2004)

Name	Unit	1981	1985	1990	1995	1999	2000	2001	2002	2003	2004	2005
Washing machine	ea.	6.0	48.3	78.4	89.0	91.4	90.5	92.2	92.9	94.4	95.9	95.51
Refrigerator	ea.	0.2	6.6	42.3	66.2	77.7	80.1	81.9	87.4	88.7	90.2	90.72
Color TV	ea.	0.6	17.2	59.0	89.8	111.6	116.6	120.5	126.4	130.5	133.4	134.80
Camera	ea.	4.3	8.5	19.2	30.6	38.1	38.4	39.8	44.1	45.4	47.0	46.94
Motorcycle	ea.	-	-	1.9	6.3	15.1	18.8	20.4	22.2	24.0	24.8	25.00
Video-recorder	ea.	-	-	-	18.2	21.7	20.1	19.9	18.4	17.9	17.6	15.49
Music center	ea.	-	-	-	10.5	19.7	22.2	23.8	25.2	26.9	28.3	28.79
Air conditioners	ea.	-	-	0.3	8.1	24.5	30.8	35.8	51.1	61.8	69.8	80.67
Shower	ea.	-	-	-	30.1	45.5	49.1	52.0	62.4	66.6	69.4	72.65
Hood	ea.	-	-	-	34.5	48.6	54.1	55.5	60.7	63.6	65.6	67.93
Player	ea.	-	-	-	-	24.71	37.5	42.6	52.6	58.7	63.3	68.07
Home computer	ea.	-	-	-	-	5.9	9.7	13.3	20.6	27.8	33.1	41.52
Video camera	ea.	-	-	-	-	1.1	1.3	1.6	1.9	2.5	3.2	4.32
Microwave	ea.	-	-	-	-	12.2	17.6	22.3	30.9	37.0	41.7	47.61
Fitness Equipment	ea.	-	-	-	-	3.8	3.5	4.0	3.7	4.1	4.2	4.68
Family Car	ea.	-	-	-	-	0.3	0.5	0.6	0.9	1.4	2.2	3.37
Mobile telephone	ea.	-	-	-	-	7.1	19.5	34.0	62.9	90.1	111.4	137.00
Ordinary telephone	ea.	-	-	-	-	-	-	-	93.7	95.4	96.4	94.80

(Sources: *China Statistical Yearbook 1987, China Statistical Yearbook 2004, China Statistical Abstract 2005, China Statistical Yearbook 2006.* Note that since 2003, some traditional statistical indicators have been removed by the National Bureau of Statistics.)

The family car will be discussed later. What we discuss here are only consumer durable goods represented by electronic appliances. These waves of consumer durables, led by electronic appliances, have shown that since the reform and opening up, urban residents in China have continuously engaged in the pursuit of new and updated consumer durables. This trend has several distinctive features. First, consumer durables, represented by electronic appliances, are constantly being upgraded. Product replacement is mainly due to technological innovation. The information and digital technology revolution has accelerated product upgrades, and shortened the product replacement cycle. The time when China began to open itself up to the outside world coincided with the start of the information and digital technology revolution. Product importation, technology transfer and introduction of similar domestically built product lines made consumer durables available in China at the same time as in foreign markets. Thus, in the West, it took consumers many decades to upgrade their televisions from black-and-white to color ones. In China this took only about 10 years to complete. Similarly, it took Chinese urban consumers much less time to switch from fixed telephone lines to mobile phones than it took Western consumers.

Second, the distribution of consumer durables over time follows a pattern, starting in isolated spots to becoming widespread, as consumers move from demonstrating to imitating. This process has gone through several phases. The first phase is often the time when products from the developed countries are in demonstration. When new appliances became available overseas, they were often brought back by the returning Chinese visitors or returned overseas workers (in the 1980s through the 1990s, a state rule says allowed bringing back 8 large foreign appliances duty-free) or these foreign products were made known to the domestic consumers through the media and other channels. The second phase is the import stage. Because of the high duty, the price of foreign products is usually high and only high-income groups can afford them. These consumer durables are usually purchased and used first by a small number of people, later becoming more widely used. While a certain level of understanding needed to utilize some products, the main reason for the delay is price. The third phase is the product line introduction stage. With introduction of foreign production lines into China, more electronic appliances are domestically made. The production cost was reduced and the price dropped, making the appliances popular among the mass class. When prices are high, only a few high-income groups can afford to buy. This leads to the phenomenon of product demonstration by elite consumers. It stimulates desire of those groups that are for the moment unable to afford the product. Then, as the price of a particular home appliance drops, consumer desire is stimulated, and the customers who have not yet purchased but have strong desire to do so will quickly follow the trend and complete a purchase. This stage is called the mass imitation stage. Table 5-5 uses the examples of washing machines, refrigerators and television sets to show how the household penetration of the "big three" in different years depends upon income. No matter which year, high-income consumers are always the leaders in home appliances purchases while low-income people are always followers. There is a certain time lag between the leaders and the followers (Table 5-5). Although income and other factors are important in determining the ownership rate of appliances by different groups, there must also be other influences. Otherwise it would not be possible to explain why, in the early stages, there are a considerable number of people in the highest income groups not buying these home appliances. Obviously, the desire to own or not own is a very important reason. Product demonstration by the elite group of mainstream society is one of the ways to provoke the desire to own something. The fourth phase is the stage of joining World Trade Organization (WTO). After joining the WTO, China was more open to the outside world. Tariffs were lowered and the prices for many foreign durable consumer goods were lower than before. More consumers could afford them. This phased process from international product demonstration, demonstration by domestic elite's and subsequent mass imitation, led to the boom in consumption of home appliances and other durable goods in China.

Table 5-5 Ownership of the Three Major Applicances by Income Level, per Hundred Urban Households, 1986~2004

Item	Years	Total Average	Lowest Income household	"Hardship" Household	Low-Income Household	Below-Average Income Household	Average Income Household	Above-Average Income Household	High-Income Household	Highest Income Household
Washing machine	1986	59.70	38.46	33.82	49.84	54.23	60.56	64.93	69.04	69.14
	1995	88.97	78.14	76.04	82.81	86.42	90.36	93.03	93.61	95.55
	2005	95.51	81.68	76.56	88.95	93.38	96.89	99.50	101.54	103.84
Refrigerator	1986	12.71	4.38	4.61	7.47	8.43	9.83	11.42	14.11	19.16
	1995	66.22	47.86	44.84	53.39	61.88	67.32	72.89	76.68	80.12
	2005	90.72	65.33	58.72	79.99	87.84	94.08	97.36	99.76	104.10
Color TV	1986	27.41	10.86	10.82	17.47	19.19	25.31	31.00	37.76	48.19
	1995	89.79	72.01	69.30	79.36	86.52	91.71	95.51	96.95	102.12
	2005	134.80	107.26	103.73	118.14	123.94	133.73	142.50	152.62	172.30

(Sources: *China Statistical Yearbook 1987, China Statistical Yearbook 1996, China Statistical Yearbook 2005, China Statistical Yearbook 2006.*)

Third, with the information and digital technology revolution, the life cycles of products incorporating information and digital technology are shorter. The time required for the price of an item to drop has been shortened, greatly speeding up the adoption rate of associated consumer goods. For example, when new models of computers, mobile phones or digital televisions are introduced, the initial prices are often set very high. Only high-income groups can afford them. However, because these products become "outdated" ever faster, their prices fall quickly, making them affordable to medium and low-income people as well. However, there is a clear time lag between the high-income leaders and the mass income followers in adopting these products.

Fourth, when consumer durable goods are new or just introduced, because of high prices that are beyond ability and willingness of the ordinary working-class to pay, they are often defined as "luxury" goods. As prices decrease over time, these consumer durables are redefined as "necessities." For example, our interviews show that washing machines, refrigerators and color televisions were, in the early 1980s, generally considered "luxuries." Today, these former "luxury" items have all become "necessities" and their ownership essentially democratized (Table 5-5). This process from "luxury" to "necessary" leads to the continuous racheting-up of urban resident's desire in China. For example, China's urban residents have experienced the evolution of their consumption pursuit from "old three pieces" (bicycle, watch and radio), to the "new three pieces" (television, refrigerator and washing machine) plus the "two small pieces" (tape recorder and camera) to today's "new, new three pieces"(house, car and plasma television). This process by which the level of desire constantly increases can be called "the desire ladder."

It can be said that the consumption boom in home appliances and other durable goods constitute materialism after the reform and opening up. There are many factors leading to the formation of such materialism, for example, the state's policy of opening up to the world, tariff policy, industrial and consumer policy, the revolution in new technologies, international product demonstrations, product demonstration by the elite and the mainstream consumers, the evolution of consumer durables toward more features and lower prices, urban resident's income rise and so on. All these factors have significant impact on the formation of this materialism. In this, people's desire for home appliances and other durable goods is not built primarily on the basis of what is absolutely necessary, but on the basis of relative need, which instigated by product demonstration by elite reference groups. Using electronic home appliances and other durable goods as symbols, people engaged in a contest of consumption and status competition against each other, which led to an unprecedented desire to possess these goods. It is true that home appliances can give us comfort and enjoyment of life. But this is only one aspect of the reasons that generate such desire. A more subtle and important reason is the formation of social relationships around these goods. As Bourdieu said, the products become the symbolic "distinction" of class.[449] If the high-income class distinguishes themselves from the others by being the first to possess and use "luxury" appliances and other durable goods, the medium and low-income classes would aspire to end their "relative deprivation" by obtaining these goods, thereby reducing their distance from "mainstream society".

What are the consequences of this materialism? In the early stage of the reform and opening up, there were still tensions between the state and individuals with regard to such materialism. For example, in the early days of reform and opening up, when the nation had no ability to produce color televisions, refrigerators, washing machines, etc., domestic consumers nonetheless had a strong desire to obtain these products. But the state had adopted a tariff policy to restrict the importation and consumption of these products. This situation soon was changed. When the nation developed the capability to produce electronic appliances through the introduction of technology and production equipment, and in particular when there was excess production capacity, the state began to encourage the consumer desire for consumer durables. Therefore, in the late 1980s, a new wave of consumption of home appliances (refrigerators, color televisions and washing machines) surged in Chinese cities. The consumer became a powerful force promoting domestic economic development and the development of the home appliance industry. Thus, in the consumption of consumer durables, the state and citizens have reached consensus.

The boom in household electronic appliances has not only greatly advanced the Chinese home appliance industry, but has had political consequences. Why? Since the reform and opening up, with the unavoidable international product demonstration, domestic consumers are eager to have these consumer goods. If they are denied these products for a long time, they will inevitably be disappointed. Therefore, the introduction and popularity of home appliances have become objective physical evidence and proof of the improved standard of living, and thus helping to re-establish the state's legitimacy resources.

Consumption of household electronic appliances and other durable goods evokes people's enthusiasm and vision of a happy life. With the tangible emergence of home appliances and other durable goods, the empty idealism advocated in the past is no longer attractive to people. People's attention has shifted to the pursuit of material goods and the possession of these items, as these products directly improve and enhance the quality of life, and at the same time provide an experience of "social participation".

2. The Ideal of Happiness: "Owning a House and Car,"

In the era of Mao Zedong's planned economy, social mobility was mainly tied to family background, party membership and political performance. Because most people had similar spending patterns, consumer goods were not main evidence of social mobility and status.[450] Since the reform and opening up, the mechanism of social mobility has fundamentally changed. The social transformation caused by the reform and opening up has allowed an individual's capability to supplant family background, and business performance rather than political performance has become the primary key to social mobility. In this new environment, market transformation has created many opportunities for upward mobility, enabling a middle class to rise in the cities (though its size relative to the total population is still small). For the rising classes, possession and consumption of consumer durable goods has become evidence of their social mobility and social status. The kind of house someone lives in, and the type of cars they drive are direct perceptual indicators, identifying their social status. Thus, the quest for a house and car is not only to satisfy a material need, but also to satisfy the individual's social and psychological needs.

In the early stage of the reform and opening up, through the media exposure (e.g., film, television), people realized that "owning a house and a car" were a way symbolizing the wealth of Western countries. Today, the people themselves are beginning to be to pursue such an idealized life. It can be said that private housing and cars have been incorporated into the middle-class ideal of life and are indispensable symbolic elements of the middle-class lifestyle. Therefore, people wanted to own houses and cars, not just for the convenience of living and traveling but because owning a house and car demonstrates their "successful" status and their middle-class lifestyle. When people want to become members of the middle class, they naturally desire to be private owners of houses and cars. It can be said that worshiping the ownership of a "house and car" is a way of worshiping the middle-class lifestyle. In this sense, the desire to have a house and car gives new impetus towards upward social mobility. Working towards a "house and car" instead of older utopian ideals has become a new calling. Our interviews have many such examples: "(Interviewer: What kind of lifestyle do you want to have?) Middle-class. (Interviewer: Can you describe it? Have a house and a car, then buy the latest electronic products, taste the food in Guangzhou, and travel around the world."(B07-M-25, credit guarantee corporation account manager) "(Interviewer: What kind of life do you aspire to?) At least I would like to a house, the kind of small villa, two-story house, separate rooms, not an apartment. (Interviewer: In addition to a house, anything else?) Cars, of course, at least one, I own it." (B02-M-23, sales clerk at a private technology company) "We can afford houses and cars, and a little money left to travel. Of course we will have some family funds, ah, our own children always need money to go to primary and secondary schools. So we'd best save some for them. ... This is my greatest motivation to work hard."(B12-F-23, customs employee) "It is a sure thing that we must have a house and cars. Life has to be at a certain level."(B14-F-22, bank employee)

Clearly, for young people, the spirit of idealism, of "devoting oneself to the motherland", the norm during Mao Zedong's era, has given away to materialism, which is a kind of material idealism symbolized by owning a "house and car." It can be said that for young people in contemporary society, their individual ideals are personalized, materialized and symbolized. The so-called ideal personalization means that people's efforts are no longer centered on the state's macroeconomic goals and collective vision, but on personal interests and wellbeing. The so-called ideal materialization means that to large extent the ideal of personal happiness is achieved increasingly through the possession of consumer durables. The so-called ideal symbolization is that people's pursuit of happiness is reflected in their pursuit of symbolic objects. In this sense, people pursue ownership of a private house and car because the house and car are symbols of a middle-class lifestyle.

Between a house and a car, a house is more "essential" in nature. Not only that, but from the perspective of durability, a house is longer lasting and may appreciate over time, while a car depreciates continuously. Thus, comparing the wish to own a house with to own a car, the wish to own a car reflects a stronger tendency towards materialism. According to a survey by Hu Xiaojun (sample size 25017), urban and rural residents show a strong desire to own cars (Table 5-6). People giving the answers "have a car," "buying a car," "will buy in one or two years", "will buy within three to five years," "will buy within five to ten years," account for the following percentage of those surveyed: in Beijing, Shanghai and Guangzhou: 70.3%, in the provincial capital cities and coastal cities: 65.7%, in inland cities and coastal developed counties: 57.8%, in inland counties and rural areas: 51.6%. It can be seen that in large cities more than seventy percent of the population already has a car or wants to buy a car in near or more distant future. Even in the inland counties and rural areas, the number is over half (see details in Table 5-6).

Table 5-6   National Consumer Willingness to Purchase Cars in Various Regions and Over Various Timeframes

	Existing car	Buy Now	Buy in 1~2 years	Buy within 3~5 Years	Buy within 5~10 Years	No plan
Beijing, Shanghai and Guangzhou	12.8	3.3	13.8	25.1	15.4	29.7
Provincial capitals and coastal cities	6.9	2.2	8.8	25.2	22.6	34.3
Common inland and coastal counties and cities	4.0	1.3	7.0	19.2	26.4	42.2
Inland counties and rural areas	0.5	0.2	5.2	15.4	30.0	48.6

(Source: Hu Xiaojun, Zhang Xiliang, [Jiankun], "Consumer Intention Survey and Influencing Factors on Family Car Purchase", *Consumer Economy*, **3**, 2007, 23~26.)

The symbolic function of houses and automobiles has become a large part of the stimulus that pushes young "self-interested" people to work hard and actively. They have become the expectations of the younger generation. Whether they can obtain them directly affects their future self-identity and social recognition. Therefore, the desire for home and car ownership raises expectations about the future, and the opportunities for people to be frustrated have also increased. The reason is simple. The higher expectation, the lower the probability of achieving it. As social stratification leads some people to have difficulty in realizing their expectations, their frustration is bound to increase. There are dual consequences of the materialism symbolized by a "house and car". It can encourage people to work hard to realize their own "perfect happiness". It can also increase frustration and resentment. In this sense, materialism is actually a "love-hate relationship".

3. Dreams of Cars

For a long time in China, a car was part of an official's perquisites. It represented power, status and identity, something ordinary people could not expect. Before 1984, not all ranking officials were eligible for cars. In accordance with the provisions of the time, only senior officials of the party and state were eligible for dedicated cars. The officials with county and lower governmental units were only allowed the use of jeeps and bicycles. In 1984, this restriction was canceled. The authorization of a car was extended to officials at county or group level. Ever since, governmental car services have has runaway popularity. In 1985, the state imported 200,000 cars and vans, costing nearly $2 billion, more than the sum total in the previous 30 years.[451] Dedicated governmental car services for officials become symbols of power and status. Official's access to cars at government expense is a demonstration of their power based upon their position.

In the middle 1990s, government official's monopoly on access to cars was broken. To build the automobile industry into a pillar industry of the national economy by 2010, the state began to encourage individuals to buy cars. In 1994, the State Council promulgated the "Automobile Industry Policy", which states: "Gradual changes must be made to the consumption structure of state administrative agencies, organizations, government institutions and state-owned enterprises by which they use the public funds to buy and use cars." (Article 46) "The state encourages individuals to buy cars. And according to the development of the automotive industry and market changes in consumption structure, the country will develop specific policies in due course." (Article 47) "Any localities and departments shall not use administrative and economic means to interfere with the purchase and legitimate use of personal vehicles. They should take positive measures to support and assure this by means of license management, parking, gas stations, driving training schools and other facilities." (Article 48) Very soon, those in the elite, high-income classes such as sports stars, film and television stars became the leaders in private ownership of cars. Their car ownership, a symbol of their economic and social status, played a strong demonstration role for the middle class. The systematic barriers preventing individuals from owning cars were eliminated. People's desire for cars begins to ferment, surge and expand. Although because of the high price, many people were able to purchase a car, they quietly formed a desire to own one (Table 5-1). Evidence of this is that many people learned to drive and obtained driver's licenses before they owned their own car. The expansion of desire for cars encouraged those having the economic means to accelerate joining the purchasing group, converting themselves from "car-free families" into "car families". According to the study by Tian Jun, since 1998, more than 50 percent of vehicles were privately purchased, which is now the main force in car consumption.[452]

In 2002, in order to join the WTO, the Chinese government made commitments to substantially reduce the regulatory overhead of the automotive industry and loosened it protectionist policy, essentially allowing free competition in car manufacturing. Multinationals accelerated their entry into China's automobile industry, and private capital investment in the industry increased. During this time there was a dramatic increase in the demand for cars.[453] However, after joining the WTO, the state's "Automobile Industrial Policy" of 1994, was no longer appropriate for the current realities of the automobile industry. Therefore, "to adapt and constantly improve the socialist market economic system and to adapt the domestic auto industry to the new situation after joining the WTO," "and to make our auto industry in 2010 to become a pillar industry of national economy,"[454] in 2004, with the approval of the State Council, the National Development and Reform Commission on 1 June 2006 promulgated the "Automotive Industry Development Policy". At the same time, the National Development and Reform Commission also announced to the termination of the "Auto Industry Policy" of 1994 under the State Council document [2004] number 30. The new automobile industry development policy directs "to guide consumers to purchase vehicles that have low fuel consumption, small-displacement engines, and use new energy sources" (Article 61). "Under the premise of ensuring the safety of credit, the state allows consumers to use the car they purchased as collateral for their auto loans," (Article 65). "To foster and develop the second-hand car market," (Article 66), "to ensure smooth traffic, easy parking and the convenience of driving, actively improve the planning and construction of parking facilities," (Article 70). A favorable environment had to be created for the promotion of private car consumption in all its aspects. Private car consumption is recognized as a national goal, part of building the car industry into the country's pillar industry, and is encouraged by national policy. Because of the state's encouragement of low end, highly economical cars, also its efforts in nurturing and developing a second-hand car market, the price threshold for personal cars was greatly reduced. More people were able to afford cars.

Although currently private car ownership in China is not high, still being much less than in developed countries, encouraged by national policy, private car consumption grew rapidly in the late 1990s, especially after China's accession to the WTO. According to the National Statistic Bureau (Table 5-4), in the years from 1999 to 2005, the rate of car ownership per one hundred Chinese urban households was respectively 0.3, 0.5, 0.6, 0.9, 1.4, 2.2, and 3.4. Private car ownership in some big cities has reached a considerable fraction. For example, in 2004, the number of cars owned per one hundred households in Shenzhen and Beijing was 21.5 and 12.64, respectively.[455]

Within China's urban areas, private car consumption is still limited to a small number of high-income groups, and remains in the demonstration phase. The desire to own a car among other income groups is in a fermentation stage. Even within the highest income groups, private cars are not yet universal. For the low-income groups, the private car ownership rate is even lower (Table 5-7). It can be said that private car ownership is a new wave of materialism supplanting the popularity of consumer electronics. It is still in a development stage. In some cities, car ownership has reached a state of rapid expansion (e.g., Shenzhen, Beijing, Shanghai, Guangzhou). The ultimate evolution of this materialistic trend follows the familiar model, a cycle in which the elite demonstrate to mass consumer groups, and the mass consumer groups subsequently imitating the elites.

**Table 5-7 Ownership of Cars at Year End by Income Level,
per Hundred Urban Households,   (2003~2005)**

Income Years	Total Average	Lowest Income Household	"Financial Difficulty" Household	Low Income Household	Below Average Household	Average Income Household	Above-Average Household	High Income Household	Highest Income Household
2003	1.36	0.20	0.11	0.25	0.42	0.62	1.00	1.97	6.57
2004	2.18	0.13	0.07	0.69	0.64	0.81	1.93	3.45	10.79
2005	3.37	0.29	0.16	0.64	0.91	1.73	3.26	5.57	16.20

(Sources: *China Statistical Yearbook 2004, China Statistical Yearbook 2005, China Statistical Yearbook 2006.*)

Besides adding to the enjoyment of life, improving the quality of life and showing a type of "social participation", cars, like electronic household appliances, led to new experiences and expanded individual freedom of action by breaking the limitations of public transport for daily personal activities. The possession of a car reflects the consciousness of contemporary "self-interested" people (i.e.: the exclusiveness in possession and use of material goods). To the middle class, a car not only brings a spatial experience but also creates a symbolic sense of social status. Therefore, it is not only a physical carrier, but also a social vehicle, signifying a certain social status.[456] Personal control of a car is akin to a feeling of control over one's own destiny. And this feeling is exactly what the rising middle class is eager to have as they acquire more economic power. Clearly, before the car became available to the masses, people's consumed cars not only for transport but also (at least subconsciously) as a social symbol, because the car represents freedom, comfort, speed, a radius of movement, success, identity, pride, and so on. In other words, people's desire for cars was not entirely built on the basis of absolute necessity, because public transport can also solve the problems of traffic. Their use of cars was mainly based on an individual concept of freedom (e.g., convenience), a desire to escape a sense of relative deprivation (not to appear to be out of date, abject, "to be old fashioned", constrained, shabby, "to have fared poorly", etc.) Or it was based on the pursuit of "success" and "identity". Therefore, the formation of the desire for car consumption is on one hand based on incentives established by national policies, and on the other hand is partly due to social demonstration by elite or interactive groups, which leads to personal imitation and following the examples of the reference groups.

The formation of the desire for car consumption follows a "point" to "surface" process. In the early stage, the rate of family car ownership is not high, but consumer spending on cars constitutes a demonstration "point", while other sectors forms the "facets" of the emerging desire for car consumption. According to our interviews, we can divide people into three categories based upon their relationship to automobile consumption: "having a car", "desiring a car" (the group that does not own a car but wants to) and "opposed to having a car "(the group that does not have a car and does not want to buy a car). The group having a car has satisfied their desire and relies upon the car psychologically. The group eager to own cars desires one but has difficulty in satisfying their desire to own one. The group rejecting cars does not have a desire to own a car.

In China, especially before China's joined the WTO, the first group of private car owners was a high-income group, mainly due to high tariffs on cars, which, along with various fees and taxes resulted in high car prices. For some brands of cars, the sales price in China was much higher than that abroad. Therefore, unless they were in a strong economic position, consumers had a hard time realizing dream of car ownership. A private enterprise chairwoman described her experience: She first bought a model called a "Maxima" second-hand, drove it for four years, then she changed to a Honda made in Guangzhou, but she did not like it. She then replaced it with BMW. All these car purchases were one-time cash payments. "Well we feel that we have money, buying a car or buying a house is quite normal. ... Also we need a brand name for cars too." (B33-F-37, chairwoman and managing director of private company) Because of her high-income, she desires to buy brand name cars. During the interview, in her own words driving a car was not only a pleasure, but also "status". A car is an important symbol allowing high-income consumer groups to distance themselves from other "normal" consumer groups. With the increasing number of car owners, the pursuit of a brand name car is an approach by which high-income groups can further distance themselves from the ordinary group of car owners.

The possession of a car can lead to the formation of dependence on it. As cars become a way of life, without a car, some would feel at a loss. "A few years ago we felt people owning a car were better than people who did not have cars. Now we think car is just a part of life. One day a friend borrowed my car, I felt as if my legs were gone. I just did not want to go out. When buying the first car, we felt that we gained face and position, and now we have no feeling. I've changed cars twice, this is the third one."(B15-M-42, owner of a private business)   As car prices slowly fall, and with the development of credit services for automobile purchases, in addition to high-income groups, some working-class people can afford cars too. Automobile loans are available from financial institutions. A car brings convenience to many people's lives. "Its use (my car) is a little high. It is more than 100 kilometers every day. I have to pick up and send my wife to work, drive myself to work, and go out socializing, the average daily (use) about 100 to 150 km. ... I bought this car that has room to put a lot of things. I like sports. I can put sports gear inside the trunk. My friends call me to play ball. I will drive there straight without going home first. My car almost becomes my traveling home, very convenient, not like a motorcycle ride or bus that is not convenient. "(B29-M (2)-33, policeman) This improved consumer experience makes the car owners behavior irreversible. It is no way for them to return to riding a motorcycle or waiting for the bus in the sun or rain. In other words, the desire for car consumption has become a normalized desire that is taken for granted. It is a desire beyond riding a motorcycle or taking the bus.[457] Stepping up the ladder of desire makes car owners feel that their cars are indispensable.

Among our respondents, when talking about buying a car, the most used keyword is "convenience." Survey data by Hu Xiaojun and others also shows that more than 75 percent of respondents believe that it is "convenient to have a vehicle".[458] "Convenience" expresses two meanings: on the one hand, it reflects the convenience to have a car in daily life. This convenience is often relative to taking the bus, "calling cabs" or self-driven motorcycles; on the other hand, the "convenience" is in fact the expression of "personal freedom in transportation": "I can go to wherever I want to," "I will go whenever I want to go." It shows that people with cars tolerate less of traffic constraints (time constraints, space constraints). More and more, they take for granted personal freedom in transportation. They more and more internalize and naturalize this "personal freedom".

The external effect of "car owners" on car consumption is their demonstration effect and the group pressure they exert on those without cars. Consequently, ever more people without cars desire private cars. In the late 1990s, favored by national policies, such as the consumer lending policy, car ownership began to expand beyond those powerful politically (e.g., national cadres) and the economic elite (e.g., private entrepreneurs, etc.). Car ownership became more accessible to the middle class. For them, it was not a matter of whether they should own a car, but rather a matter of time, because their desire to own a car has become very clear, all that remains is to realize this ambition over time. "I want to buy a car and just signed up for a driving school. I would like to buy a car. With money I definitely want to buy it. In fact, everyone sets up his or her target. At this stage you want to have something, and at the next stage you will want to have something. ... Here in Guangzhou, you cannot always rub shoulders like this on the crowded bus. "(B35-M (2)-28, advertising designer) "In fact buying car is a kind of consumer attitude. From the perspective of consumerism, we are all young people. We should enjoy when we are able to, not wait to be too old and then enjoy. We should learn from foreign consumer attitudes. Driving is actually a casual way of relaxation. When going to play, taking bus is never as convenient as driving by myself. The third point, if you have a car, or in the future have the potential to get a car, it is also an incentive. I have been driving and I would like to progress in this direction."(B30-F (2)-32, community services manager). "China's population is so big. Someone has calculated that if each Chinese has one car, there would not enough parking space in the world and the cars have to be parked in the sea. Moreover, Chinese road construction can never keep up with the pace of the development of the car industry. ... Car consumption in China should not be vigorously promoted. (But) I will definitely buy a car. I want to be the part of the first rich group. Paying a bit more than two hundred thousand yuan to buy a car, I should be able to meet my own car needs." (C12-M-26, university administrator)

In the medium term, car will remain beyond the financial means of many people. However, given their expanding economic power, the middle-class is finding it much easier to buy cars. At least three factors have accelerated the ability to afford a car: First, middle-class incomes have risen. "I'm thinking of spending our own money (a one-time payment to buy a car) ... compared to buying a house, it is a relatively small amount. ... And it is a one-time payment, not a big problem after years of savings." (B31-M-31, newspaper editor) Second, car prices have declined, especially with the introduction of low cost, entry level cars, to the point that majority of middle-class families can afford them. "Buying a car in China is not difficult these days. It is about 100,000 yuan, ... anyway, it is not expensive to buy a car now." (B27-M-34, government official) Third, the establishment of an automobile loan system has greatly enhances people's ability to purchase cars. "With some level of savings to provide security and backed by continuous salary income, I will spend a bit more ahead of time, and get car loan to buy a car." (C20-M-30, customs employee) Fourth, one can adjust one's budget, setting priorities that will permit satisfying the desire for a car. "Now the car is also a lot cheaper. Relatively speaking, buying a car is much easier than buying a house, which accounts for my buying a car." (C23-M-24, clothing salesman) It is precisely this affordability factor that drives people's desire for cars. It is no longer a daydream, but an item built into the household budget.

The desire to own a car is surely because a car can solve the personal transportation problem. But when public transport is available, especially if the cost of maintaining a car is higher than the taking taxicabs, the purchase of a car is not merely for transportation; it must provide some other kind of "value". In our interviews, all respondents who had cars rationalized their purchase with an assertion of the "value" it provided. After analysis and classification, we can put these "values" into five categories: (1) "convenience" and expanding the radius of accessible activities; (2) experience and entertainment; (3) identity and status; (4) group pressure; (5) business needs (an instrumental type of purchase).

The "convenience" of traveling, so as to expand the scope of social activities and contacts, was the motive expressed by most of the respondents we interviewed. On the surface, this motivation seems to be "instrumental", but in fact, this surface reflects a deeper motive, which is "personal freedom." The so-called "convenience", is mainly by comparison to that provided by bus or taxi. On the one hand, with a car, you can basically go whenever you want and wherever you want. This is the superficial meaning of "convenience". On the other hand, by having your own car, you do not have to take a bus or taxi. With a car, there is space for individual freedom in action. The scope and radius of personal activities expand, and restrictions are lifted. "Owning a car is convenient, certainly more than taking the bus or calling taxi." (B23-M-31, survey and design institute engineer) "During rainy days when you cannot get a cab, you really want to own a car. For example, going to work, if I am a bit late, after half past seven, the traffic in Guangzhou Bridge area really jams. And if I have a car, I know it is bad ahead, I would not go the route of Guangzhou Bridge. I would take the Haiyin Bridge. When it is really hot, I just want to stay inside the car to be comfortable. Another reason is that with the car, you can change the location of your home. You can live further out. You sell the old house and re-invest. With the car, your area of activities is enlarged, including your personal circle and your working circle."(B31-M-31, newspaper editor) So the deeper meaning of "convenient" is still "personal freedom", which means eliminating the constraints involved when taking a bus or taxicab. As people's income levels have increased, the personal freedom associated with such spatial activities is given "value" and "meaning", therefore becoming a "need" having value.

In addition to convenience, many respondents also said that their reason for buying a car was to experience the pleasure of driving, or for travelling to entertainment, for socializing, or go on outings. "(Interviewer: Why do you want to buy a car?) Because I have a driver's license. And I like the feeling of driving. In particular, I like to drive fast. Oh, I feel very HIGH. I really enjoy that kind of pleasure, very exciting." (B41-F-24, retired woman) "I bought a car primarily to go out to play, for example on weekends I can go to far places. I do not use much of the car when I am at work. I own the car out of both work and entertainment needs." (B28-M-35, university teacher)

Cars are also symbols of success, identity and status. Therefore, the desire to own a car is not only for the convenience it provides for transportation and travel, but also to illustrate to society a person's success, identity or status. According to the survey by Hu Xiaojun, about 20 percent of respondents across different income groups expressed that "a car is a sign of success."[459] In this sense, car consumption is a kind of social communication. The car as a symbol conveys information about the success or status of the car owner. Because of this, ambitious members of the middle class are often eager to have a car. Although some people interviewed verbally denied that they bought a car to show off their status or success, subconsciously, these motives do exist. But some people frankly acknowledge that they own a car to show their success, identity and status. Others use a more tactful tone to express the same motivation. "I think the people out there driving fancy cars are all women. This way, even if people don't think the woman is beautiful, they feel the woman is very high up. I am actually envious of this kind of life. But I know that it is impossible for me to have such kind of life." (B41-F-24, unemployed) "(Interviewer: How do you feel when you drive your own car?) A sense of accomplishment. I graduated three or four years ago. If I can buy a car within five years, it counts a small success. It is not a big success, but at least it makes other people feel that you are doing okay, at least having ability, right?" (B35-M (2)-28, advertising designer) "More or less, cars bring people a sense of vanity. Since you drive a car, people may think you are doing very well, which brings you a sense of vanity. ... If the car does not bring you social status, it would at least be a symbol of your success." (B21-F-24, accountant) "When I buy a car, a world famous brand of course would be the best, still, it depends on my economic situation. (Interviewer: Why are the world-famous brands are the best?) One is quality. The other is that people relate it to your identity and recognition. Buying a house is mainly for your own use, a brand is relatively less important, but a car is often driven out to show to others." (C06-M-29, director at China Mobile)

The desire to own a car also comes from the pressure of the community. A person, when all the members of his or her reference group (participative reference group) all have cars, he or she is bound to feel pressure from this peer group to own a car. Or, when most people have cars, it will inevitably create a trend to attract car-free families to join the ranks of car owners. Therefore, owning a car is a relative need, formulated according to whether "other people have one or not". "(Interviewer: You seem very interested in a car, why do you consider buying a car?) Convenience. With a car, your thinking will change. Your circle of friends will be expanded, like to the (Pearl River) Delta. One reason is social, and another factor is to follow the group. Many of my friends have bought cars. Their economic situation is not very comfortable. But with a little tight budge, we can afford buying cars. Our reason of buying cars is for the convenience of making friends more easily, also a bit out of our own vanity." (B26-M (2)-34, cadre)   "(Interviewer: Why learn to drive?) We all learn. I learnt about science before you. There are always opportunities to buy cars and the opportunity to use them." (B23-M-31, surveying and design institute engineer) The desire to have a car is to certain extent to avoid the "relative deprivation" and exclusion from mainstream social circles, in which owning a car is a symbol of membership in mainstream society.

In addition to the reasons above, some people need to buy cars for business purposes. For them, buying a car is not consumption, but an investment. "(Interviewer: Why do you buy a car anyway?) Because I own hotels. To provide a convenience to guests, I need to run a shuttle bus service. ... Buying a car for me is an investment, not consumption. We calculate the return for any investment. If this investment can bring greater benefits, I will buy a car."(B39-M-30, freelancer)

The temptation to purchase a car is great. But not all urban residents want to buy a car (see Table 5-1). These people do not want to buy a car for many reasons. The following categories summarize the main ones: (1) a purely physical or personal reasons (e.g., motion sickness, phobia, or simply do not like cars), (2) inadequate income, (3) budget constraints, (4) poor driving environment, (5) high cost of maintenance, (6) other alternatives available, (7) values (awareness of the environment). Some are simply in an uncertain state and are waiting.

The formation of materialism, in addition to the factors of rising incomes, a rich supply of goods and services and changes in values, is also shaped by the institutional arrangements of the state. One of these that had revolutionary effect was the systematic support of consumer credit. It paved the way for the formation of materialism, sweeping away all obstacles. The consumer credit system was introduced by the state in the late 1990s to promote economic and real estate development and the development of the automobile industry. It allowed consumers to borrow against their own future income, in the form of a mortgage to purchase large consumer durables, avoiding the long process of savings and allowing the enjoyment of these products much sooner. This system allows consumers to maximize their pleasure within a certain time horizon (rather than delaying enjoyment). Therefore, the consequences of introducing he consumer credit system were revolutionary. It led to the emergence of new consumption patterns, namely: getting loans from banks or other financial institutions, to purchase or use consumer durable goods or consumer services, and then paying in installments, repaying the bank debt. In addition to this mortgage system, the consumer credit system also includes a credit card system, which allows consumers to make purchases in their daily lives on credit, promoting and expanding the desire to consume.

We can say that consumer credit is a systematic "booster" of materialism. Prior to the credit system, people's consumption was limited by their current income. This limited their ability to pay for the most consumer durable goods or services. The emergence of the consumer credit system has solved this problem. It changes consumption as a function of current income to be a function of income over time. This revolutionary change promotes and expands the consumer's desire to spend, especially that of young consumers. With the consumer credit system, people's desire for material possessions and consumption level can extend significantly beyond their current ability to pay. Thus the time over which a particular unit is consumed or enjoyed is extended. Since the emergence of the consumer credit system, items that were previously remote materialistic dreams (e.g., a house or a car) have been brought within reach. It has been possible to satisfy people's desire more easily. Because of such psychological anticipation, the desire for material possessions will inevitably expand. In this sense, the consumer credit system has become a "booster" allowing the middle-class and other groups to pursue materialism. It has led to a quantum jump in the desire for material possessions: from the enjoyment of everyday products to the possession and consumption of large amounts of consumer durable goods.

In addition to household appliances and private cars as discussed above, materialism is also reflected in many other items, such as: clothing, furniture, kitchenware, decorations, pets and more. However, due to space limitations, we do not discuss them here. Household appliances and private cars were examined sufficiently to show that after 20 years of economic reform, materialism has replaced idealism as the new goal for which people to strive. Materialism has become a new kind of incentive for social transformation. Moreover, materialism has become a mechanism that people use to give their lives meaning, because materialism to a large extent has become a symbol of idealized happiness.

With respect to the process by which materialism was formed, household appliances provided consumers with a widely open space in which they exercised their unbridled enthusiasm for the pursuit of material goods. This process therefore not only reconstructed the state's legitimacy resources, but also encouraged people's expectations for the reform and opening up. However, when materialism moved to the stage of car consumption, car consumption made apparent social stratification. The purchase of cars, building on the foundation of consumer's enthusiasm for household appliances, has renewed people's enthusiasm to consume. Finally, the emergence of the consumer lending system has allowed people to upgrade their material possessions and accelerate their purchases.

B. Ethics of Pleasure

The "sense of possession" or materialism as described above, is inseparable from the sense of pleasure. In other words, possession of an object also means enjoyment. It can be said that the characteristics of consumer culture not only include materialism (the desire to possess the material good) but also the ethics of pleasure. The so-called ethics of pleasure refers to the fact that once pleasure becomes legitimate, it becomes a goal pursued by people. In other words, pleasure becomes an important motivation for people's action. The concept of pleasure has existed since ancient times. However, in traditional society, the pursuit of pleasure has always been restricted to a small, privileged circle within the upper class. In the United States, Britain and other countries, the mainstream of society follows the traditional Protestant ethic. This ethic advocates asceticism and postponing enjoyment, opposing extravagance and waste; it is the opposite of "carpe diem".[460] In modern society, the ethic of pleasure or romance became a new kind of belief or code of conduct derived from the Protestant ethic of conviction.[461] A major cause of the rise of the ethics of pleasure is economic prosperity and expansion of the middle class. Not until the stage of developed productivity can the ethics of pleasure have an economic foundation and can it be put into economic orbit. At the same time, only after the expansion of the middle class can the ethics of pleasure find a social base and be accepted by the mainstream of society.

As many sociologist's studies revealed, the population structure of Chinese society in general is still far different from that of the Western society, with its "olive" shaped income distribution, i.e. the size of the middle-class is too small.[462] However, if we focus on the cities, the middle class has already grown to a significant fraction. Now their income level enables them to pursue the ethic of pleasure. The emergence of the consumer credit system has further promoted this. But we cannot say that in Chinese cities, the traditional ethic of frugality has given way completely to the ethic of pleasure. This is because not only do those with lower incomes continue to live frugally, but also among the population pursing the ethic of pleasure, it may be necessary to adopt frugal practices in order to reach a particular goal of enjoyment. In other words, for this group of people, the ethic of pleasure and frugality can "peacefully coexist". For example, they may take out bank loans to buy a house and car, while at the same time, in order to repay the those loans, they save moderately and limit their daily consumption (i.e., "amphibious" consumption").[463]

1. From Ethics of Thrift to Ethics of Pleasure

The so-called ethic of thrift refers to the attitudes, beliefs and habits of consumption that address how to manage individual economic resources in the most frugal way under the condition of economic shortage. People believing in frugal ethics often control their desire, cut spending, and reduce their consumption to the minimum physical needs. Opposed to the ethic of thrift, the ethic of pleasure is a set of consumer attitudes, beliefs and habits that address how to manage individual economic resources to maximize pleasure under the condition of economic excess. People obeying the ethic of pleasure seek to maximize consumer pleasure by using a variety of budget strategies that permit staying within budget constraints. Here, pleasures include both immediate pleasure and long-term pleasure. There are three different budget strategies in addressing the relationship between immediate-term pleasure and long-term pleasure: (1) satisfying the immediate pleasure, regardless of the long-term pleasure (strategy of enjoying the pleasure on spot); (2) at the expense of the immediate-term pleasure, satisfying the long-term pleasure (strategy of delayed gratification); (3) seeking balance between the immediate-term pleasure and long-term pleasure (strategy of equilibrium in pleasure-seeking). Over time, the first budgeting strategy leads to less pleasure over longer time periods, so it is not the best strategy to achieve maximum pleasure over a lifetime. The second budget strategy achieves the goal of obtaining ultimate pleasure by inhibiting immediate enjoyment. This is a rational inter-temporal budget strategy under the condition in which resources are substantially constrained, and is also a strategy to maximize overall pleasure under those conditions. The third budget strategy is used to achieve the maximum pleasure over a lifetime if resources are unconstrained, and is often adopted in modern society. One reason for the third strategy's popularity is the rise of the consumer credit system. As financial institutions issue loans to consumers, consumers can use the money, according to their expected income and repayment ability, buy consumer durable items that would otherwise require long-term savings. This way, the "delayed enjoyment" budget strategy is converted to a "balanced pleasure seeking" one. In other words, people no longer have to live frugally for a long time in order to save enough money to purchase of major consumer durables (e.g., residential housing). By obtaining bank loans, they are not only able to purchase durable consumer goods sooner, but also they need not sacrifice immediate-term pleasure. The consumer credit system comes into play exactly when there is excess economic capacity and consumer demand has become an important force driving economic growth. Therefore, the ethic of pleasure, supported by the consumer credit system, is a system of consumer ethics under the condition of economic surplus. Of course, in addition to consumer credit system, the rise of the ethic of pleasure is also related to other institutional and structural conditions.

As I have discussed in the third chapter, in the era of Mao Zedong's planned economy, asceticism was a policy direction by the state, and it institutionalized a particular lifestyle and set of consumer ethics. As we have already analyzed, under the conditions of limited resources, the state prioritized the development of heavy industry, which required controlling the consumption level of the urban residents by limiting the supply of goods to them. In order to ensure the successful implementation of this policy, the state had to promote asceticism by means of the national discourse, for instance using the slogans "plain living" and "hard work, diligent and thrifty." During that period of time, behaviors and attitudes that indicated the pursuit of personal pleasure were treated as heretical acts and people who engaged in them were considered morally stigmatized. For example: "pleasure-seeking" was a term with negative moral implications, which was used to criticize those seeking personal pleasure. Moreover, behaviors indicating a pursuit of pleasure were also often escalated to the political level, to be denounced as a "bad idea", or "the pursuit of bourgeois lifestyle," and those engaged in them "being captives of bourgeois ideology."

Therefore the asceticism (or ascetic culture) of that time was not only the lifestyle determined by the national policies that curbed consumption, but was also an ethic of consumption deeply engrained in people's consciousness. In the society dominated by this ethic, frugality was not only seen as a virtue, but was a set of habits and principles rooted in national psyche. Under this ethic of frugality, people not only found ways to save, but they also could not tolerate other people's pursuit of "luxury" and hedonic behavior. Therefore, if someone paid attention to what they ate, drank or wore, he or she would often be criticized by the political leadership or public. In such social and moral soil, the pursuit of pleasure not only lacks an economic foundation but cultural legitimacy.

In the society with this moral atmosphere of asceticism, thrifty behavior is not only legitimate but it is reasonable, because it allows people to balance their limited income with their expenditures. "Simplicity", "thrift" and "savings" became affirmations of people's morals. Thus, to obtain political advancement (e.g., membership in the party youth league or the party itself), people consciously foreswore advocating the values and behaviors of pleasure seeking. There were even those who "conspicuously exhibited their frugality." This kind of conspicuous thrift often earned a positive moral evaluation.

The main spiritual pillar supporting the ascetic life was idealism. With an ideal vision of future happiness, people were able to accept and follow an ascetic life for the time being. However, once disillusioned, asceticism loses its spiritual support. The ascetic becomes "tragic." As shown in the previous data, in the late period of the Cultural Revolution, idealism began to fail. Asceticism not only could not survive, but also caused the collapse of the state's legitimacy resources. It was under such circumstances that the reform and opening up began.

When Deng Xiaoping's famously said that, "Poverty is not socialism," he endorsed wealth, consumption and legitimized pleasure seeking. Those people who get "rich first" have the ability to purchase luxurious products, and to pursue pleasurable lifestyles. This class of people had demonstrative effects on the other classes. As an economic surplus developed in the late 1990s, the state adopted a policy of stimulating consumption. By establishing the consumer credit system, the pursuit of pleasure not only gained legitimacy but also obtained financial support from the system. The ethic of pleasure was an inseparable part of the country's economic trajectory. It became a cultural force to stimulate market demand and economic growth. Seeking pleasure was no longer an act subject to moral condemnation. On the contrary, due to its positive economic function, it gained unprecedented legitimacy. For many people, the pursuit of pleasure became the pursuit of personal freedom, becoming in turn the ethical basis of consumer behavior.

Clearly, the changes from thrift to the ethic of pleasure follow a certain internal logic. In the era of planned economy, to achieve the goal of industrialization under extremely resource-poor conditions, the state adopted a policy of suppressing private consumption. A consumer ethic of frugality was an integral part of this policy, in order to serve the need of the country's industrial development. However, after 20 years of reform and opening up,

China has reached a stage of "excess" production. The previous ethic of thrift conflicts with the new national goals, because now consumer demand is the force driving economic growth, and the ethic of frugality prevented this force from contributing to the national goal. Thus, in order to achieve economic growth, the state not only tried to increase incomes to improve people's ability to consume, but also tried to use the consumer credit system and other financial leverage (e.g., interest rate policy) to stimulate consumption. An important cultural motivation that can be used to stimulate consumer enthusiasm is the ethic of pleasure. Ethics of pleasure or hedonism are an important attribute of the subject of contemporary consumption.

2. Legitimacy of Ethical Pleasure

To understand the rise of the ethic of pleasure, it is necessary to understand the social space of its existence, namely: the existence of distinct social classes. To this end, it is necessary for us to see it from a subjective point of view, to understand people's views on pleasure. Our data has clearly shown that the ethic of pleasure has formed within certain groups and classes. It has become a subject of consciousness, where ethic of frugality has given way to ethic of pleasure. However, this does not mean that ethic of frugality has absolutely no "market". Instead it means on the one hand, that the specific content of ethical frugality has changed; on the other hand, the believers in the ethic of thrift and practitioners of frugality in the traditional sense are primarily limited to the lower and bottom classes. Therefore, the rise of the ethics of pleasure means a divergence of consumer ethics, because in different classes and groups, people believe in and practice different consumer ethics.

A sign of the rise of the ethic of pleasure is that it no longer has a negative moral connotation; it has gained cultural legitimacy. The so-called legitimacy of the pursuit of pleasure refers to people's wide acceptance of pleasure as being legitimate, justifiable, and worthwhile pursuing. Only when pleasure gained legitimacy, could people confidently pursue pleasure, and follow an ethic of pleasure. Our interviews show that in people's minds, pleasure is no longer considered shameful as it was in the past.

When being asked whether "pleasure is shameful," all of the respondents who replied disagreed with this view. "(Interviewer: in the past, the pursuit of pleasure was considered shameful. Do you still agree with this opinion?) I do not agree. People just need to know work, as well as enjoyment. ... Now people all have learned well about enjoying things. It would be totally fine if they pursue adequate amount of pleasure. There is not much money left on my bankcard. I spent almost all. My salary is not high anyway."(B01-F-23, civil servant) People believe that as long as someone's consumption stays within his capability to pay for it, it would be reasonable for him to pursue it. "It would be rational and reasonable if individual's personal capabilities can support that. I think my spending even reasonable ah, although my older sister and my mother thought I should have been more frugal, but I think I am very happy. Ah, happiness is reasonable." (C11-F-25, actor in advertising)

As people were able to justify consumption, how did they justify the enjoyment of it (legitimization)? The reasons given can be divided into the following classes: (1) pleasure is the purpose of life; (2) pleasure is a means to reduce work stress; (3) the pursuit of pleasure is a virtue to strive for; (4) pleasure is the return for one's efforts; (5) enjoyment is allowed and encouraged by the state.

Our respondents illustrate the different justifications that are given to legitimize pleasure. The first view is that pleasure is an end. Money is to be earned and to be used for pleasure, if one has money why should one live poorly? As long as the source of the money is legitimate, it does not really matter how people pursue pleasure. "(Interviewer: In the past, the older people believed that the pursuit of pleasure is shameful. Do you still agree with this opinion?) I do not agree, as long as you have economic capacity, you can pursue whichever way you'd like. So long that you are able to make money, you should be able to enjoy it. Money earned is to be spent. (B10-F-30, leisure center cashier) "How could the pursuit of pleasure be shameful? Now everyone looks for pleasure, ah, people are not making money to be poor, right? It just needs to be legitimate pleasures, not extravagance, certainly not over indulgence."(B36-M (1)-30, doctor)

The second view is that pleasure is a way of releasing the pressure of work. On the one hand, people want to work, on the other hand, it is also necessary for them to relax and pursue pleasure. "I never believed it so, 'that the pursuit of pleasure is shameful.' Because people must have a place to decompress, different jobs having different troubles. It is necessary to have some level of enjoyment." (B05-F-35, hotel room service staff) "There is a saying I quite agree with. It is 'learning to spend money well, will allow you to make money better.' If you did not know how to spend money, always splitting a penny into half to spend, you would never know how to make it back in the future. The way I feel about pleasure is that if it is for appropriate relaxation, especially after too much work pressure, an adequate level of pleasure should not be a problem."(B13-F-22, kindergarten teacher)

A third view is that the desire for pleasure constitutes the driving force of economic and social development. The advancement of society requires desires. The pursuit of pleasure can promote the development of better products and economic growth. If there was no desire for pleasure, more advanced products would not sell and society would not advance. "If there is no consumption, how can there be development and needs. A society or individuals must have desire in order to have drive, to push society forward. (B15-M-42, owner of a private company) "I think as long as that it is not over-indulgence, stimulating the pursuit of pleasure is entirely for the advent of better products and the increase of productivity. "(B07-M-25, credit guarantee corporation account manager) "Subject to the context of social ethics and legality, any consumption can be understood and accepted, as long as they are not contrary to this premise. If there were no consumption, there would not be social advancement. If the products produced did not sell, it would affect technological progress and social development. Taking driving as an example, if I am happy with a tractor, the Mercedes-Benz and BMW will not sell. "(B08-M-28, joint venture manager)

The fourth view sees pleasure as a reward for working or living. People pay in order to get a benefit. The pleasure of consumption is a type of benefit. "Why sometimes do we Chinese people work to death, which is the tradition for thousands of years? ... I think the pursuit of pleasure should be a reward in our lives. Usually, if my sources are legitimate and my income is legitimate, my going after pleasure is the fruits of my labor. I take this for granted. I don't think it being anything shameful."(B29-M (1)-32, policeman) "I think the pursuit of pleasure is a human need, just like your relaxing in your spare time after work, a proper level of spiritual enjoyment is necessary, so is the case of some material pleasure. If you want to pursue higher-level spiritual enjoyment, consumerism is certainly a part embedded inside it. At a certain level, people talk about different things. According to their individual income level and capacity, people should reward themselves a little within a range."(B30-F (1)-32, community services manager) "It is normal to pursue the sense of pleasure. I feel that while you are making big efforts, you will need to learn how to get paid back, right? You need to learn to enjoy. Only working hard but not knowing how to enjoy is not enough. But your enjoyment should be limited within your economic conditions. You can enjoy. Nobody is against you being able to enjoy these days."(B25-M (1)-29, military logistics driver)

Finally, there is the view that advocates examining pleasure from the perspective of its social environment. Whether pleasure is justified must be linked with the social environment. In the past, pleasure was a deviant thing. In today's social environment, the pursuit of pleasure is the individual freedom permitted by the state. One of the respondents expressed his view on this: "In fact, when we say someone is pursuing pleasure, we mean someone seeking materialistic enjoyment. In the previous environment when there is a great spiritual wealth, your pursuit of material pleasures, of course, was seen as a deviant.

Now what the state and the society have taught to us is more an individual point of view. Thus a person seeking pleasure is not to be controlled by others. And nobody can control it. It is unlike the previous centralized environment where people will and are able to interfere with you."(B35-M (1)-28, advertising agency owner and designer)

Once the ethic of pleasure becomes a part of consumption ethics, the criteria to judge a particular consumption being worthy or legitimate is no longer whether it meets the functional requirement of being "essential", but whether it agrees with people's values with regard to pleasure. Because spending on tourism is consistent with the value of pursuing pleasure, tourism as a form of consumption has unprecedented legitimacy. From this point of view, whether people see tourism as "worthwhile" reflects their perception as to whether travel is legitimate or not. The rise of the legitimacy of tourism is the best proof of the rise of the ethic of pleasure.

The transformation from frugal consumption to an ethic of pleasure is a profound change. This change is not only because of the increase in people's disposable income, but also because of morphological changes in desire within the contemporary social structure. People's desires are no longer externally or internally inhibited or constrained, instead they may freely act on their desires, which led to the ethic of frugality being replaced by the ethic of pleasure. So, dining out or traveling, traditionally considered "luxury" consumer expenditures, are now considered justified, even necessary. Even if people still believe in saving or thrift, this belief has no conflict with pleasure. It is to better achieve the goal of enjoyment. When short of economic resources, people can even practice an ethic of thrift in one particular area in order to support the satisfaction of desire in another area ("amphibious consumption").

C. Performance Will

The third dimension of consumerism is expressionism or the performance of will. Here the word "performance" here is not so-called "performance" of Mao Zedong's planned economy era (i.e., political performance, performance of activism), but the "expression", "embodiment", "display" (presentation), the exchange and dissemination (communication) or "representation". From consumption people derive a pleasurable experience and get satisfaction of functional needs. But it is also to express something. Performance can be divided into two types, the first being conscious and the second unconscious performance. The so-called "unconscious performance" refers to spontaneous behavior that inadvertently reveals to others someone's desires, ideas or identity. The so-called "conscious performance" occurs when a person realizes that they are expressing something to others. "The performance will" I am to discuss here refers mainly to a "conscious performance."

In Mao Zedong's planned economy era, the space available for people's performance was greatly limited politically. At that time, the interests of the workers, farmers and other manual labor classes considered to be members of the revolutionary proletariat had achieved the highest level of legitimacy,[464] while the lifestyles of the urban and petty bourgeoisie were the objects of criticism . As a result, people conducted themselves based upon a model of extreme homogeneity, being afraid to "deviate half an inch." In the area of consumption, it is almost the case of the "same face for thousands of people", the norm being identical lifestyles. Obviously, at that time, consumption could not be a means for expressing individuality and identity.

The reform process not only improved people's living standards and consumer autonomy, but it also allowed consumption become a means for expressing individuality and identity. Spending more integrated into the so-called "symbolic consumption" logic, as a symbol of constructing social distinction and self-identity. Thus, people not only consume physical products and services but also the symbolic meanings carried by those goods and services. These two processes of consumption are called the "duality of consumption." Because of this duality, in consuming a physical or tangible products or service, people also build a recognizable social image and identity. Consumption then becomes a means of social communication and self-expression of the main subjects.

1. Interior Decoration, Furniture and Furnishings: Expression of Taste, Interest and Style

In the planned economy era, products typical of Western consumer markets (e.g., lipstick, perfume, suits, etc.) were often connected with the bourgeois lifestyle and criticized. When the state was promoting a spirit of hard work, it also established virtual taboos in many consumer areas. One of the taboos was not allowing people to pursue the so-called "bourgeois lifestyle." Paying attention to tastes in dress, leisure or style, was considered part of the bourgeois lifestyle and therefore banned. Today, this type of consumer taboo has been eliminated. Urban residents gained the opportunity to freely express their own tastes. For example, tableware, interior decoration and furnishings, clothing, jewelry, food, music and art and so on, are beginning to suit a particular taste, interest and style.

What best reflects a person's taste, interest and style, is probably the area of interior decoration, arrangement and furnishings. In the planned economy era, the house was a kind of public property and a benefit form the state. There was at that time had no private ownership. Housing conditions were relatively simple. So residents either did not want to decorate their homes or did not have the economic capability to do so. With the privatization of housing and creation of the real estate market, people began to obtain residential property. Temporary housing was no longer a simple place of habitat. As a result, people adapted the space to express their own tastes, interests and style. People began to consider the taste and style of their home interiors.

Our home decoration is relatively simple, but it is considered to have great taste and class. My husband really likes other people saying that he has class and taste. In fact, it has been fit into place, mainly furniture and furnishings. (C08-F-40, cadre)

In a sense the interior decoration has become a kind of celebration of the right to own private residential property. Because only with the rights to the property, are people willing to decorate the interior, expressing their own taste, interest and style. In this sense, the decoration of the interior is a particularly grand ceremony.

In addition to interior decoration, people also began to consider taste, interest and style when they purchased furniture. "(Interviewer: What is your furniture style?) I prefer a little more wood products, wood flooring ah, more classical." (B33-F-37, chairman and managing director of a private company) "(Interviewer: What is your consideration of style when you buy furniture?) This is definitely yes, it is a personal preference, I like wood. I do not like leather. Color, style, ah, ah all these are to be considered in light of the overall style of the entire display. Color should be coordinated. You will feel better. I personally prefer walnut. "(B27-M-34, government cadre)" (Interviewer: Now how did you choose this furniture? What are the major factors you consider in the selection process?) We are all choosing our own, visiting store by store. Considerations, well, in general, we like the pieces that are not easily broken. And the composition is pleasing to own eyes, our own ... We like the red-brown furniture; we choose more of that. Because there is such a saying: Black is always a high-end. "(B28-M-35, university teacher) One of the respondents described in detail how to sell furniture in line with her own taste:

As we buy furniture, we are quite critical, and my husband is even pickier. We have a relatively higher standard of furniture. We went to all the high-end furniture stores in Guangzhou, almost breaking our legs. ... We then bought and brought them back. People really see us having certain taste. ... We are very particular about the furniture. Our home furniture is all solid wood, rarely compound board. My husband is very particular in shopping. I feel tired even when I think about it now. For that set of sofa, we thought a bit over ten thousand yuan should be okay. We actually settled for a set of more than twenty-five thousand yuan. But our family is not the most expensive consumer. It is mainly my husband that wants to pursue his own feeling, and taste. See the house across from us? They bought sixty thousand dollars of furniture. It is not as good-looking as ours (laughs). There must be a little personal style, a little taste. (C08-F-40, cadre)

In addition, interior decoration and furnishings have become a place for the expression of taste, interest and style. Housing is no longer a place for the owners to put their things, but a space in which to express their taste and style.

Moreover, this taste, interest and style have a unity, because people are asked to express their consistent taste, interest and style in all consumer goods. McCracken calls the harmonization of taste, interest and style the "Diderot unity" or "Diderot effect."[465] For example, in the planned economy era, every time a family moved, all the old furniture was moved to the new home. Style is not an issue with the move. However, recently people have formed a concerted awareness of the requirements of style. "(Interviewer: At that time did you consider style when you were purchasing furniture?) Taking into account the overall coordination, certainly we choose our favorite, more practical ones, with guaranteed quality." (B30-F (2)-32, community service manager) "(The purchase of furniture) must be in coordination with the overall style, to match the color of the home. " (B28-M-35, university teacher)

This sense of taste and style is a cultural change brought about by social transformation. In the ascetic society, taste, interest and style that were linked to Western civilization and the Western style of consumption were often treated stigmatized. Rather, the tastes of the "working class" became dominant taste that was used to evaluate the correctness of consumer behavior. Such a "dictatorship" of taste, interest and style, implies the supremacy of national macro-objectives and the requirement for residents to live frugally. Thus, consumer behavior and attitudes have never been isolated subjects. They are closely related to social structure and ideology. After the reform and opening up, consumption became a way for the country to reconstruct its legitimacy resources. Accordingly, consumers have gained unprecedented autonomy and space in which they can freely express their personal taste, interest and style. It can be seen that the rising of such a performance culture has an inherent logical connection with the institutional transformation.

2. Apparel Consumption: Image Consciousness and the Expression of Identity

In modern times, clothing has become one of the largest consumer items. "I actually spent with a lot of money on clothes, a wardrobe full of all my clothes." (B16-F-27, insurance company clerk) "(Interviewer: What are the main objects your consumption these days?) The main thing is the purchase of clothes. It is my major spending. It accounts about three thousand yuan or so a month. (Buying designer clothes?) Yes, certainly. My clothes are brand name. I added up all the clothes in my closet. It is almost a hundred thousand yuan. I bought definitely better clothes, not bad clothes. "(C12-M-26, college administrative staff) Not only is clothing a significant expenditure, but clothing consumption has a direct impact on people's feelings: "Sometimes the more they are satisfied with their own clothes they wear, the better their whole mood will be. Whomever I see at work, I feel very happy." (B38-F-40, university office clerk) "(Interviewer: What is the impact of clothes on you?) It does affect me. It makes me feel more spiritual, and I feel better, more efficient. Being an individual, I have more confidence." (B19-F-24, state enterprise worker) In addition, more and more people pursue individuality in clothing, avoiding duplication with other people. "For example, when you buy a dress, you have to consider that many people will buy these clothes. It would be very embarrassing if someone wears the same clothes. We should take this into consideration to avoid embarrassment, as we don't want to wear the same clothes as others do. "(C16-M-25, institution staff)

In comparing today's clothing consumption to that prior to the reform and opening up, the effect of cultural change is even more apparent. All who lived through the era of Mao Zedong's planned economy understand how dull of clothes were then. Everyone remembers how their clothes resembled everyone else's.[466] Clothing that expressed personal taste, interest and style was often seen as demonstrating "bourgeois ideology"; it was "fancy dress". This taboo on the consumption of expressive clothing reflected the integrative mechanism prevailing under ideology of "uniformity". After the market-oriented reforms, this ideological objective of uniformity was neither necessary nor possible. The market economy is characterized by division of labor and exchange. It is also guided by consumer preferences. It encourages people's personality and self-awareness. Therefore the personalization and styling of clothing precisely reflected the end of such "uniformity". Clothing, once politicized and ideological objects were quickly absorbed by the logic of the market. An important logic of the apparel market is to make clothing symbolic, branded, stylish, fashionable, so as to make the garment represent a person's self-image and identity. People also increasingly recognize the symbolic meanings of clothes, brands, style and the features of fashion.

Therefore, in today's clothing consumption, people see ever more value in the style of clothes and material from which they are made. Clothing has developed symbolic and visual elements. After a certain amount of mix and match, clothing shows a certain spirit and shapes self-image. "What clothes mean to me is certainly not just to keep out the cold. I think it a question of image to have people see it as being very comfortable." (B38-F-40, university office clerk) "(Clothing's) styles, colors, fabrics are important. (All of these) meaning the visual effects and the comfort of the exposed skin, which is very important. ... (Interviewer: What is the main consideration when you buy clothes?) Or your own style is most important. It means that the style that fits you, which is the premise, determines where you buy; identity is rarely considered; age? Age cannot be considered separately. Style is the main determinant. The second is that style determines where to buy."(B33-F-37, chairman and managing director of a private company)" (Interviewer: What does clothing mean to you?) It means a mental state, in line with temperament, the publicity of your personality. Color must suit the temperament. It is very jarring to see two colors clashing. The whole body should be coordinated."(B31-M-31, newspaper editor)

As income levels increase, there is growing emphasis on the symbolic meaning of clothing, especially a focus on apparel brand. People buy designer clothes for two reasons. The first is for their quality and comfort when being worn. The other is to demonstrate their taste in order to perfect their self-image.

I think for a brand to become famous, there must be a certain the truth in it. It is assurance of quality and quality. If you truly want to compare, you would think that it really is not worth the price. The price for a brand-name product is indeed much higher than its intrinsic value. But I think the brand still has its intangible asset, which is its value. ... When being students, we go to Giordano, Baleno to buy clothes. Now we all work in such an environment, everyone pays attention to his or her image. And you see, people working in the office all very much pay attention to their images. ... No other way. You have this job. You (dress code) must be like this. (C04-F-24, employee at a foreign enterprise)

The main restraint on the purchase of designer clothes is personal income. People purchasing brand-name clothing are often those whose income has reached certain level. But those earning less can afford brand-name clothing by taking advantage of the opportunity to buy discounted designer clothes when the season changes. "I also like to shop for clothes. But I was so-called family housewife. And I consider economic factors a lot when I buy clothes. I often buy comparatively cheaper clothing. Of course I buy brand-name clothing too, but generally at the season change time when the clothes can be a lot cheaper (laughs), with more discounts." (B38-F-40, university office clerk) For many people who are unable to afford designer clothes, it does not mean that deep from their heart they do not want to wear designer clothing. At least they do not want to dress badly. "I will not pursue brands too much, because I know (buying) the big names is not what I can afford. I cannot afford most famous brands or above average brand names. But if it is too common brand, people on the street all wear them. I do not like that either. I will not buy." (B41-F-24, unemployed) Of course, many people are indeed careless about brand name clothing. It is also partially because of their limited financial means. But what is certain is that people's knowledge of and desire for brand-name clothing have built a common fashion culture.

Regardless of whether they seeing value or not in brands, people still use clothing as a symbol to express their self-image and social identity. Veblen said: "There are other ways to effectively prove a person's financial status, and these methods are always ambiguous. But there is strength of spending on clothing as compared to other methods. That is, our apparel is always evidence. We can let people see our financial status at a glance by seeing our clothing."[467] In his view, clothing provides most prominent, straightforward and direct evidence of someone's financial status. Although today not all people are like Veblen's "conspicuous consumers", which he described as vain and boastful, his assertion that clothes express personal information is an irrefutable fact.

Today, clothing is a "language" for expressing our individual and social identities. Individual identity is personally relevant. It is the level of positioning and acceptance of "Who am I?" "What kind of a person am I?" Social identity is about the positioning and acceptance of "what is the group is like and what kind of people should be in it?" It is a group identity, including age, gender, occupation, class identity and so on. Any individual identity is a combination of various components of social identity, such as: age, sex, occupation, class and so on. At the same time social identity can only be manifested through individual recognition. Dialectical relationship exists between the two.[468] Regardless of the type of social identity, it can be reflected in clothing.

First, clothing represents age identity, reflecting a person's sense of membership in an age group. "(Interviewer: Why do you prefer the casual type of clothing?) Because the leisure-type makes people look younger, more energetic, spirited. ... I don't want people to feel that I am being very old." (B19-F-24, state owned enterprise worker) "For me being a professional women, I need to dress up decently, openly, but also taking into account of my age. I cannot wear too sexy or too exposing clothes."(B38-F-40, university office clerk) "Of course I want to wear clothes in line with my age. ... I want to wear clothes in line with my own identity, looking a little younger, spiritual even glowing a little. Quite often we can see a person's taste and spirit from what he or she is wearing."(No. B30-F (2)-32, community service manager) While people age, the group they belong to and the answer to "how should I be?" also change accordingly:

In the past, every year people hope to have a more elegant, fashionable (garment), in pursuit of the youthful spirit. Now people seek meaning inside, which is a change. There was shopping around before, because in the past there were few good things. So it's necessary to look around, to find something new. Now, even Beijing Road[469] and the "Guang-Bai"[470] we rarely go to. Place like "Shangxiajiu"[471] would not suit me anymore. When I was young, I'd like to buy beautiful clothes, attracting attention and praise. Now I have no such mentality. Now I just want to look more to my temperament, more rational. Although I still like the other's favorable comments, I was not like the wish I had before. Before people said, wow! You are so pretty, ah! I would be very happy. Now when people say that I am beautiful, I fully understand, at my age. But now I hope your comments about my clothes right to the point. I feel very comfortable then (laughs). I think people at different stages, expect different evaluations from others. (C08-F-40, government institution cadre)

Clothing has also become the expression of gender group identity. During the Cultural Revolution, the state ideology stressed equality of the sexes, consistency between men and women. It was agreed that "women can hold half the sky", which highlighted the status of women. The sense of being female was diluted, the female being identified with the male: "Chinese people have peculiar talents. We do not like the pink and red stuff, but love the armed forces." (Mao Zedong) Reflected in fashion, the female gender was deliberately concealed. Clothing to some extent denied the characteristics of female image. After the market-oriented reform, women escaped the neutral identity imposed upon them by the "national patriarchy," and brought back gender identity. Fashion became the symbol of female group identity. "I'm wearing more casual clothes, want to wear a bit more feminine clothes. There is increasingly consideration of this along with aging. Mood has changed. It not because of popularity or out of work needs. A person's choice of clothing should be complementary to her or his temperament. And during this period of time, I find wearing women's clothes makes my temperament better."(C03-F-24, employee at foreign garment company) "I am more biased in favor of a girlish taste, a little elegant, a bit romantic, a little casual, a little enriched."(B33-F-37, chairman and managing director of a private company)

Clothing can also play a role in supporting role group identity. The role of groups, especially the role of group identity in the professions, is to determine how people act and dress up. Although such awareness also existed in the planned economy era, differentiation in dress was not significant. After the market reforms, there was more diversification by role. Dressing according to one's role leads to a wide range of differentiation.

Clothing has also become the direct visual expression of class identity. People's attitude toward clothing differs based on their class identity. In our respondents, some people have accepted and are conscious of their lower class status. They dress up more casually, without feeling stress.

However, for most people, their consumption of clothing agrees with their social class. Such a class identity is not necessarily an objective class position. Instead people subjectively position their social class. Since many people position themselves as "middle class", they tend to make clothing consumption agree with the image they associate with their social class. In other words, consumption of "middle class" clothing reflects people's expression of identity.

Obviously, the middle class is the group holding certain economic capital and high cultural capital. This social class status determines their class identity. And people belonging to this class dress themselves according to their class identity: neither too "extravagant" nor too "shabby". They tend to choose "mid-range brands" in order to associate themselves with the middle social class. Here, the brand's status and the buyer's class status have formed a corresponding relationship. A particular brand becomes a symbol reflecting a particular class position and identity.

In summary, the rise of consumerism in Chinese cities is an integral part of the social transformation of Chinese society. It is also the result of the state's rearrangement of the system of consumption. To study the changes of consumerism of the contemporary social structure since the reform and opening up, we must understand at the same time the state of faith and labor motivation in the social structure. The states of belief, work motivation and the consumer concept have developed an intertwined relationship among each other. With the utopian disillusionment, the holy faith of the past faded away. The weakening of the faith led to ideological changes in people's work motivation (people changing from being dedicated to being self-interested). It has also led to changes in people's consumption concept (consumption becoming a new source of happiness and giving meaning to life). The rise of the mass of consumers in turn affected people's attitude towards life and work motivation.

Although there are still those who adhere to the doctrine of thrift, this adherence is especially stratified socially; the doctrine of thrift still has a specific social class (migrant workers, laid-off workers and other such groups) as its carrier. Therefore consumer attitudes still have some degree of continuity. In general, there have been tremendous changes of in the consumption concept among contemporary urban residents. The most important manifestation of these changes was the rise of consumerism. It consists of three dimensions: the consciousness of possession (materialism), the ethic of pleasure (hedonism) and performance of will (expressionism). The rise of consumerism since the reform and opening up is a reflection of dramatic change in the social structure and spiritual world of human beings. And this change in the spiritual world is embodied in the replacement of the sacred world by the secular world, namely: a utilitarian orientation, and the principles of self-interest and consumer desire replacing sacred faith, dedication and the ideal of frugality.

Chapter Six

Conclusion and Discussion

Consumption is an important window through which to observe social structure and cultural movements. The reason we say this is that not only does consumption record the transformation of social structure and other cultural changes. But consumption itself constitutes an important mechanism of social transformation and cultural migration. Therefore, to examine social and cultural changes in urban China from the point of view of the consumer provides a new perspective on the study of social and cultural changes. This book's basic argument is that from the consumer's point of view, since the establishment of the New China, Chinese society has gone through a transformation from an ascetic society to a consumer society. This book, respectively from the perspectives of system transformation and social structure transformation, explored the situation and logical path of the ascetic society's migration to a consumer society.

The first two parts of this chapter will be a brief summary and conclusion of the basic ideas in the book. The latter four parts of the chapter will expand and extend some important issues and discuss them in depth.

The Logic of Consumption System Transformation

The transformation of the system of consumption is an integral part of social migration and transformation. From a sociological point of view, the book analyzed the transformation of the consumer system and its laws of the Chinese cities from the early 1950s to the early 2000s.[472] The book predicts that consumption system is one of the key systems embedded in the social and economic system, which labor incentive system. Therefore, the book analyzed how the state made institutional arrangements around urban resident's lives, and considered how the state's institutional arrangements were connected with resident's labor motivation. As I said before, I used the method of analyzing government policy documents.

In totalitarian countries, the change of the consumption system is at least in part the consequence of the state's efforts to mobilize social and other resources. On the one hand, the state, in order to achieve its historic mission, the goal of socialist industrialization, needed to fully mobilize people's work enthusiasm and labor productivity so that workers will give their maximum efforts. On the other hand, because of the extreme shortage of material, the state had to devote all resources to the completion of industrialization. To this end, the state asked residents to "live plainly", "tighten their belts", and "tighten their belts for the construction", which means that the state implemented a policy of curbing consumption in order to improve its resource mobilization capacity.

However, there was a conflict between inhibiting consumption and labor incentives. How did the state resolve this contradiction? Or, under the policy of curbing consumption with when there were extreme material shortages, how should the state have mobilized people's enthusiasm and labor productivity? From the perspective of the institutional arrangements in the 1950s, the state used non-material incentives as the form of labor motivation under the conditions of severe material constraints. The main form of non-material incentives was spiritual stimulation (honor and the opportunity to rise). It was effective, largely due to the state being rich in "legitimacy resources." It reflected that the state still benefitted from the "liberation effect" ("national liberation and independence," "the emancipated working people, the masters," "eliminating exploitation and oppression," the "equality" of the socialist system) and the "shelter doctrine" (a full range of free benefits, social security, including life-long job security), which burnished the party and state's reputation. Specifically, the state and urban residents had two hidden exchanges: the first, "national mercy" in exchange for the gratitude of workers (labor enthusiasm); second, a national commitment (the promise by the state of an ideal future) in exchange for urban resident's accepting curbs on their consumption.

At the operational level, after the institutional arrangements for curbing consumption were made in the early 1950s, the state gradually built a set of "sacred incentives" relying on its legitimacy resources. One premise was that human nature could be altered and transformed through ideological and political education, and that self-interest could be overcome. Once the spiritual power was mobilized, it could become great physical force.

The system of sacred incentives was principally reflected in the following measures: (1) The state's ideological propaganda and the ideological and political mobilization of urban work units (usually in the form of the political unit's routine learning activities, talks, etc.). At the same time, work units also conducted criticism and education of incorrect ideas and attitudes (or self-criticism). (2) The system of labor competition, appraisal and the recognition of activists and progressive elements. Through labor competition and the selection and commendation of "advanced producers", "model workers", the state established role models for labor. (3) The system of the exemplary demonstration by party members and cadres. By having "advanced" workers help the "backward" improve, the overall labor enthusiasm of the workshop and work unit increased. (4) The free welfare system and full employment, which showed that the party and state cared about the workers, and which further demonstrated the superiority of the socialist system, and evoked people's sense of gratitude and dedication.

We can say that because of sacred incentives, around the time of the founding of the People's Republic (70 years ago) individuals are not only able to tolerate an impoverished material life, but also maintained "positive" labor enthusiasm and "strong" drive. A "marriage" was formed between the "ascetic culture", characterized by frugality, and the "culture of dedication" which was characterized by selflessness and "self-sacrifice."

The effectiveness of sacred incentives depends on two premises: first, the divine goal, ideal or object cannot be tarnished. Second, the national commitment should not be broken, because such a promise is a sacred goal. In the late stage of the Cultural Revolution (1971~1972 onwards), the mechanism of sacred incentives began to lose its effectiveness. Part of the reason was that the two premises of the sacred incentives fell into crisis during the Cultural Revolution. First, the brutal reality of the political struggle during the Cultural Revolution caused the sacred ideals and objectives, originally so appealing, to lose their former charm. Second, the state's promises were never realized. Actual living standards for most workers declined. The supply of consumer goods deteriorated. The rise of privileges and "back door" phenomenon began to spread.

Once sacred incentives became less effective, there was a new relationship between consumption inhibition and labor motivation. In other words, as living standards were resistant to improvement, people did not want to work as desperately hard as they did in the past. Chronic poverty and the "perceived" inequality of wage income (there were eight wage categories), made workers in a certain age groups begin to slack off, and labor enthusiasm began to decline. In Walder's words, the labor force began to "moralize."[473]

The failure of sacred incentives caused a decline in labor productivity and the persistence of poverty, consuming the state's original legitimacy resources. So the new generation of State leaders who were out of favor during the Cultural Revolution or afterward had to find a new incentive mechanism to replace sacred incentives. What was this incentive mechanism? Whether it was merely expedient or fundamental, it could only be secular incentives, meaning it had to be a system of material incentives. The replacement of spirituality by materialism defined the new form of labor incentives.

From the standpoint of policy orientation, that the state was able to implement its system of consumption curbs (which continued until right before the reform and opening up) during the early days, was because of the state's high reputation, namely: the rich legitimacy resources it could draw on as a policy support. At the national level, the national goals were above everything else and they were related to the fundamental and long-term interests of the whole country. It was necessary for a whole generation to make sacrifices at the consumer level. Therefore, the state's policies on consumer desire follow "rational logic" (Table 7-1). Why? It appears to the state that inhibiting people's consumption is necessary to achieve industrialization and therefore a rational choice to achieve national objectives. Even though such an arrangement may have led to resentment among the people, the state still nevertheless pursued this system. The most characteristic reflection of rational logic in consumption is the system of "unified purchase and sale" of food.

In the 1950s, precisely because the party and state leaders at the time had very high reputations and a wealth of legitimacy resources as policy support (and also because of the country's totalitarian social organization), the state could minimize social resistance to their promotion of consumption inhibition and were able to implement the institutional arrangements of "curbing consumption" at low-cost. Such institutional arrangements played an important role in improving the state's resource mobilization capacity, and further improved the state's social mobilization, establishing and strengthening the planned economic system.

However, in late years of the Cultural Revolution, after twenty years of curbing consumption, the standard of living had not improved but actually declined. In other words, the state's "commitment" was broken, which led the country into a crisis of legitimacy resources. It is not difficult to see that in order to understand the consumption system implemented after the reform and opening up, we have to take into the consideration the critical background preconditions before the reform and opening up when the state was facing the exhaustion of its legitimacy resources.

It can be clearly seen in government documents from the beginning of the reform and opening up, that the party and the state leader Deng Xiaoping launch of the campaign for reform and opening up was inherently related to the crisis of legitimacy resources that he and the collective leadership were facing. A key factor leading to the party and the state's decline in popularity and prestige was that people had been living in poverty for a long time. The poverty in everyday life virtually undermined the official discourse of "the superiority of the socialist system." And the "superiority of socialism" is precisely the state's main legitimacy resource. Therefore, it appeared to the party and state leaders that one option for resolving the state's crisis of legitimacy resources was to develop the economy, increase worker's incomes and improve people's living standards.

It is not difficult to understand why during the early stage of reform and opening up (1979~1988), the state adopted the policy of subsidizing private consumption. According to National Statistics Bureau, from 1978 to 1981, the proportion of consumption in the GDP rose from 62.1% to 67.5%; Accordingly, the ratio of savings to GDP proportionally fell from 38.2% to 32.3%. At the same time, the government raised the wages of urban workers and re-established the bonus system. The state also raised the purchase price of agricultural products, boosting farmer's incomes, and correspondingly subsidized purchases by urban residents of agricultural and food products.

It can be said that the implementation of incentives and subsidies during the early days of the reform and opening up, not only mobilized labor enthusiasm but also improved labor productivity, rebuilt the labor motivation mechanism (i.e., material incentives). Due to the improved supply of consumer goods and improved consumer life, the party and state quickly restored and further improved their reputation, in large part overcoming the crisis of legitimacy resources. Therefore, in the early stage of the reform and opening up, the state's policy toward private consumption followed "legitimacy logic". Clearly from the pre-reform days to the early stage of the reform and opening up, policies on private consumption and institutional arrangements respectively followed different logics, namely: they changed from rational logic to legitimacy logic (Table 7-1).

After the founding of the country, the state gradually established a social welfare system (health, housing, education, insurance for work-related injuries, pensions, maternity insurance, etc.) in cities and towns, and implemented a full employment policy to protect workers and provide them with a full range of benefits. Relative to the level of economic development at the time, the national implementation of the social welfare policy (collective consumption) was clearly beyond what the economy could support. Of course, to certain extent, the social welfare policy compensated for the "low wage" policy. Nevertheless, this welfare policy clearly could not be explained by rational choices.

In fact, the state's implementation of social welfare policy at the time was not based primarily on economic considerations, but on political and ideological considerations, namely: the consideration of legitimacy. The social welfare policy was a system initiative to demonstrate "the working people being the masters" and the "superiority of socialism". Thus, in the pre-reform days, the state's policy on collective consumption (mainly welfare and social security) follows "legitimacy logic" (Table 6-1). In some sense, the social welfare system performed the task of generating and maintaining the state's legitimacy resources. Moreover, it constituted an integral part of the sacred work incentives.

After the reform and opening up, because of the improvement in individual's living standards, the party and state's prestige were restored, and the state's legitimacy resources were effectively reconstructed. In this case, the importance of "legitimacy" generation by means of collective consumption (social welfare and security, mainly in cities) has decreased compared to the traditional planned economy era. Furthermore, because of the state's adoption the policy of "stability overriding everything" since 1989, the state is no longer worried about the problem of legitimacy resources. Thus, in the late 1990s the state conducted liberal-style reform of the social security and welfare system. This reform of collective consumption followed rational logic (i.e., the logic efficiency) instead of "legitimacy logic" (Table 6-1).

Table 6-1   reform the system before and after consumption of the logic of transformation

Stage	Private Consumption	Collective Consumption
Pre-reform	Rational logic	Legitimacy logic
After Reform and Opening up	Legitimacy logic(1980s)	Rational logic(Late 1990s)

The liberal reform of collective consumption efficiently supplied the resources for collective consumption, but at the same time, it widened gaps in the income distribution. Reforms in the areas of collective consumption were not effective in reducing the gap between the rich and the poor. Instead, due to the unequal social rights, the reforms increased the gap between the rich and the poor, and indirectly suppressed consumption by the lower-middle class, leading to dual-track consumption. A contradiction existed between the suppression of consumption and the state's policy of expanding domestic demand. One reason leading to such contradictory results was the instrumental orientation of national policy, which was that the formation of the state's social policy (collective consumption) followed rational logic (giving priority to efficiency considerations) rather than legitimacy logic.

It can be seen that in a totalitarian state, consumption cannot be completely understood at the individual level. It is largely the result of national policy and institutional arrangements. The national institutional arrangements for consumption are closely related to labor incentives. And the evolution of the relationship between the consumption system and labor incentives is intrinsically linked to the state's legitimacy resources. From the trends of growth and decline in the state's legitimacy resources, it is easy to identify the logic trajectory of the institutional system created by the state for consumer life and labor incentives.

Logic of The Main Structural Transformation

Any system needs to be reflected in people's daily activities. People are the main actors, namely: their behavior as the initiators and implementers of actions. The manner in which a person acts, reflects what kind of social structure he or she has. The so-called social structure refers to the composition of various subjective factors that affect a certain mode of people's behavior. From a national perspective, as some kind of institutional arrangements must be implemented, they must match the social structure of the system, because the system is implemented and reproduced through actions of the social structure.

As a totalitarian country controls all media and propaganda mechanisms, and screens out any threatening information, from the perspective of information dissemination, the totalitarian state is essentially a closed society. In such a society, the social structure is more easily shaped. Through ideological control and information shielding, the state can shape the social structure of its citizens according to the desired national prototype. By shaping the specific mode of the social structure, the state's institutional arrangements can be reproduced through citizen's customary thinking without hesitation and their voluntary actions (in other words, the state's will can be translated into individual free will). The type of systematic structure determines the type of social structure. Conversely, the kind of social structure decides the kind of systematic structure. There is a dialectical relationship between institutional structure and the social structure.

Because the social structure plays such an important role in maintaining the systemic structure, during the planned economy period, the state greatly emphasized ideological and political education. The so-called ideological and political education, in essence, was the process of building the social structure of the populace in accordance with the subject prototypes established by the state. The more that institutional arrangements appear to be in conflict with human "nature" (e.g., self-interest), the more important the transformation of the social structure becomes. In the fifties, the state's policy of curbing consumption was in conflict with human "nature" (or conventional nature). Therefore, in mobilizing people's enthusiasm for work while simultaneously curbing consumption, ideological education and political mobilization (i.e., the process of shaping the social structure) become of paramount importance. Because of the importance of building the social structure, the state had to maintain an idealize environment in which to shape it: suppressing and shielding people from all "threatening" ideas and information and maintaining a closed society. It was only by means of this social closure, that ideological control could be effective and successfully create a social structure aligned with the institutional arrangements to curb consumption.

With the reform and opening up, institutional arrangements became more aligned with human "nature" (e.g., self-interest, profit). Subsequently, ideological and political work became less important than they were during the pre-reform days. This is one of the reasons why the state could loosen its ideological control to some extent. With the weakening of national ideology and ideological control, as well as China's movement from a closed to an open society, a variety of unofficial discourse, including public discourse, began to appear on the media stage. This began to play a role in shaping the social structure of the populace. Therefore, after the reform and opening up, the ways of shaping the social structure became more diverse. Correspondingly, the social structure of has been transformed: people who were once ascetics became consumers. Overall, such a transformation of the social structure is synchronized with the transformation of the system, and generally consistent with the system transformation.

Obviously, the kind of social structure in which people exist or in what mode they think or act, are not entirely the products of individual's own self-will. To a large extent, they are formed as a result of the national discourse system and social discourse system. Therefore, to study the transformation of the system we must also examine the transformation of the social structure, because in the transformation of the system, the restructuring and transformation of the social structure is an interdependent and inseparable aspect of the same process.

Based on our interviews with two generations (the generation growing up and joining the workforce before the reform and the generation growing up and joining the workforce after the reform and opening up), we found that the two different generations have clear differences in their social structures, with an especially significant difference in their concept of consumption and concept of work (two basic factors of the social structure). The root cause leading to this variation was the transformation of the social structure.[474] Although the new generation inherited some of the main factors of the older generation, in comparing the new generation to the older one, there were significant changes in their consumption concept and labor concept. From the perspective of an ideal type, the consumption concept of older people is ascetic (following a doctrine of thrift), as opposed to the new generation of consumers whose consumption concept is consumerist (materialism, an ethic of pleasure and performance will). From the same perspective of ideal type, the older people's labor concept is a dedicated spirit without caring much for compensation, while the labor concept of the new generation is self-serving (sense of trade, contractual awareness, awareness of their rights, maximizing returns). And the deeper elements determining the change of the concept of consumption and the concept of labor are the status of faith or ultimate value. It forms the core of the social structure, dominating the formation of the concepts of labor and consumption. Therefore it constitutes the soul of the social structure, and the focus of intervention for national ideological and political work. From the perspective of an ideal type, before the reform and opening up, the older generation's belief was mainly sacred idealism. After the reforms, the new generation's faith was weakened and secularized. The value system of secular realism replaced sacred idealism (Table 6-2). Of course, no doubt, this change was a gradual, evolutionary process, not a sudden occurrence.

Table 6-2   Changes in the Main Structure Before and After the Reform and Opening up

Stage	Belief state	Consumer spirit	Spirit of labor
Pre-reform	Idealism	Asceticism	Dedication
After reform and opening up	Pragmatism	Consumerism	The principle of self-interest

Clearly, comparing before the reform and opening up to afterward, the most essential difference in the social structure is the difference in faith. Because of the differences in main beliefs, the main decisions on labor and consumption, followed different logics of action. From the perspective of an ideal type before the reform and opening up, the main body adhering to idealistic beliefs followed the sacred logic in the field of work (work being honorable and noble), while in the field of consumption it followed instrumental logic (consumption is mainly a means for the reproduction of labor). Also from the perspective of an ideal type, after the reform and opening up the new, pragmatically oriented, generation followed instrumental logic in the field of labor (work being primarily a means of livelihood), and followed sacred logic in consumption (consumption embodying "a happy life") (Table 6-3).

Table 6-3   Before and After the Reform and Opening Up the Main Structure's Logic of Action Transformation In Consumption and Labor

Stage	Belief type	Consumption	The field of labor
Pre-reform	Idealism	Instrumental logic of action	Sacred action logic
After reform and opening up	Pragmatism	Sacred action logic	Instrumental logic of action

At the time of the reform and opening up, the transformation of the logics of action in consumption and labor were basically synchronous with the transformation of the country's macro system. Before the reform and opening up, on the one hand, the state had to mobilize all resources to achieve socialist industrialization and to lay a solid material foundation for the realization of communist ideals. On the other hand, the state faced the problem of limited resources, and asked people to tighten their belts, curb consumption and save in order to support socialist industrialization. In the state's eyes, the realization of lofty communist ideals and goals, as well as the industrialization that lays the material foundation for these objectives is the divine and supreme task. Consumption was irrelevant, useful only as a means for the reproduction of labor, so it could be suppressed. As Liu Shaoqi said, "Under conditions that we are not cold, not hungry and able to maintain normal healthy conditions, we shall save as much as possible and spend a little less so that the funds can be accumulated by the state to speed up industrialization."[475] Thus, the social structure the country desires to shape is one emphasizing labor and downplaying consumption. It is a social structure that depicts labor as a noble, the purpose of life, and consumption as vulgar (e.g., as pleasure-seeking or shameful) and a means. The social structure upholds idealism as faith utilized instrumental logic in consumption and sacred logic in the field of labor, which was in line with national needs.

After the reforms, as economic construction became an overwhelming national task, and also with shift of labor incentives from sacred motivation to secular motivation at lower transaction costs, the state harnessed "human nature" (people's self-interest and profit-seeking behavior) to stimulate labor enthusiasm and promote economic development. As a result, the state no longer needed people to adhere to the spirit of "dedication" and "sacrifice". Also, during the early stage of reform and opening up, the state faced a crisis of legitimacy resources. Improving people's consumption became an important means to re-establish the state's legitimacy resources. In the late 1990s, with consumption playing a more significant role in economic growth, the state objectively began to require citizens to expand their consumption. All of this broke the taboos and restrictions on consumption that had existed in the planned economy. People's consumption gained a positive sense. The weakening of state ideological control encouraged a rise in public discourse. Consumption was constructed as an activity with sacred significance (e.g., the goal of owing "a house and car"). Therefore, the pragmatic new generation after the reform and opening up followed sacred logic in consumption and instrumental logic in labor. This was in unison with the transformation of the country's macro system.

The social structure prior to the reform and opening up was mainly idealistic belief in the core spirit of the subject. This was primarily a product shaped by the state's ideological machine. Although the social structure contained many traditional elements, the main components of the social structure came from the state ideology. Therefore, from the spiritual perspective, the social structure and ideology very much overlap. After the reforms, with marketization and development of the social division of labor, social systems integration (Lockwood) and the enhancement of organic solidarity (Durkheim), the ideological control system played a less significant role in forming the social system. With the state focused more on economic construction and the related issues of system control, the state's ideological control was relatively weakened. Market discourse became an integral part of the system that generated the state's legitimacy resources, creating a relatively independent public discourse that began to shape the people's social structure. Thus, in the new social structure, the elements of state ideology are reduced, and elements of public discourse are increased. The citizen has changed from an idealist to a pragmatist, shifted from asceticism to consumerism, from being a devotee to being self-interested. In short, the social structure of the citizenry has undergone profound transformation. The transformation of the social structure is a reflection of the macro-system in the form of a micro system. And the macro-system transformation constitutes a micro-foundation.

The Significance Given to the Mechanism of Transformation

The existence of an ultimate meaning of life, a view of the world, and other beliefs (an ultimate faith) is a product of social civilization. It is also a condition that distinguishes people from animals. It is an important mechanism for maintaining social order, for example, providing the ultimate foundation for the role that religion plays in maintaining social order. As Durkheim said in his book "Basic Forms of Religious Life," the so-called "God" is but a synonym for "society". People need God, because people need the social order. People's faith in God constitutes the ultimate meaning of life. The ultimate significance of this forms the basis of the traditional social order. Therefore, the control of the source of ultimate meaning has been the way that traditional society maintains social order. It is also the means by which the state maintains power. So, in traditional society, any deviant will be severely punished. The institutional supply of ultimate significance constitutes the "mechanism which gives meaning" to personal life. For example, religion is a system or mechanism for giving meaning to personal life in traditional society.

The western modernization process, in a sense, is the transformation process of meaning-giving mechanism. As Althusser said, in medieval society, the meaning giving mechanism was mainly religion. However, in modern society, the meaning giving mechanism is mainly a modern educational system.[476] As Weber pointed out, with the rise of the spirit of rationalism and the great strides made in science and technology since the Enlightenment, the social world went through a process of "disenchantment", the role of region was gradually weakened, and social activities and arrangements moved increasingly towards the rational and secular. This rationalization and secularization was also reflected in the modern education system. Modern education not only instills knowledge and skills but also an order associated with capitalist values (ultimate meaning), e.g., individualism, personal freedom, and individual rights. So modern education was integrated into the capitalist system, constituting a part of social integration.

Rational and secular society is both a catalyst for and a product of modernization. This is mainly because along with the advances in science and technology from modernization, the development of the capitalist market economy and industrialization, the formation of social order is ever more dependent on the integration of the system itself. The power of the system (mainly the market and industry) replaced religious authority, and became the main guarantor of social order. Social rationalization and modernization made the integration of the system play a stronger role in maintaining the social order. And the traditional supplier of ultimate meaning (religion) played a diminishing role in maintaining the social order.

Clearly, the modernization of western society changed the meaning giving mechanism: First, the role of the traditional meaning giving mechanism (religion) in maintaining the social order was relatively weakened. The transformation relied upon the strength of system integration. This trend is fully reflected in the rationalization and secularization of western society. Second, the monopoly of the meaning giving mechanism was broken. The sources of ultimate meaning were diversified. This trend is also reflected in the rationalization and secularization of western society. In this process, the monopoly of religion held ultimately collapsed. Businesses, public education, mass media and popular culture are all new suppliers of ultimate meaning. Western modernization was a process in which the role of the priest, the original provider of the ultimate meaning of life, was given over to the businessman.[477] Third, the type of ultimate meaning provided by the meaning giving mechanism has undergone a fundamental change. In traditional society, ultimate meaning is about the afterlife or the intentions of the gods. The purpose of this supply of ultimate meaning is to enable individuals to better endure abstinence and suffering. In modern society, ultimate meaning is often secular and personal. The purpose of this supply of ultimate meaning is to encourage people to "legally" pursue personal pleasure, personal desires and individual freedom.

The occurrence of this transformation was closely related to people's ability to control external world. In traditional society, people have little ability to control nature. Therefore, a dominant feature is the scarcity of materials. In this case, the resources people are able to obtain from nature are not adequate to fully satisfy their internal desires. Since people's control over external nature is low, they naturally want more control over their internal natures (physical instincts and desires). For example, improved self-control is the only way to achieve a balance between individuals and their external world. An effective means of self-control is to provide ultimate meaning in the form of a particular "reasonable" explanation of the world and life (e.g., fatalism, atonement theory, a theory of the afterlife, a theory of heaven). For example, in the view of Christianity, suffering in life comes from "original sin". It is only through redemption in physical world that one can get rid of sin, and go to heaven after death. This means that people must endure hardship and suffering in life, hoping for a happy life in heaven after death. In a traditional society with severe material deprivation, the mechanism of religion certainly helps give individuals psychological comfort when they experience difficulties and enhances their tolerance of suffering, which also helps to maintain a particular social order.

The decline of religion during modernization is mainly because of the improved control of the external world. In modern society, with the advancement of science, technology and the industrial revolution, humanity's ability to control external nature has made a revolutionary leap forward. This is because the design of the capitalist system and human nature are not at odd. Rather they have an affinity to each other. As Hirschman said, "Using some relatively harmless desire to balance some other more dangerous and destructive desire"[478] constitutes the secret power of capitalism. (The former includes: the accumulation of wealth through commerce. The latter are, for example: robbery, piracy, war, murder and other violent means to obtain wealth). When productivity, like a magician's hand, continuously draws more and more wealth out of nature, desire, especially the desire for consumption, is no longer the object of ethical condemnation. On the contrary, it becomes the main psychological dynamic for the formation and expansion of the modern market, and is integrated into capitalist economic logic. Thus, in capitalist society, the "relatively harmless", "non-destructive," natural desires (such as: greed for wealth) are no longer a "plague". On the contrary, these desires are given a positive meaning, and are seen as part of human nature. Human nature constitutes the basis for organizing the modern social order. In other words, the social order in a modern society is not built upon the basis of suppressing human nature, but on the basis of responding to and adapting to human nature. Therefore, the main task of society is not to suppress human nature, but to improve humanity's capability to conquer the external world, and to develop businesses and industries able to continuously satisfy people's endless, "relatively harmless", desires. Therefore, the mechanism traditionally supplied an ultimate meaning, which advocated suppressing human nature (i.e., religion), was inevitably weakened. The ultimate meaning provided by modern society (humanism) has developed some degree of consistency with human nature, which is also reflected in the design of its system.

Undoubtedly contemporary Chinese society moves in orbits different from those of Western society. However, regarding the supply of ultimate significance and social attitudes toward human desires, the contemporary Chinese society has gone through a similar transformation of the meaning giving mechanism.

At the beginning, just after the founding of the People's Republic, one of major difficulties facing the country was a serious shortage of material goods. Once developing heavy industry was established as a strategic objective and given priority, the inhibition of the consumption was a rational choice. However, the inhibition of consumption created a certain tension with the resident's expectations after liberation (e.g., the expectation of rapidly rising living standards). Therefore, in order to effectively to control "excessive" consumption, while also at the same time preserving "active" labor enthusiasm, the state had to provide some level of sacredness in its supply of ultimate meaning to overcome this tension. In fact, the state was unwilling to provide, or simply did not have the material to make, products for human consumption (priority was given to goods for socialist industrialization). Ultimate meaning resided in the lofty ideals and goals of communism. The state tried to uses these lofty ideals and goals to give people ultimate meaning in their personal life. The national leadership told the people that the vision and goals would not be realized automatically. It was to be achieved through the people's hard work over the long term. The national leadership believed that, as long as people truly believed in these ideals and objectives, they could tolerate and accept immediate and temporary poverty. It can be seen that providing a sacred sense of ultimate significance helped the state implement its strategic and institutional arrangements (e.g., curbing consumption) for developing heavy industry as the top priority of socialist modernization.

For the above reason, the state placed great importance on providing and monopolizing ultimate meaning. While the institutional arrangements to curb consumption reflected a rational decision by the state, in order to implement their socialist industrialization plan in the face of a serious lack of funds and resources in a backward agricultural country, such a decision also had to be supported by the people wholeheartedly. Otherwise, if labor enthusiasm suffered a setback, the socialist industrialization program would not have the necessary social momentum to achieve its goals. The national leadership believed that it was absolutely necessary to explain to the people, to do ideological work on the people, so that people all across the country could be drawn together. Only in this way, given the lack of funds but abundant labor resources, could China successfully achieve the goal of socialist industrialization. Clearly, the state's emphasis on ideological and political education was not without cause. It was closely linked with national objectives. It was a rational measure that the country took to address the tension between the national goals and the lack of adequate material means to achieve those goals. The core mission of ideological and political education was to promote to the people and educate them to understand the sacredness of this ultimate meaning, which was the state ideology.

This is why ultimate meaning was provided by and monopolized by the state. The mechanism, once supplied meaning (i.e., the institutional agencies which provided ultimate meaning), was controlled by the ideological apparatus of the state. Specifically, they were the party's propaganda department, media, schools, cultural institutions and the educational systems under the political units that were controlled by the state and the party. The state invested much manpower and material resources in in this mechanism for giving ultimate meaning. The purpose was to monopolize and control the production and dissemination of the ultimate meaning, to establish common beliefs and ideological standards among the whole of society. It aimed to ensure that the whole population, the party and the state made coordinated efforts, had the same beliefs and thoughts, and moved at a consistent pace to achieve the great ideal and objectives of communism as soon as possible.

Since the state lacked sufficient material means to achieve its goal of industrialization, it could only rely upon the abundant labor resources. Therefore, it was a rational choice for the state to ask people to "tighten their belts" and be spiritually dedicated. Only in this way could socialist industrialization be achieved at minimum cost, and the country's lofty ideals and goals be realized from their paper blueprint. This shows that achieving the national goals was to a large extent dependent on people's thinking and associated labor motivation (whether there was labor enthusiasm and spiritual dedication). Under the institutional arrangements for curbing consumption, doing good ideological education of the people (in other words, establishing the faith or ultimate meaning), so as to mobilize people's enthusiasm and labor productivity, was a key to implementing the nation's goals. This situation could be called the contingency of national goals on people's "work motivation."

The contingency on labor motivation made the state vigilant to suppress any information that potentially threatened its established ultimate meaning. Perhaps this is why the state had a low tolerance for "heretical" thoughts during the planned economy. So on the one hand, the state engaged in strong ideological propaganda and indoctrination of the people. On the other hand, the state criticized and lashed out vigorously at all incorrect thinking. Implemented at the micro level, ideological and political work became a core task of the work unit. Therefore, on the one hand, a person's ideological and political performance became the main factor when the unit evaluated an individual's overall contribution. It also became the major evidence used to assess a person's application to join the party, join the Communist Youth League, get promoted or obtain other forms of "advancement" (e.g., the state's political rewards to individuals who are politically and ideologically compliant) and obtain distribution of certain benefits (e.g., housing, bonus). On the other hand, an individual showing "backward" thinking, or a bad attitude, is often to be criticized by their work unit leaders and colleagues. In the "fight for progress", there began race among people, judged in terms of personal ideological "correctness" and "purity". The contest for "ideological correctness" led to rising standards of political performance. The competition in "purity of thoughts" had the result of encouraging abstinence as a national norm. Although these contests eventually led to the divergence of "positive elements" and "ordinary people", in such a highly pressured ideological environment, the ordinary person rational choice was to keep up with the prevailing standards. This explains the characteristic feature of the time, identical consumption and cultural life styles, with all people sharing the same appearance and habits. Clearly, the mechanism that gave of ultimate meaning prior to the reform and opening up, portrayed people as revolutionary ascetic (both firmly believing in and fearing the breach of taboo, while remaining true to asceticism). The society before the reform and opening up was truly an "ascetic society."

I have already discussed the systematic logic of the transformation from an ascetic society to a consumer society. What we need to ask here is how was the mechanism for giving ultimate meaning transformed along with the social transformation? I believe the meaning giving mechanism has undergone three major changes: First, the role played by the meaning giving mechanism has changed. As the strategy to realize the nation's goals changes from "dependency on labor motivation " (i.e., through ideological and political work to stimulate labor enthusiasm and productivity) to "harnessing labor's material interests" (i.e., secular work incentives), the role of the meaning giving mechanism in achieving national objectives became weaker. Second, the sources of ultimate meaning have changed. With the state's attention focused on economic development, the state was increasingly inclined to use economic means to solve the many problems they faced, rather than relying on ideological work as they had in the past (as well as administrative measures). Thus, the state relatively weakened its ideological control. The monopoly on ultimate significance was broken, and other forces (e.g., marketing, religion) were included into the supply of ultimate meaning. The sources of ultimate meaning became more diverse. Third, the content of ultimate meaning changed. Before the reform, ultimate meaning was often about ambitious goals and ideals for the future. The purpose of establishing this kind of ultimate meaning was to encourage the spirit of delayed gratification. Through this approach of looking toward the future, the state made people to tolerate their immediate poverty (abstinence) while maintaining strong labor enthusiasm and a spirit of dedication. After the reform and opening up, the content of ultimate significance gradually shifted from abstinence and moderation to personal happiness and enjoyment. Here I will discuss these three changes in detail.

Why was the role of the meaning giving mechanism relatively weakened? On the one hand, on the eve of the reform and opening up, after twenty years of a planned economy, the state had failed to deliver on its commitment. Although the state had some level of achievement in macroeconomic development, people still lived in widespread poverty. In addition to that, people were subjected to more constraints both vertically and horizontally. This situation led to many people to have doubts about the ultimate meaning before the reform and opening up. The state's "non-material incentives" (sacred incentives) lost its effectiveness over time. Labor productivity and enthusiasm decreased. This in turn exacerbated economic shortages, which further heightened doubts of the ultimate meaning.

In order to break this cycle, the state's new generation of leaders had to find another way, by diluting the role of "non-material incentives" and using material incentives to mobilize labor enthusiasm and productivity. The use of material incentives implied a fundamental change in the national leader's view of human nature: human nature and material desire should no longer be suppressed. To the contrary, it is something that the state could and should take advantage of. By taking advantage of people's material desires labor enthusiasm and productivity were greatly increased, the national economy improved, and people's living standards improved swiftly as well. Obviously, adopting material incentives to satisfy people's material desires led to an economic, social and political success. The original role of the ultimate meaning inevitably declined. In other words, taking advantage of people's desire for material pursuits, the state obtained a favorable social dynamic for economic development. The state did not need to depend heavily on ideological and political work (i.e., the meaning giving mechanism), which is costly both labor and time, to secure the social dynamic for economic development.

On the other hand, since economic development was the main way for the party to rebuild its legitimacy resources, to solve its traditional problems and to address a new set of economic and social problems, and because the new generation of state leadership disliked the frequent political campaigns, the party and the state soon made economic development their central task. The party and state quickly shifted their attention from "class struggle" and political movements to economic construction. As part of this shift, the state launched the "emancipation" movement. As a result, the state ideology changed: from the old doctrine of building a utopia to an economic (economic development is the central task of the party and state) and experimental doctrine ("feeling for the stepping stones while crossing the river"). The ideological shift to the economic and experimental doctrine creates a conflict with traditional ideology. However, the variety of new ideas and new measures proved useful for economic development, and were tolerated by the country. The relaxation of thought-control made the supply of ultimate meaning no longer a state monopoly. External forces (e.g., marketing) became involved in providing ultimate meaning. Moreover, after the economic reforms began to progress, complicated economic issues and routine administrative matters consumed much of the energy of the party and government leadership. They had no time to focus on the supply of ultimate meaning. Leaders realized that the supply of "bread" (livelihood) had become more urgent than the supply of ultimate meaning, and could not afford to be delayed. The shift of national attention to worldly affairs and the economy meant that the state needed, to a certain degree, to give up its monopoly on supplying ultimate meaning. It also provided an opportunity for the forces and powers "outside the system" to get into the supply of ultimate meaning.

So what are the sources "outside the system" of ultimate meaning? As the reform and opening up changed the Chinese economy from a planned economy to a market economy, the market sector became a new, powerful supplier of ultimate meaning. The market economy led to the rise of salesmanship and marketing. The nature of marketing is not only to identify the existence of a market, but also to shape the market, namely: using advertising, fashion and other marketing means to establish or change ultimate meaning (including the world, life, etc.). Because marketing is an integral part of the market economy, and because marketing identifies ultimate meaning with economic development, the supply of this "outside the system" ultimate meaning, was not only endorsed by the state but also encouraged objectively by it. The market sector no longer provided the ultimate political significance. Instead it provided "de-politicized" and secular ultimate meaning.

This "de-politicized" ultimate meaning is mainly reflected how it is linked to the national macro goals. Since the state relaxed its monopoly on the supply of ultimate meaning, and forces "outside the system" (e.g., marketing, public discourse, etc.) got involved in interpreting and reconstructing ultimate meaning, people no longer had to get their individual ultimate meaning from the state's goals and ideals ("meaningful life"). On the contrary, because of the diverse supplies of ultimate significance, particularly because of the institutional arrangements for material incentives (to encourage people to pursue material interests), people adopted the pursuits of individual freedom, personal interests, personal happiness or enjoyment as their own ultimate significance. Thus, the original kind of ultimate meaning, characterized by abstinence and dedication, gradually gave way to an emphasis on ultimate meaning revolving around individual and personal interests.

In contemporary society, the most important promoter of "de-politicized" ultimate meaning is the consumer culture and its associated marketing.[479] The so-called consumer culture is the symbolic system of consumer goods and consumption constructed to supply an ultimate meaning of life, by the organizations of production, management and capital by use of marketing tools (e.g., advertising, fashion). In the consumer culture, the meaning of consumer goods and consumption has changed from its original economic meaning to a sociological meaning. As Baudrillard said, consumer goods and consumption have changed into system of symbols and are included into the logic of social and cultural movement.[480] This consumer culture becomes a new meaning giving mechanism that gives people today their meaning of life.

The rise of consumer culture fundamentally changed the landscape of contemporary Chinese society. It meant that people were released from the state's totalitarianism and allowed reconstruct an ultimate meaning of life relatively independently of the state ideology. People reconstructed their personal lives and pursued individual autonomy and freedom. Consumer culture directs people's attention from politics to spending, shifting it from utopian ideals to real life. Consumer culture was also rebuilt with "sacred" and "secular" content. What was formerly enshrined as a "sacred" and "noble" was now thrown out of the shrine. What was formerly disparaged as "vulgar" was now given "sacred" status. For example, in the past, "pleasure-seeking" was considered shameful. Now, pleasure is not only considered natural, but a "sacred" right.

Consumer culture has changed people's social relations. On the one hand, because of the rise of consumer culture, human relations have become ever more "abstract". On the other hand, the relationship between persons and things is getting closer. In other words, in consumer culture, a relationship between people and goods increasingly becomes an alternative to a relationship between people. As Bowman said, as people's ability and willingness to forming relationships, maintaining social relations (i.e., social skills) and mending relationships when conflict arises are degraded, people tend to have "market dependency syndrome", specifically appearing to rely more on the marketing of products and services, which is to use the goods and services purchased as an alternative to resolving interpersonal problems.[481] As Jean Baudrillard pointed out in his book "Consumer Society" contemporary people are surrounded by objects, unlike in the past when people were surrounded by people.[482]

We can say that in the planned economy era, "political discourse" had the dominant position; in the market economy, "commodity discourse" has replaced the previous dominance. The initiator of "political discourse" is the state. Its aim is to mobilize productivity (e.g., the "Great Leap Forward", the "Agricultural Learning From Da Zhai" movement, and thee "Industrial School Learning from Daqing" Campaign). By contrast, the initiator of "commodity discourse" is the market. Its purpose is to stimulate labor enthusiasm. In the era dominated by "political discourse", our duty is defined to be "labor" and "dedication" (e.g., the spirit of Lei Feng and the "Iron Man" Wang Jinxi spirit). In the era dominated by "commodity discourse", our "obligation" is defined as "spending." Thus, in a consumer society dominated by goods, the status of consumer goods is "totemized". Consumption, at least some types of consumption, has become a "quasi-religious" sacred activity.

In this sense, the emerging consumer culture becomes the mechanism to give meaning to people's lives. This is because in the consumer culture, consumer goods have been endowed with meanings. Why? According to McCracken's point of view, owning certain items means owning the significance of those items.[483] Williamson also pointed out that in modern western society, "people are identified by what they consume, not by what they produce."[484] Similarly, as China's urban society changed into a consumer society, people's social and self-identities were more and more defined by what they spent on rather than by what products they produced. In fact, consumption can create a "false position",[485] in which people's identity as producers in society is weighted relatively less. Because material products are increasingly symbols representing social significance, they ever more become the symbols that give meaning to life.[486] For example, for many people, owning a house and car is the same as being "successful", having "social status" and being "upper-class." Having a television, refrigerator and automatic washing machine is the same as having a "modern" family life. Having a cell phone is equal to participation in social interaction. On Valentine's Day, having roses, chocolates and champagne, is the same as having "romance." At the wedding, the bride gets a ring from the groom, which means access to each other's "commitments", "responsibility" and "loyalty." Examples like these go on endlessly.

So where does the meaning of products come from? McCracken believes that it is transferred from the world of culture, with advertising and fashion playing a "bridging" role. Because advertising and fashion transfer the sense of cultural world to products, the products become symbols of social and cultural significance.[487] The commodity discourse manipulated by market is actually a process of symbolizing products, namely: advertising and fashion magazines have consumers to establish a customary association between products and their particular meanings, so as to make the products become symbols representing such meanings. However, the process of this meaning transfer is selective rather than mechanical. By choosing an approach that helps merchandising and is profitable, marketing selectively constructs its "cultural and social significance." In this sense, the commodity discourse is ideological in nature. It is marketing ideology.

In consumer culture, consumption is a dual process. One is the dominant process, which is the functional consumption of the product's usable value. The other is the hidden process, which is the cultural-social spending of the product's symbolic meaning. In the former case, people's consumption follows natural laws and functional logic. The natural properties of materials satisfy people's natural desires and emotional needs. In the latter case, people's consumption follows the logic of symbolism. The symbolic properties of the products satisfy people's needs in building their own social identity, cultural identity and self-identity. At the same time, this is also an objective in line with the requirement for profit.

Admittedly, the market itself cannot arbitrarily manipulate the symbolic significance of commodities. In fact, the significance given to products by advertisers and fashion planners is not necessarily the same as consumer's interpretation of the symbolic values of the products. This is because the symbolic meaning of goods not only comes from the marketing staff in their planning for the products, but also comes from the consumer's social interactions, including the demonstration effect of consumption, the imitation of consumption, consumer competition, conspicuous consumption, consumption trends, and so on. In such an interactive process, the goods are given specific social and cultural significance. It is also through the process of these interactions, that the significance of goods is constantly defined, updated, redefined, and updated again. Clearly, the process of giving significance to consumer goods is a dynamic, not a static process. It is a continuous, not one-off process. For example, the in emergence of fashion, it is precisely people's interactions that have led to the meaning of goods being constantly updated. But no matter how smart consumers are, they always have difficulty in completely escaping control by marketing and consumer culture. At the moment when they pursue consumer autonomy and freedom, they have already been affected by consumer culture in a hidden way. In fact, "consumer choice" or "freedom of choice" is also prefabricated phenomenon constructed by consumer culture.

For consumers, a product has a "life".[488] As consumption has a dual nature, an object often has two "lives": the physical life and social life. The physical life refers to the product's period of usable value, which is determined by its natural or functional properties. For example, for a non-disposable consumer product (e.g., clothing), as long as its value is still present (i.e., the clothing is not damaged), its physical life continues (i.e., the clothing can still be worn). When its value is lost (i.e., the clothing is dilapidated), its physical life reaches an end (i.e., it can no longer be worn). The so-called social life means the period of time the social implication of an item represents or meets an individual's needs. As a result of social interactions the symbolic meaning of a product changes, making the social life of the product shorter and shorter. As a result, the end of a product's social life often comes before the end of its physical life. For example, when a garment without any damage (still possessing usable physical life) becomes "outdated" or "old fashioned", the consumers feel that they "cannot wear it anymore" (its social life is ended). Fashion has led to shorter and shorter social lives for products, with the frequency of replacing consumer products becoming greater.[489]

One important feature of consumer society is the mechanism for the formation of fashion. It gives consumer society a new social order and social integration. This mechanism of fashion has caused the ever shorter "social life" of products compared to their "physical life".[490] Fashion is precisely a new type of consumer exploitation mechanism created by marketing. People's pursuit of fashion is superficially the pursuit of social identity and personal freedom. But the result is the accelerated exhaustion of a product's social life, wherein consumers unwittingly play a role in assisting the exploitative function of fashion.[491]

This result means that in a consumer society, consumption life follows a new logic that is different from that in an ascetic society. In an ascetic society, because of the short supply of goods, people's attitude towards consumption is practically oriented. At the same time, because of the constraints imposed by the state ideology, the symbolic function of products is very restricted. Moreover, due to the relatively egalitarian income distribution and the policy of "psychological egalitarianism," people do not need to differentiate themselves from others by resorting to spending. So, in general, consumption life during that period follows economic logic or functional logic. According to this logic, its purpose is to maximize the physical life of consumer products (as the prices for major products are set by the state, rather than determined by the market, they cannot be changed, which makes the pursuit of the lowest price impossible). In other words, people pay more attention to the physical properties of the product and its physical life, rather than the symbolic properties and social life of the product. The main embodiment of this economic logic in consumer's lives is frugality. The so-called thrift and moderation is not only the curbing of desire, but is an attempt to extend the usable life of the product (i.e., its physical life).

In the consumer society, as the supply of good required for subsistence becomes adequate and eventually expands to surplus, and because of the weakening of the state's ideological control, people follow mainly symbolic logic in consumption life. Of course, people also follow economic logic, for example, to buy a given product at the lowest possible price in the market. However, at least for the middle class, symbolic logic is equally as important as economic logic. The so-called symbolic logic means that when people purchase a product, they not only considers its cost and quality (physical attributes), but also consider whether the product "fits" or appropriately "represents" their self-image, aesthetic needs, their social interest and social status. To consumers, consumption in a certain sense is a reconstruction or reproductive activity of social recognition and self-identity. The reason that consumption has such a social function is because the products we use are often symbols or representations of our social role, identity and status. Through a certain model of consumer choice and behavior, we create or reproduce our social identity and self-identity.[492] And fashion is a collection of symbols and consequences reflected by different expressions of social identity and the individual pursuit of self-identity. In this process, once a product ceases to carry its most relevant symbol, "matching" a consumer's social identity and self-identity, its social life reaches an end. Therefore, in the consumer society, the middle class, despite their concerns about a product's physical attributes, are also concerned about the symbolic attributes of a product (e.g., how it reflects trends and taste). The product's symbolic representation goes beyond the physical attributes of the product, namely it possesses social attributes and self-attributes, such as: the purchaser or user's interests, habits, social role and social status. In Bourdieu's words, consumption is segmentation. It is to separate classes and groups with different taste and habits by distinguished symbols.[493] Or in the words of Jean Baudrillard, consumption is the "logic of social distinction".[494] Following symbolic logic in consumption, consumers use products as symbols to intentionally or unintentionally express or conceal certain social information and self-information of themselves. For example, a consumer can cover up their low social status through certain kind of consumption to create a false position. Also consumers can take the initiative to enhance their social image through consumption that expresses their social identity and self-identity.

The symbolic expression process is a "sense-making" process, a process that people use to give meaning to their lives. From a sociological point of view, the real consumption activities are meaning-construction activities. Personal construction of meaning is possible, because consumer culture has already transformed the commodity system into a symbol system. Consumers choose and combine various symbols and elements from this symbolic system to create a personal meaning. Obviously, this consumer culture is a newly emerged "sense giving mechanism" that has entered Chinese society since the reform and opening up. In significant contrast to the planned economy period, which had a "metaphysical" ultimate meaning supply mechanism, in consumer culture the mechanism for giving ultimate meaning no longer supplies a "metaphysical" meaning, instead it gives a "physical" meaning. When people no longer believe in "metaphysical" possibilities, "physical" meaning becomes an alternative to "metaphysical" meaning.

Consumer culture makes consumption activities follow not only economic logic but also symbolic logic. What consequences do symbolic logic in consumption leads to? One significant consequence is the change of people's ideological desire, namely: the change from asceticism (or frugality) to consumerism. In the ascetic community, people's desire for consumption is simple and relatively fixed, because the desire to expand consumption can only create failure and frustration. During that period, desire is not only constrained by the shortage of goods, but also by hard ideological constraints. Internal factors (the traditional frugal habits) and external factors (economic resource constraints and ideological constraints) together result in consumption that shows a relatively stable form of desire and features of self-suppression. This frugal desire is a necessary and appropriate doctrine for these conditions.

With the transformation of an ascetic society into a consumer society, consumer's desire went through fundamental changes: their desire changed from the form of asceticism into the form of consumerism. In a consumer society, the formation of people's desire is no longer based solely on what they can currently afford, but also on reference consumer groups, reference standards and anticipated future income. Therefore, to determine whether a particular item is needed, it is necessary to consider not only whether it meets natural needs, but also whether reference groups, especially those participating reference groups (e.g., neighbors, colleagues, etc.) have had such items. For example, when neighbors generally have interior decorations in their home, often a tenant who has not yet renovated, will have to obtain interior decoration as well, even if their house is still livable without interior decoration.[495] It is because consumer desire is relative to other's consumption level (a relative need), rather than determined by absolute or natural needs that in a consumer society, consumption desire appears to be in a forever changing and never-ending state. This form of modern desire is consumerism.[496]

This dynamic expansion of consumer desires has a variety of forms. One of its manifestations is materialism. So-called materialism is the consumer's never-ending desire for the possession of new products emerging into the marketplace. There are two types of products being pursued. One is the new product that did not exist before. It is the first of its kind on the market, such as the mobile phone that appeared for the first time in the 1980s (commonly known as the "Big Brother"). Another is the replacement product, for example, the new alternative to the old "Big Brother" mobile phone. Materialism is embodied in the pursuit of these two types of products. In China, the popularity of new home appliances and their replacement is the embodiment of materialism. The appearance of "car hype" reflects the upgrade of middle-class desire. It can be said that for many of today's members of the middle-class, materialism has replaced the grand idealism of the past and has become the goal for individuals to strive for. The focus on products becomes a sink of people's attention. It constitutes a driving force for people to work hard, and the goal of life. To certain extent, people's consumption goals (e.g., "owning a house and car") bring meaning and power to their lives.

Contemporary desire is another form of hedonism. Hedonism refers to the endless desire for pleasure and enjoyment. As the philosopher Schopenhauer said, once a desire for pleasure is fulfilled, another new desire for pleasure will soon come up. Hedonism is related to people's view on life and value system (the system of ultimate meaning and beliefs). The hedonist sees life as being short and therefore one must seek to maximize pleasure. Pleasure is the purpose of life. As a result, the allocation of consumption resources must be to maximize the pleasure obtained during a lifetime. There are two types of pleasure, these being sub-sensory pleasure and spiritual pleasure. No matter which kind, their common feature is the constantly changing requirement for pleasure stimulation. Consumer goods and consumer services constitute such kind of pleasure stimulation. If we say that life is a monotonous stimulus program, then pleasure is an approach to relief, regulation, and going beyond the routine of monotonous stimulation. At the same time, daily life is full of pressure, and pressure leads to tension and anxiety. Pleasure is a way to relieve anxiety and relax. It is in this context, that pleasure is given a purposeful meaning. The cost paid for a pleasure, is legitimized and naturalized. For example, dining out, compared to eating at home, and traveling, compared to family leisure, both are expensive, yet they are considered to be irreplaceable consumption. Such consumer spending is a worthwhile activity. Hedonic consumption is also a focus of the "absorber." It is a kind of activity periodically giving meaning to people's lives.

Another form of modern desire is expressionism. So-called expressionism refers to people, according to their own will, expressing by means of spending taste, interests, culture, style, personality, psychological tendencies towards identity and social status. In Mao Zedong's planned economy era, the state defined the interests of working people as the highest standard of taste, and established "plain living" and "elegant simplicity" as the highest legitimate pleasures. With this standard, the state denounced the interests of the middle-class masses as a "bourgeois" or "petty bourgeoisie" lifestyle. Therefore, in those days, spending hardly had space to be exhibited. After the reform and opening up, the state gradually abandoned its intervention in private consumption life, consumer culture started to rise and consumption eventually gained the space for demonstration. In particular, with the social differentiation and social stratification caused by the market economy, people's social identity and status has experienced steep ups and downs. It is not only possible, but is urgently necessary for people to use the products they consume to pass on to others certain social information, an thereby express their own identity, social status, and interests and taste corresponding to their social position. Residential housing, interior decoration, clothing, jewelry, perfume, cars, etc., are all commercial products that can express some kind of social information. Consumption performance thus becomes the way of constructing the meaning of life.

The Transformation from "Goal Oriented" to "Means First"

From the perspective of institutional arrangements, China's social transformation from before to after the reform and opening up can be summarized as being from "goal oriented" to "means first". In the "goal oriented" period, the main problem facing the country was that it lacked the means necessary to achieve the national goals. In the "means first" period, the main problem facing the country was the ambiguous target and the ideological crisis that followed from such ambiguity.

In the planned economy period, prior to the reform and opening up, the entire society was organized around the overall ideological objectives. With respect to this overall objective, everything else was means. The state was not to consider cost in its effort to achieve the overall objectives. Because of its economic backwardness and lack of resources at the time, China lacked sufficient material means to achieve its overall objectives. To address this shortage of resources, the state made appropriate policy choices: First, it centralized control of all scattered resources and to establish a command economy system, so as to enhance the state's capacity to mobilize resources. Second, it curbed people's consumption level, reduced the consumption fraction, and proportionally increased savings. It used extraordinary measures to achieve socialist primitive accumulation. Third, it compensated for the shortage of material resources by leveraging the strength of China's abundant labor resources. To fully mobilize labor resources and improve social mobilization, it was necessary to improve the "power of command" over the workers. To this end, the state set up work units in urban areas, people's communes in rural areas, to force people to organize themselves in a rigidly similar way. By increasing its capabilities in organization and mobilization, the state's capabilities in social mobilization are increased.

However, these measures do not solve the problem of labor motivation. The work unit system improved the state's power of command over the workers (solving the problem of labor obedience), thereby increasing social mobilization. But there was no way to guarantee worker's initiative, creativity and enthusiasm. The institutional arrangements of the command economy and curbs on consumption improved the state's capability to mobilize resources, but there was no way to guarantee worker's initiative, creativity and motivation. Therefore, after implementing the command economy system, the system for curbing consumption and the work unit system, although resource and social mobilization were improved, there was still no way to solve the problem of "labor showing up but not contributing", namely, the labor motivation problem, and inhibiting consumption also dampened worker enthusiasm. It is clear that during the planned economy, the main problem facing the country was: "How could labor incentives be possible under a command economy system which had implemented policies to curb consumption?"

To solve this problem, the state carried out a systemic innovation by establishing a grass-root ideological and political work system. On the one hand, this ideological and political work system makes the state's ambitious goals to be sacred, so as to convince people to treat national goals as the individual's own goals. It provided individuals with a sense of sacred ownership, a sense of mission and responsibility that motivated them to work enthusiastically to achieve these goals. Such incentives can be called "sacred incentives." On the other hand, by means of humiliation and labeling, by criticizing and condemning the human desire for material goods and self-interested performance, the state shackled "inappropriate" material desires and made them taboo, and associated "hedonism" with a sense of sin or shame, thereby improving people's self-suppression of their desire for material goods.

However, the cost of ideological and political work is great. This is mainly because "blocking" measures were adopted to control people's natural desires rather than "smoothing" measures. In other words, the state used ascetic measures. This involves the transformation of human nature, which cannot be achieved in a short time. Instead it is a long-term task. At the same time, it is not a local thing, but a global consideration. This means that to implement such a system, a whole set of matching systems are required to be in place. For example, the egalitarian system was a complete system in the field of distribution. This system eventually became one that encouraged laziness.

The effectiveness of ideological and political work system relies upon its consistency with official discourse (the discourse of ideological and political work), namely: the capability to interpret reality. But quite often, official discourse clashed with reality, losing its effectiveness in explaining reality. For example, in the 1970s, after twenty years of practicing socialism, the discourse on "the superiority of socialism," clashed with the reality that the people were still living in poverty. The "National commitment" never materialized, the "persuasive power" of official discourse decreased. Another example, due to the difficulties in transforming human nature, was the spread in the 1970s of "back door" procedures and other irregularities and the growth if the cadre's privileges, which were in conflict with the official discourse of "working people being the masters." It can be said that in the late 1970s, the ideological and political work became a form of red tape. Not only did the official discourse not have the effect of stimulating labor enthusiasm, it also caused a level of resentment, because the official discourse had become "false, big and empty" words, losing their "persuasive power." Because of the constraint of its ideological dogma, the state was unable to change or amend the official discourse to accord with reality.

Once sacred incentives lose their effectiveness, the state faced the problems in achieving its ambitious goal of not only insufficient material means but also the lack of worker's labor motivation. And this problem was fatal. The state's intention was to mobilize worker's initiative, creativity and enthusiasm to make up for the lack of material means. But now they also had to face the lack of labor motivation. It can be said that during the command economy period, the state did not solve the problem of generating labor enthusiasm and productivity under the condition of curbed consumption. In short, while the state, is "goal oriented", it could not find means adequate to achieve its objectives. The state tried to stimulate worker's enthusiasm through sacred incentives in order to compensate for the lack of material means, but this eventually proved to be a failure.

In the "goal oriented" environment the state lacked the material means to achieve its objectives. In this case, human resources were the only national means that could be activated to compensate for the lack of material resources. This often led the state to see people as a means rather than an end. Since people were a means to achieve the national objectives, national leaders stressed that people must carry the tasks forward, not be afraid of hardship, be willing to sacrifice, be willing to live plainly, to save on clothes and food, to work diligently and hard like a "screw", an "ox", during the construction of socialism. From the national perspective, individual rights had to give way to duty. Therefore, all contents in he official discourse that related to individual rights described them as the "care" and "grace" from the country to its people. That is to say, it is a "gift" from the state, not necessarily a right people "should have". Obviously in a situation where people are treated as means, "individual rights" would not have a place in the official discourse. Therefore, in the command economy period, if personal rights were trampled on, it is hardly surprising.

Reform and opening up, in fact, was the historical response by its initiators to a problem that the state was unable to effectively address during the period of the planned economy: the possibility of labor incentives under the condition of curbed consumption. At that time, the state had set up ambitious goals but could not find adequate means to achieve its objectives. Therefore, means had become the key issue. To reduce the huge gap between objectives and means, the initiators of the reform and opening up (a new generation of national leaders) adjusted in two ways. On the one hand, they adjusted the national goal. The ambitious goals of the past were reduced to be operational and manageable, while specific enough to achieve. The specific target was modernization. This goal could be quantified by per capita GDP. With regard to these ever more ambitious goals, the new generation of state leaders maintained a strategic silence. On the other hand, the state also adjusted its means. After the state loosened the shackles of ideological dogma (the emancipation movement), they further weakened the already ineffective sacred incentive system (ideological and political work-based) and relied upon the means of material incentives to promote modernization.

Resorting to the means of material incentives with a commodity or market economy, the state succeeded in finding a social dynamic for modernization. Different from spiritual incentives (sacred incentives), material incentives encourage people's natural desires with "smoothing" measures rather than "blocking" the desires. Therefore, this kind of incentive system has some affinity with human being's natural desires, not only reducing greatly the cost to implement the system, but also improving its effectiveness. When hundreds of millions of workers were stimulated to work for their own personal gain and wealth, the result was a whole macro-economy and society full of vitality.

The new generation of national leadership realized that "development is the final word" (Deng Xiaoping). In China, a country with a low economic level, departing from the foundation of economic development, would render everything else meaningless. In accordance with Deng Xiaoping's view, and to settle the legitimacy issue left behind by the planned economy on "socialism's superiority", socialism was only feasible through economic development, strengthening national forces, and by improving people's standard of living. Thus, economic development was not only a means to achieve the goal of modernization, but in fact was the solution to the crisis of the state's legitimacy resources. Many legacy social problems left from the past could only be solved by economic development. Since economic development plays such an important role, Deng Xiaoping repeatedly emphasized that economic development should become the Party and the state's central mission and focus.

Since economic development is a major contributor to the state's legitimacy resources, the importance of economic development was raised by the state to the level of official ideology (i.e., economic ideology), and was turned into the primary means of motivating cadres. Beginning in the 1990s, the GDP indicator became an important basis to evaluate and promote local officials. The separation of local taxes from state taxes in 1994, made the GDP index an important indicator for local officials to work on improving, because economic development had expanded local revenue sources. Between local governments, there were fights over the GDP numbers, which made local officials pursue the goal of their GDP indicator being "GDP index first." Since GDP is only a means of modernization, the "GDP index first" goal is one kind of "means first."

"GDP index first" (means being first) led local officials to only care about the result of the GDP index, regardless of the cost to obtain that results, including environmental costs (e.g., environmental pollution) and social costs (e.g., social equity). They were only concerned about economic development, neglecting social development (e.g., social security and welfare). Since the introduction of investment projects (foreign and domestic) is to promote local economic development, thereby increasing local revenue measures, local government policies or their implementation favored investors, ignoring the public responsibility of protecting basic labor rights. In sum, "GDP index being first" made local governments into a main body with self-interest and relative autonomy. This main body to a certain extent became self-serving. This is why many of the policies from the central government were derailed once they were carried to the local level.

"Means being first" was not only reflected at the local government level (e.g., "GDP index being first"), but also at the central government's policy level. At the end of 1993, in party documents, the central government proposed to implement the principle of "giving priority to efficiency and considering fairness" in the area of income distribution. Here, the "efficiency" as a means is given a higher status than "fairness" as the universal value (objective). Therefore, "giving priority to efficiency and considering fairness" is nothing but a veritable "means being first." This "means being first" led to a huge loss of state-owned assets during the reform process of state enterprises. At the same time, during the process of restructuring the state-owned enterprises, workers were not given fair treatment. For instance, many of them were forced to accept low-cost "buyouts" and being laid-off. From a macro point of view, "means being first" caused polarization of the income distribution, where wealth was increasingly concentrated in a minority and the majority of people were unable to enjoy the same share of the fruitful results of reform and development. Therefore, since the 1990s, the "means being first" type of radical economic reform as led to the emergence of dual trends. Consumerism and a doctrine of thrift co-exist and move forwards through the main structures of Chinese society.

"Means being first" was also reflected in the reforms of collective consumption during the late 1990s. The supply of public goods in collective consumption, including social security and welfare, was originally the government's responsibility. Because of "means being first", the government saw social security and welfare as a governmental burden rather than a governmental obligations. Therefore, the reform of collective consumption followed the same principle of "giving efficiency priority and considering fairness". The government cut financial investment in social security and welfare and partially deregulated the supply of collective consumer goods while charging market prices, collecting high monopoly prices from consumers. Such a policy arrangement will inevitably cause the main departments supplying collective consumption to become self-interest groups, forming their own monopolies and taking advantage of their ability to set policy, charging consumers high monopoly prices to maximize their self-interest rather than social welfare. The collective public goods whose function was to redistribute income became the means for the supply departments of mass consumer consumption to maximize the benefits for themselves. Therefore, the reform of collective consumption did not have the effect of redistributing wealth on the contrary, it aggravated the division between rich and poor, making many low-income or vulnerable groups unable to afford medical coverage, unable to afford a house, and unable to pay for school for their children.

"Means being first" was also reflected in the social exclusion of migrant workers.

Despite the large number of migrant farm workers in the cities, they did not have access to the household registration system, thus it is difficult for them to become city residents. Resident's household registration status determined whether they were eligible for collective consumption of public goods. For example, the children of migrant workers would not be allowed to share the city's mandated public goods. The social housing system in the cities was not open to migrant workers. Medical care for migrant workers was often unavailable. The problem of migrant workers was actually a derivative phenomenon of "means being first." Cheap migrant workers provided China with a comparative advantage in the world economy. The existence of cheap migrant labor ensured price competitiveness of products "made in China", and constituted a competitive advantage in attracting foreign direct investment. Many liberal economists put it bluntly that if the wages and corresponding rights of migrant workers were to increase, it would threaten the competitive advantage of China's economy. Therefore, to maintain low-cost migrant labor, implementing "social exclusion" in the field of collective consumption of public goods has become an important means for the economic development in the eastern coastal areas. Migrant workers have thus become the main representatives of frugality in the dual-track society.

The essence of "means being first" lies in the fact that after finding the effective material means to achieve modernization (the commodity or market economy), people lost their faith in the goals, direction and practice of the state at the operational level. Before the reform and opening up, the main problem facing China was material deprivation, namely: the state lacked effective material means to achieve its goals. Then two-decade reform program solved this problem. However, since the 1990s, while the state has overcome its lack of materials, at the same time they have created a new shortage, namely: the lack of fairness. This stems from the policy direction of "means being first", namely, the policy of "giving priority to efficiency and considering fairness". Therefore, the question to the state since the reform in the nineties has been: "how can social justice be possible once effective means of modernization (market efficiency) are found?" The party and state leadership are fully aware of the issue. In 2007 there was an appropriate response in the documents of the Party's 17th congress.

The origin of "means being first" was in the state's ideological crisis. The ideology of the planned economy period had developed an increasingly tense relationship with the real world. It lost its power to explain and predict events in the world. Continuing to adhere to such a dogmatic ideology (e.g., the "two whatevers") would be no different than political suicide. This is why a new generation of leaders needed to launch an "emancipation" movement in the early days of the reform and opening up, which for ideological reasons deconstructed the old dogma. After the state loosened the shackles of dogmatism, the new generation of national leaders upheld a "realistic" spirit. In the formulation of policy they have taken a pragmatic approach. However, the state is not willing to abandon traditional socialist ideology and social "orthodoxy." A number of specific reform measures have come into heated conflict with traditional socialist ideology. In implementation of many policies this leads to the dilemma of it being possible to do something, without being able to say why (i.e., to discuss the ideological underpinnings). Thus, one can only question the means. As to the questions of ultimate values, ideals and goals, people try to avoid these much as possible. It can be seen therefore that behind the nation's pragmatism, is truly the crisis of state ideology. The state had no chance to create a new ideology that had explanatory power. In the absence of the support of ultimate beliefs, values and goals, the pragmatic approach will inevitably lead to the "means being first" phenomenon. However, we can see from the party's documents at its 17th congress, that through the proposed "harmonious society", "people-oriented" development, "scientific development" and other programs in that spirit, the party and state leadership are taking steps to correct this tendency of "means being first". The key to correcting "means being the highest priority" is to rebuild ideology, particularly by the establishment of common doctrine of faith and values. Under the new value system people should seen as ends rather than means.

Overall, the country before the reform and opening up was a "mission-oriented country". This state saw liberating the whole of China (and even the world) and realizing communism as its historical mission. And all state institutional arrangements were initiated and built around this mission. The "mission-oriented state" had a strong faith and sense of direction, but it suffered from a lack of material means. Thus, driven by its sense of mission, the "mission-oriented state" adopted institutional arrangements with general doctrines that concentrated all human and material resources in order to raise the state's social and resource mobilization capacity, so to better complete its historical mission. The secret of the "mission-oriented state" is its supreme "command of power" and its persuasive power over the masses. But ultimately it was unable to continuously mobilize people's enthusiasm to work, and unable to guarantee the efficiency of economic operation. The beginning of "mission-oriented state" was often good, but the results were often contrary to the original intention.

After the reforms, the "mission-oriented state" transformed into a "production-oriented state." A "production-oriented state" gives up unrealistic utopian goals. Instead it seeks achievable, operational goals. The goal is modernization. To achieve this goal, the "production-oriented state" focuses on economic construction. Economic construction becomes the central task of the state. National institutional arrangements are basically made around economic development. This was the case in the 1980s with the separation of government from the state-owned enterprises, the decentralization of authority, and increased personal responsibility, as well as in the 1990s with the introduction of the modern enterprise system, the commoditization of labor, securities trading and other elements of the modern market system. Economic growth is not only a means to solve social problems, but also becomes a source of state legitimacy. In addition, economic growth increases revenues for all levels of government. Thus, economic growth became the top priority for all levels of government to pursue. However, economic growth was achieved at high social and environmental cost. Therefore, after the reform and opening up, the state resolved the issue of labor incentives and economic efficiency (market economy), but at the same time the government neglected their obligation to provide fairly for environmental protection and the collective consumption of public goods.

A sign emerged after the 17th Congress that the "production-oriented state" is in transition to a "service-oriented state". In this type of state, the state is no longer directly involved in economic development, but provides fair rules and order for the market, and makes up for market failures in the supply of public goods to the whole society, including providing for the collective consumption of public goods. In the "service-oriented state", policies of particularism (e.g., social exclusion) will give way to a policy of universalism, the "people being the means" approach will give way to the "people being the end" approach. Local and short-term thinking will give away to an overall and long-term rational doctrine.

Towards A Civil Society[497]

This book discussed the transformation process of Chinese urban society from an ascetic society to a consumer society. From the perspective of individual freedom and autonomy, whether in an ascetic society, or in a consumer society, human development has not reached its final stage. The direction of social development should be toward a civil society.

In the ascetic society, almost every aspect of the individual was under social surveillance. Individual privacy was substantially denied by the state (e.g., private property being destroyed, private consumption being suppressed, the right of private consumption being limited). An individual's private space was severely restricted, and activities pushed into public space. However, even in public spaces, individual rights were limited. People enjoyed lifetime job security, social security, welfare and other social benefits, but at very elementary level. People's activities in the public forum were mainly political activities, for example, political education, political movements, political rallies and so on. However, these were not the people's spontaneous, unselfconscious activities. They were performed at the command of higher authority. Therefore, in the public space, people were not exercising public rights. Instead, it was the state exercising its power to mobilize the nation's populace. Thus, in the ascetic society, most of the private nature of individuals was lost. Individuals were forcibly transformed into "state people" (or "system people"), a transformation that was not voluntary. In the institutional arrangements in the ascetic society, because once one is "outside the system" it is almost impossible to secure basic resources. People who left their work units were almost unable to survive. It led to "syndrome of work unit dependency" or "institutional dependency". The identity of a "state person" is mainly reflected in two aspects: on the one hand, individuals in their work units are an extension of the power of the state and are obligated to accept the state's authority and recognize its chain of command. On the other hand, individuals are protected by the work unit and given "asylum" (employment protection, guarantee of survival resources, social welfare) and enjoy the "welfare grace" the state gives to "state people." But this "asylum" and "grace" are at the expense of individual freedom. Clearly, in a society where personal life and privacy are almost gone, personal private spaces for social freedom, personal freedom and autonomy are difficult to maintain.

The deprivation of privacy in the ascetic society is linked to the supremacy of the state's goals. To achieve the national ideological goals under the condition of a shortage of material means, the nation's leadership realized that it had to fully exploit and mobilize its human resources. Therefore they had to have all labor resources under a national command system in order to improve their capability to organize and mobilize social resources. Once the individual is included into the national command structure (i.e., the work unit), the individual becomes a "state person" or a "system person" because he or she has been included in the state power chain. To improve the state's power of command over individuals, the individual's privacy must be taken away: on the one hand, individuals are not allowed to own private property; on the other hand, the subsistence consumption necessary for personal survival is only available from supply channels within the system, eliminating the possibility to go "outside the system," for subsistence consumption. The reason for the elimination of privacy was that privacy sows the seeds of "selfishness". And selfishness, under the conditions of the state's suppressing consumption, was in contradiction to the institutional arrangements of non-material incentives. Therefore, the abolition of the private sphere was what the state needed to do to eradicate the seeds of "selfishness" from the system. But the abolition of the private sphere inevitably leads to people ("state people") becoming "system dependent": they must be attached to the system, subject to system command. "State people" with "institutional dependency" have a very high compliance. But it is difficult for them to have sufficient personal freedom and autonomy.

In the consumer society, individual privacy is revived. Specifically: on the one hand, private property was recognized and affirmed by the State, and the pursuit of the personal possession of private property obtained unprecedented "legitimacy"; on the other hand, the state abandoned its monopoly of the supply of subsistence consumption and corresponding social control. Consumer production and supply were gradually organized on the market principle. The supply and distribution of the consumer resources necessary for survival "outside the system" weakened people's dependence on "inside the system" resources. The consumer society transformed individuals into "consumers" in the modern sense. It not only gave consumers freedom of choice, but autonomy in their private lives. Thus, the private sphere repressed in the ascetic society returns in the consumer society. The revival of the private sphere, to a certain extent, increased individual freedom and personal autonomy.

The recovery of the private sphere was also related to the national decision to give up on intervening in personal, private lives. In the ascetic society, an individual has almost no private life. Almost all aspects of personal life are monitored and controlled by the "organization", colleagues and neighbors. In the popular saying of the time: "people's eyes are sharp." Individuals do not choose activities in private life, including a personal lifestyle, freely. Instead, they must meet the "correct" standard as defined by the national ideology. Otherwise, they would be subject to criticism by the leaders of their work unit and their colleagues. Therefore, at that time, the state took the approach of deep involvement and intervention in people's private lives. However, after the reform and opening up, the state gradually abandoned this program of deep involvement and intervention. On the one hand, in the wake of the state's ideological transformation, the state relaxed ideological control. On the other hand, the state had to focus on economic construction and other public affairs. It neither saw the necessity nor had the energy to interfere with the freedom of private life. As the state backed out of private life, businesses began to intervene in this area, because people's private lives formed part of their efforts to identify and develop the marketplace. Therefore, in a consumer society, not only is the privacy of the individual restored, but also that due to their roles in business discourse, "privacy" and "private life", which in the past were defined as "vulgar", acquire sacred meaning.

However, while in consumer society the private sphere is reconstructed, people's public nature has deteriorated. This public nature is embodied in two aspects: one being public rights and the other, public obligation. On the one hand, individual's public rights have been weakened. A typical example in this regard is the decline of individual's social rights. Social rights are part of individual's public rights. They refer to individuals, as citizens, having the right to benefit from collective consumption of the public goods (mainly social security and welfare) provided by the state. The weakening of social rights is related to the state's change in its ideological orientation toward social security and welfare (collective consumption of public goods). In the planned economy period, social security and welfare were "proof" of the "superiority of the socialist system" and "working people being the masters." Although the state implemented a policy of suppressing private consumption, in collective consumption, because of its ideological commitments, the state provided a modest level of social security and welfare for much of the population. After the reforms, especially in the 1990s, the state shifted its ideological position on social security and welfare (i.e., it adopted the liberal-style ideology). In the state's view, the traditional social security and welfare system was inefficient. The reform of the social security and welfare system was a question of how to more effectively allocate resources rather than a question of an individual's social rights. Therefore, the state took measures to reform social security and welfare, introducing market (profit for suppliers) and private (the user paying) factors, thereby reducing the government's investment and financial burden. From the national perspective, on the one hand, there should be profits for suppliers so as to increase the efficiency of the supply of collective goods for collective consumption, and to improve the efficiency of resource allocation. On the other hand, the individuals now have to bear part of the cost for collective goods (social security and welfare). Private individuals should therefore value efficiency in the consumption of collective resources by reducing waste. However, a result of the reform of collective consumption led suppliers of collective goods to seek "maximum the benefits for their departments" (e.g., as in the medical sector) rather than maximizing social welfare. So public goods for collective consumption, originally provided out of the government's public funds, were transferred to the private sector and became a private burden. Superficially, the reform of the collective consumption system seemed to improve its efficiency. But in fact fairness was lost, and the social rights of citizens were especially neglected. The individual as a private citizen now has the burden of supplying public goods for collective consumption, which should have been the responsibility of the public purse.

The weakening of the individual's public nature was reflected in the weakening of the individual's sense of public obligation. People focus to a greater extent on personal matters. A sense of indifference to public affairs is growing. The lower level of individual political participation and participation in public affairs, often leads to a personal sense of powerlessness. Since people feel powerless to change the status quo, this inevitably leads to a sense of indifference to public affairs. Public affairs are seen as a governmental responsibility, which can be taken for granted. As a result, people have adopted an attitude of passivity toward public affairs. For example, the amount of charitable donations and the number of volunteers as a proportion of the total population is far lower in China than in the United States or European countries.[498] Although the reasons for this phenomenon are very complex (involving a web of interrelated reasons), it is undeniable citizens approach public affairs with a certain degree of indifference. The weakness of the public sense of duty is also reflected people's lack of cooperation in complying with the law and maintaining of public order." For example, the proportion of Chinese people ignoring the rules of traffic is relatively high. For example, many pedestrians are not accustomed to obeying red lights, and the proportion of drivers running red lights is also not small. Drunk driving, speeding, and overloading violations are often repeated.

In the consumer society, the weakening of individual's public nature is related to the state's "means first" policy. On the one hand, in order to improve the efficiency of resource allocation, the state reformed the collective consumption of public goods (social security and welfare) by implementing a "quasi-market" (liberal style) system, passing on a considerable part of the cost to supply collective consumer goods (including costs of monopolized pricing), to the private consumer. It hereby reduced the burden on the government's finances. The government used the "savings" to expand domestic demand and stimulate economic growth (simultaneously, consumption by the government itself was growing rapidly). Consequently, individual's social rights have been devalued and individual's public natures have been damaged. On the other hand, the state has only warily injected itself into political and public affairs. Since Beijing went through a political crisis in 1989, the state adopted a "stability overrides everything" policy, trying to avoid social unrest and maintain social stability. In this context, the state allows citizens to focus on consumer and other private affairs, both to divert their attention and energy to "safe" areas and to promote economic development, thereby increasing the state's legitimacy resources, because economic development and improving private consumption have always been the way the state has reconstructed and improved its legitimacy resources since the reform and opening up. In this sense, the rise of consumerism is the transition of the country into a civil society. It is a result of the alienation of people's livelihood in exchange for "social stability."[499.] Clearly, the radical market-oriented reforms after 1992 not only led to the emergence consumerism as a by-product, but also exacerbated the decline in individual's public nature. In other words, individuals are increasingly focused on the private sphere (private life and private affairs), and show an increasingly indifferent attitude toward public affairs.

It is clear that in an ascetic society, an individual's public nature suppresses his private nature. In a consumer society, an individual's private nature crowds out his public nature. Neither the disappearance of private nature or the weakening of public nature is a complete state of personal development. As a complete individual, the person should have both private and public natures. The private and public natures of the individual should be unified. On the one hand, the individual's private space is the space for individual freedom and autonomy. As Hegel said in "On Philosophy", private property is self-affirmation. So for people to have personal freedom and autonomy, they must have material security by owning private property. At the same time, an individual's autonomy is reflected in his private life and private affairs being protected from intervention by authority. On the other hand, the public nature of the individual is expressed in the quality of public (or social) life. People's political participation and participation in public affairs, constitute the necessary conditions for the people to have a quality public (or social) life. People's social rights (the rights to social security and welfare) become direct reflection of the quality public (or social) life. At the same time, the public nature of the individual also requires people to perform public duties so as to enhance the quality of public (or social) life. Improving the quality of public life will, in turn, encourage the private sector to enhance the quality of life. Thus, the individual's public nature is not only a necessary condition to perfect the private nature of the individual, but it is also the guarantee of individual freedom and autonomy. The society in which both the private and public natures of individuals are recognized is civil society. On the one hand, it avoids the flaw of the ascetic society, which suppresses the private nature of individuals. On the other hand, it avoids the flaw of the consumer society, which weakens the public nature of individuals. The individuals in a civil society are not the "state people" of the ascetic society. They have sufficient private nature, private life and personal freedom. Individuals in the civil society are not the "private people" of the consumer society (only concerned with private affairs and private consumption). They have sufficient public nature, having the right of public participation, and demonstrate positive enthusiasm for performing their public obligations. When "private people" pursue consumerist lifestyles, they often hold aloof attitudes toward the negative consequences to the social and natural environment caused by their consumption. In contrast, the "citizen" consumers of the civil society, when they pursue their private rights and freedoms in consumer choice, will not accept the adverse social and environmental consequences caused by their consumption. On the contrary, they will take action to change their consumption choices, resisting consumption that has negative or destructive consequences for the social and natural environment. They will adhere to green or sustainable consumption patterns. In other words, in the civil society, an individual's rights and obligations are an organic unity.

Notes

1. J. M. Keynes, *The General Theory of Employment, Interest and Money*, Chinese ed. (Commerce Press, 1963).

2. For an introduction to the theory of consumption function, see: Xueheng Zang, *China's Consumption Function Analysis* (Shanghai People's Publishing House, 1994), chapter 1 and Angus Dayton, *Understanding Consumption*, trans. Jingbei Hu and Chang Lu (Shanghai Finance University Press, 2003).

3. Francesco M. Nicosia and Robert N. Mayer, "Toward a Sociology of Consumption," *Journal of Consumer Research* **3**, no. 2 (1976), 65~75.

4. Mary Douglas and Baron Isherwood, *The World of Goods: Towards an Anthropology of Consumption* (London: Routledge, 1979).

5. Zheng Hong-E believes that there are two paths of theoretical research on consumer attitudes domestically and overseas: economic determinism and cultural hegemony theory. The former sees the concept of consumption being determined by economic conditions, while the latter sees the concept of consumption being created by cultural domination in capitalist society. She believes that both theories are biased. Therefore, she proposed a "recognition and build" theoretical perspective (Zheng Hong-E, *Social Transformation and Consumer Revolution* (Beijing University Press, 2006), 12~31.) From the literature, it seems that "economic determinism" mainly exists in economic circles, and the "cultural hegemony" theory belongs to the field of sociology.

6. Thorsten Veblen, *The Theory of the Leisure Class*, Chinese ed. (Commerce Press, 1997).

7. Harvey Leibenstein, "Bandwagon, Snob, and Veblen Effects in the Theory of Consumer's Demand," *Quarterly Journal of Economics* **44**, no. 2 (1950), 183~207.

8. Juliet B. Schor, The Overspent American: Upscaling, Downshifting, and the New Consumer (New York: HarperPerennial, 1998).

9. Georg Simmel, "The Philosophy of Fashion", in *Consumer Culture Reader*, ed. Gang Luo and Zhong-Chen Wang (China Social Sciences Press, 2003), 241.

10. Georg Simmel, *Philosophy of Money*, 2nd enlarged ed., trans. T. Bottomore and D. Frisby (London: Routledge, 1990), 461.

11. Grant McCracken, *Culture and Consumption* (Indianapolis: Indiana University Press, 1988), 93. In this book, McCracken criticized Simmel's the top-down fashion theory.

12. Pierre Bourdieu, *Distinction: A Social Critique of the Judgement of Taste*, trans. Richard Nice (London: Routledge, 1984).

13. Jean Baudrillard, *Selected Writings*, ed. Mark Poster (Cambridge: Polity Press, 1988), 22.

14. Baudrillard, *Selected Writings*, 41.

15. Max Horkheimer and Theodor Adorno, "Culture Industry: Enlightenment as mass deception", and "Dialectic of Enlightenment," trans. Jing-Dong Qu and Wei-Dong Cao (Shanghai People's Publishing House, 2003), 134~187.

16. Herbert Marcuse, *One-Dimensional Man*, trans. Ji Liu (Shanghai Translation Publishing House, 2006).

17. "Antonio Gramsci," in Tony Bennett, Graham Martin, Colin Mercer and Janet Woollacott, eds., *Culture, Ideology and Social Process: A Reader* (London: B. T. Batsford, 1981), 185~218; Chantal Mouffe, "Hegemony and Ideology in Gramsci," in *Culture, Ideology and Social Process: A Reader*, 219~234; Antonio Gramsci, *The Prison Notebooks*, trans. Lei-Yu Cao, Li Jiang and Xian Zhang (Beijing: China Social Sciences

Press, 2000).

18. Marcuse, *One-Dimensional Man*, 6~12.

19. On consumer's practices to counter capitalism, see Michel de Certeau, *The Practice of Everyday Life*, trans. Steven F. Rendall (Berkeley: University of California Press, 1984).

20. For example, the British School of thought believes that the Frankfurt School treats consumers as a passive, easily deceived and "taken advantage of." This view devalues the consumer's autonomy, initiative and rebellious nature.

21. Deborah S. Davis, "Urban Consumer Culture", *The China Quarterly* 183 (2005), 692~709

22. Zheng Honge, "China's Consumerism and Beyond," *Academic Forum* 11 (2005), 119.

23. Colin Campbell, *The Romantic Ethic and the Spirit of Modern Consumerism* (Oxford: Basil Blackwell, 1987).

24. Russell W. Belk, "Third World Consumer Culture" in *Research in Marketing, Supplement 4*, "Marketing and Development: toward Broader Dimensions" (Greenwich: JAI Press, 1988), 103~127.

25. Jeffrey James, *Consumption and Development* (New York: St. Martin's Press, 1993), 111~136.

26. Leslie Sklair, *Sociology of the Global System* (Baltimore: Johns Hopkins University Press, 1991), 129~169.

27. Leslie Sklair, "The Culture-Ideology of Consumerism in Urban China", in *Research in Consumer Behavior*, ed. Clifford J. Shultz II, Russell W. Belk and Ger Guliz (Greenwich: JAI Press, 1994), 259~292.

28. Deborah S. Davis, ed., *The Consumer Revolution in Urban China* (Berkeley: University of California Press, 2000).

29. Zheng Hong-E, *Social Transformation and Consumer Revolution - Changes in Consumer Attitudes in Chinese Cities* (Peking University Press, 2006), chapter 3.

30. Friedrich Hayek, *The Road to Serfdom*, trans. Ming-Yi Wang and Xing-Yuan Feng Xingyuan (Beijing: China Social Sciences Press, 1997), 146.

31. Chen Nabo, "Debate Overseas on China's Market Transition: Reviews of the Fifteen-Year Literature, *Sociological Research* 5 (2006), 205.

32. Margaret Levi, "The State of the Study of the State." in *Political Science: the State of the Discipline*, ed. H. V. Milner (Washington, D. C.: American Political Science Association, 2002), 33. Cited by Chen Nabo, "Debate Overseas on China's Market Transition: Reviews of the Fifteen-Year Literature", 205.

33. Regarding the concept of "Macro-Actor", as far as I know, it was first put forward by Mouzelis; see: Nicos Mouzelis, *Sociological Theory: What Went Wrong? Diagnosis and Remedies* (London: Routledge, 1995).

34. Regarding the Introduction of qualitative research methods, see: Xing-Ming Chen, *Qualitative Research Methods and Social Science Research* (Beijing: Education Science Press, 2000), Anselm Strauss and Juliet Corbin, *Basics of Qualitative Research: Techniques and Procedures for Developing Grounded Theory*, 2nd ed. (London: Sage, 1998), John W. Creswell, *Qualitative Inquiry and Research Design: Choosing among Five Traditions* (London: Sage, 1998), Catherine Marshall and Gretchen B. Rossman, *Designing Qualitative Research* 3rd ed. (London: Sage, 1999), Norman K. Denzin and Yvonna S. Lincoln, eds., *Collecting and Interpreting Qualitative Materials* (London: Sage, 1998). Uwe Flick, *An Introduction to Qualitative Research* 2nd ed. (London: Sage, 2002).

35. Pertti Alasuutart, *Researching Culture: Qualitative Method and Cultural Studies* (London: Sage, 1995).

36. Flick, *An Introduction to Qualitative Research*, 2nd ed.

37. "Generation" or "Group of Generations" as a noun, are both Chinese translations of the English word "generation". They both talk about one generation of people or the same generation. However, "generation" also has the sense of a quantifier. To distinguish the quantifier-type "generation", the translation here takes the meaning "group of generations".

38. Karl Mannheim, "The Problem of Generations," in *From Karl Mannheim*, 2nd expanded edition, ed. Kurt H. Wolff (London: Transaction Publishers, 1993), 351~395.

39. Wang Ning: "Representative or Typical? - Talking about the Logical Base of Case Study Methodology,"

Sociology 5 (2002), 123~125.

40. Douglass North, "New Institutional Economics and Development," in *Transition, Rules and Institutional Arrangements*, ed. Kuan-Ping Sun (Social Sciences Academic Press, 2004), 10.

41. Victor Nee, "Sources of New Institutionalism," in *The New Institutionalism in Sociology*, ed. Mary C. Brington and Victor Nee (Stanford: Stanford University Press, 1998), 8.

42. Tong En-zheng, *Man and Culture*, (Chongqing Press, 1998), 10.

43. Wang Ning, *Consumer Sociology - An Analytical Perspective* (Beijing: Social Sciences Academic Press, 2001), chapter 9.

44. Wang Ning, "Consumption and Identity - Sociology of Consumption, an Analytical Framework to Explore," *Sociology* 1 (2001), 4~14.

45. The view that people have learned "delayed enjoyment" during the course of human civilization is detailed in: Sigmund Freud, *Civilization and Its Discontents*, ed. J Strachey, trans. J. Riviere (London: The Hogarth Press and the Institute of Psycho-analysis, 1963).

46. Weber's *Protestant Ethic* and its analysis is a typical example. See: Max Weber, *The Protestant Ethic and the Spirit of Capitalism*, 2nd ed., trans. Talcott Parsons (London: George Allen & Unwin, 1976).

47. Albert Auch Seaman, *Desire and Benefits: Political Debate Before Capitalism to Victory*, trans. Li Xinhua, Zhu Jindong Zhu (Shanghai Literature & Art Publishing House, 2003).

48. Levi, "The State of the Study of the State," 33.

49. Chen Nabo, "Debate Overseas on China's Market Transition: Reviews of the Fifteen-Year Literature", 205.

50. Levi, "The State of the Study of the State."

51. T. H. Rigby (1964), "Traditional, Market, and Organizational Societies and the USSR," *World Politics* 16, no. 4 (1964), 540. Cited by Franco Wavelet Jan, *State: Nature, Development and Prospects*, trans. Yao Chen (Shanghai People's Publishing House, 2007), 167~168.

52. For details, see Michael Oakeshott, *On Human Conduct* (Oxford: Clarendon Press, 1975).

53. Mao Zedong, "On Coalition Government," 24 April 1945, in *Mao Zedong's Selected Works*, vol. 3, 2nd ed. (People's Publishing House, 1991), 1059.

54. Mao Zedong put forward a description of the general guidelines in, Mao Zedong, "Speech at Chinese Communist Party National Conference: Opening Remarks," 21 March 1955, in *Selected Works*, vol. 6, 389.

55. Mao Zedong, "The Changes of Revolution and the Party's General Guidelines During the Transition Period of Time", in *Selected Works*, vol. 6, 316.

56. Mao Zedong, "Guidelines During the Transition Period of Time."

57. Mao Zedong, "On Coalition Government."

58. Mao Zedong, "On Coalition Government."

59. Zhou Enlai, "General Guidelines of the Transition Period," 8 September 1953, in *The Selected Works of Zhou Enlai*, vol. 2 (People's Publishing House, 1984), 109~110.

60. Li Fuchun, "The Report on the First Five-Year Plan of National Economic Development" (extract) (5 July 1955 report at the second session of the First National People's Congress), in Hong Zhou, ed., *The PRC National History Chronicle (1949~1956)*, 788.

61. Chen Yun, "A Few Points On the First Five-year Plan," 30 June 1954, in *Selected Works of Chen Yun (1949~1956)*, p. 241.

62. Zhou Enlai, "Government Work Report," 23 September 1954, in *Selected Important Documents Since the Founding of the Country*, vol. 5, 585~586.

63. National Bureau of Statistics, *The Great Ten Years - the Statistics of the People's Republic Economic and Cultural Achievements* (People's Publishing House, 1959), 1~2.

64. International Statistical Bureau (National Comprehensive Economic Statistics Division), *Collection of Statistical Information from Fifty Years of New China*, (China Statistics Press, 1999).

65. Zhou Enlai, "Government Work Report," 23 September 1954, 607.

66. Zhou Enlai, "Government Work Report," 23 September 1954, 586.

67. Since Max Weber proposed three types of legitimacy (legal-rational, traditional and charismatic), "legitimacy" has become a very important concept in political science and sociology. There are many analyses and discussions about legitimacy theory. This book does not intend to review those documents. For convenience of analysis, I will define legitimacy as a kind of capital that can be increased or decreased and expended. For Max Weber's discussion of legitimacy, see: Max Weber, *Economy and Society*, vol. 1, ed. Guenther Roth and Claus Wittich (Berkeley: University of California Press, 1978), 212~216.

68. The First Five Year Plan was chaired by Zhou Enlai and Chen Yun. The preparation started in 1951 and was not completed until the first half of 1955. It was passed in July 1955 at the second meeting of the First National People's Congress. The "First Five" was actually a project formulated and implemented while being continuously modified. The final implementation period of the plan was determined to be from 1953 to 1957, see: Hong Zhou, ed., *The PRC National History Chronicle (1949~1956)* (Red Flag Publishing House, 1993), 368.

69. Li Fuchun, "The Report on the First Five-year Plan of National Economic Development," 789.

70. Li Fuchun, "The Report on the First Five-year Plan of National Economic Development," 789~790.

71. National Bureau of Statistics, *China Statistical Yearbook 1992* (China Statistics Press, 1992), 158.

72. Lin Yifu, Fang Cai and Zhou Li, *China Miracle: Development Strategy and Economic Reform*, updated ed., 38.

73. Zhou Enlai, "Opinions on Wages Reform and Labor Welfare Policy," 26 September 1957, in *Selected Important Documents Since the Founding of China*, vol. 10, 574.

74. Lin Yifu, Fang Cai and Zhou Li, *China Miracle: Development Strategy and Economic Reform*, 42.

75. "The Central Government's Decision on Implementing Planned Food Acquisition and Supply," 16 October 1953, in Hong Zhou, ed., *The PRC National History Chronicle (1949~1956)* (Red Flag Publishing House, 1993), 699.

76. Chen Yun, "To Improve Conditions of Food Production and Sales," 28 November 1953, in *Select Works of Chen Yun (1949~1956)*, 224.

77. Chen Yun, "To Improve Conditions of Food Production and Sales," 223.

78. Chen Yun, "Strengthening the Market Management and Transformation of Private Enterprises," 13 July 1954, in *Select Works of Chen Yun (1949~1956)*, 252.

79. Chen Yun, "On the Planned Purchase and Supply," 23 September 1954, in *Select Works of Chen Yun (1949~1956)*, 256.

80. Pang Song, *Concise History of the People's Republic* (2001), 19; Sun Jian, *Chinese Economic History*, vol. 2, 1499~1500.

81. Chen Yun, "Stopping the Surge of Prices," 13 November 1949, *in Select Works of Chen Yun (1949~1956)*, 29~31. See also Zhou Hong, ed., *The PRC National History Chronicle (1949~1956)* (Red Flag Publishing House, 1993), 15.

82. Quoted from *Select Works of Chen Yun* (1949~1956), 52.

83. Chen Yun, "To Unify Financial and Economic Management," 28 December 28, 1949, in *Select Works of Chen Yun (1949~1956)*, 48~50.

84. Chen Yun, "To Unify Financial and Economic Management", 49.

85. Chen Yun, "Finance Workers Should Raise Own Consciousness," 13 February 1950, in *Select Works of Chen Yun (1949~1956)*, 61.

86. Chen Yun, "1951 Key Points of Financial and Economic Work," 4 April 1951, in *Select Works of Chen Yun (1949~1956)*, 136.

87. Chen Yun, "1951 Key Points of Financial and Economic Work," 130.

88. Of the work done by Chen Yun in early days of the founding of China, in 1956, Mao Zedong spoke highly of what Chen Yun did. He said: "As Comrade Chen Yun ... I see him being a good man. He is quite fair, competent, relatively safe. He saw problems with vision. I did not know him well in the past. In the past few years since we moved into Beijing, I worked with him and learned more about him. Do not think that he only looks very peaceful. He sees the problems with acumen, right to the main points." Mao Zedong, "On Vice Chairman of the Country and General Secretary of the CPC Central Committee," 13 September 1956, in *Selected Works*, vol. 7, 112.

89. Mao Zedong, "The Issue of Centralized Food Purchase and Sale," 2 October 1953, in *Selected Works of Mao Zedong*, vol. 6 (People's Publishing House, 1999), 295.

90. Mao Zedong, "The Issue of Centralized Food Purchase and Sale," 295.

91. Mao Zedong, "The Issue of Centralized Food Purchase and Sale," 297.

92. "The Order from the Central People's Government Administration Council on Implementing the Planned Food Purchase and Supply", in *Selected Important Documents Since the Founding of China*, vol. 4, 561~564.

93. Chen Yun, "Centralized Purchase and Sale of Grain," 10 October 1953, in *Selected Works of Chen Yun (1949~1956)*, 202~206.

94. Chen Yun, "Centralized Purchase and Sale of Grain," 206.

95. Chen Yun, "Centralized Purchase and Sale of Grain," 216.

96. Chen Yun, "Centralized Purchase and Sale of Grain," 206.

97. Chen Yun, "Centralized Purchase and Sale of Grain," 207.

98. Chen Yun, "Centralized Purchase and Sale of Grain," 208~209.

99. Chen Yun, "Centralized Purchase and Sale of Grain," 210.

100. Chen Yun, "Centralized Purchase and Sale of Grain," 210.

101. Chen Yun, "Centralized Purchase and Sale of Grain," 212~213.

102. Chen Yun, "Centralized Purchase and Sale of Grain," 212.

103. Chen Yun, "Centralized Purchase and Sale of Grain," 213.

104. Chen Yun, "Centralized Purchase and Sale of Grain," 212.

105. Chen Yun, "Centralized Purchase and Sale of Grain," 213.

106. Chen Yun, "Centralized Purchase and Sale of Grain," 214~215.

107. Chen Yun, "Centralized Purchase and Sale of Grain," 213.

108. Chen Yun, "Implementing Centralized Purchase of Cotton Cloth," 7 December 1950, in *Select Works of Chen Yun (1949~1956)*, 124~125. (This is what Chen Yun drafted for the Financial and Economic Committee of the Government Administration Council as the "The Decision On Centralized Purchase of Cotton Cloth", promulgated on 4 January 1951.)

109. Chen Yun, "Strengthening the Market Management and Transformation of Private Enterprises," 13 July 1954, in *Select Works of Chen Yun (1949~1956)*, 246.

110. Chen Yun, "To Improve Conditions of Food Production and Sales," 226.

111. Chen Yun, "To Improve Conditions of Food Production and Sales," 227.

112. Chen Yun, "On the Planned Purchase and Supply," 260.

113. Zhang Peigang and Liao Danqing, *China's Grain Economy In the Twentieth Century* (Huazhong University Press, 2002), 500~501.

114. "Interim Measures for Food Rations in Cities", in *Selected Important Documents Since the Founding of China*, vol. 7, 115~122.

115. Zhang Peigang and Liao Danqing, *China's Grain Economy*, 502.

116. Chen Yun, "On the Planned Purchase and Supply," 260 (originally published in People's Daily, 24 September 1954).

117. Chen Yun, "On the Planned Purchase and Supply," 260~261.

118. For an analysis of the consolidation and strengthening of the planned purchase and sale system, see *Contemporary Work on the Chinese Food System* (China Social Sciences Press, 1988), 104~206.

119. Zhang Peigang and Liao Danqing, *China's Grain Economy*, 552.

120. For details see Zhang Peigang and Liao Danqing, *China's Grain Economy*, 555. (Note that the 1978 total consumption data for cities and villages are questionable.)

121. *Contemporary Work on the Chinese Food System*, 536~537.

122. Zhang Peigang and Liao Danqing, *China's Grain Economy*, 561.

123. "The Common Program of Chinese People's Political Bureau," 29 September 1949, in *Selected Important Documents Since the Founding of China*, vol. 1 (Central Government Academic Press, 1992), 1~13.

124. "Labor Insurance Act of People's Republic of China," 23 February 1951, in *Selected Important Documents Since the Founding of China*, vol. 2 (Central Literature Publishing House, 1992), 55~67. This act was passed at the 73rd Political Administration Meeting of Government Administration Council and announced on 26 February 1951.

125. "Administration Council's Decision on several amendments to 'Labor Insurance Regulations of People's Republic of China'" in *Selected Important Documents Since the Founding of China*, vol. 2 (Central Literature Publishing House, 1992), 68~69. (Passed on 2 January 1953 at the 165th session of Administration Council Meeting.)

126. For the evolution of social security for urban workers, especially public health, welfare and social security for women (maternity insurance, worker protection, etc.), see Zhen Gongcheng et al., *China's Social Security Changes and Assessment* (People's University of China, 2002).

127. On state "paternalism", see Janos Kornai, *The Socialist Structure. The Political Economy of Communism*, trans. An Zhang (Beijing: Central Government Compilation and Translation Press, 2007), 51, and Gongcheng Zheng et al., *China's Social Security Changes and Assessment*, 15.

128. Zhou Enlai, "The Great Ten Years," 6 October 1959, in *Selected Important Documents Since the Founding of China*, vol. 12, 609.

129. Zhou Enlai, "The Great Ten Years," 609.

130. Mao Zedong, "Adhering to Hard Work, Having Close Ties with the Masses" (March 1957), in *Works of Mao Zedong*, vol. 7 (People's Publishing House, 1999), 285.

131. *People's Daily*, "All Efforts Towards Achieving the Country's General Guideline - 1954 New Year's Message," 1 January 1954, reprinted in *Selected Important Documents Since the Founding of China*, vol. 5, 4.

132. Zhou Enlai, "The Great Ten Years," 613~614.

133. "CPC Central Committee's Instructions for Increasing Production and Savings in 1957," in *Selected Important Documents Since the Founding of China*, vol. 10, 27. (Passed by the Politburo on 8 February 1957.)

134. Mao Zedong, "The Sixty Working Methods (Draft)," January 1958, *Works of Mao Zedong*, vol. 7, 344.

135. Mao Zedong, "Introducing a Cooperative," 15 April 1958, in *Selected Important Documents Since the Founding of China*, vol. 11, 275.

136. Liu Shaoqi, "The Political Report at the Eighth National Congress of the Chinese Communist Party," 15 September 1956, in *Selected Works of Liu Shaoqi*, vol. 2 (People's Publishing House, 1985), 241.

137. Zhou Enlai, "The Great Ten Years," 588.

138. *People's Daily*, "Striving to Realize Ambitious Goals of Socialist Industrialization - to Celebrate the Fourth Anniversary of the People's Republic of China," 1 October 1953, reprinted in *Selected Important Documents Since the Founding of China*, vol. 4, 409.

139. *People's Daily*, "To Meet the Task in 1955," 1 January 1955, reprinted in *Selected Important Documents Since the Founding of China*, vol. 6, 1.

140. Li Fuchun, "The Report on the Drafted 1960 National Economic Plan," 30 March 1960, in *Selected*

Important Works Since the Founding of China, vol. 8, 155.

141. Mao Zedong, "Introducing a Cooperative," 274.

142. Zhou Enlai, "The Great Ten Years," 607.

143. Mao Zedong, "The Report at the Second Plenary Session of the Seventh Central Government Committee Meeting of the Communist Party of China" (5 March 1949), in *Selected Works of Mao Zedong*, vol. 4 (People's Publishing House, 1991), 1438.

144. Ekkehart Schlicht, *On Custom in the Economy*, (Oxford: Clarendon Press, 1998), 35.

145. Schlicht, *On Custom in the Economy*, 36.

146. Schlicht, *On Custom in the Economy*, 36~37.

147. Hayek, *The Road to Serfdom*, 146.

148. Kornai, *The Socialist Structure*, 49~50.

149. People's Daily, "Striving to Realize Ambitious Goals of Socialist Industrialization - to Celebrate the Fourth Anniversary of the People's Republic of China," 1 October 1953, reprinted in *Selected Important Documents Since the Founding of China*, vol. 4, 407~408.

150. Zhou Enlai, "Government Work Report," 26 June 1957, in *Selected Important Documents Since the Founding of China*, vol. 10, 345.

151. Mao Zedong, "On Coalition Government," 1094.

152. Mao Zedong, "On Coalition Government," 1094~1095.

153. Mao Zedong, "Speech at the Shaanxi-Gansu-Ningxia Conference" (6 November 1941), in *Selected Works*, vol. 3, 809.

154. Mao Zedong, "The Status of The Chinese Communist Party in the National War", in *Selected Works*, vol. 2, 522.

155.Mao Zedong, "On Coalition Government," 1096.

156. Mao Zedong, "The Instruction of the People's Liberation Army Headquarters on Re-enacting the Three Disciplines and Eight Attention Points," 10 October 1947, in *Selected Works*, vol. 4, 1241.

157. Mao Zedong, "Against Bureaucracy, Command Doctrine and Lawlessness," 5 January 1953, in *Selected Works*, vol. 6, 254.

158. Mao Zedong, "Cadres Should Appear As Ordinary Laborers," 29 May 1958, in *Selected Works*, vol. 6, 378.

159. Mao Zedong, "Getting Organized," 29 November 1943, in *Selected Works*, vol. 3, 932~933.

160. *People's Daily*, "Marching Along as on the Beachhead," 1 January 1964, reprinted in *Selected Important Documents Since the Founding of China*, vol. 18 (Central Literature Publishing House, 1997), 5.

161. *People's Daily*, "Marching Along as on the Beachhead," 5~6.

162. "CPC Central Committee's Instructions on Continuing to Pay Close Attention to the " Five Antis" Movement – Two Documents Resent Originally to the North China Bureau and the South Bureau" (22 March 1964), in *Selected Important Documents Since the Founding of China*, vol. 18 (Central Literature Publishing House, 1997), 319.

163. Li Fuchun, "The Report on the Drafted 1960 National Economic Plan," 160~161.

164. "CPC Central Committee Approved and Transmitted to Anshan Municipal Government 'Report on the Industrial Front of Technological Innovation and Revolution Campaign report's," 22 March 1960, in *Selected Important Documents Since the Founding of China*, vol. 13, 109~110.

165. "The Report by Anshan Municipal Government on the Industrial Front of Technological Innovation and Revolutionary Movement," 11 March 1960, *in Selected Important Documents Since the Founding of China*, vol. 13, 110~124.

166. "CPC Central Committee's Instruction on Carrying out Campaign around Securing Grain and Steel and Increasing Savings," 14 August 1960, in *Selected Important Documents Since the Founding of China*, vol. 13, 536.

167. Mao Zedong, "To Serve the People," *Selected Works*, vol. 3, 1005.

168. Mao Zedong, "Hard Work Being Our Political Nature," 15 November 1956, *Selected Works*, vol. 7, 162.

169. Mao Zedong, "On the Ten Major Relationships," 25 April 1956, in *Selected Readings from the Works by Mao Zedong* (People's Publishing House, 1986), p. 726.

170. Zhou Enlai, "Government Work Report," 23 September 1954, in *Selected Important Documents*, vol. 5, 607.

171. Mao Zedong, "Combat Liberalism," 7 September 1937, in *Selected Works*, vol. 2, 360.

172. Mao Zedong, "Combat Liberalism," 361.

173. Mao Zedong, "The Chinese Communist Party's Position in the National War," 14 October 1938, in *Selected Works*, vol. 2, 522.

174. Mao Zedong, "In Memory of Norman Bethune," in *Selected Works*, vol. 2, 660.

175. Mao Zedong, "Report at The Second Plenary Session of the Seventh Congress of the Communist Party of China's Central Committee," 5 March 1949, in *Selected Works*, vol. 4, 1438~1439.

176. Mao Zedong, "Cadres Should Appear as Ordinary Laborers," 378.

177. "Qi Yanming's Report Forwarded by the CPC Central Committee in Beijing on Senior Cadres and Intellectual's Need of Special Supply," 9 November 1960, in *Selected Important Documents*, vol. 13, 683~684.

178. Liu Shaoqi, "The Report Made at Expanded Central Working Conference," 27 January 1962, in *Selected Important Documents*, vol. 5, 68.

179. Liu Shaoqi, "The Party's Task on the Propaganda Front," 23 May 1951, in *Selected Important Documents*, vol. 2, 292.

180. Liu Shaoqi, "The Party's Task on the Propaganda Front," 302.

181. "Instruction Approved by the CPC Central Committee and transmitted to the Youth League of Central Committee 'About Carrying out Training of Young Communist Morality in Order to Resist the Erosion by Bourgeois Ideology' for the Instruction of the Local Party Committee," in *Selected Important Documents*, vol. 7, 171~183.

182. "CPC Central Committee's Instructions on Continuing to Pay Close Attention to the " Five Antis" Movement – Two Documents Resent Originally to the North China Bureau and the South Bureau," 22 March 1964, in *Selected Important Documents*, vol. 18, 323.

183. Zheng Xiaohan, "How Lei Feng Was Found," *Biography* 6 (2003).

184. "CPC Central Committee's Instructions on Paying Close Attention to Socialist Education in Rural Areas," 10 May 1963, in *Selected Important Documents*, vol. 16, 294.

185. "CPC Central Committee's Instructions on Paying Close Attention to Socialist Education in Rural Areas," 298~299.

186. "CPC Central Committee's Instructions on Continuing to Pay Close Attention to the " Five Antis" Movement – Two Documents Resent Originally to the North China Bureau and the South Bureau," 22 March 1964, in *Selected Important Documents*, vol. 18, 321.

187. Mao Zedong, "The Conversation with Mr. Snow," 9 January 1965, in *Selected Works*, vol. 8, 407.

188. Mao Zedong, "On Coalition Government," 1093~1094.

189. Mao Zedong, "Speech at the Second Session of the First CPPCC Congress: Closing Remarks," 23 June 1950, in *Selected Works*, vol. 6, 82.

190. Mao Zedong, "Speech at the Third Session of the CPPCC National Congress: Opening Remarks," 23 October 1951, in *Selected Works*, vol. 6, 184.

191. Mao Zedong, "Speech at the Chinese Communist Party National Conference: Conclusion," 31 March 1955, in *Selected Works*, vol. 6, 406.

192. Mao Zedong, "Dialogue With the Business Community," 8 December 1956, in *Selected Works*, vol. 7, 174~175.

193. Mao Zedong, "Speech at the Chinese Communist Party National Conference on Propaganda Work," 12 March 1957, in *Selected Important Documents*, vol. 10, 125.

194. Mao Zedong, "Speech … on Propaganda Work," 126.

195. "The Communiqué of the Communist Party of China's Central Committee Eighth National Congress Tenth Plenary Session," 27 September 1962, in Selected Important Documents, vol. 15, 653~654.

196. The CPC's Central Committee pointed out: "Socialist education movements in urban and rural areas, are in the future to be referred to as the four cleans: clean politics, clean economy, clean organization, clean thinking. In the past, the socialist education movement in the city was known as the five antis-movement, but later was generalized as the 'Four Clean' movement, replacing the name of 'five-antis'." See: "Some Issues Raised in the Current Rural Socialist Education Movement," 14 January 1965, in *Selected Important Documents*, vol. 20, 22.

197. "CPC Central Committee's Instructions on Its Efforts to Increase Savings and Fight Against Corruption and Theft, Against Speculation, Extravagance, Waste, Decentralization and Bureaucracy", in *Selected Important Documents*, vol. 16, 172~173.

198. Giddens's "Structuration Theory" is a brilliant exposition of the relationship between structure and action, see: Anthony Giddens, *Central Problems in Social Theory* (London: Macmillan Education, 1979); Anthony Giddens, *The Constitution of Society: Outline of the Theory of Structuration* (Cambridge: Polity Press, 1984).

199. Norbert Elias, The History of Manners (The Civilizing Process, vol. 1) (Oxford: Blackwell, 1978); Norbert Elias, Power & Civility (The Civilizing Process, vol. 2) (Oxford: Blackwell, 1984).

200. Pierre Bourdieu, *Outline of a Theory of Practice* (Cambridge: Cambridge University Press, 1977).

201. Louis Althusser, *Essays on Ideology* (London: Verso, 1971), 1~4.

202. Althusser, *Essays*, 4~5.

203. Althusser, *Essays*, 5~6.

204. Althusser, *Essays*, 6~7.

205. Althusser, *Essays*, 16~19.

206. Althusser, *Essays*, 25~31.

207. Another variable related to labor productivity is labor discipline and supervision. For example, under the foreman's discipline, even those workers who want to slack off, will find it difficult to do so. Here, our conclusion is based on the variable to be controlled.

208. Althusser, Essays, 41~43.

209. Althusser, Essays, 44~45.

210. Althusser, Essays, 48~49.

211. Althusser, Essays, 50.

212. Althusser, Essays, 56.

213. Oakeshott, *On Human Conduct*.

214. Hayek, *Serfdom*, 88.

215. Hayek, *Serfdom*, 146. Some individual terminologies were modified.

216. Hayek, *Serfdom*, 146~147.

217. Hayek, *Serfdom*, 152.

218. Freud, Civilization and its Discontents.

219. Althusser. *Essays*.

220. Andrew G. Walder, *Communist Neo-Traditionalism* (Berkeley: University of California Press, 1986), 122.

221. Walder, *Neo-Traditionalism*, 123.

222. Data in this paragraph are from Hu Fangzhi, *Wage Studies During China's Economic Take-off* (Beijing: China Economic Publishing House, 2005), 95~96.

223. By the prevailing regulations at the time, children's health care was only reimbursed 50 percent.

224. Zhou Enlai, "A Number of Tasks in the Current Construction," 3 April 1961, in *Selected Important Documents*, vol. 14, 250.

225. *People's Daily*, "Meeting the Task in 1955," 1 January 1955, reprinted in *Selected Important Documents*, vol. 6, 1.

226. Li Fuchun, "The Report on the Drafted 1960 National Economic Plan," 30 March 1960), in *Selected Important Works*, vol. 13, 155.

227. Zhou Enlai, "Government Work Report," 23 September 1954, in *Selected Important Documents*, vol. 5, 607.

228. Deng Xiaoping, "More Liberal Ideas and Faster Pace of Reform," 25 May 1988, in *Selected Works of Deng Xiaoping*, vol. 3 (People's Publishing House, 1993), 265.

229. Deng Xiaoping, "Summing up History Is to Open up the Future," 5 September 1988, in *Selected Works of Deng Xiaoping*, vol. 3, 272.

230. Walder, *Neo-Traditionalism*, 191~201.

231. Walder, *Neo-Traditionalism*, 197~201.

232. Walder, *Neo-Traditionalism*, 205.

233. Walder, *Neo-Traditionalism*, 205.

234. Walder, *Neo-Traditionalism*, 208.

235. Walder, *Neo-Traditionalism*, 212~219.

236. Walder, *Neo-Traditionalism*, 219.

237. See also Georgi Plekhanov, *On the Question of the Individual's Role in History*, trans. Wei Zhen (Beijing: Joint Publishing, 1964).

238. Deng Xiaoping, "The Immediate Priority of the Third-Generation Leadership," 16 June 1989, in *Selected Works of Deng Xiaoping*, vol. 3, 310.

239. Jiang Zemin, "Accelerating the Pace of Reform and Modernization, Winning Greater Victory of Building up the Socialist Cause with Chinese Characteristics - the Report at the Fourteenth National Congress of the Chinese Communist Party," 12 October 1992, in *Selection of Important Documents at All Plenary Meetings Since the Third Plenary Session of the Eleventh National Congress Party Central Committee (Second Half)* (Central Government Literature Publishing House, 1997), 154.

240. Fang Aiqing, Fan Jianping, Zhu Xiaoliang et al., eds., *The Trend of China's Consumer Demand and Research on Chinese Consumer Policy* (Beijing: China Economic Publishing House, 2006), chapter 1.

241. Deng Xiaoping, "Market Economy Allowed Under Socialism," 26 November 1979, in *Selected Works of Deng Xiaoping*, vol. 2, 233.

242. Deng Xiaoping, "The Current Situation and Tasks," 16 January 1980, in *Selected Works of Deng Xiaoping*, vol. 2, 268

243. Deng Xiaoping, "Transforming and Managing Enterprises with Advanced Technologies," 18 September 1978, in *Selected Works of Deng Xiaoping*, vol. 2, 130.

244. Deng Xiaoping, "Ideological Guidelines and Political Guidelines Ensured by Realizing Organizational Guidelines," 29 July 1979, in *Selected Works of Deng Xiaoping*, vol. 2, 191.

245. Deng Xiaoping, "Market Economy Allowed Under Socialism," 231.

246. Deng Xiaoping, "Market Economy Allowed Under Socialism," 231.

247. Deng Xiaoping, "The Current Situation and Tasks," 251.

248. Deng Xiaoping, "Socialism Must First Develop Productivity," 5 May 1980, in *Selected Works of Deng Xiaoping*, vol. 2, 312

249. Deng Xiaoping, "Adhering to Socialism, Adhering to the Policy of Peace," 4 April 1986, in *Selected Works of Deng Xiaoping*, vol. 3, 157.

250. Deng Xiaoping, "Accelerating the Pace of Reform," 12 June 1987, in *Selected Works of Deng Xiaoping*, vol. 3, 241.

251. "Communiqué at the Third Plenary Session of the China's Eleventh National Congress of the Chinese Communist Party," 22 December 1978, *Selected Important Documents Since the Third Plenary Session* (People's Publishing House, 1982), 4.

252. Deng Xiaoping, "The Situation Forcing us to Further Reform and Opening Up," 22 June 1988, in *Selected Works of Deng Xiaoping*, vol. 3, 269.

253. Deng Xiaoping, "Socialism Must Get Rid of Poverty, 26 April 1987, in *Selected Works of Deng Xiaoping*, vol. 3, 223.

254. Deng Xiaoping, "Uniting the People with a Firm Belief," 9 November 1986, in *Selected Works of Deng Xiaoping*, vol. 3, 190~191.

255. Deng Xiaoping, "Reform and Opening up to Make China Alive," 12 May 1987, in *Selected Works of Deng Xiaoping*, vol. 3, 235.

256. Deng Xiaoping, "Talking Points In Wuchang, Shenzhen, Zhuhai, Shanghai and Other Places," 18 January – 21 February 1992, in *Selected Works of Deng Xiaoping*, vol. 3, 372.

257. Deng Xiaoping, "Talking Points," 370~371.

258. Deng Xiaoping, "A Few Comments on the Economic Work," 4 October 1979), in *Selected Works of Deng Xiaoping*, vol. 2, 194.

259. "Communiqué at the Third Plenary Session," 1.

260. "Communiqué at the Third Plenary Session," 4.

261. Deng Xiaoping, "Comments on the Economic Work," 195.

262. Deng Xiaoping, "Market Economy Allowed Under Socialism," 26 November 1979, in *Selected Works of Deng Xiaoping*, vol. 2, 234.

263. Deng Xiaoping, "Message at the Fourth Chinese Literature and Art Workers Congress," 30 October 1979, in *Selected Works of Deng Xiaoping*, vol. 2, 208~209.

264. Deng Xiaoping, "Sticking to the Party Line, Improving the Working Methods," 29 February 1980, in *Selected Works of Deng Xiaoping*, vol. 2, 276.

265. Deng Xiaoping, "The Current Situation and Tasks," 16 January 1980, in *Selected Works of Deng Xiaoping*, vol. 2, 250.

266. Deng Xiaoping, "Building Socialism with Chinese Characteristics," 30 June 1984, in *Selected Works of Deng Xiaoping*, vol. 3, 64.

267. Deng Xiaoping, "Our Ambitious Goals and Fundamental Policy," 6 October 1984, in *Selected Works of Deng Xiaoping*, vol. 3, 77.

268. Deng Xiaoping, "Reform to Liberate the Productive Forces, Science and Technology System," 7 March 1985, in *Selected Works of Deng Xiaoping*, vol. 3, 107.

269. Deng Xiaoping, "Building A Socialist Material Civilization and Spiritual Civilization," 29 April 1983, in *Selected Works of Deng Xiaoping*, vol. 3, 28.

270. Deng Xiaoping, "Market Economy Allowed Under Socialism," 26 November 1979, in *Selected Works of Deng Xiaoping*, vol. 2, 236.

271. Deng Xiaoping, "Socialism and Market economy Have No Fundamental Contradiction," 23 October 1985, in *Selected Works of Deng Xiaoping*, vol. 3, 148~149.

272. Deng Xiaoping, "Both Planning and Marketing Are Methods of Developing Productivity," 6 February 1987, in *Selected Works of Deng Xiaoping*, vol. 3, 203.

273. Deng Xiaoping, "Talking Points," 372.

274. Jiang Zemin, "Accelerating the Pace of Reform and Modernization, Winning Greater Victory of Building up Socialist Cause with Chinese characteristics - the Report at the Fourteenth National Congress Chinese Communist Party," 12 October 12, 1992, in *Selected Important Documents at All Plenary Meetings of Since the Third Plenary Session of the Eleventh National Congress Party Central Committee (Second Half)*

(Central Government Literature Publishing House, 1997), 169~170.

275. Deng Xiaoping, "The Current Situation and Tasks," 250.

276. Li Xiannian, "Speech at the Central Government Work Conference," 5 April 1979, in *Selected Important Documents since the Third Plenary Session (First Half)* (People's Publishing House, 1982), 112.

277. "Communiqué at the Third Plenary Session," 8.

278. "Communiqué at the Third Plenary Session," 140~186.

279. Li Xiannian, "Speech at the Central Government Work Conference," 5 April 1979, in *Selected Important Documents since the Third Plenary Session (First Half)* (People's Publishing House, 1982), 112~113.

280. Li Xiannian, "Central Government Work Conference," 113.

281. Li Xiannian, "Central Government Work Conference," 121.

282. Li Xiannian, "Central Government Work Conference," 127.

283. Li Xiannian, "Central Government Work Conference," 124.

284. Li Xiannian, "Central Government Work Conference," 114.

285. Li Xiannian, "Central Government Work Conference," 133~134.

286. Li Xiannian, "Speech at the National Planning Conference," in *Selected Important Documents since the Third Plenary Session (First Half)*, 297~298.

287. Zhao Ziyang, "Several Issues on Adjusting National Economy," 16 December 1980, in *Selected Important Documents since the Third Plenary Session (First Half)*, 610~611.

288. Zhao Ziyang, "Adjusting National Economy," 620~621.

289. Zhao Ziyang, "The Current Economic Situation and Future Economic Development Policy," 30 November – 1 December 1981, in *Selected Important Documents since the Third Plenary Session (Second Half)*, 1034~1035.

290. Zhao Ziyang, "The Current Economic Situation," 1012.

291. Zhao Ziyang, "The Current Economic Situation," 998.

292. Zhao Ziyang, "The Current Economic Situation," 1003~1004.

293. Zhao Ziyang, "The Current Economic Situation," 1038.

294. "The Central Government's Proposal for the Seventh Five-Year Plan of National Economic and Social Development," 23 September 1985, in *Selected Important Documents Since the Twelfth National Congress (Middle Part)* (People's Publishing House, 1986), 804.

295. "Seventh Five-Year Plan," 804.

296. "Seventh Five-Year Plan," 828~829.

297. "Seventh Five-Year Plan," 829.

298. "Seventh Five-Year Plan," 829.

299. "Notice from the State Council on Implementing Incentives and Piece-rate Wage System (excerpts)", People's Network, Law and Regulation Libraries: http://www.people.com.cn/item/flfgk/gwyfg/1978/L35801197803.html.

300. Kang Shiyong, "The Evolution of Wage Reform and Policy Options for Continuous Reform - Commemorating 20 Years of Wage Reform in China," *News of Beijing Municipal Labor Management Institute*, no. 4 (1999), 24.

301. Hu Fangzhi, *Research on the Wage Level during China's Economic Take-off* (China Economic Press, 2005), 107; Kang Shiyong, "Evolution of Wage Reform," 24.

302. Hu Fangzhi, "Research on the Wage Level," 107~108; Kang Shiyong, "Evolution of Wage Reform," 25; Song Guangda, "50 Years of China's Wage Reform," *China Labor*, no. 12 (1999), 5.

303. Kang Shiyong, "Evolution of Wage Reform," 25.

304. Kang Shiyong, "Evolution of Wage Reform," 25.

305. Hu Fangzhi, "Research on the Wage Level," 109.

306. Jiang Zemin, "Holding High the Great Banner of Deng Xiaoping Theory, and Building the Socialism with Chinese Characteristics into the 21st Century," 12 September 1997, in *Selected Important Documents Since*

the Fifteenth National Congress (First Part) (People's Publishing House, 2000), 24.

307. Hu Fangzhi, "Research on the Wage Level," 110~111.

308. Hu Fangzhi, "Research on the Wage Level," 112~113.

309. *Work on Contemporary China's Food System* (China Social Sciences Press, 1988), 173.

310. "Communiqué at the Third Plenary Session," 8.

311. *Contemporary China's Food System*, 182.

312. "Notice Issued by CPC Central Committee and State Council to the State Agricultural Committee on 'Developing Diversified Enterprises in the Rural Areas'", in *Selected Important Documents Since the Third Plenary Session (Second Half)*, 741~742.

313. *China Agricultural Yearbook* (China Agriculture Press, 1985), 22~23. Quoted in Zhang Peigang Zhang and Liao Danqing, *China's Grain Economy In the Twentieth Century* (Huazhong University Press, 2002), 565.

314. Zhang Peigang and Liao Danqing, *China's Grain Economy*, 567~568.

315. Zhang Peigang and Liao Danqing, *China's Grain Economy*, 569~572.

316. Zhang Peigang and Liao Danqing, *China's Grain Economy*, 572~574.

317. Zhang Peigang and Liao Danqing, *China's Grain Economy*, 611~612.

318. Tang Zhong and Song Jiqing, *Food Stamps and Food Prices*, (Chinese People's University Press, 1992), 55.

319. Tang Zhong and Song Jiqing, *Food Stamps*, 3~13.

320. Tang Zhong and Song Jiqing, *Food Stamps*, 619.

321. Li Peng, "Government Work Report," 5 March 1998, in *Selected Important Documents Since the Fifteenth National Congress*, vol. 1, 213.

322. Chen Huai, ed., *Surplus Economy! Surplus Economy? - Situation and Counter-measures* (Economic Science Press, 1998).

323. Data from Li Tongpin, *Studies on the Institutional Changes of China's Consumption* (Economic Science Press, 2005), 133.

324. Zhu Rongji, "Good Governance, Clean and Efficient, Doing Good Work for the Generation of Government for the Next Century," 24 March 1998, in *Selected Important Documents Since the Fifteenth National Congress*, vol. 1, 267.

325. The main argument for the points from the second to fourth sections is from Wu Jinglian, *Contemporary China's Economic Reform* (Shanghai Far East Press, 2003), 365~366.

326. Jiang Zemin, "Holding High the Great Banner of Deng Xiaoping Theory and Building Socialism with Chinese Characteristics into the 21st Century," 12 September 1997, in *Selected Important Documents Since the Fifteenth National Congress (First Half)* (People's Publishing House, 2000), 29.

327. Jiang Zemin, "Do A Good Job on Domestic Economy, Enhance the Ability to Withstand Risks," 26 February 1998, in *Selected Important Documents Since the Fifteenth National Congress (First Half)*, 205.

328. Zhu Rongji, "Good Governance," 271.

329. Zhu Rongji, "Good Governance," 272.

330. Zhu Rongji, "Government Work Report (Report at the Second Meeting of the Ninth National People's Congress)," 5 March 1999, in *Selected Important Documents Since the Fifteenth National Congress (First Half)*, 773.

331. Zhu Rongji, "Government Work Report (5 March 1999)," 778.

332. Jiang Zemin, "Further Mobilize the Party and Society, to Win the Victory of the Decisive Phase of the 1987 Attack on Poverty," 9 June 1999, in *Selected Important Documents Since the Fifteenth National Congress*, vol. 2 (People's Publishing House, 2001), 850~851.

333. Zhu Rongji, "Government Work Report (5 March 1999)," 1174.

334. "Central Government's Proposal for the Tenth Five-Year Plan on National Economic and Social Development," 11 October 2000, in *Selected Important Documents Since the Fifteenth National Congress*

(Middle Part), 1392.

335. Jiang Zemin, "The Whole Party to Participate, to Mobilize All Social Forces and Work Together to Guarantee the Basic Livelihood and Re-employment of the Laid-off Workers of the State-owned enterprises," 14 May 1998, in Selected Important Documents Since the Fifteenth National Congress, vol. 1, 357~371; Zhu Rongji, "A Few Issues Regarding the Basic Livelihood and Re-employment of Laid-off Workers of the State -owned Enterprises," 16 May 1998, in Selected Important Documents Since the Fifteenth National Congress, vol. 1 372~379.

336. Li Tongpin, *Studies on Institutional Changes of Chinese Consumerism* (Economic Science Press, 2005), 174~175.

337. Zhu Rongji, "Government Work Report (5 March 1999)," 1174.

338. "Tenth Five-Year Plan," 1392.

339. Li Tongpin, *Institutional Changes*, 184.

340. "The State Council's Notice to Further Accelerate the Development of Tourism," 11 April 2001, in *Selected Important Documents Since the Fifteenth National Congress (Second Half)* (People's Publishing House, 2003), 1761.

341. Li Tongpin, *Institutional Changes*, 178.

342. "The State Planning Commission's Views on Several Measures in Accelerating the Development of Service Industry During the Tenth Five-Year Plan Period," 3 December 2001, in *Selected Important Documents Since the Fifteenth National Congress (Second Half)* (People's Publishing House, 2003), 2138.

343. Zhu Rongji, "Government Work Report (Report at the Fifth Meeting of the Ninth National People's Congress)," 5 March 2002, in *Selected Important Documents Since the Fifteenth National Congress (Second Half)* (People's Publishing House, 2003), 2265~2266.

344. Li Lanqing, "According to the Requirement of 'Three Representations', Transform the Functions of Government to Further Improve the Socialist Market Economic System (Speech Given to the Students of the Central Party School)," 5 April 2002, in *Selected Important Documents Since the Fifteenth National Congress (Second Half)* (People's Publishing House, 2003), 2319.

345. Jiang Zemin, "Building A Moderately Prosperous Society and Creating A New Situation for the Socialist Cause with Chinese Characteristics (Report at the Sixteenth Chinese Communist Party National Congress)," 8 November 2002, in *Selected Important Documents Since the Sixteenth National Congress (First Half)* (People's Publishing House, 2005), 16~17.

346. Jiang Zemin, "Building A Moderately Prosperous Society," 25.

347. Zhu Rongji, "Government Work Report (Report at the First Session of the Tenth National People's Congress)," 5 March 2003, *in Selected Important Documents Since the 16th National Congress (First Half)* (People's Publishing House, 2005), 269.

348. Wen Jiabao, "Government Work Report (Speech at the Second Session of the Tenth National People's Congress)," 5 March 2004, in *Selected Important Documents Since the Sixteenth National Congress (First Half)*, 363.

349. See also: He Fan, "The Origin, Evolution and Decline of the Traditional Planned Economy System," in *The Transition from Planned Economy to Market Economy*, ed. Jing Weimin (Nankai University Press, 2003), 3.

350. Zheng Gongcheng et al., *China's Social Security System Changes and Assessment* (China People's University Press, 2002), 340.

351. Zheng Gongcheng et al., *Social Security System Changes*, 341~342.

352. Lu Feng, "Unit: A Special Form of Social Organization," *China Social Science*, no. 1 (1989), 75~76.

353. "The State Council's Notice on Continuing to Actively and Steadily Carry out the Reform of Urban Housing System," 7 June 1991, in *Selected Legal Documents and Legislation on Housing Reform* (The Chinese Construction Industry Press, 1998), 9~10.

354. "The Central Government's Proposal on Setting up the 7th Five-Year Plan on National Economy and Social Development," 23 September 1985, in *Selected Important Documents Since the Twelfth National Congress (Middle Part)* (People's Publishing House, 1986), 804~805.

355. "The State Council's Notice on the Implementing the National Urban Housing System Reform in Phase and by Group," 25 February 1988, in *Selected Legal Documents and Legislation on Housing Reform* (The Chinese Construction Industry Press Society, 1998), 1.

356. "Implementing National Urban Housing System Reform," 2.

357. "Implementing National Urban Housing System Reform," 2~3.

358. "Implementing National Urban Housing System Reform," 4~6.

359. "Implementing National Urban Housing System Reform," 8.

360. "The State Council's Notice on Continuing to Actively and Steadily Carry out the Reform of Urban Housing System," 7 June 1991, in *Selected Legal Documents and Legislation on Housing Reform* (The Chinese Construction Industry Press, 1998), 10~11.

361. "Actively and Steadily Carry out the Reform," 11~12.

362. "The State Council's Decision on Deepening the Urban Housing System Reform," 18 July 1994, in Selected Legal Documents and Legislation on Housing Reform, 13.

363. "Deepening the Urban Housing System Reform," 13.

364. "Deepening the Urban Housing System Reform," 13~14.

365. "Deepening the Urban Housing System Reform," 17.

366. Zhu Rongji, "Good Governance," 279.

367. "Deepening the Urban Housing System Reform," 20.

368. "Deepening the Urban Housing System Reform," 20.

369. "Deepening the Urban Housing System Reform," 21.

370. "Deepening the Urban Housing System Reform," 21.

371. "Deepening the Urban Housing System Reform," 23.

372. "Deepening the Urban Housing System Reform," 20~24.

373. Liu Shaoqi, "Report at the Expanded Central Government Working Conference," 27 January 1962, in *Selected Important Documents Since the Founding of China*, vol. 15 (Central Literature Publishing House, 1997), 71~72.

374. Walder, *Neo-Traditionalism*, 205.

375. Deng Xiaoping, "A Few Comments on Industrial Development," 18 August 1975, in *Selected Works of Deng Xiaoping*, vol. 2, 30~31.

376. Deng Xiaoping, "Adhering to the Principle of Distribution According to Work," 28 March 1978, in *Selected Works of Deng Xiaoping*, vol. 2, 101.

377. Deng Xiaoping, "Reform of the Party and State Leadership System," 18 August 1980, in *Selected Works of Deng Xiaoping*, vol. 2, 337.

378. Deng Xiaoping, "Emancipating the Mind, Seeking the Truth, Being United and Looking Ahead," 13 December 1978, in *Selected Works of Deng Xiaoping*, vol. 2, 146.

379. Deng Xiaoping, "Distribution According to Work," 101.

380. Deng Xiaoping, "Transform the Enterprises with Advanced Technologies and Management," 18 September 1978, in *Selected Works of Deng Xiaoping*, vol. 2,130.

381. Deng Xiaoping, "Interview by Italian Correspondent Oriana Fallaci," 21 August 1980, in *Selected Works of Deng Xiaoping*, vol. 2, 351~352.

382. "CPC Central Committee's Decision on Accelerating Agricultural Development (Fourth Plenary Session of the Eleventh CPC Central Committee Meeting)," 28 September 1979, in *Selected Important Documents Since the Third Plenary Session (First Half)*, 183~184.

383. Li Xiannian, "Speech at the National Planning Conference," 20 December 1979, in *Selected Important Documents Since the Third Plenary Session (First Half)*, 298.

384. Deng Xiaoping, "Adhering to Socialism," 157.

385. Deng Xiaoping, "Speaking Out with Facts," 28 March 1986, in *Selected Works of Deng Xiaoping*, vol. 3, 155.

386. Deng Xiaoping, "Emancipating the Mind," 152.

387. "CPC Central Committee's Decision on Economic Reform (Passed at the Third Plenary Session of the Twelfth Meeting of the Chinese Communist Party' Central Committee)," 20 October 1984, in *Selected Important Documents Since the Twelfth National Congress (Middle Part)* (People's Publishing House, 1986), 577.

388. "Decision on Economic Reform," 577~578.

389. Deng Xiaoping, "To Be United Relies First upon Ideals and Secondly upon Discipline," 7 March 1985, in *Selected Works of Deng Xiaoping*, vol. 3, 110~111.

390. Deng Xiaoping, "Talking Points," 373~374.

391. Deng Xiaoping, "To Be United," 110.

392. Deng Xiaoping, "Implementing the Policy of Adaptability to Ensure Stability and Unity," 25 December 1980, in *Selected Important Documents since the Third Plenary Session (First Half)*, 640~642.

393. Li Xiannian, "Speech at the Central Work Conference," 5 April 1979, in *Selected Important Documents since the Third Plenary Session (First Half)*, 139.

394. "CPC Central Committee's Decision on A Number of Issues Regarding Establishing A Socialist Market Economic System," 14 November 1993, in *Selected Important Documents of All t Previous Plenary Sessions of the National Party's General Assembly Since the Third Plenary Session of the Eleventh Assembly* (Central Literature Publishing House, 1997), 269~270.

395. Deng Xiaoping, "Emancipating the Mind," 145.

396. Deng Xiaoping, "The Working Class Must Make Outstanding Contributions to the Four Modernizations," 11 October 1978, in *Selected Works of Deng Xiaoping*, vol. 2, 135.

397. Deng Xiaoping, "Emancipating the Mind," 150

398. Deng Xiaoping, "Reform of the Party," 328.

399. Deng Xiaoping, "Emancipating the Mind," 150~151.

400. Deng Xiaoping, "The Working Class," 137.

401. Deng Xiaoping, "Emancipating the Mind," 151.

402. Deng Xiaoping, "Emancipating the Mind," 151.

403. Deng Xiaoping, "Emancipating the Mind," 150.

404. Deng Xiaoping, "Distribution According to Work," 102.

405. "CPC Central Committee and State Council's Decision on Overhauling the State-owned Industrial Enterprises," 2 January 1982, in *Selected Important Documents since the Third Plenary Session (Second Half)* (People's Publishing House, 1982), 1082~1083.

406. "Overhauling the State-owned Industrial Enterprises," 1083.

407. "The State Council's Temporary Rules on Expanding the Autonomy of State-owned Industrial Enterprises," 10 May 1984, in *Selected Important Documents Since the Twelfth National Congress (First Half)* (People's Publishing House 1986), 463~464.

408. "Temporary Rules on the Labor Contract System for the State-owned Enterprises," issued 12 July 1986 by the State Council, in *Selected Important Documents Since the Twelfth National Congress (Second Half)*, 1067~1075.

409. "Interim Provisions on Recruiting Workers by the State-owned Enterprises," in *Selected Important Documents Since the Twelfth National Congress (Second Half)*, 1076~1078.

410. "Interim Provisions on Dismissing and Disciplining Employees by the State-owned Enterprises," issued on

12 July 1986 by the State Council, in *Selected Important Documents Since the Twelfth National Congress (Second Half)*, 1079~1080.

411. "Provisional Regulations on Unemployment Insurance for State-owned Enterprise Workers," issued on 12 July 1986 by the State Council, in *Selected Important Documents Since the Twelfth National Congress (Second Half)*, 1081~1085.

412. "Establishing A Socialist Market Economic System," 528.

413. Wang Ning, "The Take-off of Desire and Thrift Doctrine – Desire and Consumption in A Two-tracked Society," *The Sociologist Café*, no. 5 (2007).

414. This document presented for the first time in the official media the concept of "subjectively for ourselves and objectively for others" (i.e., the unity of self-interest and altruism). It questioned and challenged the main model of unconditional self-sacrifice and dedication that shaped the traditional past.

415. On 7 February 1977, Hua Guofeng approved the editorial article "Studying Documents by Grasping the Outline" that was published by two newspapers and a magazine: the "People's Daily", "Liberation Army Daily" and "Red Flag" magazine. He openly proposed the "two whatever" policy, namely: "We are determined to maintain all decisions by Chairman Mao; and we are determined to follow whatever instructions made by Chairman Mao."

416. On 10 April 1977, Deng Xiaoping, in name of a veteran Communist Party member, wrote to the CPC Central Committee about the "two whatever" policy: "We must guide our Party, Army and People for generations with accurate and complete thoughts of Mao Zedong, so as to advance the socialist cause and international communist movement to victory." Deng Xiaoping's criticism of the "two whatever" policy anticipates the emancipation of the Party's mind. On 3 May, the CPC Central Committee forwarded this letter and confirmed the views of Deng Xiaoping. In December, the CPC Central Committee appointed Hu Yaobang as the Head of the Central Organization Department. Following the Party's principles of seeking truth and correcting mistakes, Hu Yaobang launched campaign at all levels of party organizations, cadres and the masses, to investigate wrongdoings and resolutely redress injustices. This, in effect, broke the constraints of the "two whatevers". From May 1978 onwards, a great discussion was started nationwide on the criterion of truth. In December of the same year, at the Third Plenum of the Eleventh CPC Meeting, the discussion on the criterion of truth was fully affirmed. It affirmed the need for a complete and accurate grasp of the scientific system of Mao Zedong's thought, and strongly criticized the "two whatever" policy. Data cited from Xinhua website: "Error of 'Two Whatever' Policy," http://news.xinhuanet.com/ziliao/2003-01/20/content_698196.htm.

417. On 13 January 1988, a "Forum between Young Education Experts and Shekou Youth" was held in Shekou, Shenzhen. Three nationally-known experts in youth education from Beijing and other places (Yanjie Li, Xiao Qu, Qingyi Peng) attended the forum along with nearly 70 young people from Shekou. At the meeting, the Shekou youth and experts engaged in a fierce debate on issues such as life values. One point of contention centered on the "Gold Digger" argument. One expert mentioned in her speech that some people were coming to Shenzhen for their own purposes, to benefit from the wealth created by others. There are the very small number gold diggers. The Special Economic Region does not welcome such gold diggers. The Shekou youth, however, argued that though the "gold diggers" were coming to make money, it was not against the law. They are not at fault. Although the "Gold Digger's" direct motivation is to make money in Shekou, objectively they benefit the construction of Shekou. There is nothing wrong with the "Gold Diggers". ... The youth education experts were greatly displeased. On 1 February "Shekou Communications News" reported on this symposium in an article titled "Shekou: A Fierce Clash Between Stale Preaching and Modern Ideology". Since then, the article was reported or reproduced by many papers both at home and abroad. Different points of view were discussed on the new era of young people's ideological and political work. The debate lasted more than six months, causing quite some sensation in the country (the "Shekou Storm"). Although the debate was mixed, its significance goes beyond the storm itself. Several reporters contributed to guide the youth. After the "Shekou Storm" their report was still in demand. Data

cited from People's Network: "'Shekou storm' – Discussion Triggered by 'Youth Education Experts and Shekou Youth Forum'," http://www.people.com.cn/GB/shizheng/252/7955/7959/20020422/714400.html.

418. From 18 January until 21 February 1992, Deng Xiaoping made his southern tour of Wuchang, Shenzhen, Zhuhai and Shanghai, and delivered an important speech. Deng Xiaoping's speech during his southern tour of China played a key role in promoting economic reform and social progress in the 1990s. Deng stressed that we would be more courageous by reforming and opening up, and daring to experiment. Seeing the right target, we shall venture boldly and take bold actions. He said that, without a little bold spirit, without "daring" spirit, without courage, there would not be a good way to find and shape a new road, or to create new cause. Probably in another 30 years, we would be able to form a set of more mature systems. Principles and policies under such a system would also be more stereotyped. He said that the fundamental reason for the pace of reform and opening up being slow was the fear of capitalism, fear of taking the capitalist road. The key issue is 'capitalist' or 'socialist'. The determinative standard should be whether it is beneficial to the development of productivity for the socialist society, whether it helps to enhance the overall strength of the socialist countries, whether it is conducive to improving people's living standards. Deng Xiaoping said that some people think that with a little more foreign investment, there would be more capitalism. More "three capital" enterprises, there would be more capitalists, which is would be to develop capitalism. These people do not even have basic common sense. Deng Xiaoping made it clear that a little more planned economy or a bit more market economy, is not the essence of socialism or capitalism. The planned economy is not equivalent to socialism. There is planning in a capitalist economy. A market economy is not equal to capitalism. There is a market in socialism. Planning and a market are both economic means. From: People Net, "Deng Xiaoping's Speech on His Southern Tour," http://cpc.people.com.cn/GB/33837/2535034.html.

419. Deng Xiaoping, "Talking Points," 372.

420. Deng Xiaoping, "Talking Points," 370~371.

421. Deng Xiaoping, "Talking Points," 372.

422. Deng Xiaoping, "Talking Points," 373.

423. Chen Sheng, "The Channel of Desire – the Analysis of 20 Years of Advertising Content of *Yangcheng Evening News*," master's thesis, Zhongshan University (2003).

424. Stuart Even, *Captains of Consciousness: Advertising and the Social Roots of the Consumer Culture* (New York: McGraw-Hill, 1976), 97.

425. Robert Goldman and Stephen Papson, "Advertising in the Age of Accelerated Meaning" (1996), in Juliet B. Schor and Douglas B. Holt, eds., *The Consumer Society Reader* (New York: The New Press, 2000), 81.

426. Goldman and Papson, "Advertising," 82.

427. Goldman and Papson, "Advertising," 95~96.

428. Juliet B. Schor, *The Overspent American: Upscaling, Downshifting, and the New Consumer* (New York: HarperPerennial, 1998).

429. Of work that provides "external return" an example is: "(Interviewer: You think a good job should pay higher wages, right?) Yeh, a bit of hard work does not matter. Our coming out to work is to make money. (Interviewer: In addition to money, are there any other requirements?) No, nothing else. " (B06-F, 28-year-old garment factory worker).

430. An example of work giving "internal return": "I always thought that the police were a more noble profession, I set it as an ideal, the ideal since I was a child. And now the police are treated well, leaving nothing for us to worry about ... I need more spiritual recognition from our community, more focus on spiritual rewards." (B29-M(1)-32, policeman).

431. An example of work providing "a unity of external and internal return": "A satisfactory job is to reflect my value. It is not necessarily about money or material performance, I think the main thing is a comprehensive thing, spiritual satisfaction, recognition by the others, plus income, together which should be proportional to

my efforts and should not be too far from the original settings." (B40-F-23, bank account manager).

432. Wang Ning, "The Take-off of 'Desire' in A Transformational Society - the Sociological Theoretical Analysis the Rise of Consumerism in China", in Blue Book 2006 of Guangdong Social and Demographic Development (Guangzhou: Guangdong Economic Press, 2006.), 67~81.

433. Thus began the discussion of the four phases of the concept of consumerism, see Wang Ning, "National Alienation Theory: the New Proposition of the Causes of Chinese Consumerism," *Sun Yat-sen University Journal (Social Science Edition)*, no. 4 (2007).

434. Steven Miles, *Consumerism: As a Way of Life* (London: Sage, 1998), 4.

435. The reason for saying "quasi-popular" is because in China there are a considerable number of people still in poverty. However, in the cities, the concept of consumerism has rather broad popularity and support.

436. Peter N. Stearns, *Consumerism in World History: the Global Transformation of Desire* (London: Routledge, 2001), ix.

437. Pasi Falk, *The Consuming Body* (London: Sage, 1994), 94.

438. Belk, "Third World Consumer Culture," 105.

439. Jukka Gronow, *The Sociology of Taste* (London: Routledge, 1997), 2.

440. Veblen, *The Theory of Leisure Class*; Bourdieu, Distinction; Schor, *The Overspent American.*

441. Falk, *The Consuming Body.*

442. Colin Campbell, *The Romantic Ethic and the Spirit of Modern Consumerism* (Oxford: Basil Blackwell, 1987).

443. Ping Huang, "Lifestyle and Consumer Culture (Preface)", in Xin Chen, ed., Redemption and Consumption: Consumerism in Contemporary Chinese Daily Life (Jiangsu People's Publishing House, 2003), 7.

444. Colin Campbell, *The Romantic Ethic.*

445. Chen Xin said: "Conceptual high consumption means that due to economic constraints, consumption is still far from actual high consumption, but it has been aggressively pursued or imitated in terms of the lifestyle of the high consumption group. This often goes even beyond actual economic capacity, or is suppressed to meet basic needs." Chen Xin, *Redemption and Consumption: Consumerism in Contemporary Chinese Daily Life*, (Jiangsu People's Publishing House, 2003), 8.

446. Wang Ning, "Sociological Analysis of 'Amphibious' Consumer Behavior", *Sun Yat-sen University Journal (Social Science Edition)*, no. 4, (2005).

447. Xin Chen, *Redemption and Consumption*; Xiaohong Zhou, ed., *Survey of China's Middle Class* (Social Sciences Academic Press, 2005), chapter 2.

448. For discussion of the desire for consumption in traditional society, see: Colin Campbell, "Consuming Goods and the Good of Consuming," in *Consumer Society in American History*, ed. Lawrence B. Glickman (Ithaca: Cornell University Press, 1999), 19~32.

449. Bourdieu, *Distinction.*

450. However, entitlements for officials (e.g., housing, cars) are strictly hierarchy-based. Such treatment is evidence of their social class status.

451. *Xinhua Net*, "To End 'Governmental Car Corruption' Cancel Car Services?" 9 November 2005, http://www.bj.xinhuanet.com/bjpd-wmhd/2005-11/09/content_2803041.htm.

452. Tian Jun, ed., *Report on Market Research on China's Mainstream Consumers* (Beijing: Enterprise Management Press, 2003), 69.

453. Zhao Ying, "Automotive Industry Policy Review and Outlook," *Economic Information Daily*, 27 May 2003.

454. *Xinhua Net*, "Automotive Industry Development Policy," 1 June 2004, http://news3.xinhuanet.com/auto/2004-06/01/content_1501777.htm.

455. The data for Beijing are from *China Statistical Yearbook 2005*; Shenzhen data are from Shenzhen Statistical Yearbook 2005.

456. Henry Lefebvre: "The car is a status symbol. It represents comfort, power, prestige and speed; in addition to its practical uses, it is primarily a symbol to be consumed; because it is a symbol of consumption and consumers, it is a symbol of happiness and it stimulates joy with symbolic objects. So the inherent contents of cars are intertwined. They reinforce each other and cancel each other." (Quoted in John O'Neill, *Body Shape: Five Types of Bodies in Modern Society*, trans. Zhang Xuchun, (Spring Arts Press, 1999), 96.) John O'Neill also says, "A car is a kind of symbolic good. It is not only a tool to carry the body, but also a kind of transportation tool emphasizing the value concepts of privacy and freedom. So a car not only carries its load of things, it also carries personal ideology." (O'Neill, *Body Shape*, 95.)

457. Starting 1 January 2007 motorcycles were banned in Guangzhou from roads in urban areas.

458. Hu Xiaojun, Zhang Xiliang and He Jiankun, "Survey of Family Car Consumption Trends and Influencing Factors," *Consumer Economy*, no. 3 (2007), 25.

459. Hu Xiaojun, Zhang Xiliang and He Jiankun, "Family Car Consumption," 25.

460. Weber, *Protestant Ethic*.

461. Campbell, *Romantic Ethic*.

462. See studies of social stratification by domestic scholars. There are many studies with fruitful results on social stratification of China, such as Liu Xue-Yi, ed., *Report of Studies of Contemporary Chinese Social Classes* (Social Sciences Academic Press, 2002); (2) Li Peilin, Li Qiang, Sun Liping et al., *Social Stratification of China* (Social Sciences Academic Press, 2004).

463. Wang Ning, "Amphibious Consumer Behavior," 71~76.

464. Cheng Wei, "Luxury: The Symbolic Value of Consumer Goods," *End of the World*, no. 3 (2003), 165~172.

465. McCracken, *Culture and Consumption*, chapter 8.

466. Of the dress code during the Cultural Revolution, Dr. Peidong Sun has done a detailed study. Sun Peidong, "Fashion In Totalitarian Context," Ph.D. dissertation, Zhongshan University (2007).

467. Veblen, *Leisure Class*, 167.

468. On identity theory, see Wang Ning, "Consumption and Identity," *Sociology Research*, no. 1 (2001), 4~14. See also Qing Wu, "Consumer Identity", Ph.D. dissertation, Zhongshan University (2007).

469. Refers to a pedestrian shopping street in Guangzhou in which there are many clothing stores.

470. Refers to the Guangzhou Department Store.

471. Refers to Guangzhou Upper Nine and Lower Nine Roads, which are pedestrian commercial streets. Many clothing stores have opened there.

472. This book is only an analysis of the formal consumption system, not an analysis of the informal system.

473. Walder, *Neo-Traditionalism*, 211.

474. For a discussion of the relationship between generation and social change, see Karl Mannheim (1993) "The Problem of Generations", in From Karl Mannheim, 2nd expanded edition, ed. Kurt H. Wolff. (London: Transaction, 1993), 351~395; June Edmunds and Bryan S. Turner, Generations, Culture and Society (Buckingham: Open University Press, 2002).

475. Liu Shaoqi, "Industrialization of the Country and the Improvement of Living Standards," in Selected Works of Liu Shaoqi, vol. 2, (People's Publishing House, 1985),   7.

476. Althusser, *Essays*, 25~31.

477. Zheng Yefu believes that whether one is in the East or in the West, there has been transformation from politicians defining the concept of life to businessmen defining concept of life. Zheg Yefu, *Post-materialistic Era* (Shanghai People's Publishing House, 2007), 6~9.

478. Albert Auch Seaman, *Desire and Benefits* (Shanghai Literature & Art Publishing, 2003), 15.

479. In this book, "consumer culture" is different from "consumerism." Consumerism is a more abstract concept. It refers to all elements related to consumer culture. Therefore, it exists not only in modern society, but also in traditional society, and is a common historical and cultural phenomenon. The consumer culture is modern

consumerism. It exists only in the modern or post-modern society. It does not exist in traditional society. The appearance of consumer culture is accompanied by the rise of modern "consumers".

480. Baudrillard, *Selected Writings*, 22.

481. Zymund Bauman, *Legislators and Interpreters* (Cambridge: Polity Press, 1987), 164~165.

482. Baudrillard, *Selected Writings*, 29.

483. McCracken, *Culture and Consumption*, 84~89.

484. J. Williamson, *Decoding Advertisements: Ideology and Meaning in Advertising* (London: Marion Boyars, 1978),13.

485. The idea comes from C. Wright Mills, *White Collar: the American Middle Classes* (Oxford: Oxford University Press, 1951).

486. Of the symbolic function of objects, Veblen, Bourdieu, and other Western scholars have had deep discussions. For a review of the symbols of material consumption, see Wang Ning, *Consumer Sociology* (Social Sciences Academic Press, 2001), chapter 7.

487. McCracken, *Culture and Consumption*, 71~83.

488. About the view of product having a "life", see The Sovereign Era of Consumers, trans. Dong Zhengde (Yuan-Liou Publishing, 1989), 89.

489. The analysis of the distinction between the "physical life" and "social life" of goods, see Wang Ning, *Consumer Sociology*, 6~7; Wang Ning, *Consumer Desire - Sociological Interpretation of Chinese Urban Consumer Culture* (Southern China Daily Press, 2005), 68~70, 149~152.

490. Wang Ning, *Consumer Desire*, 68~70.

491. "Fashion as a mechanism of consumer exploitation," is discussed in Wang Ning, Consumer Desire, 66~70.

492. On the relationship between consumption and identity, see Wang Ning, "Consumption and Identity – An Exploration of Analytical Framework on Sociological Consumption," *Sociology Research*, no. 1 (2001), 4~14.

493. Bourdieu, *Distinction*.

494. Baudrillard, *Selected Writings*, 41.

495. Wang Ning, *Consumer Desire*, 113~116.

496. The discussion on desire being a modern form of consumerism, see Wang Ning, "National Alienation Theory."

497. The view in this section was inspired by the article by Peiyun Xiong, "How to Become Citizens from Consumers," Phoenix Net, 20 February 2008, http://news.ifeng.com/opinion/200802/0220_23_405728.shtml. I am grateful for the inspiration.

498. Li Xin, "Some Thinking about Developing China's Charity Cause," *Fujian Forum (Humanities and Social Sciences)*, no. 10 (2006), 162~165; Liu Cheng, Liu Zhiwei and Ye Bo, "Improving the Institutional Arrangements of China's Charitable Work and Donations", *International Economic Review*, no. 5~6 (2006), 41~44; Wu Wei, "Charitable Donations, Volunteering to Provide Public Goods, and Non-profit Voluntary Organization", *Financial Theory and Practice*, no. 4 (2007), 78~82; Liying You, "Analysis of Sino-US Enterprises Fulfilling Their Charitable Obligations," *Productivity Research*, no. 8 (2007), 79~81.

499. Wang Ning, "National Alienation Theory," 1~7.

This book is the result of a co-publication agreement between Social Sciences Academic Press and Paths International Ltd

----

The Rise of the Consumer in Modern China
By Wang Ning

ISBN: 978-1-84464-100-0

CPSIA information can be obtained at www.ICGtesting.com
Printed in the USA
BVOW061958210413

318645BV00006B/14/P